The Erosion of the
American Sporting Ethos

The Erosion of the American Sporting Ethos

Shifting Attitudes Toward Competition

JOEL NATHAN ROSEN

McFarland & Company, Inc., Publishers
Jefferson, North Carolina, and London

LIBRARY OF CONGRESS CATALOGUING-IN-PUBLICATION DATA

Rosen, Joel Nathan, 1961–
  The erosion of the American sporting ethos : shifting attitudes
toward competition / Joel Nathan Rosen.
    p.   cm.
  Includes bibliographical references and index.

  ISBN-13: 978-0-7864-2917-2
  softcover : 50# alkaline paper ∞

  1. Sports—Moral and ethical aspects—United States.
  2. Sports—Social aspects—United States—History.
  3. Competition (Psychology)—Social aspects.   4. Competition
(Psychology)—Public opinion.   I. Title.
  GV706.3.R67   2007
  175—dc22   2007013022

British Library cataloguing data are available

Cover art ©2007 Wood River Gallery

Manufactured in the United States of America

*McFarland & Company, Inc., Publishers
  Box 611, Jefferson, North Carolina 28640
  www.mcfarlandpub.com*

For Bubbie, Aunt Lynn, and Uncle Bob

Acknowledgments

This project, which has been percolating in my head for the past ten years, has in actuality encompassed well over six years of writing time over two continents alongside countless phone calls, e-mails, and other contemporary forms of communication with a host of well-informed and selfless individuals who have proven their mettle time and again. For that, I'd like to take this moment to offer a few brief yet heartfelt expressions of appreciation.

Starting in the United Kingdom, I would like to thank Frank Füredi of the University of Kent, whose wisdom, guidance, and presence has seen me through some of the more frenetic points of the project. I would also like to extend my appreciation to Dr. Ralph Fevre of the University of Cardiff, who graciously donated his time and his considerable talents in talking me through the rough patches. Additionally, I would also like to extend a further note of thanks to Duleep Allarajah, a true sport genius, and to Grant Dyer, whose voice continues to resonate in my mind after all these years.

In the United States I would like to pay homage to the many people who have lent their thoughts and other considerable contributions to this project. First of all, I would like to thank Mohamed D. Turay at Savannah State University and William Dickinson, both of whom helped give life to many of the stagnating thoughts locked inside my head during the long periods of self-imposed isolation, and to Tim Harrington in Arizona and Lance Hatten of Washington, D.C., both of whom at one time or another listened and somehow allowed me to prattle on at length about sport and culture and such, irrespective of the moment at hand.

In Houston, Texas, there was my good friend and former colleague Peter Fogo, who at the most opportune moment helped me find the words for which I had been searching. My summer at the University of Mississippi in Oxford brought me back in touch with old friends and former colleagues whose assistance is apparent within, including Kevin Bales, Mark Tew, James Payne, and Max Williams. I would also like to offer up my appreciation to the many members of the North American Society for the Sociology of Sport who have offered their scholarly critiques and their friendship over the years, especially Earl Smith of Wake Forest University and John Phillips of the University of the Pacific, both of whom have read segments of this work as often as I have.

To my wife MaryKay and our son Travis, who have so diligently helped me circumnavigate the often rough waters of such an undertaking and have watched me disappear for long stretches hither and yon, I offer my love, appreciation and my apologies for anything I might have said, done, or overlooked during these past few years. You have been my rocks.

And finally, to my parents, Stanley and Ida Rosen in Las Vegas, Nevada, your loving support and financial generosity have made all this possible, and for that and many other reasons too numerous to name here, I am eternally grateful.

Contents

Preface

The importance of sports to contemporary American culture was manifest. It could be measured by the many hours that fans spend riveted to television screens, by the column inches in newspapers devoted to sports, and by the samplings of cocktail conversations. Novelists, poets and dramatists increasingly turned to sports for motifs, and scholars began to execute minute investigations of the psychological, philosophical, and social significance of sports. As in the past, twentieth-century sports mirrored fundamental social divisions of the United States. Simultaneously, sports have joined the electronic media, bureaucratic structures, and mass consumption as one of the new sinews holding together modern society.[1]

It is certainly true that one can learn the value of teamwork, hard work, and sacrifice from sports, but those lessons can also be learned from many other activities and events.[2]

If little Timmy sees that his friend earned an A on his essay, he will feel jealous. Hence, Timmy will feel like an underachiever.... We all heard poor Timmy's final voice as he committed suicide.[3]

The following is meant to be a comprehensive analysis of the nature of competition in contemporary American sport in response to a perceptible withdrawal from the more traditional American competitive spirit. Critical to this assessment is my intention to transcend standard responses to sport-related subject matter in order to explore through the prism of athletic competition how this retreat is reflected in many other societal institutions. While competitive sport will serve as the backdrop of this work, the more substantive aim is to underscore how changing social and political interpretations of modern life have co-opted the contemporary discussion of competition and what this divergence suggests about life both within and without the sporting environment.

In exploring this aspect of American culture, I have sought to evaluate and engage a considerable number of sources often obscured by more conventional sport-related investigations. To be quite candid on this point, while many commentators work through a wide range of complex social phenomena with regards to competitive sport, the nature of competition itself is rarely if ever engaged directly within the literature, which suggests that within both popular and academic circles there exists an apprehensiveness, if not outright rigidity, when it comes to sport-related discussions. Furthermore, what passes for challenging albeit provocative discussion regarding contemporary sport often degenerates into a predictable condemnation of such activities built on a wide range of a priori cultural assumptions.

The genesis of this project lay in the typically banal responses to modern sport-related phenomena as captured primarily in popular commentary emanating from both print and electronic media. That the driving forces behind these analyses came not necessarily from academic sources, but rather through a mix of scholarship often juxtaposed to popular assessments, should help to underscore America's more distinctive changing disposition toward competitiveness and competition itself. The overwhelming numbers of scholarly works within the field of sport criticism have long held sport socially, politically, and culturally suspect, a uniformity that remains apparent today. On the other hand, the changing nature of popular assessments demonstrates a dramatic departure from the nineteenth century tendency to spread the gospel of physical activity or the twentieth century trend toward promoting sport on both a sociopolitical as well as consumer-based level, creating a tension that highlights a much more intriguing direction in this particular set of circumstances.

Whereas the theme of sport reporting had once centered around athletic skill and guile, the emergent echo of post–Cold War era sport seemed weighted down by a range of concerns that ran parallel to non-sporting institutions. Discussions of, for example, labor-management disputes and salary concerns, waters that had long run deeply within professional sport, seemed to find a greater degree of resonance during this period, as would issues of morality, health, criminality, and the increasingly frequent elevation of tangential or alternative competitive environments thought by some commentators to be more compliant and sensitive to building expectations. Additionally, what these same critiques also tended to exhibit was a noticeable turn toward the introspective, which in the normally detached, often curt, sports world, marked a major departure in its own right.

As I began to explore these shifts in greater detail, I was struck by many of the parallels popular criticism demonstrated relative to more scholarly assessments of sport. Specifically that, similar to the more notably unfavorable academic treatments of competitive sport — assessments that had been typically rejected within popular commentary — it was becoming increasingly obvious that by the mid-1990s even popular commentators were finding it difficult to defend sport without tempering that defense in some manner or another. This increased focus often manifested itself in a much more astonishing discounting of sport's perceived contributions to American life, marking another radical detour within the various reaches of popular discourse.

Having had spent several years researching elements of this altering perception through my work in the field of sport radio broadcasting,[4] I noticed an equally palpable anti-competition bias emanating from various corners of sport industry media as well. These seemed to correspond in part to the weighty coverage of the murder charges tendered against retired football superstar O.J. Simpson in 1994, which came on the heels of former heavyweight boxing champion Mike Tyson's highly public conviction and subsequent incarceration for sexual assault in 1992. To be clear, popular conjecture that held sport to be suspect was already advancing into the mainstream well before the Tyson and Simpson stories broke, but the suggestion that this direction constituted anything more than an aberration was quickly invalidated by a seemingly endless torrent of similarly controversial, prurient, and otherwise non-sportive content.

Beyond the "What have you done for me lately?" tone of popular sport discussion so evident today lies the concern that sport has lost both its primacy and its relevancy to the culture because it can no longer serve as a breeding ground for constructive behavior and a tolerable degree of morality as expressed in the modern worldview. The dearth of unapologetically positive assessments of competitive sport still in existence today, such as the Reverend Jesse Jackson, Jr.'s claim that "[s]port teaches teamwork, loyalty, dedication, and respect from players and citizens,"[5] are counterbalanced by the bulk of popular sentiment that seems heavily weighted toward assessments of sport that portray it to be both anachronistic and certainly more in line with an assertion that hearkens back to the nineteenth century: that it is, in the words of one critic, "Darwinism misrepresented as survival of the most belligerent rather than the most adaptable."[6] Whether or not this perceived failure is alleged to mark an offense to traditional modalities, that is, national unity or goal-orientation, or to the more modern constructs ranging from matters of physical and or psychological discord to ideals expressed in the thrust toward a more egalitarian society, a thread of apprehension continues to haunt the contemporary vision of competitive sport while threatening its place as an institution with a viable future in American life away from the stigma of controversy.

When juxtaposed to the more traditional relationship between popular commentary and sport, these critical popular assessments that seek to portray sport in a cynical and often dismissive fashion indeed marked a major development in the field. This contradiction, coupled with the increasing exposure sport receives in public spaces, also suggested that while Americans continued to tune into sport broadcasts and identified themselves as sport aficionados, the collective response to the games, their governance, and the athletes themselves was often marked by an equally perceptible hostility toward virtually every corner of the sporting world. In this respect, it had become increasingly obvious that popular and academic sport criticism has come to find much more common ground then ever before and especially at the level of a shared distrust of the competitive arena that had yet to be demonstrated so visibly at any other time in America's past.

In taking on this task of both tracing the contemporary nature of competition in American sport while also attempting to reconcile its significance, I have uncovered many avenues of exploration from which I was able to formulate a handful of useful working questions. The most notable points include:

- Has there been a shift in America's acceptance of competitive sport?
- If so, can this shift be traced through a parallel discussion of changes taking shape away from the sporting milieu?
- What sort of effect would a recoiling away from the traditional competitive ethos have on a nation once indelibly committed to its competitive bearing?
- What might a shift away from and an overarching distrust of competitive circumstances suggest about America's collective self-image during a period of often dramatic flux?

Toward these ends, I have compiled a wide variety of sources that have allowed me to explore these matters in a rational and coherent fashion.

Material used in this analysis was drawn from primary sources, such as American and international newspapers, periodicals, personal interviews with industry insiders, and even the occasional pamphlet, official document, event program, or hand-out. Additionally, I have also employed a variety of electronic media sources including television, popular film, documentaries, and various local and national radio broadcasts, all of which remain major contributors to the discussion of American sport.

The reader will also notice that a significant portion of the source material included in this study was uncovered at various Internet sites. The availability of such source material has been of inestimable value given the nature of this work, the ever-evolving ideals within sport, and the changes that manifest in society at large. Access to various local, national, and international newspapers and periodicals posted online, not to mention the wide range of Web sites and home pages that offer regular or sporadic commentary on sport and social issues, have been extremely important toward the completion of this work, and every effort has been made to identify contributors as well as verify the information offered.

In the sequence of chapters I have fostered what I believe to be a logical and reasonable presentation of my inquiries. In the first chapter, I purposely avoid sport, attempting to tease out the context from which contemporary criticism of athletic competition emerges in a much broader sense by exploring notable changes taking shape within early 21st century society. Inherent to this discussion is tracing the evolution of 1960s era countercultural ideals into the mainstream of contemporary life while placing them squarely within the context of shifts within post–Cold War culture. These shifts, I would argue, constitute the most central theme toward understanding the nature of the advancing withdrawal from not only the traditional competitive spirit but from many other markers of American tradition that are thought to have been born of unsavory and even antiquated ideals. Moving back into athletic competition chapter two offers a more comprehensive overview of the traditional interpretation and application of sport and sport-related motifs in American life. While many parallels do indeed exist between then and the now, it is also apparent that in terms of the popular arena, the thought that sport can no longer serve society in any practical sense marks a dramatic departure from sport's more traditional pose, a point that I develop throughout this particular chapter.

In chapter three I look specifically at the treatment sport garnered during the height of the Cold War era. Of particular importance herein is the influx of countercultural critiques that seek to both undermine traditional sport values and offer an increasingly angst-ridden social order alternative modes for expressing its dissatisfaction through demonstrably countercultural initiatives.

Chapter four marks an attempt to lend insight into some of the more central themes within contemporary sport-centered debates, including concerns regarding sportsmanship, aggression, and the increasingly omnipresent discussion of off- and on- field behaviors relative to the role model question, and the more recent frenzy concerning doping and doping allegations. The tensions apparent in these discussions highlight a much more extensive vision of a once-vaunted institution no longer perceived to be able to measure up to changing societal expectations. Likewise, in chapters five and six, I seek to uncover mounting anxieties relative to the contemporary perception of an uncontrollable youth sport apparatus and its inability (or unwillingness) to respond to contemporary expectations regarding character-building and the health-driven acquisition of increasingly valued self-concepts in youth participants, all discussions reminiscent of a bygone era but with a notably different tenor.

In chapter seven I attempt to add varied analyses to a progressively more fractious modern sport advocacy that was once united in the struggle for equality and opportunity within sport but is no longer capable of moving beyond each other's territorial divide. It may well be that this schism within traditional alliances, namely the forces of feminism and anti-racism, has become a metaphor for the advancing and more commonly held conclusion that sport can no longer be held as a paean to American culture.

The epigraphs that adorn each chapter and subsection are intended to introduce each new theme or direction by highlighting the often extreme vantage points relative to the varying sides of the debates. My choices for these particular reflections were often tempered by the knowledge that while they were by and large germane to the analysis as a whole, they often had no real place in the actual text beyond the periphery. Moreover, I also found them to be quite useful if for no other reasons than to attempt to inject both a sense of clarity and, at times, a brief moment of levity to an often moribund venture. Caught in a vise between what it should be and what it has become, we seem all too prone to forgetting that at the end of the day, sport is also about the elevation of the human spirit and a soaring of the human imagination, matters that seem all but lost in the countless debates regarding politesse and character. Thus, while I concur with Christopher Lasch's assertion that we rarely seem to take the essential elements of sport seriously enough,[7] I likewise concur with those frank sentiments emanating from the African American oral tradition that remind us that sometimes laughing is the only way to keep from crying.

Introduction

*As the hallowed force of capitalism and the principle of most public rit-
ual in modern society (sport and politics), competition organizes individuals into rule-governed action that sets individuals against each
other until a winner is created. Competition is ideally suited to balance the forces of democracy and aristocracy, of egalitarianism and
elitism, for through competition some individuals can be determined
to be superior to others.[1]*

*For most of us, the dream of becoming a champion remains a fantasy,
but for a special few, it is very much a reality. We live through them.
Athletes are our last warriors.[2]*

Once a manifestation of behaviors that a proud and resolute nation nur-
tured among its citizenry, competition, and most specifically athletic competition, in the early 21st century seems far removed from its previously vaunted
place in the American consciousness. The growing tendency to view competition, especially in its most recognizable form as competitive sport and its associative elements, as anathema to progress as well as antithetical to the values
of a progressive people is today fueled by a proliferation of books, articles, and
broadcast reports that indicate that sport in the modern context can no longer
measure up as either a beneficial or even serviceable feature of American culture.

Sport in its modern context, once publicly revered as a wholesome expression of American values and politically exploited as a means to further the
process of nation building, has increasingly come under fire from a variety of
ideological perspectives with a wide range of motivating factors. Set against a
backdrop of tradition, contemporary American sport is thought to have reached
a stage of degeneration similar to the stage-managed theatrics inherent to professional wrestling and day time talk shows, both of which have made entertainment niches for themselves by appealing to the baser values of an either
bored, disillusioned, or entertainment-starved public intent on watching someone else become a target of popular scorn.[3] In many popular and philosophical circles, the more modern sporting environments are considered to be fraught
with inexcusable and unmanageable quandaries perpetrated by a host of ill-

Figure I.1. Attendance Trends in Major American Sports

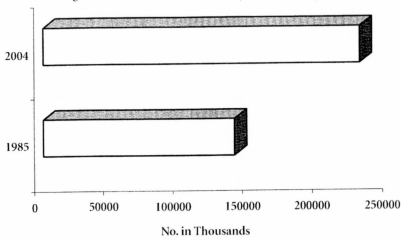

No. in Thousands

This compilation of attendance figures includes Major League Baseball, men's and women's Division I college basketball, the National Basketball Association, Division I college and National Football League football, and the National Hockey League.[4]

mannered athletes, self-absorbed administrators, and their ham-fisted, often sycophantic supporters. Few if any are willing to defend, let alone endorse, competitive sport without broodingly qualifying one's response while tempering it with an apologist's brush. And yet, while the discussion tends to center around the bleak, the irony is that in terms of pure athleticism alone, American sport has entered into one of those rare and vaunted Golden Ages with resulting numbers that suggest that in spite of increasing antipathy, both revenue and attendance continue to soar (see figure I.1 and Appendix).

With athleticism, competitiveness, and sport's popularity hovering at such a lofty peak, one might expect the discussion of sport to be overwhelmingly represented by gushing approval of the competitive spirit and a zest for what modern athletes are able to accomplish on the playing surfaces of various sports and what this suggests about human efficacy at its essence, but this simply is not the case. The sport and front pages of newspapers, the ubiquitous sports broadcasts on television, radio, and the Internet, and both the popular and academic work of the early twenty-first century are replete with lurid tales of corruption, sexual misconduct, and wistful appeals for a more morally sound, competitive milieu, though admittedly even this reflective and certainly romanticized view of sport has come under fire in more recent assessments.[5] As John Gerdy was to note in his portentous sounding *Sports: The All-American Addiction*:

> As much as I would like to forget about sports' problems and simply enjoy the games, I cannot. Sports' influence on our lives and culture is simply too great for

such concerns to be swept under the rug. Everywhere we turn, sports-related images, attitudes, and behaviors are pervasive — from the workplace, to the schools we attend, to what we see on television, to the taxes we pay. Sport has an impact on and influences, in one form or another, virtually every aspect of our lives. It is simply too important to stand by as it continues to evolve into something that we are no longer comfortable with and no longer feel good about.[6]

What is obvious is that the contemporary discussion of competitive sport rarely concerns all the things that sport is. Rather, this discussion tends to underscore all the things sport is not, a point not lost on the American public, who, in spite of its more noticeable disgust for most things sportive, seems to pine for what prominent sport historian Allen Guttmann once advanced as "nothing better than to dream on of a pastoral world where the grass is green, the sun is bright, and the crisp spring air carries the delightful sound of bats and balls."[7] Thus, while this contradiction is indeed extraordinary, what is also unmistakable is that so much of modern discussions about competitive sport revolves around competition's inability to foster high moral functioning through the teaching of lessons deemed to be invaluable within the contemporary frame of reference, a frame of reference that is often informed by a robust and resilient sense of nostalgia.

Popularizing the Debate

[The] drive to compete and to be a "winner" has always been part of the American psyche. Our early ancestors were aggressive and competitive to begin with. They knew they were pitted against amazing odds, but they also felt they were a select group.... We worship the victors. But why? The Dutch don't especially, nor the Swedes, neither do the Danes, the Swiss, or the English, and they all seem like fairly civilized people.[8]

Football has acquired a social significance it never previously enjoyed. Football is discussed by the chattering classes; universities run degree courses in football studies; bookshops overflow with new football writing; the government has even set up a football taskforce.[9]

Pervasive images of disorder coupled with repeated pronouncements of gross misconduct seem far removed from the once idyllic image of American sport. Nevertheless, is quite recognizable that this has made up the flow in contemporary analyses of competitive sport, and especially within the popular commentary. What stands in place of a once inviolate American sporting consciousness is an overt sense of frustration, a frustration that seeks to assign culpability while systematically acknowledging that in addition to playing upon the fears and insecurities of a society in flux, competitive sport also demonstrates the capacity to irreparably shape the nation's collective character through unacceptable behaviors perpetrated by those in and around the sporting terrain. As Fred Engh, an increasingly omnipresent and outspoken advocate of youth sport reform, explains:

> The lack of appropriate philosophy on our playing fields, as well as all the other negative factors ... makes it very clear that we need to change the system. The present situation in place nationwide actually facilitates the emotional and physical abuse of children and encourages inappropriate behaviors. The message is clear: organized sports needs much more than a minor tune-up; it needs a complete overhaul.[10]

The placement of competitive sport within this extremely untenable and certainly ill-favoring context has come to be something of a given in more modern analyses. Modern sporting environments, in sharp contrast to their previously recognized incarnations as principal vehicles for the proper socialization of American youth, exist alongside the suggestion that they operate well beyond impropriety and so much so that in many cases municipalities and even high-profile sporting circuits themselves have taken extraordinary measures to at least attempt to reign in sport's more public face in order to assuage public rebuke. For example, some American sport venues have constructed operational municipal courts that have complete legal authority to monitor and restrict spectator behavior, including the sentencing of enforceable jail terms.[11] Similarly, as discussed in greater detail elsewhere in this work, local sport organizations are seeking equally extreme measures to restrict sport-related interactions, such as in New Brunswick, New Jersey, where the principal authorities of their youth sport program have constructed what they have termed a parent-proof stadium intent on keeping at arm's length an increasingly more problematic yet increasingly stereotypical figure in American life, the so-called little league parent.[12]

As reviewed in much greater detail in chapter two of this work, sport's increasingly more customary focus, as overseen by official and unofficial social governance, and well beyond its inner dynamic of fun and exhilaration, was to both test and reinforce America's established values and to further instill the ideals of courage and masculine virtue through physical supremacy bathed in a disciplined and resolute competitive light. At the dawning of the new century, however, as so many of America's traditional values are being called into question, competitive sport's relationship to those same values are also being revisited. This, in turn, serves to subject sport to standards that no longer hold excellence and self-discipline as fundamental elements of a well-rounded citizenry, while competitive sport further conceived as problematic and out of touch with an evolving impulse that today is often driven by emotion and an emphasis on self-awareness, two contemporary conceptual models that are at odds with a nascent competitive ethos.[13]

While at times predictable, the work of many noted academic sport researchers also reflects these sorts of dramatic responses to sport's more modern and popular portrayal. For example, David Light Shields and Brenda Light

Bredemeier, co-directors of Notre Dame University's influential Center for Sport, Character, and Culture, contend that sport in the modern context has become a refuge of sorts for both social irresponsibility and, increasingly, immoral conduct. They maintain that "the reality is that many actions that may be seen as totally illegitimate in everyday life — such as inflicting pain on another human being — may be accepted and even embraced as a routine part of some sports."[14] Consequently, they conclude:

> What we found is that many athletes, certainly not all, saw sport as a time of letting go of everyday life concerns, including, at least to a limited extent, moral concerns. They wanted to throw themselves into the sport experience, thinking only about their own interest, and perhaps that of their team. This fits the description of sport ... as an institution of release.[15]

They further note:

> [Sport] is a sphere of activity that is not only "set aside" spatially and temporally from everyday life, it "sets aside" or releases concerns of everyday life. Indeed, part of the appeal of sport is its relative freedom from daily concerns. That "moral release" theme is recurrent in many of our interviews.[16]

Support for measures that would effectively deter what Shields and Bredemeier assert are illegitimate behaviors has become so widespread that in some ways it would appear that open debate is superfluous, leaving substantive discussions of the nature of the contemporary competitive environment to be regarded in some circles as both fixed and off-limits to further critique. In this respect, what controversial sports writer-turned-critic John R. Tunis once noted in the mid-1970s, that the mythology surrounding sport is "a fiction ... [telling us] that competitive sport is health-giving, character-building, brain-making, and so forth,"[17] seems to wield much greater influence in modern debate. Or as *Time* reporter Andrew Ferguson has observed in more popular and certainly modern terms:

> Most sports programs, despite their excesses, manage to promote the old virtues: self-confidence, personal responsibility, teamwork, persistence, the ability to win and lose with grace. Of course, the traditional virtues come wrapped in the garb of the less than traditional 1990's when prosperity is at an all-time high and leisure at an all-time low.[18]

These sorts of accounts regarding contemporary manifestations within the more traditional competitive culture suggest that past treatments of competition must have been steeped in folly, and this is most telling in the more popular depictions of contemporary sport. While academia has always expressed a degree of mutual distrust with the competitive dynamic, it has long been in the public/popular sphere where competitive sport wielded its greatest power. Thus, many critics, and most specifically those who would have been more apt to defend and even promote competition, are more likely to focus their analyses on concerns that are more in keeping with the sort of fashionable critiques that have historically emanated from academic circles. In this regard, the growing popular concern that a more traditional competitive schema is marred by both anti-human and anti-progressive behaviors is where the most dramatic shift appears in early twenty-first century discourse.

A Clash of Culture Finds Contemporary Sport

America is in the midst of a culture war that has had and will continue to have reverberations not only within public policy but within the lives of ordinary Americans everywhere.[19]

Lower your expectations and reduce anxiety. Expect nothing and your dreams will come true.[20]

Son, take my advice. If you have to take up a sport, take up horseshoes where you don't have to be perfect.[21]

Whether they are professional, semi-professional, amateur, or youth-oriented in nature, competitive sports in North America as a whole, and specifically in the United States, the perceived focal point for North American sport, have been catapulted into an atmosphere of uncertainty and doubt. Nowhere is this more apparent than in the world of high-profile professional and elite college sport, which for the sake of clarity we will define herein as men's professional baseball, basketball, football, and hockey alongside collegiate Division I men's football and basketball and, to a lesser extent, college baseball and hockey. We can also include on this list, given more recent developments, women's professional and collegiate basketball, soccer, hockey, and softball. Regardless of the form it may take, however, there exists a strong undercurrent of condemnation that places competitive sport in a defensive position that forces it to both justify its presence and defend its worth amidst rising skepticism.

As I will argue throughout, modern competition's oppositional elements consist primarily of two distinct entities whose differences often pale compared to their similarities. From the left, and spearheaded in many instances by the work of self-professed *humanist* sport researchers, there are those who are influenced by remnants of Cold War era countercultural thought. These commentators form their critiques around the most basic assumption that because competition possesses what can be interpreted as a repressive past, it is incapable of adapting a progressive design, in which athletic competition is simply a test of acumen, without some overtones of authoritarianism and a notably tradition-laden power imbalance. There are some who even go so far as to argue that anytime competition exists, and even under the most managed conditions, it presents inherently anti-human conventions that threaten cooperation and the spirit of solidarity while encouraging aggression and even violence among the participants.[22] Furthermore, in a climate of distrust, as engendered by older strains of Cold War era, antiestablishment rhetoric, the divisiveness inherent to competition renders sport incapable of adapting to changing notions of inclusion and leads to debates surrounding enduring concerns over race, gender, and class relations. Within this strain of criticism, competition can be linked to the idea that it is an impediment to progress while remaining an anachronistic tool of power, the manifestations of which are often demonstrated through the presentation of high-profile sport. As scholar/critic Thomas Keil once noted, "[Sport] is activity which constitutes and reconstitutes a given social formation in ways that are consistent with other social practices in that formation,"[23] and the contemporary left seizes upon this supposition by focusing on sport's longstanding relationship to nationalism, heterosexual masculine domination, and its notably intolerant past.

From more conservative sectors, competitive sport in its modern guise presents a challenge to what remains of the *status quo ante* in terms of power relations and matters of Victorian-derived civility from an ostensibly less cluttered past. A conservative backlash against competitive sport reeks of the sort of nostalgia that is reminiscent of a time when athletes were perceived to behave in such a way as to imply a humble and wholesome demeanor. As an integral component of character education and behavior initiatives through sport dating back to the nineteenth century, an athlete was expected to merit public adulation. The behavior of some of today's more impetuous or ambitious athletes, however, many of whom no longer fit the traditional mold in terms of deference and obeisance (the discussion of which is often wrapped in fairly overt racial terms), threatens the once inviolable nature of athletic competition while drawing additional focus on the sordid external dynamics surrounding sport that few were made privy to or even wanted to know existed. In this respect, Steven Overman's description of the American sport culture cloaked in a resolutely traditional Sunday School atmosphere,[24] an image that once resiliently and indelibly attached itself to America's sporting ethos, has undergone a severe and very public admonishment. Still, irrespective of the pervasive coverage of contemporary sport, one is hard pressed to find anything about modern sport that was not evident during previous periods in American life.

While the differing sides present contrasting images in terms of the role that sport should play in contemporary life, it becomes equally apparent that these often competing visions also share remarkable similarities in their scope. The common thread that binds left and right in this case is that competitive sport in the context of modern life cannot and must not continue along on its current pace without wholesale changes ahead, changes that seem to intersect with a mutual conviction that at the root of sport's debasement lies nothing less than America's future, especially given the revitalized focus on the importance of character building in children, who are thought to be inestimably influenced by sport. Indeed, the thought that sport can be rescued from this era of spiraling decay, a notion astonishingly reminiscent of attitudes dating back to nineteenth century Victorianism, glares outward from this analysis and on all sides of the debate and has emerged as a sort of nexus from which varying political orientations may coordinate their efforts in spite of their traditional animosities. Thus, it is from within this nexus that we shall launch this journey in the pages to follow.

1

Contemporary Sport in the Broader Social Context

On consecutive nights in October 2000, television's Fox Sports Network and Home Box Office (HBO) aired programs that chronicled what both maintained to be the sad state of sport today.[1] These reports centered on some of the more scandalous aspects of modern sport, including player arrests, on- and off-field altercations, and drunken and belligerent spectators, giving rise to an increasingly more widespread conviction that sport has shed the last remaining vestiges of its once proud heritage and has become prone to a displacement motif that values spectacle and mayhem in the pursuit of increased revenue and all at the expense of civilized behavior and basic human decency. Still, what made these particular reports so fascinating was not necessarily the shocking images and depictions of belligerent participants and spectators they presented to a justifiably dismayed and horrified viewing public — effective though they may have been — but that they were merely two examples of a more recent trend to present sport in such a negative light within the context of a general and overarching breakdown in American social values. As Brian C. Anderson and Peter Reinharz of *The City Journal* read it:

> Once upon a time, after all, the public — and coaches and team owners too — expected athletes to stand for certain ideals of civility, self-mastery, respectability, and fair play that provided an example for all citizens. But when pro football players are implicated in brutal murders, or a millionaire basketball star assaults his coach (perhaps we should mention George Shinn![2]) — such incidents now seem to crop up weekly — it's a sign that something has gone awry in sports and in the culture as a whole. It suggests, too, that sports have become not just a reflection of cultural decline but an active agent of debasement.[3]

While there is little use denying that sport of late has demonstrated that like other elements of the popular world, it too can present itself as ill-mannered and objectionable in the face of mounting criticism, it is equally evident that behind many of the supercharged depictions and analyses of contemporary sport there exists a more common and certainly more cynical interpretation of sport that reflects other, more wide-ranging discussions of contemporary social phenomena. The implication is that in spite of sport's well-chronicled

15

excesses, the clash between the sport-induced competitive ethos of yesteryear and the spirit of modern society is not inevitably based on an apparent rash of unseemly behaviors in the sporting milieu but rather on variations that exist within the relationship between sport and modern society itself. The fact is that while many Americans might feel disgusted by what they see in contemporary sporting circles, it is not so much a matter pertaining directly to sport or the world of sport itself but rather the way in which a society in transition views itself through a particular form of self-evaluation.

There is every reason to consider that the war being waged in terms of the role that sport plays at the dawn of the twenty-first century may be a struggle between competing ideals as expressed by a traditional as well as a modern reading of that function. Still, that sport finds itself betwixt and between these competing visions should not be all that surprising given the temper of modern times, a disposition that seems ready to support the notion that sport itself is less the issue. Rather, society, it would appear, has entered into an age in which the optimism and hope once assigned to modernity has given way to a tangle of pessimism and disillusionment regarding the future of the civilized world, a view that would certainly render a significant impact on a host of social institutions, including sport with its competitive base, its assumed masculine posture, and its tenacious insistence upon excellence.

This contemporary treatment of sport stems from a more general shift in public attitudes that have turned away from the traditional American competitive ethos, extending to a variety of institutional settings and demonstrating in a much broader sense that persistent disenchantment predominates in the modern world while at the same time rendering a host of once-cherished features of American culture incapable of arousing the public's collective imagination. To be sure, the level of contestation that takes place on the various playing surfaces and the tallying of scores and statistics, hardly matters of grave importance in the scheme of things, should not be confused with more pressing issues facing modern man, but as indicators of where contemporary society exists, these abrupt departures from one of America's most revered conventions do seem to indicate a notable change in public sentiment as it exists in the modern cultural landscape. Thus the question presents itself: How is it that sport, an institution historically regarded as above the fray in such debates, and in fact long considered to be a factor in shaping the nation's political, cultural, and moral character, could become caught up in the contemporary pattern of distrust and discontent so prominent in modern society?

This chapter will seek to shed light on this issue by presenting an analysis of the social milieu from which contemporary sport criticism and the changing perception of sport's place in American society emerge. Throughout, I will explore various shifts in American culture that took shape following the end of the Cold War and identify how these shifts inform an increasingly more angst-driven discussion that seeks to reinterpret the meaning of competitive sport in contemporary American life.

Post–Cold War Anxieties and Countercultural Values

America has always been a nation given to public idealism. Unlike the nations of Europe, its identity was never rooted in the millennia of tradition. America compensated for this lack of a long national history through the construction of great myths about its origins and loftier visions of its calling in the future... Even in secular political discourse, America has long been portrayed in the most moralistic terms.[4]

As the twenty-first century dawns, American culture is, quite simply, in a mess.[5]

In an article written in August 1990 for *Atlantic Monthly* entitled "Why We Will Soon Miss the Cold War," noted University of Chicago political scientist John J. Mearsheimer offers a conspicuously alternative assessment of a matter that many once believed was supposed to have assumed a decidedly different course:

Peace: it's wonderful. I like it as much as the next man, and have no wish to be willfully gloomy at a moment when optimism about the future shape of the world abounds.... To be sure, no one will miss such by-products of the Cold War as the Korean and Vietnam conflicts. No one will want to replay the U-2 affair, the Cuban missile crisis, or the building of the Berlin Wall. And no one will want to revisit the domestic Cold War, with its purges and loyalty oaths, its xenophobia and stifling of dissent. We will not wake up one day to discover fresh wisdom in the collected fulminations of John Foster Dulles. We may, however, wake up one day lamenting the loss of the order that the Cold War gave to the anarchy of international relations.[6]

In a distortion of what was once conceived of as popular logic, Mearsheimer's response to what most Americans had imagined would be the dawning of the age of new freedoms, lasting peace, and global prosperity might have seemed unusual in an age of perestroika and glasnost and the optimism expressed over the dismantling of the Berlin Wall. Still, there is little mistaking that in terms of what has actually transpired since the end of the Cold War, Mearsheimer and others who have since shared a similar degree of foreboding seem to have ably predicted the systematic unraveling of the once popular fantasy of universal post–Cold War potency. This more than anything else has proven to have a significant effect on the direction that American cultural patterns have taken hence.

In the years following the end of the Cold War, American society has observed a steady erosion of international and intranational relations, suggesting that the envisioned new age has been anything but idyllic. On the contrary, the so-called New World Order has been plagued by an often atypical state of affairs poised to threaten esteemed notions of global solidarity that at one time marked the zenith of ambitions expressed in the most general post–Cold War vision. In place of Cold War era repression and surreptitious operations perpetrated in the name of national security, however, the post–Cold War world appears ready to justify Mearsheimer's fear of an anarchic condition brought about by the unraveling of an apparatus that may have run its course but was, nevertheless, solidly in place and effectively able to help maintain a sense of order in spite of its limitations and contradictions.

Groups displaced by Cold War posturing and looming debates over such concerns as individual freedoms and ethnic identities were effectively and efficiently held at bay by the enormity of Cold War politics, but in the aftermath of such unprecedented and certainly curious stability, what has followed is a wave of conduct suggesting that marginalized individuals and issues once easily brushed aside by Cold War rhetoric have reemerged in the contemporary world with a thunderous roar. As British researcher Kenan Malik has suggested in his erudite yet dispassionate tracing of racialist thinking within the Western tradition, the disappearance of the bonds fostered by a shared focus on anti-communism that once carried Western culture through the era has given way to a dramatic weakening of cohesion and stability. This decline has in turn generated a well-spring of once artificially suppressed discontent that serves to highlight a variety of political and social insecurities once buried beneath the established Cold War routine.[7]

The instabilities of the post–Cold War order have led to a general collapse in both the international as well as intranational arenas. Internationally, these changes are reflected in outbreaks of wars and conflicts thought to have emanated from more ancient animosities, though in actuality many of these struggles seem to have very modern roots spearheaded in part by remnants of Cold War era engagements.[8] To be sure, adversarial nations whose once open insecurities were often obscured by the Cold War dynamic often found themselves embroiled in modern-day conflicts that appear on the surface to have few viable solutions, while interethnic rivalries that had lain dormant during much of the era seem destined to threaten whatever sense of order that may have existed before these changes were manifest. In this respect, the return of active military engagement that has evolved in the absence of the often muted stand-off between the Cold War superpowers seems to have awakened fears of future entanglements seemingly destined to reignite nationalist interests that threaten to further erode international relations. While looking primarily at the issue of race under these conditions, Malik's reflections seem to encompass an emergent malaise:

> The breakdown of the postwar consensus has swept away the rules which governed social discourse over the past half-century. Like an orchestra without a con-

ductor, society is becoming more discordant. At the same time themes and attitudes that had previously been considered unacceptable are no longer seen as illegitimate.[9]

Within post–Cold War America, the presumed breakdown of what had generally been seen as a shared American vision is thought to have manifested itself in a flurry of social debates that are poised to occupy the decades to come. These debates tend to illustrate a general lack of coherence in terms of a unified or universal voice and can be viewed in part as the result of the frustration and confusion once caused by the outward dismissal of particularist interests during the Cold War in favor of the more tightly wound focus on keeping international communism at bay. At the center of these philosophical constructs is a reinterpretation and in many cases a refutation of commonly accepted Western ideals such as anthropocentrism, universalism, and other conceptual standards reminiscent of Enlightenment thought. In place of Enlightenment ideals, post–Cold War era critiques often consider alternative interpretations of events, focusing instead on matters of subjectivity, individual perspective, and a general rejection of modernity, culminating in a more contemporary stream of ideas with a more critical view of the significance of modern man and the future of shared political ideologies. As cultural critic James Heartfield argues in *The 'Death of the Subject' Explained*, the result of such countercultural rejections marked a retooling of philosophical thought intent on justifying what he deems to be a postmodern nihilism that reaches beyond predictably marginalized segments of the population.[10]

Indeed, the post–Cold War period seems awash in such modern-seeming interpretations of social affect, most notably in its embrace of identity and the acceptance of individual experience. Once valued external expressions of solidarity or nationalism with their resulting group identity that could be hitched up alongside Cold War ideology have taken a backseat to internal markers of feeling and limited perspective based on a litany of individual concerns that have their roots in 1960s era countercultural debates. Coalitions that had once lined up to be recognized for both their unique contributions to American life and for the hardships they have endured had spent the majority of their time being ignored by powerful Cold War authority who could effectively use the enormity of the threat of pending nuclear disaster as a shield against such interests. Afterward, however, many of these same groups would reemerge energized and resonate powerfully with a weary populace while proclaiming that, after decades of neglect and marginalization, they had become forces with which to be reckoned. This turnabout has resulted in a veritable explosion of identity-oriented struggles in many parts of the nation that seem to have left Americans overwhelmed by the resulting fragmentation in both common ideals and political implementation, an effect that British sociologist Anthony Giddens explains is the result of a sort of "detraditionalization" of modernity.[11]

As alluded to in the Mearsheimer comment above, these circumstances have often made it difficult for various social forces to either interpret or navigate the new rules for social or political engagement. For Giddens, the noted degree of destabilization endemic to the rather abrupt shift from Cold War to post–Cold War life has systematically altered perceptions of what was once believed to mark the best courses of action in a given context. Thus, it can be noted that Giddens's notion of "manufactured uncertainty"[12] results from these dramatic changes, leading some to question the very nature of modernity while seeking newer means with which to interpret the conventions of contemporary life. As he observes, "In a detraditionalizing society individuals must become used to filtering all sorts of information relevant to their life situations and routinely act on the basis of that filtering process."[13]

In contrast to Giddens, Terry Eagleton, Thomas Wharton Professor of English at the University of Oxford, struggles with this move toward an identity-based politic, posing it not as a discernible banding together of similarly-minded stalwarts compelled by a shared ideology but as evidence of a general breakdown of traditional political ideologies, coupled with a spirited but often ill-defined search for innovative standards amid the chaos of a changing social order. Eagleton's criticism of the emergent philosophical constraints leads him to contemplate the significance of a rejection of universality, a rejection that he claims has its roots in countercultural debates regarding power imbalances. And though Eagleton sympathizes with those more typically cast aside by the divisive rhetoric of a previous age, he also perceives little practical value in aggravating matters through what he deems to be the atomizing effects of individual posturing meant to replace a more traditional and relatively more inclusive political process.[14]

In *The Illusions of Postmodernism*, Eagleton notes that a shift toward a politicized sense of individual identity has a tendency to create further disintegration rather than offer society its desired galvanizing respite, a situation that he claims often ends up subverting the aims of the divergent factions in question. Within this arrangement, he explains, groups that might normally operate in tandem have become adversarial, which ultimately serves no one's quest for consideration during the search for reasonable interpretation under new social guidelines. He notes:

> When such enterprises are baffled, it is hardly surprising that these oppositions should rip open with such compulsively repetitive force. In the epoch we are imagining, what might gradually implode, along with a faith in the kind of reasonably certain knowledge we in fact enjoy all the time, would be the idea of a human subject unified enough to embark on significantly transformative action.[15]

The radical-seeming challenges that Eagleton criticizes are often informed by a dual thread of cynicism as well as an inherent sense of risk and impending danger from a host of potential but often undefined assailants. By turning inward, groups seeking relief from the burdens of inequality have grown less tolerant of others also operating within these spheres, creating a heightened sensitivity that often leads to a competitive underpinning that penetrates virtually all sectors of modern life.

Also apparent in these more contemporary debates is the dual notion of risk and risk aversion, impulses that can also be traced back to countercultural ideologies. In lieu of the more traditional perils as expressed within the vocabulary of Cold War relations, a Pandora's box of fears, built often upon a foundation of moral panics, have replaced thoughts of imminent danger emanating solely from Washington and/or Moscow. This in turn has grafted an illusion that despite the dramatic transformations taking shape since the end of the Cold War, the world remains an inherently more dangerous and perhaps even more disingenuous place than before, further exacerbating tensions that suggest that in the midst of far-reaching change, there is little that can be construed as positive. As Frank Füredi observes in his myriad reflections on such matters, the concentration of perceived risks inherent to the modern world seems immeasurable, a matter that might seem inconceivable this close to the previous epoch when the threat of an imminent nuclear war was thought to supersede any other pressing debates. For Füredi, whose analyses tend to look comparatively at changes within the United States and Great Britain, this descent into a risk aversive interpretation of modern life has created a sense of stagnation that permeates nearly every facet of American and British culture, creating newly manifest divisions within segments of society that have been rendered incapable of interpreting the nature of these changes while lapsing further into the sort of degeneration and upheaval once thought to be unimaginable.[16]

Füredi is one of many critics who have traced a similar tendency for such glum and cynical accounts of the future streaking across the post–Cold War landscape. American cultural historian Morris Berman, for example, contends that amid the chaos of the new age, America has been caught flat-footed by these striking transformations and has fallen into the throes of a sort of psychic and perhaps ideological recoil that threatens to relegate the once-vaunted American Dream into a distant nostalgic haze. For Berman the inexorable decline in solidarity is often manifest as a dissolution of shared cultural values that has led Americans to look inwardly for responses to questions that until very recently had been universally acknowledged. Lacking external indicators and shared objectives, Berman's composite America seems ripe for the emergence of schisms within the modern order that have the capacity to jeopardize future stability while enabling the process to spiral further into decay.[17]

Giddens, too, wrestles with these sorts of manifestations and contends that much of the uncertainty of the modern age can be attributed in part to the dismantling of Cold War institutions and the encroachment of left-leaning ideas brought about by a more efficiently globalized modern order. For Giddens, the interconnectedness of modern economies that in part marks the general make-up of the post–Cold War condition fuels conflict through the emphasis of more tightly bound social relations that give historically common-place activities a much broader scope. He argues that in a situation in which local actions can hold international significance, it is a much more difficult task to steer clear of conflict, which he claims is intensified by the globalization effect that conversely stands poised to block attempts for individuals to move closer toward one another. He notes:

> Globalization is not a single process but a complex mixture of processes, which often act in contradictory ways, producing conflicts, disjunctures and new forms of stratification. Thus, for instance, the revival of local nationalisms, and an accentuating of local identities, are directly bound up with globalizing influences, to which they stand in opposition.[18]

These chaotic-seeming backdrops lend themselves to the impression that the post–Cold War order offers not concrete responses but tenders instead further abstractions and upheavals to an age of transition. In this respect, what once characterized the appearance of a semi-united front in support of Western values and was thrust together by the consequences of the East-West divide has slipped into an increasingly muddled perception that Americans, the subject of this particular work, no longer seem able to recognize what it is that actually constitutes national values or perhaps even a progressive political ideology in an age of mounting uncertainty and ambiguity, an ambiguity made even more challenging by more recent tensions between Western and Muslim societies.

This confusion that permeates both remaining and developing aspects of American culture has resulted in a struggle among competing moral visions with links to Cold War era struggles that sociologist James Hunter and others have dubbed "a culture war"[19] taking shape both at home and abroad. Hunter notes that "[o]ne of the chief tasks of a public philosophy centers around the problem of national identity — deciding who we as a nation have been, coming to grips with who we are now, and defining what we should aspire to become in the future,"[20] a matter that might prove exceedingly problematic for a society unable to fully address such queries while leaving both Right and Left to reinvent their individual theoretical foundations as each searches for both relevancy and legitimacy in a chaotic age. It is specifically this sort of ambiguity that has led American sociologist James Nolan to concede that when it comes to American leadership today, "the erosion of the older sources of state legitimation, along with the continued expansion of the state, make particularly poignant the problem of legitimation and particularly pregnant the need for a new source of legitimation."[21]

To be sure, conservative elements have also struggled with these new variants in its search for order and definition amid the changes, but it is the more left-leaning factions that assume the most distinctive character in this clash by virtue of their inability to demonstrate a coherent summary of left-wing ideology amid the new social and political conventions. As popular culture critic

Todd Gitlin points out in his assessment of such contemporary cleavages, the Left has become mindful that a general distrust of existing institutions is preferable to overt complacency.[22] Still, without a coherent baseline for what constitutes a just cause, this conspicuous denunciation of tradition has become rooted in an austere, almost nihilistic critique of modernity that gives rise to Giddens' position that modernity has witnessed a veritable switching, or at the very least melding, of the traditional left-right divide, though few would contend that the basic language of the Left and the Right have been altered all that significantly.[23]

Nevertheless, Gitlin further contends that in lieu of the commonality of what had once been marked by the cause of universal freedom, modern-seeming political commentary comes across as introspective and self-affirming to the point of being overtly self-aggrandizing. Furthermore, guided by a historical perspective that has removed an objective interpretation of sociopolitical affairs while replacing it with a decidedly subjective understanding of historical phenomena, self-styled progressive elements respond to the modern world through both a portentous dread of the future and a flippant disregard for previously effective tools for encouraging solidarity. What results, perhaps ironically, is a competitive struggle between those who seek to preserve the past and those intent on erasing it altogether, under the guise of equality and justice.

Gitlin concedes that the changes manifest by the modern renegotiation for power have left a void that neither side has been able to fully grasp:

> For all the self-congratulation, the collapse of Communism rattled America — not just the consciously held ideas of what America had won and why we had won it, but also deeper, barely articulated ideas of what America was and how Americans were attached to each other. It was as if for half a century the nation had been a tug-of-war team, held together largely by the force of the adversary pulling against us. When the other team dropped their end of the rope and fled the field, what was there to hold us up?[24]

Or as Füredi contends, following the end of the Cold War, "[t]he mood of society is characteristically one of millennial doom."[25] And nowhere is this articulated more readily than in terms of what this holds for the coming generations of Americans who appear destined to be raised without the gallant struggles of the past to serve as a common thread that may bind them, as was the case with previous generations. This image is conspicuously thrust into the center of an oftentimes mordant and stark assessment of America's future, the implications of which can appear staggering and can be felt in a variety of political and cultural spaces.

The move toward a more reflective interpretation of social and political affairs coincides, thus, with the dramatic changes brought about by the end of the Cold War. Amid the uncertainty, strains of countercultural political ideology, once effectively kept at arm's length by the repressive nature of anti-communist initiatives, have quickly seeped into the chaos of an emergent post–Cold

War order. Thus, what appears to have begun in conjunction with the social and political unrest inherent to the more critical periods of the Cold War, namely the 1960s and 1970s, as a critical response to injustice and the continued repression of individual liberties has resulted in a significant shift in the basic strategies of those seeking to build a better world, a matter that seems oddly more visible elsewhere, including the cultural expectations found in the administration of competitive sport.

Risk and a Nascent Cult of Victimization

There is, in fact, a manly and lawful passion for equality that incites men to wish all to be powerful and honored.[26]

Risk taking can be in many different circumstances a highly charged test of character.[27]

On today's show, will boxing ever be safe?[28]

In a particularly poignant article written for the German daily *Frankfurter Allgemeine Zeitung*, Detlef Junker, professor of modern history at the University of Heidelberg and holder of the prestigious Engelhorn chair in American History, addresses what he deems to be "the American culture of remembrance."[29] Junker claims that modern American culture seethes with contemporary angst and chooses to look backward, reliving old injuries and reveling in previous successes while assigning them a more recent context that hastily and inexplicably overlooks modern phenomena in its scope. He contends that in their attempts to provide a voice for those who have historically been marginalized or maltreated by dominant forces, which in this particular article reflects Holocaust victims, modern elements operating under the progressive mantle have in turn elevated the aggrieved to a status that was once typically reserved for conquerors or heroes. This, according to Junker, has given rise to a more common refrain in contemporary social exchange that regards those who have struggled and lost to be heroic in spite of a more traditional reading of the concept. In other words, by assigning a primary voice to those society has traditionally overlooked or dominated through the traditional power imbalances inherent to modern societies, modern commentary has learned to offer legitimacy and authority by repositioning the victim as the new and more politically expedient mark of distinction.

In Junker's estimation, this perceived cultural manifestation seeks to reemploy the language of oppression and liberation in strikingly and notably introspective terms, and inherent to this transformation is the very notion of human activity as it pertains to the construction of what some have deemed a deification of the victim. In parallel to this perceived elevation of the victim is an increasingly accepted tendency to indict humanity rather than established social systems for events that have taken place throughout modernity. Continued dismay over the role that humans played in such horrific events as, for example, the African slave trade, the fascist experience, the atomic bombing of two Japanese cities during World War II, and even the more recent 9/11 attacks with its resulting effects, has reached the point that the stream of ideas that propel these discussions has presented these matters as a component of a more contemporary condition. Paradoxically, these historical phenomena are often aimed at a level of dialogue that cloaks the past in a modern context and presents historical events in terms of the failure of human activity that can be utilized and justified in today's debates on the grounds that human beings are unlikely to have moved on from these decidedly horrific points.

A distinctive feature of this treatment is to both relativize human activity (all behavior is culturally based and, therefore, beyond criticism) and condemn it (human behavior is intrinsically bleak and sinister), a treatment of human agency offered time and again in popular idioms ranging from film to television as well as in both literature and popular music. Furthermore, by imbuing contemporary discussions with a sense of morbidity and alarm, this progressive-seeming direction often renders the consideration of human solutions to social problems as steeped in a marked degree of hubris and is, hence, wholly inconsequential and woefully beside the point. In Eagleton's assessment of this phenomenon, which he couches in terms of a postmodern turn, the tendency to indict humanity across the board is indicative of an overtly mechanistic, even romantic, inclination toward discrediting so-called modernity while impeaching human behavior by virtue of its ambivalence to lasting social justice through attempts to theoretically interpret social interaction as politically ineffective as well as ultimately inconsequential.[30] As Gitlin explains, "People think within the intellectual and cultural currents that surround them —currents with histories, even if the sources cannot be seen from downstream,"[31] rendering what he fears is a form of "intellectual parochialism"[32] that has seized the contemporary imagination and steered it "toward an objective grid"[33] that suggests that truth can only be found in the experiences of the storyteller.[34]

Risk-taking and the idea of testing limits, once staples of American culture as well as marks of distinction customarily worn with both delight and self-assurance by the general population, have taken a severe beating under these increasingly widespread outlooks. Whereas Americans might have assumed enormous pride in their indomitable spirit as a nation of "live wires" and "go-getters,"[35] today's live wire is more likely to be thought of as overextended, bowled over by expectations, self-inflated, and potentially a hazard to him- or herself and others.

In the social climate of the early twenty-first century, the strikingly aggressive and take-charge attitude as expressed in the folklore of American convention has fallen prey to a rejection of the types of attitudes it once took to affect change and steer the course of new ideals. Principally, we can account for these changing perceptions in part because these approaches are thought to reflect traditionally hegemonic ideals at a time when these notions seem conspicuously out of touch and dangerously nostalgic and are no longer thought of as productive and virtuous, a reinterpretation of modern values that seem to hover about cultural artifacts such as competitive sport. Thus, for example, while President Theodore Roosevelt might once have argued that the value of competitive athletics lay in the stressing of "more virile virtues,"[36] the contemporary notion of traditional virtue, defined in terms of its masculine character alongside such masculine-driven behaviors as aggressiveness, goal-orientation, and a fervently expressed desire to excel, is regularly depicted as being anachronistic within the context of modern social expectations (see below).[37] In this regard, the idea of taking chances, whether it be through the active implementation of new ideas or the attempt to radicalize older ones as a means of reinventing social custom, has been replaced with passivity and inactive contemplation, with an emphasis placed on the belief that in the midst of swirling discontent, human activity can only serve to make matters worse.

In *Arrested Development: Pop Culture and the Erosion of Adulthood*, British popular culture critic Andrew Calcutt argues that this tendency to eschew the decidedly more traditional take-charge veneer in favor of a sort of cautious, safety-first approach is looked upon as an advancing virtue in the modern climate. He contends that this renewed focus is discernibly the product of a pop-cultural embrace of childishness brought about in part by the elevation of the child and childlike attributes near the center of the modern debate.[38] In a chapter entitled "Safe," Calcutt notes that a fascination with childlike purity and innocence, which is often expressed through both a celebration of childhood and a sort of conscious unwillingness to act (as one might suppose a confused child would when challenged), intersects with a growing disregard for human activity as expressed in current debates functioning within both the United States and the United Kingdom. He writes:

> Widespread infatuation with pop culture is underpinned by the common experience of impasse, i.e. the equally widespread recognition that we are living in a society which cannot understand the problems of its own making, still less overcome them. Standing before the elephantine chaos of today's world, we all have a tendency to feel like children; and pop culture is the focus of everyone's attention because it embodies the pervasive sense of childlike vulnerability which we experience in the face of social problems which seem to be as imponderable as they are gigantic.[39]

This notion of childlike vulnerability, as Calcutt has branded it, indeed marks a radical departure from more characteristic American responses to social phenomena. In this respect, the modern American is often presented not as the predictably over-ambitious zealot, as often caricatured by other world cultures, but rather as ineffective progeny befuddled by adversity and paralyzed by the fear and the responsibility of having to somehow make matters right.[40]

Correspondingly, the modern conception of the notion of risk exists in terms of its potential for dangerous outcomes or at the very least harmful side effects. This matter is typically highlighted by a perceived disruptive character and the likelihood that imminent danger rather than a reasonable solution seems the more likely outcome, leaving the proof in the examiner's accusation rather than the inverse. As University of Southern California sociologist Barry Glassner, who also wrote a critique of modern risk obsession entitled *Culture of Fear*, notes, albeit sarcastically:

> When it comes to a great [story], a journalist will behave like the high school nerd who has been approached by the most popular girl in school for help with her science project. Grateful for the opportunity, he doesn't bother to ask a lot of questions.[41]

At the same time, this thread seems poised to fuel — rather than mitigate — the insecurities of an already anxious social order by virtue of a celebration of cultural paralysis, which can often be viewed as a preferable choice when faced with the notion of doing things in error. Still, the modern discussion of risk can be offset by a much more subtle character and, according to some theorists, has the potential to be a decidedly more insidious feature of the contemporary world than one might infer given the modern climate. Füredi, for example, troubled by the notion of a further endorsement of what he deems "a diminished sense of humanity"[42] at the expense of "the human potential for improvement,"[43] places the modern obsession with risk and safety at the root of a predatory armory of cultural consciousness:

> The celebration of safety alongside continuous warnings about risks constitutes a profoundly anti-human intellectual and ideological regime. It continually invites society and its individual members to constrain their aspirations and to limit their actions. The call for restraint can now be heard everywhere, be it in discussions on science, school results or living standards. Such continuous lowering of expectations can be justified through an exaggerated presentation of the destructive side of science, or through the projection of people as fragile individuals who cannot be expected to cope.[44]

A general move toward adopting an overarching sensitivity to human suffering, either real or imagined, corresponds to these changes and has made it difficult for individuals to view things as being anything other than intrinsically dangerous, reaffirming the notion of an increasingly menacing victim status serving as something of a baseline for contemporary life. A tendency to express a hypersensitivity,[45] whether it pertains to physical or even emotional threats, cuts across all elements of society, to the extent that the most innocent remark or the most banal transgression is subject to analysis that assumes vicious intent first, often leaving those "targeted" to feel victimized by the experience, while the more insidious impediments to personal safety or even issues of individual liberties are left unchallenged. As Glassner acknowledges in his critique, one of the paradoxes operating within this cultural shift is that serious problems remain widely ignored even though they give rise to precisely the dangers that the populace most abhors. Furthermore, and as Glassner insists, even those who have historically been considered among the more dominant figures in society imagine themselves feeling victimized by discussions of privilege and power. And yet, given the new standards that dominate social conduct, these responses seem perfectly valid.[46]

Recoiling from Excellence

America has always been a nation given to public idealism. Unlike the nations of Europe, its identity was never rooted in the millennia of tradition. America compensated for this lack of a long national history through the construction of great myths about its origins and loftier visions of its calling in the future.... Even in secular political discourse, America has long been portrayed in the most moralistic terms.[47]

We live in an age that is deeply pessimistic about the human condition; an age that more often than not sees human activity as a force for destruction rather than for betterment.[48]

And thus spoke Zarathustra to the people: "The time has come for man to set himself a goal. The time has come for man to plant the seed of his highest hope."[49]

The shift toward the acceptance of victim as a mark of distinction, coupled with a withdrawal from behaviors that constitute risk, has demonstrated a profound influence on contemporary society to the extent that in many circles, the victim/loser has superseded the hero/victor as the model for what constitutes the admirable. This situation often reveals a potential to render human subjects as tragic figures unaware of the extent to which they remain powerless while they are condemned to struggle further in their anguish with a potentially devastating outcome. As one particularly beleaguered journalist puts it, "Through the elevation of suffering, passivity becomes sanctified, even celebrated. People are cast in the role of *objects* to whom things are done, rather than *subjects* capable of doing the business themselves [italics in the original]."[50]

If humans are incapable of acting alone or affecting change without creating further chaos, then the more traditional ideals relating to human efficacy and calculated risk-taking in the name of progress are a feature of contemporary society that seems to be unresolved. This situation involves an evolving tendency to present human behavior, no matter how benign or even bizarre, as both pandemic and well within a paradigm of riskiness, with the emphasis being that in the more modern and chaotic social climate (and to draw from an old adage), it is morally more acceptable to be safe rather than sorry. As Füredi reminds, "No opportunity is missed ... to remind the world that humanity has gone too far."[51] Or as the self-proclaimed contrarian Christopher Hitchens muses:

> Is it so true, as we are often assured, that we're lucky to live in an age that needs no heroes? Survivors of megalo-supermen like Napoleon might understandably agree. What a blessing to live in a society that doesn't encourage the rise of a charismatic and ruthless leader.... How much more fortunate to be able to cultivate one's own garden and pay intermittent attention to the doings of prophets and politicians. Except that ... isn't there something banal about it?[52]

One critic that presaged the clash of ideals operating within the framework of an increasingly angst-ridden modern order was the late Christopher Lasch, a consistent if not omnipresent critic of shifting cultural values as expressed within Cold War era America. In *The Culture of Narcissism: American Life in an Age of Diminishing Expectations*, Lasch seemed convinced that the contemporary American struggle for cultural supremacy would be shaped by a countercultural resistance to mainstream ideology during the zenith of America's pursuit of Cold War initiatives.[53] Beyond his depictions of a culture in retreat from itself, Lasch advanced his analysis by underscoring the seriousness with which modernity and a collective future might be imperiled by this retreat, which he considered to be, among other things, a retreat from both human efficacy and established standards of excellence.

Anticipating the work of many of the post–Cold War's harshest social critics, Lasch depicted Cold War era American society as teetering on the brink of exhaustion that would, in turn, materially threaten the very future it only fears in the abstract, a theme that he and others would address in decades to come.[54] He portrayed modern man in such a way as one might expect a psychiatrist would describe a neurotic patient: an increasingly pathetic figure in a seemingly perpetual state of despair and foreboding who lacks either the ability or the willingness to consider self-assurance or to seize upon the mechanisms for moving beyond self-absorption. In the interim, he would further describe an apprehensive, uncertain, and envious order whose collective lack of a satisfactory self-image threatens the very social stability it craves.

For Lasch, the increasingly modern position, as assumed by both the counterculture of the day and the more conservative elements with whom they battled, was driven by a dramatic shift in America's cultural reserve that seemed determined to replace the energy of a nation traditionally fortified by thoughts of infinite possibilities with an acknowledgement of limits, boundaries, and a deepening fear of the future, which he felt offered both intellectual as well as salutary concerns. He argued that while the collective, conservative frame of reference was nearing collapse, within the radicalism of the countercultural Left there existed a degree of self-absorption that encouraged such notions as living for the present in the face of an increasingly desolate and narrow future while seeking to reinvent the social order through a shared interpretation of what it means to feel good about oneself and one's environment in the midst of mounting chaos and confusion. Citing an acknowledged failure of the traditional means for engendering activity to stir the public's imagination past the desperation and listlessness of the age, Lasch maintained that following the exhaustion of the countercultural project in Cold War America, holdovers such as instant gratification and living for the present were considered by the Left to be the mark of a progressive people. In contrast, Lasch noted that the Right continued to fight to hold on to more traditional measurements of success and achievement through more traditionally narrow (and perhaps more manageable) straits as part of a larger acquiescence toward a distinctive goal orientation that the Left sought to portray as elitist and exceedingly unjust, spearheading further division between those who advocated active human engagement and those who followed more passively expressed principles.[55]

Lasch's nod toward countercultural concerns was intended to position an increasingly vulnerable society that had grown to accept a mounting conviction that an aggressively pursued goal orientation had the potential to leave the individual prone to disappointment and rejection and would mark, thus, a decidedly precarious and potentially life-threatening condition. Equally as vital was his assessment of the notably humanist stance, as fomented by nascent countercultural critics, which he argued added fuel to the assumption that mankind lacked the capacity to either move forward or overcome mounting obstacles without inviting some sort of cognitive, physical, or psychic injury or some variation thereof. Additionally, Lasch maintained that regardless of a wide range of extant or perceived inequities as chronicled by many of the era's critics, the one component of traditional American life that must stand resistant to change was the standard of excellence as established within many venerable institutions. Looking specifically at competitive sport in this case, Lasch feared that in the place of excellence, a fashionable political element stood poised to reinterpret the concept of excellence as elitist and inherently discriminatory, fostering an erosion of standards in the name of creating a more egalitarian ideal to which Lasch took great exception. As he would observe, such a move would "[confuse] socialization with indoctrination."[56] Or as Morris Berman notes angrily, "The inevitable result of [an erosion of standards] is the inability of the American public to distinguish garbage from quality."[57]

Without the constancy of Cold War conformity, the loss of cultural moorings as expressed through a once fervent anti-communism and an engineered, though effective, display of nationalism has augmented a remarkable denigration of the historically renowned American spirit. This in turn has tendered an appreciably predictable course of evaluation and reevaluation of the nature of human activity, the meaning of productivity, and a reinterpretation of a number of shared American values. Given these changes, it should come as little surprise that as the twenty-first century continues to unfold before us, we can find parallel, albeit particularist, shifts taking shape throughout the vast cultural milieu that marks everyday life.

Masculinity Reconsidered

Men are not my favorite critters. Straight men can be crude, violent, hateful, misogynist, and insensitive. But they do things. They go out in the world and work. They make things. They compete with one another without getting bitchy.[58]

I am tired of men. Sick and tired of men and their ethos of violence. Truly I am and figuratively. Male violence is an integral part of our culture.[59]

The feminism around me in classrooms, conversations, and student journals was not the feminism I grew up with.... All of the sudden feminism meant being angry about men looking at you in the street and writing about "the colonialist appropriation of the female discourse."[60]

The increasingly more distinctive atomization of the population, coupled with its growing distrust of the traditional mechanisms for initiating lasting and substantive change, suggests that American cultural patterns have taken a notable turn toward the introspective, causing some critics to wonder aloud about the future of shared social activity. As Berman concedes, somewhat dramatically, the stagnation brought about by this steady stream of evaluation and reevaluation places the nation on a course in parallel with the waning days of the Roman Empire. In turn, he forecasts further breakdown brought about by what he reasons to be sincere yet misguided attempts to forcibly assemble a more open society without attacking its roots.[61]

Looking specifically at issues pertaining to educational standards and their effects on America's youth in this environment, Berman asserts that the consequences of challenging previous social standards with what he deems to be floating standards may end up exacerbating the problems already in question, that is, racism, gender inequality, power imbalances, and so on, while at the same time threatening to deplete what remains of the nation's cultural assets altogether. Echoing the nineteenth century admonitions of Tocqueville, Berman posits that in an effort to create a more inclusive social order free of both Cold War era conformity and the sort of stratification emblematic of capitalist social relations, cultural excellence is left exposed to the encroachment of lower expectations. Moreover, he contends that this condition has the potential to thrust the nation into what he deems to be a sort of postmodern barbarism that considers excellence to be little more than an elitist lie and a remnant of a once venerated masculine hegemony, conditions that often find themselves at odds and at the center of debates staged across an increasingly fragile cultural terrain. Toward that, Berman maintains that a "so-called [period] of democratization is not an attempt to get the less able to stretch themselves a bit; rather, it is a reduction of everything to the lowest common denominator and the regarding of that as some sort of political triumph."[62]

Berman's analysis emerges from an increasingly held perception that an allegiance to the individual rather than the collective has the potential to redraft the foundations of modern life. Though controversial, this shift toward the elevation of the individual and the importance of self-perception stands poised to place the internal impulse of feeling rather than an externally grafted achievement ethos at the forefront of contemporary social thought. This in turn has the potential to render modern criticism benign primarily because in its traditional guise it seems to intersect with the cultural or social orientation of the individual, while threatening whatever cultural space he or she may have earmarked along the way. This experience is reflected in a variety of social or cultural settings, resulting in endless debates regarding the efficacy of existing institutions that feature emotionally charged debates concerning their potential to contribute positively to the general well-being of a nation increasingly prone to self-absorption.

In many contemporary critiques, the predominance of the self, which has historically been linked to feminine social patterns and cultural themes, coincides with discussions pertaining to the role that men and masculinity have played in shaping modernity. Indeed, there is an escalating mode of thought that suggests that the foundations for the problems facing modern society stem not from fateful turns of global events but from the traditional stranglehold that a patriarchy and its resulting interests have long assumed over sociopolitical debate. In this respect, there is a growing segment of the population that assumes that an ongoing crisis in masculinity lies at the root of social pathology, which puts so-called masculine tendencies and behavioral traits in a sort of limbo state if not in outright jeopardy. As Heartfield notes:

> Masculinity is increasingly seen as a problem.... The expectations of what it means to be a man today are confused and uncertain, or even held to be a problem. 'Masculine virtues' like assertiveness, self-possession, comradeship and courage were once seen as traits whose virtue was beyond question. Many of the 'manly virtues' that were once seen as evidence of a healthy natural order, today seem to be interpreted as inherently pathological conditions.[63]

By contrast, if masculinity is responsible for societal upheavals, the reasonable turnabout is that a feminized future is the answer, which further underscores the growing divide between a progressive and a regressive worldview that is often couched as a matter of male versus female virtue. Füredi, writing in a now-defunct British publication once known for polemics, queries:

> Many experts have identified an inexorable trend towards the economic enfranchisement of women. The popular media is fascinated by the feminisation of cultural life ... where lesbianism and androgyny can be presented as fashionable. Social scientists point to the feminisation of public attitudes towards everything from parenting to TV violence, and argue that "macho" aggression has now been widely rejected in favour of the values of caring and sharing. They suggest that one of the fundamental features of the postmodern age is the renegotiation of the traditional relationship between men and women.[64]

More decidedly modern assaults on masculinity and masculine comport-ment also have their roots in the social unrest of the 1960s and the reinvigora-tion of a fragmented women's movement into what has been called a second wave. This second wave sought to build upon the advances of what had been a long-dormant movement that seemed to have scattered between the world wars and weakened beneath the supposed conformity-driven dynamic of the 1950s. The success of such monumental works as Betty Friedan's *The Feminist Mys-tique*,[65] however, shook feminist attitudes from their dormancy, culminating in a much more broad-based and far-reaching attempt to extricate women from the margins of modern life and thrust them into the center of the increasingly contentious debates of the Cold War era.

The successes of the second wave are marked by the encroachment of women into such traditionally masculine spheres as the workplace, academia, and even competitive sport, but in the aftermath of the post–Cold War period, there are indications that this second wave of feminism has become weighted down by notable fracturing within the circle of modern feminism at various levels, ranging from a general lack of a coherent vision to an outright clash of ideologies. For example, writing in the introduction to a collection of postmod-ernist essays on sport, editor Geneviève Rail of the University of Ottawa con-cedes that while much of feminism and postmodernism have forged an alliance in the past decade, there are some factions within modernizing feminist debate that have not come on board with more modern shifts in feminist discourse, most notably those stemming from the more liberal circles and the Marxists.[66] She notes that a continued allegiance to the Enlightenment tradition, to which modern feminism had once been wed, has left many feminist thinkers either unwilling or unable to forge a relationship within the more popularly heralded academic disciplines. She maintains, thus, that the "postmodern conceptual-ization of subjectivity as permanently discontinuous, displaced, and destabi-lized"[67] has proven to be challenging for a good portion of feminists who might have, at least at one time, been considered on the radical edge of the feminist frontlines but are at present more likely to be seen as products of an increas-ingly conservative approach.

Others, however, refute Rail's central premise that competing ideologies are to blame for a more decidedly fractious feminist project. For instance, Camille Paglia, writing in *The Chronicle for Higher Education*, notes that assign-ing a dual theoretical premise to a modern feminist ideology assumes a muted yet arguably chic cultural Victorianism that promotes what she deems to be a sloppy essentialist pose that lacks a basic consideration of scientific inquiry.[68] In the face of mounting skepticism mired in what some feminists have termed a sort of modernist backlash, Paglia, who calls herself a member of the reform wing of contemporary feminism and has emerged as an exceedingly contentious figure, muses:

Arcane French theory, based on linguistic paradigms predating World War II, looks pretty foolish these days, when most people are concerned with bread-and-butter issues such as child care, the divorce rate, drug use, and decaying public education.[69]

Others have also noted that more contemporary strains of feminist discourse seem compelled to overstep a wide range of women who might benefit from such critiques, which often leaves the movement to be perceived as exclusive, narrow-minded, and disinterested in the lives of everyday women. Mary Zeiss Stange, associate professor of women's studies and religion at Skidmore College, notes that while it had once been customary for second wave feminists to present a united front, this may no longer be the case. She explains that a dogmatic faithfulness to feminist positions is no longer fashionable but is still enforced in many academic circles, giving rise to the notion that, as she laments, "for all our talk of multiplicity and inclusiveness, [we] skate dangerously close to the edge of intolerance."[70]

These contestations within contemporary feminist thought notwithstanding, the underlying effect of the more recent awareness of the language of contemporary feminism has brought about a reconsideration of what it means to be a man and what it means to be a women in the context of what is an increasingly ill-defined social order. This resulting confusion demonstrates a remarkable and notable shift that has in many ways divided the movement into many different domains, that is, the cultural, the historical, the sexual. These myriad directions at times seem poised to refute one another rather than offer more coherent and substantive social commentary, often leaving the promotion of feminist ideals both within academic discussion and on the outside of the academy in a particularly precarious state. Where they do seem to stand united, however, is the increasingly more common contention that masculine behaviors and attitudes remain at the center of social discord.[71] As cultural critic Stephen Heath ponders:

> Men's relation to feminism is an impossible one. This is not said sadly nor angrily (though sadness and anger are both known and common reactions) but politically. Men have a necessary relation to feminism — the point after all is that it should change them too, that it involves learning new ways of being women *and men* against and as an end to the reality of women's oppression — and that relation is also necessarily one of a certain exclusion — the point after all is that this is a matter *for women*, that it is their voices and actions that must determine the change and redefinition. Their voices and actions, not ours. [italics in the original][72]

A more contemporary discussion of masculinity assigns to traditional male behaviors a formulaic array of hegemonic transgressions ranging from over-aggressiveness to a callous disregard for health, safety, and the importance of relationships. In a twist on what was once supposed to be a matter of common knowledge, men today are thought to suffer from a variety of psychological disorders that have resulted from both the unrelenting demands of living up to masculine standards and the confusion of having to reinterpret the developing rules poised to negate traditional masculine virtue.[73] The proliferation and popularity of men's self-help journals, organizations such as Promise Keepers,[74] the largely African American Million Man March, and poet Robert Bly's work in the field of masculine studies[75] highlight these convictions. These and other such organizations help further the notion that modern man is either a victim of the unrealistic standards inherent to the Western tradition or a dupe who believes that he is supposed to measure up to these same standards by resorting to unseemly behaviors that in the end have the potential, if not the capacity, to turn violent. Thus, when Giddens refers to the challenges facing a reconstruction of masculine and feminine roles in what he reasons amounts to a post-military order,[76] he must also acknowledge the degree to which these roles are ingrained, once they are juxtaposed to the many social changes to follow:

> The transformation of masculinity and femininity, or rather their multiple forms, as inherited from the past, will depend in a basic way on how far a post-military society comes into being, and what consequences flow from the changing character of work, the family and sexual relationships.[77]

A parallel discussion has formed regarding a so-called crisis of young males today. This debate further advances the notion that as society unearths additional substantiation of behaviors thought to be typically masculine, classically described as stoicism, assertiveness, and bravado, society should be acutely aware that these once esteemed behaviors are to be viewed in contemporary circles with both a weary and a sympathetic gaze.[78] In this respect, young men coming of age in the early twenty-first century are to be looked upon as both potential perpetrators of traditional masculine misdeeds and as victims of the same confusion and discordant displays expressed in older generations. Furthermore, it is also considered probable that the potential to recreate and transmit traditional masculine traits, behaviors that are thought to predictably cut against the grain of the contemporary behavioral norms as expressed in the language of modern discourse, places them squarely within the modern, albeit ubiquitous, interpretation of being *at-risk*.

Couching male youth in such terms fuels already rampant speculation that they may indeed already be victims of maladies ranging from an abnormal and elastic moral nature to an insufficient degree of impulse control and even notably poor socialization processes as employed by unenlightened adults caught unaware and ostensibly trapped in the more traditional parenting cycles.[79] Michael Gurian, a popular child-rearing author, advocate, and lecturer, observes:

> Males undoubtedly enjoy certain advantages in our culture. But they do not have the advantage of being born with an inherent path to self-worth. Their early brain development pushes their lives more outward into the surrounding world than inward into their emotional development. They push and prod and hit and miss

their way through obstacles and challenges. They know even from the first truck they hold that they must earn their place in the world. They compete and strive and can often appear to lack basic compassion as they try to do better, gain respect, and prove their worth.[80]

To be sure, the growing condemnation of masculinity has become one of the more hotly contested debates of the post–Cold War era. Still, as the sides line up in opposition to one another, the commonality of this discussion seems to be the insistence that in an increasingly modern society, one in which seeking a more egalitarian existence supersedes many other points of contention, the distance between the sexes, sometimes tendered as a gender war, is cause for alarm.

Where the line seems to be drawn is at the level of the worth of so-called masculine traits and whether or not there is a place for traditional masculinity in the envisioned liberalized and certainly less aggressively displayed and perhaps feminized future. In this case, modern feminism's most vocal critics can be found, generally speaking, in the insistence that a once respected masculine deportment is no longer welcomed in the contemporary frame. For example, John MacInnes of the University of Edinborough notes with some alarm that traditional masculine virtues such as heroism, independence, courage, strength, rationality, will, backbone, and virility have been redubbed masculine vices, with the implication being that any tangible connection to traditional masculine deportment threatens to render behavior archaic and conceivably even hazardous. On its face, this type of assessment would tend to discount the more environmental origins of what had typically been considered the marks of masculine productivity, right or wrong. Undeniably, males have long dominated the productive sphere, but this domination was the result of a socially constructed program rather than indicative of a natural order. To dismiss outright a record of dynamic and industrious conduct because it comes with untoward sociohistorical baggage suggests that a diminished capacity is an acceptable outcome if it leads to a more egalitarian order, an assessment that some would argue comes complete with unfortunate baggage of its own.[81] As Füredi has observed, "Today's anti-masculine culture condemns forms of behavior that in the past were considered elementary human virtues. Critics of masculinity have a strong distaste for the habit of self-reliance and self-control. They believe that the aspiration for heroism is ludicrous. And they are intensely suspicious of the virtues of independence, willpower, risk-taking and rationality."[82]

Behind this anti-masculine pose lies an equally spurious perception that women are themselves incapable of typically masculine behaviors and have chosen biologically, rather than having been assigned historically, to roles that are notably submissive, burdened by emotionalism, and decidedly non-heroic in spite of evidence to the contrary. This is a point that is routinely addressed in responses that seek to redress assumptions that there lurks a level of predatory masculinity behind more far-reaching explanations. For instance, in *The*

Morning After: Sex, Fear, and Feminism, a work that raised the ire of numerous feminists both within and on the outside of academia, Katie Roiphe took exception to such generalizations, contending that at the root of contemporary feminist assessments is a decidedly anti-male posture coupled with an equally disturbing denigration of the capacity of women to effectively control their own destinies. Writing on the so-called rape culture operating on American college campuses in the 1980s and 1990s, she notes:

> In this era of Just Say No and No Means No, we don't have many words for embracing experience. Now instead of liberation and libido, the emphasis is on trauma and disease. Now the idea of random encounters, of joyful, loveless sex, raises eyebrows. The possibility of adventure is clouded by the specter of illness. It's a difficult backdrop for conducting one's youth.[83]

Toward Establishing a Modern Discussion of Competition

> *If you've coached girls' or women's sports, if you've played with or against women, if you have women as friends or family, if you know a woman or are a woman — then you know the mess of contradictions they can harbor about what it means to be competitive.*[84]
>
> *In a world so fragmented, team unifies.*[85]

Some contend that given the level of the discussion relative to gender roles and faddish modern analyses, an increasingly atomized modern feminism fails in part because it brings to the forum an open contempt of men and masculine behaviors that is often validated in theory but does little to bring about actual liberation short of further separating individuals from one another. Indeed, one of the more conspicuous criticisms enveloping modern feminist debate is that it has become advocacy masquerading as scholarship, which makes for some vitriolic responses but fails to effectively debunk the myth that women are incapable of objective, unemotional, and self-reliant behavior irrespective of previous socialization patterns in evidence. To be candid, whether or not this assessment of the efficacy of modern feminist discourse is valid is clearly beyond the scope of this work, but where it does intersect in terms of the contemporary discussion of competition, a decidedly masculine trait if one can believe the overall content of sport-ordered dialogue, is the assumption that in a world conspicuously organized around manly virtues and masculine deportment, is it possible or even likely that a woman can compete either in the athletic arena or within the society itself, for that matter? Furthermore, one may also inquire as to whether or not a women's competitive nature can or should be governed by a different philosophical construct as a means to refute a tradition and a performance ethos that has long been assigned a masculine character?

Given sport's traditional relationship to matters that are often thought to constitute a decidedly male-dominated frame, including such time-honored principles as heroism, its celebration of victors, its conscious lack of sensitivity to those deemed ineffective in the competitive schema, and the unexpurgated devotion to achievement, which generally involves some element of risk, it is hardly surprising that the world of competitive athletics today finds itself bracing under the weight of increased scrutiny. Furthermore, it is from within an increasingly omnipresent shroud of heightened sensitivity along with the expectation of peril and its resulting victim status that the framework exists for more modern critiques of many existing or emerging institutions, including discussions concerning the contemporary nature of competitive sport and its perceived influence over American society as a whole.

With an eye toward caution, along with the articulated misgivings relative to traditional masculine virtues, contemporary sport criticism has come to reflect increasingly modern anxieties regarding its effects on America's subsequent generations. By portraying competitive conditions in terms of their potential for pathological outcomes, a modern paradigmatic shift can be noted whose varied content seems to have evolved in part from older ideals regarding social justice that have been reshaped and outfitted for a decidedly more contemporary outlook.

Within the emergent post–Cold War period, competitive sport, with its relationship to achievement, strength, drive, excellence, and manly virtue, has emerged as something of a straw man for the sorts of discussions as described above. The ubiquitousness of modern sport allows ample opportunity for heated exchange between traditional forces trying to make sense of the modern world and the more modern developments in social criticism trying to reconcile or in many cases negate more traditional perceptions of competition and its place within the culture. Consequently, within many of the more prevailing segments of mainstream life, competitive sport is no longer viewed simply as a reasonable symbol of an acceptable and just moral order as projected in the more customary representation. Rather, it is often looked upon adversely as a reflection of a bygone era whose ethical standards are no longer relevant to a more modern and perhaps even more accommodating epoch.

Thus, one may infer that as we advance farther into the twenty-first century while moving farther away from the Cold War dynamic, discussions regarding competitive sport's place in contemporary American society can no longer be viewed strictly in terms of the competitive terrain but through a prism of modern discussions pertaining to a more widespread dissatisfaction with contemporary cultural and sociopolitical phenomena. Debates surrounding matters brought to the surface, at least initially so, by a range of countercultural ambitions have ascended into the mainstream of contemporary thought and have circulated within an increasingly more crowded world of sport criticism.

The image of traditional sport may indeed be changing, but the enormity of these changes are enhanced by an evolving societal pathos that emanates not from within competitive sport itself but rather from within the anxieties and ambiguities of a modern order in search of a more consistent rationale with which to interpret both modern and traditional experience. The fact that competitive sport has gotten caught up in this environment is not all that unexpected given its importance to the culture as a whole and its perceived inability to adapt to the emergent trends along the periphery of modern debate; but the fact that its traditional, almost sacrosanct, place in American life is being materially threatened demonstrates in part the mounting distance between more typically accepted practices and the aspirations of more fashionable discussion of what might constitute acceptable conduct in a rapidly changing social landscape.

2

American Sport and the Traditional Competitive Ethos

There is an aspect of America's cultural heritage and the nation's self-image steeped in that heritage that seems remarkably at ease using the language and the metaphor of sport. Americans have long viewed themselves through the context of hard-fought physical and psychological confrontations that are then typically followed by attempts to draw out some moral significance associated with each challenge. Through this apparently competitive frame of reference, they have been able to construct a powerful image of national strength, pride, and unity that has been both ingrained and nourished over the course of many years, forging a relationship between sport and culture that has become almost inseparable from the nation's character. Still, while the images of sport may have been able to comfort, sustain, and even in some cases affect policy for Americans in the past, contemporary depictions assigned to sport today often bear little resemblance to the same institution that has historically been so honored and revered in the popular consciousness.

The genuine accounting of the evolution of competitive American sport, so romanticized in public opinion, was never part of the flowing and balanced narrative that many Americans have long regarded and would like to imagine still exists. Rather, an investigation into the developments leading toward a modern American sporting culture shows that it was an institution that was not free from conflict, nor has it existed over time with impunity. Its emergence and rise to prominence were from the beginning held in dispute, mired in controversy, and marked by heated exchanges concerning its place, its relevance, and its role in the evolution of an increasingly modern America. Thus, while many Americans today may look back on sport with a mixture of nostalgic yearning and romantic fascination, these accounts also tend to dismiss the fact that the rise of the American competitive sport tradition as it actually existed coincided with periods of great uncertainty, unsettling transition, and national tragedy and was certainly not without its critics and detractors at any time throughout the course of myriad developmental phases.

This chapter will serve as a structural overview of the historic place that competitive sport occupies in American culture by broadly tracing the construction of its ethos in the popular consciousness. Through a broad survey of both critical and popular commentary, I will attempt to shed light on the debates, the disputes, and the dramatic changes that have shaped American sport from the antebellum nineteenth century to the end of the twentieth century while attempting as well to highlight those areas of historical import relative to changes in the nature of contemporary American sport.

Leisure and the Closing of the American Frontier

Rooted in the material, social, and political realities of the age, sport dramatized fundamental ideas in American society. During a period of rapid social and political change, sport became a powerful medium for national self-identification as well as a metaphor for bourgeois values.[1]

I believe that sport, all sport, is one of the few bits of glue that holds our society together, one of the few activities where young people can proceed along traditional lines ... where he can learn how to win ... and how to lose.[2]

In his groundbreaking study of American recreational culture, historian Foster Rhea Dulles attempted to place America's move toward the adoption of recreational sport and a resulting sport aesthetic squarely in the context of the changes taking place during the first third of the nineteenth century. He concludes:

> [The] phenomenal expansion in the field of sports was the most significant development in the nation's recreational life that had yet taken place ... athletics provided an outlet for surplus energy and suppressed emotions that the American people greatly needed. The traditions of pioneer life had influenced them along very definite lines, and the restrictions of urban living warred against a feeling for the outdoors which was in their blood. With the gradual passing of so much of what the frontier had always stood for, sports provided a new outlet for an inherently restless people.[3]

It is precisely this period of the frontier, or the closing of that vaunted expanse, where Dulles and most other American commentators assume that the transition in America's recreational culture took shape and the American embrace of competitive sport originates.

By the nineteenth century, frontier life and the developmental processes associated with westward expansion enveloped nearly every feature of American life and was a particularly important, if not often overlooked, element of the antebellum experience. The constancy of change relative to the possibilities for great wealth and future prosperity that lay ahead spearheaded confidence that a dynamic and limitless America was not an illusion but a certainty. Irrespective of the social and political difficulties brought about by, for example, debates surrounding the spread of slavery to the West and the implications of Jeffersonian democracy on the American state as a whole, most Americans saw the frontier as a symbol of a vibrant and boundless national character. As Harvard historian Frederick Jackson Turner would observe in his landmark *The Frontier in American History* first published in 1921:

> All peoples show development; the germ theory of politics has been sufficiently emphasized. In the case of most nations, however, the development has occurred in a limited area; and if the nation has expanded, it has met other growing peoples whom it has conquered. But in the case of the United States we have a different phenomenon. Limiting our attention to the Atlantic coast, we have the familiar phenomenon of the evolution of institutions in a limited area, such as the rise of representative government; into complex organs; the progress from primitive industrial society, without division of labor, up to manufacturing civilization. But we have in addition to this a recurrence of the process of evolution in each western area reached in the process of expansion. Thus American development has exhibited not merely advance along a single line, but a return to primitive conditions on a continually advancing frontier line, and a new development for that area. American social development has been continually beginning over again on the frontier. This perennial rebirth, this fluidity of American life, this expansion westward with its new opportunities, its continuous touch with the simplicity of primitive society, furnish the forces dominating American character.[4]

The closing of the American frontier would in no small fashion mark the end of an era teeming with unbridled optimism. In its place stood a notable shift away from the vitality of the day, propelling it toward an increasingly problematic and anxiety-ridden direction that brought along with it a marked degree of skepticism regarding, among other notions, the fear of the uncharted directions that lay ahead. While on the one hand, the closing of the frontier meant that Americans had in fact manifested their destiny to conquer the entire North American continent, there was an equally strong sense that the end of this particular chapter of American advancement may also have marked the start of an extended period of stagnation. The frontier gave Americans something to embrace, a shared sense of purpose, and an understanding that American life would not be predicated on limitations but on the notion that boundaries were merely challenges yet to be overcome. Without the challenge of an ever-expanding boundary, Americans seemed to resign themselves to the possibility of decline, and this contention was extremely difficult for the people of that generation to have to contemplate. As the Turner quote above suggests, with the continent conquered, what lay ahead might be construed as mundane and agonizingly predictable, hardly a condition the still developing nation would have experienced previously. The perception that there may have been little left to strive for beyond the plodding of time left Americans feeling skittish rather than celebratory, and consternation enveloped many who less than a generation ago considered American expansion to be both a constant and a given. As de Tocqueville had already observed, and perhaps even foreseen, "In America, men never stay still."[5]

Another prominent feature of the anxieties wrought by the closing of the frontier was the unsettling and often dramatic modifications in the economic sphere, modifications that would in turn have a significant impact on the ways in which Americans would perceive the quality of their lives and the nature of their livelihoods. This was especially true in the case of production, as America began to inch closer toward its own industrial revolution. Prior to this period, the antebellum American workplace typically featured small business enterprises and family farms, hardly the picture of the immense industrial infrastructure that would come to dominate and reshape the American economy and the American workplace, especially in the increasingly urban Northeast and Midwest. But as these changes began to manifest, the more traditional workplace relationships between owners and workers and those between skilled and unskilled laborers were being altered fundamentally in the face of major technological advances.

In the days prior to the massive postbellum industrial expansion, most workers experienced activities in their daily lives that appeared capable of bridging the gulf between work and recreation. The workday for many was long and the conditions challenging, if not downright primitive and harsh. Yet, and primarily because they were made to feel a part of relatively small-scale and flexible production teams, the combination of working for the greater good while cooperatively serving in a creative capacity helped foster the illusion that one's work and presence were both meaningful and psychologically nourishing. Of course this may not have been true in the case of African slaves in the American South or women in general, nor was everyone necessarily satisfied with his or her place in the American economy. Still, generally speaking, most seemed to be able to find in these arrangements at least a modicum of satisfaction in their routines relative to their professional lives.[6]

One result of these arrangements was that leisure and recreational pursuits were often the farthest thing from the minds of the majority of so-called Middle Americans.[7] While they had participated in leisure activities long before these changes took shape, by and large, these types of activities were relegated to local custom and tended to be disorganized and practiced somewhat arbitrarily. Furthermore, given America's historical devotion to activity and production, the coalescence of physical labor and spirituality that Weber would term the "Protestant ethic,"[8] endeavors that were not directly linked to work, or at the very least to improvements in one's ability to produce more efficiently and effectively, were generally held in a negative light, leaving leisure and recreational pursuits of any sort to remain under close scrutiny well toward the middle of the century. In this regard, people who did participate in non-work related or non-church sanctioned leisure activities had to be wary of incurring the wrath of community leaders who typically frowned upon such activities and were convinced of the force that linked productivity and morally acceptable behavior. Certainly in this environment anything as non-productive as an unsupervised athletic competition would have easily fallen under the heading of frivolous and been perceived as a general waste of one's productive capacity.[9]

In sharp contrast to the European experience relative to such customs, and belying the heritage of the many immigrant cultures that were being constantly absorbed into the tapestry of American life, sport and recreation were afforded little public notice among early Americans. While there were a variety of leisure pursuits, including sport, in existence long before the closing stages of frontier life, they were for the most part incidental to daily life. As Dulles observes, any leisure activities locals might have participated in were primarily associated with country life and local ritual, though some activities such as barn-raising and beehive-husking were considered to be at least productive in spite of the typically playful tenor these sorts of events often produced.[10] Indeed, given the spread of religious custom that existed throughout the country and virtually dictated social policy, leisure that could not be linked directly to productivity was generally discouraged by often inflexible community leaders.

Eventually, however, something of an exclusive underground for sport would find its way into the folkways of a handful of either non-aligned people or populations that existed along the margins, populations that might include, for example, younger generations of landed gentry, merchants, and even journeymen craftsmen and artisans who found little wrong with supplementing a day's labor (or lack thereof) with decidedly inconsequential amusement. More troublesome for those in charge, however, was the budding recreational culture emerging from the ranks of a much rowdier cross-section of the population that featured the likes of predominantly Irish immigrants remanded to menial labor and various others of working-class extraction seeking fulfillment through leisure in what was shaping up to be a burgeoning bachelor-dominated saloon culture in the urban centers of the American Northeast.[11] These self-consciously antiestablishment mavericks, described in many accounts of this period in terms of their nonconforming and often sordid behavior,[12] existed primarily along the periphery of society. Furthermore, their unruly displays of impropriety could easily be denounced as wholly inappropriate for the times. As a result of these contributions as well as the burgeoning rural Southern pursuit of so-called blood sports such as cock- and dog-fighting and brawling, sporting interests would remain considerably outside the realm of mainstream life well into the middle of the nineteenth century. For most Americans, the principal focus of their lives remained their ability to control their individual destinies through their relationship to the American marketplace. A distinctly second-rate sporting populace, with its violent blood sports, unseemly displays of machismo, and passion for gambling, were far removed from the more typical middle-class and working-class Americans who would not find themselves drawn toward incorporating elements of sport and leisure into their own lives until the structural changes to the workplace began to manifest following, among other things, the continued escalation of industrialization and the coming of the American Civil War.[13]

Reinvestigating Antebellum Leisure

Sports gave man power over his body the same way an engineer had power over a piece of machinery. Riding a horse added the pleasure of governing another's will, physically extending one's self from the animal's ears to its hooves.[14]

In an attempt to return to some semblance of balance, late nineteenth- and early twentieth-century American bourgeois culture turned to the regulation of body and mind through organized athletics in an effort to exert control over the process of history. For the symbol of the well-regulated and disciplined body and mind of the archetypal athlete, bourgeois spokespersons soon spun new explanations and defenses of a well-regulated body politic — a modern civilization that balanced corporate and social needs through the gospel of fair play.[15]

Given the lofty place that recreation occupies today alongside its remarkable market niche, it seems extraordinary that there could have been a time in America's recent past that recreation and leisure activities, so closely aligned with the power of rejuvenation and the escape from the mundane, could have ever been coupled with the framework of the American workplace, but this was clearly the case. As an extension of older traditions, the antebellum workplace often resembled a familial setting that generally consisted of master artisans, craftsmen, and apprentices whose personal attachments and professional aspirations helped maintain at least the illusion that their lives were intrinsically linked through the production process. This often resulted in what they and others claim was an oddly satisfying relationship between work and the needs of the individual to feel as if he or she had a hand in his or her own advancement. The thought that a worker would have to arrange some sort of respite following the workday was anathema to this arrangement as regardless of circumstances, each member of the group was afforded at the very least the semblance of an opportunity to contribute in ways ranging from structural design to implementation to the pace of the work environment itself. But in the face of the changes to come, spearheaded by technology and expanding national and international markets, it was becoming evident that the illusions of broad-based satisfaction operating within the workplace were beginning to collapse under the weight of production quotas and the approaching reinvention of labor as essentially a pool of machine operators and unskilled muscle. The lasting effects on the intricate series of relationships that existed between employers, craftsmen, workers, and their markets would result in an inevitable rift, and its subsequent effect on the illusion would be calculable.[16]

These changes would come at a steady and deliberate pace, and often forced workers to respond in myriad ways. Some took matters into their own hands and found themselves caught up in a particularly novel age of entrepreneurship, but most would come to find that their autonomy, their ability to fend off managerial encroachments through organizing, and their invaluable creative processes had been usurped by the realities of large-scale production and the ensuing profits it could potentially reap. The combination of an increasingly more repressive workplace together with the blocking of the more traditional means of self-expression through creative productivity marshaled in an era in which the character of leisure and recreation were to undergo a reevaluation in the public's eye and threatened to turn free time productivity rather than workday productivity into the principal focus of a working man's day.[17]

This abrupt reinterpretation of the nature of leisure brought about by altered workplace relationships was discomfiting and problematic for most. For workers increasingly alienated from their individual contributions and unlikely to experience a creative outlet while on the job, recreational activities would grow into a welcome source for reinvigorating the spirit and mitigating the frustration and tedium born of workday drudgery.

The religious undercurrent that often served as the foundation for the older arrangements was also being diluted under the strain caused by notable spikes in productivity. Work, which for many was on par with a religious calling promising sanctuary and salvation to an exceedingly observant populace, was the primary component of America's vaunted work ethic. Under the emergent conditions, its fragmentation and increased routinization at the hands of demanding capitalists and escalating markets further eroded the private sphere, initially threatening and eventually fostering dismay and disenchantment throughout the American workforce. Whereas in the past members of the American working class were able to control their lives through the productive process, the shift from the familial shop to the impersonal yet technologically advanced factory threatened to destroy the illusion that ordinary people could control necessary aspects of their lives, drawing them closer toward behaviors that less than a generation ago might have been inconceivable.[18] As historian David Macleod notes in his formidable critique of early American leisure patterns:

> In pre-industrial America, workdays were long but the pace was irregular, and one seldom spent whole weeks stretched drum-tight by work. New economic opportunities and pressure changed that, however, so that work took on new value and intensity. Antebellum American men looked to work as an outlet for their finest strivings and as a goad to discipline and self-denial; it was a school

of character where men and boys learned to obey the marching orders of the will.[19]

In the absence of these safeguards, "[r]ecreation," he says further, "took on a new earnestness."[20]

By mid-century, being at work no longer held the same significance that it had prior to industrialization. The physical toll drawn from the increasingly perfunctory factory and the psychological effects of the mindless tedium brought about through repetition and the increasingly repressive expectations of ownership lent the workplace an unfamiliarly cool atmosphere that held little meaning to the typical employee. Many in turn began to consider work to be little more than a necessary yet unwelcome interruption to their lives and a circumstance that could no longer serve in the dual capacity of satisfying accomplishment and enriching experience. The workplace for many would instead become the symbol of repression and alienation, forcing the pursuit of satisfying and sustaining activity into an entirely different realm that in turn would bring leisure and a host of recreational activities out of the periphery and closer into the mainstream of American life.[21]

The physical and psychological significance of these rapid transformations is monumental in terms of our ability to trace the developing changes that would cause Americans to reconsider their lives in relation to leisure and recreation. As the workplace closed its doors to the more traditional relationships between production and leisure, formalized leisure activities would creep into the public's consciousness as a component of an overarching defense against the encroachment of mass production on people's lives. Competitive sport, as a specific component of the leisure equation, was simply one convention that could be effectively brought from the margins and harnessed to a larger effort to somehow replace the drudgery of the workday with something regenerative outside the workplace. In other words, those who were caught up in the inequitable arrangements brought about by the technological advances of the day looked to sport primarily because it offered a momentary reprieve from the increasingly predictable grind that had become their lives. This in turn would serve to implant early on in the American sporting environment an element of therapeutic value that would continue to develop in conjunction with the nation's overall sporting character. As physical education professor Steven Overman explains:

> The burden of work that most Americans had to bear created a need for an "escape valve," and sports and recreation provided such an escape. After-hours recreation offered a necessary palliative to the mechanization, standardization, and division of labor which were repressing human needs in the workplace.... By turning to sport, the craftsmen is able to rediscover activities where he can compensate against himself, manipulate natural forces, and actively execute the qualities of craftsmanship which are inherent in the work ethic.[22]

In this respect, Overman poses this popular shift toward both adopting and seriously embracing the dynamics of competitive sport as a reaction to the industrial forces that reshaped the workplace. By counterposing sport as a means with which labor could substitute a lopsided arrangement with one it could live with, frivolous as it might seem in the context of modern life, Overman underscores the development of a link between the shift in focus toward recreational pursuits while providing a rationale for interpreting these changes. Moreover, he further claims that this shift toward recreation would come to mark both a defense and an attempt on the part of the transformed working class to wrest control of some measure of its existence in the face of unprecedented and evidently calamitous change:

> The displacement of the work ethic into sport and recreation was a classic illustration of what happens when one social institution fails to meet the functional requirements of the system, and another institution compensates by assuming that function. The nature of industrial labor had failed to support the strongly held work ethic which equated personalized physical labor with the products and satisfaction of work … [Recreational activities] provided a counterweight to the "existential impoverishment" of industrial work by serving as a form of compensation for what was missing.[23]

Sport's rise into the public's consciousness was a feature of the new focus on leisure and recreation that the general public would turn to in the form of a compensatory amusement in order to combat the perverse effects wrought by the new relations in the workplace. With its rules, organizational qualities, and quantifiable interpretation of success and failure, sport's appeal would serve as an acceptable substitute within the context of the aforementioned Protestant ethos. Still, its rise to prominence would also be met with storms of controversy and attempts on the part of some to reign in its efficacy through the efforts of the managerial classes, political and religious leaders, and an increasingly more powerful Victorian middle class that feared that a further spread of sport's more exciting inner dynamic might have the power to erode both the moral and economic momentum already manifest in the age.

Reform and the Victorian Interpretation of Sport

The remarkably rapid growth of sport rules, associations, economies, and cultures in the nineteenth century was part of a radical redrawing of work and leisure. In preurban [sic], agrarian-based cultures, the diurnal cycle, seasons of work and rest, and the calendar of religious holidays had governed labour and respite. Both folk and aristocratic games from which our sports are derived were played in context governed by these rhythms and customs. By the end of the nineteenth century, along with the seasonal fluctuation of work … the folk games had withered away and had been displaced by sport on a mass scale.[24]

Faith in human perfectibility underlay many of the era's social causes ... Scenes of cruelty and injustice assaulted Victorian belief in an ever-brightening future. Cockfights were not just in poor taste; to those who beheld gleaming visions of a godly community and well-ordered society, such spectacles revealed a side of human behavior totally at odds with virtue.[25]

While the changes that would draw nineteenth century Americans toward rethinking the negative connotations often associated with leisure, recreation, and the sporting life continued to unfold, elements of the rather isolated and chaotic recreational culture that existed primarily along the periphery of society would continue to make their long ascent into the public's consciousness. Certainly leisure-related activities had yet to fully establish their niche in American culture by mid-century, but there were indications that sport as a developing branch of recreational culture had the potential to capture the collective imagination of an increasingly restless and disaffected public who seemed to be attracted to such endeavors.[26]

Most commentary points to the Civil War era as the formal galvanizing of America's nineteenth century sport consciousness. The more significant changes that would ultimately shape the way Americans would conceive of competitive sport in its most modern form, however, are more distinctively allied with the handling of the emerging sporting ethos through the omnipresence of an increasingly powerful postbellum Victorian middle-class that was itself driven by reform. While disenchantment continued to mount among the general public, sport in its more bucolic forms, as well as elements of sport emanating from decidedly rowdier urban environments, began to slowly filter its way out of the isolated confines of community life and merge within the developing national character. Still, these developments would not go unchallenged. To be sure, sport as a sort of working-class palliative would find itself under attack from a variety of powerful sociopolitical forces, many of which were able to effectively mask concerns over continued productivity with questions about the morality of espousing such a decidedly alternative lifestyle in which roughhousing and saloon-frequenting were so evidently capable of capturing the fancy of working men.[27] As sport historian Ted Vincent points out in his far-reaching assessment of the demise of America's communal sporting culture, "In the years of the Industrial Revolution the working classes were not expected to have fun; they were expected to work."[28] Moreover, he notes:

In the origins of American sports the control of the elite was temporarily absent; in part because sports was seen as something not to be controlled but to be repressed. A sporting world was being created in a still-Puritanical country whose gentry, clergy, and other "respectable" elements had from colonial times condemned sports and frolics as unfit for a hardworking Christian people.[29]

The catastrophic effects on working-class sensibilities brought about through industrialization would leave a fragmented and deflated populace to find its own means for post-workday diversions, something that an increasingly more powerful moralizing element in American life would view as distasteful and potentially hazardous to the moral character of the nation. The response on the part of middle-class Victorians to the newfound devotion to leisure pursuits would be both swift and direct, and, by most accounts, it was this response that led to a radical restructuring of the character of the burgeoning American embrace of sport.[30] As sport historian Steven A. Riess claims:

> The respectable urban middle class began to participate in sport at mid [nineteenth] century as they learned from immigrants, social critics, health faddists, and other social reformers that physical culture could be enjoyed free of nefarious influences, and that participation was fun and uplifting at the same time. A new sport ideology developed that promoted team sports and other athletic pastimes that were consonant with the social values of hard-working, religious, future-oriented Victorians and promised to improve health, morality, and character.[31]

Essential to understanding how Victorian values came to be embroiled within a burgeoning sporting paradigm is to consider how quickly Americans were being consumed with and by both competition and Victorianism. By the mid-nineteenth century, competitive sport had become one of the more celebrated and popular institutions in American society. This is especially true in the case of team sports, which were just starting to find their own niche among individual pursuits such as foot racing (known then as pedestrianism), horse racing, and bare-knuckle boxing. Baseball, for example, culled together from a variety of British and American ball and bat games, had become a regular feature of armed forces recreation throughout the American Civil War, spearheaded perhaps by the success of amateur baseball circuits that were in evidence by the 1850s. This was to be followed by a collegiate embrace of both baseball and yet another derivative of British sport, football, which postbellum Americans crafted from elements of rugby and other variants of British foot and ball games. In time, it would be the American strain of football and not baseball, as most might have surmised then, that would serve as the collegiate world's foremost contribution to the contemporary American sport landscape and eventually capture the imagination of American's urban population when the slowed pace of baseball failed to remain relevant by the 1960s (see figure 2.1).[33]

Whereas by the postbellum period all social classes would have found some means to incorporate sport into their culture, sport could no longer be assumed to consist simply of sadistic Southerners and drunken Northerners idly passing time, nor would it remain a measurable feature of the rural and agrarian lifestyle of Americans in the hinterlands. Rather, sport-related diversions had

Figure 2.1. What Is Your Favorite Spectator Sport?

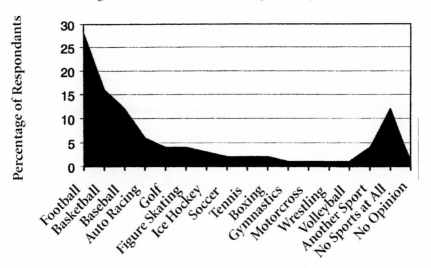

Football's rise to prominence in the United States during the 1960s, and its subsequent dominance of the American sporting landscape, due in part to its "telegenic" nature, is reflected in this random Gallup Poll assessment of contemporary spectator sport taken in March 2001.[33]

become ubiquitous with more and more Americans demonstrating a passion for sport in the dual capacities of participants and spectators both.[34]

The Victorian influences that came to dominate American social and cultural behaviors stemmed from the onset of a religious fervor that would sweep across America from the turn of the nineteenth century onward and would continue to grow in strength as the Civil War approached. The new relationship spawned between church and social mores led to an embrace of such a liaison by a self-appointed, respectable middle order that would remain a significant feature of American life well into the twentieth century. Their presence would in turn create a climate of cultural orthodoxy with an associating distrust of impulsive and non-productive behaviors, of which sport served as an example and was a matter that would need to be sorted out and quickly.[35]

Recalling the disgust reserved for the sportive saloon culture of the Northeast and the allure of blood sports in the Virginia-dominated South, an inspired American middle class sought to reinvent American social customs at the level of an asceticism normally associated with the fervor of Puritan days. In retrospect, however, it must be noted that by comparison the Puritans seemed to be much more open to bouts of spontaneous competitive play than their Victorians counterparts have shown.[36] Nonetheless, this movement was governed by an exceedingly modern and decidedly worldly understanding of what it might take to win over an increasingly fragmented American citizenry, and it aimed its collective sights on nearly every segment of the expanding American culture.

America's Victorians prided themselves on their devotion to the spread of a moral consensus. Their attacks on the immorality surrounding sport and other working-class oriented features of America's recreational culture drew on the more traditional sense that competitive sport may elicit excitement among the masses, but it also stood poised to promote idleness, frivolity, and a potentially costly lack of productivity among them as well. As oft-cited sport historian Benjamin Rader observes:

> Whether driven by religious convictions, the quest for wealth, fears of social unrest, or a combination of these motives, Victorians frowned on impulsive behavior.... Victorian moralists tried to instill in each individual an internal set of values. Ideally, an interior moral gyroscope would guide each person through the bewildering changes that were transforming American society.[37]

Still, rather than make the attempt to abolish sport altogether, Victorians showed much lustier aims. They sought instead to manipulate the course of the American sporting culture through a series of carefully constructed efforts to steer sport toward the implementation of a much more noticeably principled, ethical, and patriotic design as a means to reform what they conceived of as a decline in America's overall moral profile. And whether they realized that their best hope for successfully wresting control of the nation's collective conscience existed within the popular culture itself, or they simply got lucky, Victorians responded with an ambitious effort to build on the obvious popularity of sport and unite it to the cause of reform. This then would serve to provide them with the potential to mitigate the effects of the contemporary moral crisis while attempting to insure that future generations could be reigned in through a more proper interpretation of America's nascent competitive culture.[38]

Muscular Christianity

The strength of character that could be taught by sports was a good deal more important than calculus and Greek, which were drummed into boys by a set of sickly pedants.[39]

Before the cult of muscular Christianity and Christian gentlemanliness took hold, what passed for games in the public schools were nothing less than anarchic roughhouses. Gradually, under the influence of men who were taught at Rugby under Arnold who in turn became schoolmasters themselves, these roughhouses were replaced by organized compulsory games which had rules the strict observance of which became an essential part of the moulding of a Christian English gentleman.[40]

By the end of the Civil War, an exhausted citizenry seeking shelter from the chaos of intranational warfare gravitated further toward the excitement of sport. Sport provided Americans with a glimpse of the passion, zeal, and ingenuity of a bygone era, and while its spread may have been deemed problematic to reform-conscious leadership, Americans demonstrated a remarkable eagerness toward accepting competitive sport into their lives as evidenced by the extraordinarily swift changes in the nature of leisure pursuits throughout the later stages of the nineteenth century, a matter that was not to go unnoticed by a growing assemblage of social crusaders.[41]

A key element to emerge in the attempts toward a radical restructuring of competitive sport in America was based in part on the model presented in the elite English boarding schools, an ongoing trial in linking morality, stoicism, and masculine deportment through competitive sport that came to be known, somewhat derogatorily, as Muscular Christianity.[42] By channeling this highly influential element of elite British sport as a model against the backdrop of a perceived chaotic and unregulated sporting environment, the American Victorian element, led by physical educators and social engineers, sought to assign the growing cultural fascination with sport to several of the same ideals schoolmasters sought to instill into their all-male student bodies in the upper-class boarding schools of England —courage, patriotism, strength, and subordination to the group amid a strongly Christian orientation. As Miracle and Rees observe in their ambitious *Lessons of the Locker Room: The Myth of School Sports*, at the center of the Victorian athletic project was the issue of character building, which was doubly important in the case of elite boys whose future and the future of the nation were thought to lay in the balance.[43]

At its core, Muscular Christianity symbolized a persistent belief in the political and moral efficacy of physical activity and especially as it pertained to team sports, which were thought to contribute significantly to the development of morality and patriotism while adding a healthful vigor to future British elites. Sport in the context of the nineteenth century British boarding schools came to be equated primarily with encouraging strength while instilling moral discipline. By integrating morality into an atmosphere that appeared to be brimming with gaiety and frivolity, young men slated for important positions within British society would be exposed to the necessary rudiments that would ensure a successful transition into adulthood through a closely managed competitive environment. It was also believed that the lessons boys learned on the playing fields could be easily transferred to more likely scenarios found later in life.[44]

By all accounts Muscular Christianity would prove a monumental success in terms of its usefulness in engineering morality and gentility among upper-class British boys, but what was necessary for the successful importation of such an ideal into an American model forced it to perceptibly move away from its upper-class orientation. Though Muscular Christianity would initially appear in the United States in the similarly elite boarding schools of New England and subsequently move on to some of America's more exclusive college campuses, the bigger challenge facing America's moral guardians was in transforming the more raucous postbellum working-class environments where community sport flourished without the semblance of such meaningful and manageable interventions. Thus, while disaffected workers turned en masse to recreational pursuits that could ease the transition and perhaps mitigate the tediousness of the new rules governing productivity, many of these pursuits were deemed offensive to the sensibilities of Victorian moralists who may have in fact foreseen the potential health benefits in sport but sought, nonetheless, to wrest control of the working-class recreational culture and remake it in a much more genteel and palatable fashion. Still, these changes would not have been possible without the hold that sport had over the general population.[45] Sports may have been about fun for the working orders, but for those occupying loftier places and envisioning even loftier goals, sport had to be both regulated and meaningful.

As the American working classes expressed a growing interest in sport, the Victorian order was growing predictably despondent over what they perceived to be rough and disorderly demonstrations put on by those they often regarded as little more than thick-skinned ruffians. They viewed sporting spectacles with both fear and disdain and saw neither health nor social benefits resulting from working-class games in their current form, irrespective of the playful displays being presented in these settings. The emergent American reformist element, and especially those of the higher orders, saw little but frivolity bordering on criminality in the many cultural idioms pursued by working-class men, a condition that cultural critic and public policy consultant Varda Burstyn notes was feared by reform-minded elements who believed that "such pursuits could lead to slacking off in the factory and rebellion in the streets."[46]

Still, Victorians, driven by popular theories and consumed with strategies for alleviating the suffering of conceivably indigent and potentially idle immigrants through settlement houses and such, were poised to accept the notion that if governed properly, sport could serve to help reinvent the lower orders in the image sought by the majority of social crusaders.[47] Thus, what they tended to see within the emergent sporting paradigm was precisely what British schoolmasters saw but on a much wider scale — the potential to rein in the seemingly unruly mob. More importantly, sport in this context could be used effectively in an effort to reform what some considered to be an inherently noxious populace who were thought to be willing to accept these reforms as long as they were able to continue pursuing sport without interruption.[48]

The Victorian model of sport as an element of reform was remarkably successful, combining elements of reform with commercial requirements that called for a steady stream of healthy, strong, and energetic workers who would be more likely to accept their place in the American economy.[49] As Riess explains:

A respectable, gambling-free sporting culture was evolving, based on behavior and attitudes consonant with Victorian values that stressed the functionalism of competitive athletics. Sport was no longer merely child's play or vile amusement for the bachelor subculture, but a useful recreational activity appropriate for respectable middle-class young men who would be transformed into manly specimens, sound of body and pure of heart.[50]

Sport in its reformist ideal was based on two essentially utilitarian elements of a meaningful life: healthfulness coupled with a devotion to practicing restraint. Reformers favored a sporting life that promoted the joys of a fit, healthy lifestyle obtainable through a sporting ethic that in effect abandoned the game playing ethos. In presenting a more manageable competitive culture, reformers instead attempted to sway the public by easing them away from the less predictable (and unacceptable) behaviors associated with an overdeveloped sense of competitiveness and toward a more structured embrace of physical fitness through a focus on courteous and reflective play. Proponents may have noticed that participation in competitive challenges had the potential to frustrate and derail the masses from these pursuits, but they also came to believe that a strict regimen of physical training combined with an eye toward moderation, that is, abstinence from alcohol, tobacco products, and promiscuous behavior, would serve the lower orders well. This in turn would be enough to lay claim to sport as a positive force in American life, making it a sort of cause célèbre for those who came to trumpet the value in embracing health benefits and moral values through physical pursuits.

As the model of British Muscular Christianity demonstrated, by removing uncertainty from spontaneous play, and by regulating the competitive environment, one could espouse a goal of overall fitness while also serving to redirect the general population away from the unacceptable behaviors normally associated with rough and tumble sport, which, it was feared, remained the most basic attraction of athletic competition. Still, though they bristled at the sights and sounds coming from adult sports, moral reformers were primarily concerned with children, and especially the boys (given the prejudice that would keep young girls away from sport well into the twentieth century), who elicited the majority of the focus when it came to the duality of sport and social reform in the Victorian model.[51]

Boy Workers *and the Shaping of Twentieth Century Sport*

Child-guidance advisors, health reformers, and Muscular Christians preached — in particular to an urban middle-class audience — the necessity of athleticism for both individual self-improvement and national survival in an increasingly artificial world.[52]

The idea that a man who was moral and devout could and should also be physically fit tied in very well with prevailing middle-class values and the new sports creed.[53]

As the newer, more modern America was forming in the late nineteenth and early twentieth centuries, concern spread among Victorian elements that traditional outlets for social controls and the tools for the construction of a national ideology could be irreversibly damaged. This image left many to envision a future replete with unsupervised children roaming the urban landscape while being exposed to a host of unsavory elements, a notion that also became tied to a perceived erosion in the traditional and accepted family structure. Coupled with an increasingly widespread nativism that openly played upon the fears of a spreading contagion of foreign beliefs and ideologies flowing into the American mainstream, these fears persuaded many to believe that youth were being targeted by the worst sort of corruptive elements. For the first time since the closing of the frontier, rural life was being hailed and idealized in comparison to the idle corruption and decay of the city, though, to be fair, those in America's farm belt were becoming equally as concerned about the state of their own listless and poorly motivated youth. Nevertheless, urban churches and civic minded reformers by the 1880s sought to pave the road toward a tangible reshaping of city life, hoping to make it more conducive to, among other things, childhood living.[54]

Much of the responsibility for implementing these desired changes in urban youth was overseen by reform-minded operatives who came to be known as *boy workers*. These individuals, typically fortified with solid backgrounds in child development, along with the requisite religious and political orientations, were determined to build within their charges a more consensus-friendly and malleable character through a course of action designed to attract young urban dwellers with exciting activities intended to instill the essential virtues and morals favored by a reform-driven element. As Macleod would note:

> The character building agencies for boys which rose to prominence in the decades around 1900 were curious organizations. Their declared ideals were singularly broad and seemingly timeless, and yet these organizations were in fact quite specialized, rooted in the experience of the late Victorian and early twentieth-century middle class.[55]

Boy workers saw themselves as a buffer between the harshness of adult life and the capriciousness of childhood. They maintained towering goals of infusing of moral virtues into their charges while making little effort to obscure the fact that what they sought most was the salvaging of a generation of urban youth whose elders, it was feared, were beyond salvation. Furthermore, these individuals, filled with utterances decrying urban decay and convinced of the further collapse within America's cities, were certain that they could make citizens out of children of disparate backgrounds through the construction of these highly efficient and influential organizations.[56]

That this image of unsupervised youth aimlessly roaming the city streets would become an issue can be directly linked to the diminishing role of youth in the workforce and the increasing likelihood that more children were being steered toward public schools rather than fields and factories, once considered to be the more practical environments for young men to come of age. The appearance of increasingly formalized youth organizations paralleled a mounting debate over the nature of education for working-class youth. Many supposed that offering working-class children even the rudiments of a traditional education would be anathema to their calling, which in the United States meant manual labor or some variation thereof. To the contrary, it was believed that the better substitute for the more typical workplace experiences would be an education immersed in character building and basic work-related skills. It was further surmised that this plan would serve the country best because it had the potential to offer to prospective employers a trustworthy, morally sound, and productive workforce that would serve loyally and function without being saddled with potentially unrealistic economic or even philosophical expectations.[57]

These operatives were equally concerned with the influence education would have on their targeted demographic, but they were less consumed with the specter of adult futures and more distressed by what they perceived to be a present filled with delinquency and the lure of criminal behaviors. As these reformers would judge it, without the influence of shop foremen and bosses, a child's primary contact with adults was the largely ceremonial and notably distant student-teacher relationship, one that many considered to be an inadequate substitute and a contributing factor in the rise, perceived or otherwise, in juvenile delinquency.[58] Thus, this move to incorporate more youth-friendly activities in the community, whether it be through organized competitions or lusty outdoor recreation, was seen by many to have involved some means to keep youth free from temptation following what many believed to be an increasingly ineffective school day. Tightly organized and supervised youth activities could serve as an effective substitute, especially when it came to instilling admirable virtues without actually breaking the wills or the spirits of the boys involved. Typically these activities were conceived of under the auspices of what was often deemed a *physical education*.[59]

The attraction of sport for young men could be related to the general pleasure of participating in something spontaneous and dramatic, but there were also internal dynamics that continued to push young boys (and men) further toward adopting competitive sport as a feature of their lives. As baseball historian Ronald Story observes:

> Young males of this generation needed security and order — breathing space, respite — in a world where violence and chaos seemed the norm. But families, which might have been a refuge, were often microcosms of the outside world,

fecund sources of their own forms of unhappiness and insecurity ... needing security, young men sought it where they could, especially in the surrogate family ambience of team sports.[60]

Though what constituted acceptable character in boys existed only in the abstract, there is a general sense that these youth organizations exhibited a principal concern with what they perceived to be a lack of so-called manly behaviors. As a result, they would come to focus a great deal of their collective efforts on establishing among youth circles models for the proper degree of self-control, altruism, and a general manner that sociologist Harry Edwards has described as being civilized.[61] Part of the attraction of competitive sport, games, hiking, and other outdoor activities was that they could be structured in such a way as to encourage a coalescence of moral instruction while discouraging a sedentary lifestyle. This could also be enveloped in a play motif that would prove very attractive to youthful participants. To be sure, athletic-minded boys of the era fancied exuberant and spirited play when unsupervised, and the newly formed boys' organizations could provide and even emphasize these types of activities. In doing so they would still be able to instill the core values without having to sacrifice physical fitness while utilizing the types of amusements that would all but ensure repeated success among the targeted audience. Moreover, the boys themselves would be prone to regard their supervisors as allies who had their interests in mind rather than managers ultimately responsible for their conduct if for no other reason than these individuals were openly encouraging young men to do what they loved most — play.[62]

As troublesome as continued impropriety among boys was for some, an escalating fear of effeminacy brought about by an overly sedentary lifestyle was becoming equally disturbing. There was indeed a growing concern that in addition to delinquency, youth were falling into a pattern of listlessness and inactivity that threatened muscle tone and general health and the sort of ruggedness that had once made heroes of, for example, Andrew Jackson, Davy Crockett, and those who participated in the Lewis and Clark expeditions. Miracle and Rees point out that while middle-class suspicions regarding working-class youth gangs were assumed to be widespread and problematic to urban communities, there were also anxieties among the same middle classes that their own children were growing increasingly frail and apprehensive from long periods of inactivity.[63]

In this particular matter, the church, long the center of moral instruction, was being looked upon as a contributor to this condition due in part to its seeming inability (or unwillingness) to promote a more active lifestyle. Critics began to link the notion of sedentary behavior in children to the church's role in community life and their long accepted customs of quiet contemplation. It was thought that while the church could fill a boy with the proper ideals and behaviors, church life itself was too committed to tranquil reflection rather than a more well-rounded spirituality that would include active and physical effort, something that America's religious institutions would not address in any significant way until well into the twentieth century. Once this became a point of contention within the various churches, however, they developed an across the board interest in keeping up with the times. Church leaders sought to rid their institutions of the mantle of immobile, and, hence, "sissified" environment and began to encourage a more physically fit lifestyle for themselves and church personnel.[64] Furthermore, there may have also been a note of anti-Semitism working within this sphere as well. As cultural anthropologist Alan Klein has noted, a feature of European anti-Semitism involves an ahistorical connection between somatic effeminacy and the supposed Jewish male lifestyle, which would have been clearly at odds with Muscular Christianity and other such notions of robust physicality. The idea that Christian young men might have lapsed into such a state as to befit a Jew would have easily given rise to mounting anxieties that such a condition was both unacceptable and inherently precarious in both the secular as well as spiritual plane.[65] As a result, in the case of youth of all social standings, the focus on character building was marked by a commitment to building one's external strength as well as one's internal virtues. As Mcleod notes, by emphasizing physical activity while setting a barrier on more adult behaviors including smoking, drinking, and sexual promiscuity, boy workers sought "to conserve boys for long-term development,"[66] which helped rationalize the link between sport and a general sense of propriety for generations to come.

Of the various organizations to impact this trend in youth governance through play, the two most prominent were the Boy Scouts of America (BSA) and the Young Men's Christian Association (YMCA). Both were singularly committed to turning the spontaneous activities of youth into tightly wound and practical means of reinterpreting the image and attitudes of working-class youth. Each as well sought to offer the proper mix of benevolence combined with the sort of social controls that operatives hoped would be subtly embraced by the boys themselves. Toward that end, they steadfastly maintained the importance of God and country, morality, duty, and abstinence from all adult vices while they taught children how to play and hike and explore recreations in a highly organized and effective social environment. As Macleod acknowledges:

> If character builders were to impose authority without breaking wills, they had to find means that seemed natural to boys. What better in an age of popular Darwinism than woodsy savagery? Or what more appealing than team sports?[67]

In their attempts to shelter youth from moral contamination, the BSA and the YMCA offered alternatives that would prove favorable to children, who certainly might have played ball, hiked, and fished without their influences, while assuaging community leaders who saw in sport and outdoor recreation a convenient set of variables to exploit in the name of morality and physical fitness. Indeed, when challenged, BSA founder Robert Baden-Powell acknowledged that his primary interest in pursuing the organization's goals and directives stemmed from a distrust of unsupervised and spontaneous youth play, the mountains of obstacles that prevented a child from pursuing individual moral growth, and the belief that city boys were underworked and had an excess of energy that was desperately in need of harnessing and rechanneling.[68]

Of the two, the more sport-minded institution was certainly the YMCA (see figure 2.2), an organization that Macleod referred to as a sort of sanctuary offering Protestant young men the dual constructs of religiosity and sheltered stability.[69] The YMCA would become a staging ground for an extraordinary effort in the orchestration of acceptable behaviors through the meshing together of sport, health, and reform-driven morality. In bridging the divide between the worlds of secular physicality and spiritual obeisance, this predominantly boy work organization sought to supplant the un-Christian-like nature of unsupervised sport with an innovative sport motif capable of rewarding physical, intellectual, and spiritual excellence in spite of its attendants. While church may have been a place to commune with the spirit and the forest a place to commune with nature, the YMCA grew to become the place where one could experience the breadth of the entire human experience while getting a good physical going over at the same time. As American cultural historians Elliott Gorn and Warren Goldstein explain in their highly acclaimed *A Brief History of American Sport*, the basic premise of the YMCA

Figure 2.2. YMCA Membership 1880–1910

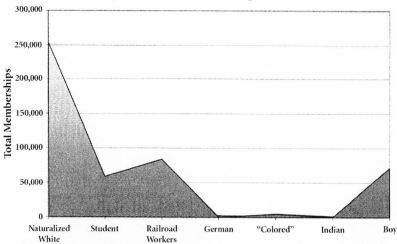

The dramatic rise in American YMCA membership between the end of Reconstruction and the onset of World War I reflects America's growing affinity for sport and its supposed benefits, especially in the case of young boys. Note: Zeros reflect either unavailability of numbers or, in the case of Germans in 1900 and 1910, an assimilation into naturalized figures.[70]

orientation featured the most sacred tenets of the Muscular Christian doctrine:

> Gymnastics made men bold, truthful, chaste; cricket engendered fortitude, endurance, and self-control; baseball promoted discipline, self-denial, and courage. Rugged masculine virtues, it was said, inhaled on the playing field with God's open air, countered the emasculation of luxurious living, the ennui of commercial transactions, and the impotence of cloistered intellection.[71]

The emphasis on inspiring proper behavior in youth through competition at the YMCA was orchestrated by G. Stanley Hall, a genetic psychologist whose prolific yet enigmatic theories on human evolution and play often placed him on the periphery of accepted science, and Luther Gulick, an ambitious former student and theoretical devotee of Hall. Collectively they sought to bring competitive sport into a more central role in matters of child development, and in America's YMCAs, they had a ready-made laboratory for testing their theories regarding proper child development through sport.[72]

Hall posed play as an evolutionary matter, saw spontaneous play in children as one of the few phases of development free from adult contamination, and insisted that adolescence marked the age in which innocence gave way to a sort of evolutionary upheaval, which, he argued, corresponded to mankind's leap from savagery to civilization. Furthermore, he came to believe that physical activity was the variable that allowed primitive men and women to survive hostile environments. He went as far as to pose the various sports of his day in their prehistorical context, calling baseball, for example, a coalescence of the past hunting instinct and the more modern concept of cooperation.[73]

What Hall sought through this analysis was to compel America's youth and their more attentive guardians to reconsider their roles in shaping increasingly negative youth behavior, such as gangs and general street thuggery, and reconnect socially through a motif filled with the imagery and the pageantry of competitive play.[74] As Rader notes, for Hall sport was the key that represented an "unparalleled opportunity for adults to encourage in boys the healthy growth of moral and religious reflexes [while requiring] the highest moral principles — teamwork, self-sacrifice, obedience, self-control, and loyalty."[75]

In collaboration with Gulick, Hall was one of the earliest theorists to present a theory of play that would promulgate the character building ideology of the YMCA. Initially Hall utilized the more traditional routine of approaching moral education through rigorous exercise, which meant non-contact and non-competitive calisthenics or gymnastics as they were then termed, but, through the urging of Gulick, who was busily tracking a tendency among young boys to gravitate toward team sports, Hall allowed himself to be convinced of the potency and potential usefulness of that particular athletic form. To be sure, many of their combined theoretical principles have proven to be flawed based primarily on what we now know about psychosocial development, motor skills, and the nature of spontaneous play among children and adolescence. Regardless, the most telling aspect of their position is their combined assessment of the role that motor skill development plays in the advance of what Hall termed "moral reflexes,"[76] which he loosely defined in modern parlance as one's conscience. Thus, the basis of their plan to incorporate athletics into the character education schema of YMCAs throughout the country involved what they felt to be the incontrovertible link between a morally sound athletic canon and the shaping of acceptable versus unacceptable reflexes through a system of appropriately conceived sport.

While Hall continues to receive a modest amount of attention in terms of his pioneering modern play theory, Luther Gulick, who engineered the more practical undertakings in the Hall–Gulick alliance and whose legacy can still be found throughout the American sporting sphere, remains the pair's most visible icon. The son of missionary parents, Gulick, who operated out of the renowned Springfield, Massachusetts, YMCA branch, is often credited (and sometimes blamed) with having turned the organization's athletic charter away from its lone focus on gymnastics and overall physical fitness into its present day embrace of competitive team sport.

Gulick was an indefatigable champion of Hall's work, and he sought to implement practically what his erstwhile mentor had amassed theoretically. He was particularly conscious of the potential for sport to improve the lives of working-class youths, but he was equally dismayed at the lack of structure and logical implementation on the part of those who simply advocated sport for the sake of recreation and competitiveness alone. He was, above all else, firmly committed to the idea that in order to be an effective and affective feature of the contemporary world, sport had to be instructive, meaningful, and resolutely ordered.[77]

Gulick was both dynamic and relentless in his quest for human perfectibility through competition in the strictest sense of the Victorian design, and his legacy would prove to be extremely influential. In addition to creating the YMCA's fêted Red Triangle, which remains the symbol of the organization's designs on creating sound physical, mental, and spiritual balance in its members, Gulick would have a hand in a number of extraordinary developments in America's competitive culture. For instance, it was Gulick who in the 1890s offered challenges to his subordinates to invent indoor games that could bridge the gap between the popular pastimes of football in the autumn and baseball in the spring. This challenge would result in the birth of both basketball in 1891 and volleyball in 1895, American sports that have been adopted around the world and are among the most popular Olympic events.[78] More on point, though Gulick would be criticized in his later years for making the YMCA too dependent on increasingly competitive team sport, he would, nonetheless, leave behind legions of like-minded supporters who would take their cues from him in their quest to provide a safe haven for potentially wayward youth through an increasingly more powerful and practically applied competitive model.[79]

A Revered Athleticism Reaches the Twentieth Century

Luther Gulick was to the captive children of the playground what Andrew Carnegie was to the exploited laborers of the steel mills.[80]

The principal goal of the high school was giving men common ideas, common ideals, and common modes of thought, feeling, and action that made for cooperation, social cohesion, and social solidarity [accomplished through] the social mingling of pupils through the organization and administration of the school [and the] participation of students in common activities ... such as athletic games, social activities and the government of the school.[81]

Whether or not competitive sport is actually capable of producing any or all of the effects desired by nineteenth century moralists is a point of contention that remains hotly debated even among modern critics. Nevertheless, by the turn of the twentieth century, the notion that a rationally applied sporting philosophy was capable of instilling a solid moral grounding among America's diverse citizenry had become one of the nation's chief articles of faith, leading Americans to be directed toward competitive sport in numbers that might have seemed altogether improbable a generation prior.[82] Sport, which had withstood nearly a half century's worth of condemnation and interference on the part of nineteenth century civic leadership and reform-minded moralists, had been wrested away from an often overzealous population raised on folk games and impulsive athletic struggles and emerged as a bureaucratized and institutionalized feature of the burgeoning American culture. Still, for most increasingly sport-conscious Americans, the only thing that really mattered was simply the ability to play.

By the turn of the century, Americans were often reminded by an evolving consumer-driven national craze for sport fortified by an increasingly sophisticated communications infrastructure that participation, or, at the very least, an interest, in competitive athletics was both an enjoyable and effective means toward building one's character and bolstering one's life chances.[83] The importance of the youth operatives and their aims for a society reared on physical education and governed by a distinctly moral vision cannot be underestimated on this point. By hitching their collective wagons to a competitive frame, America's reformist element, through its organizing of youth through sport, was able to achieve what many in governmental and spiritual leadership once thought to have been an almost insurmountable challenge to their designs on maintaining order. This in turn seems to have encouraged what many point to as a sort of individual ruggedness among the working populations during a period of increasing anxiety and social unrest. Their legacy would pave the way for even more organizations committed to the unification of character and culture, providing American sport with a remarkably favorable bearing while at the same time reinforcing the nation's embrace of sport as the twentieth century progressed. As historian Donald Mrozek notes, social reformers and politicians had come to believe that "body and soul were inextricably bound together, that moral power was directly transmutable into physical power, and that actions formed character rather than just reflecting it."[84]

By the twentieth century, sport had become an underlying feature of American life whose place seemed almost irrefutable, especially in terms of its theoretical ability to teach and govern proper behavior. While the popularity of competitive sport continued to soar, and as more Americans turned to competitive games as a primary source of recreation and leisure, those who would position themselves as the shapers and governors of America's sport consciousness seemed to grow exponentially in the early decades of the new century. Athletes had become heroic, and participation in athletic competition began to mark the road toward heroism within this particular model. Furthermore, association with the sporting world held great capital for those seeking higher visibility in public life, resulting in added organizations and even higher-profile individuals who would continue making significant contributions toward reinforcing the ideology behind a rationally governed, highly moral, character-based education through sport.

One noteworthy source of this decidedly pro-sport sentiment in the early twentieth century emanated from the American White House. From Theodore Roosevelt's rise to power through Woodrow Wilson's two terms in office, the American presidency would serve to underscore sport's place while further laying a foundation for the American public to interpret competition not only as a laudable manifestation of American culture but also as an institution that had the potential to serve the nation's interests admirably. At a time when early twentieth century Americans were beginning to think of themselves as the world's foremost nation, and in some circles humanity's last hope for survival, Presidents Roosevelt, Wilson, and William Howard Taft, who would personally initiate many of the ceremonial measures still in evidence in American sport,[85] would prove themselves to be outspoken supporters of the sporting culture. In terms of further stimulating the idea of sport as an issue of national significance, they openly, and often vociferously, championed competitiveness as a matter of national pride, strength, unity, and morality.[86]

Another contributing factor to the more widespread acceptance of the sporting philosophy of the early twentieth century was the eventual acceptance of the sporting ethos by America's religious institutions. Many in the religious communities were stung by the criticism of religious customs, especially those that led critics to maintain that traditional religious instruction encouraged youth to adopt more sedentary lifestyles and had the potential for encouraging effeminate and even self-indulgent behaviors instead of the more favorable standards of masculinity. The success of the YMCA proved to many in the clergy that the merging of faith and sport was both possible and potentially lucrative in terms of attracting once and future congregants.[87]

Perhaps banking on many of the same assumptions as boy worker organizations, which were beginning to look more like rivals, community houses of worship began hosting their own sporting events and various other sorts of competitions, subtly following Gulick's lead. The result was a surge in attendance and a proliferation of church-sponsored athletic programs attended by a notable cross-section of local faiths that appeared to be making a concerted effort to blend in more with the times. What transpired, then, was that in addition to book learning and quiet contemplation, the church began to adopt the more modern suppositions regarding athleticism and physical exercise as a means to achieve a soundness of spirit while serving to reinvent the church as an instrument of virility much in the manner that Gulick's triangle had reinvented aspects of the YMCA's charter. That Babe Ruth, arguably American sport's definitive twentieth century icon, learned his craft from a priest at the Catholic boys school in Baltimore where he was raised points to this reaffirmation on the part of the church and is equally impressive given the short amount of time the church actually had to adjust to the newer emphasis being placed on sport in religious environs.[88]

Other organizations would join with religious orders as beacons of neighborhood athletic activity and providers of constructive recreation for urban youths including the Public Schools Athletic Leagues (PSAL) and the Playground Movement, both of which liberally utilized the theoretical and practical work of boy workers and sport-minded reformers. Both of these organizations illustrate the continuing thread of liberal-minded reform placed under the care of professionals convinced of a correlation between physical education and morally acceptable deportment among youth in the best tradition of nineteenth century Victorians.[89]

The PSAL was yet another innovation of Luther Gulick, who had left the YMCA in 1900 to serve as the Director of Physical Training for the public school system in New York City. Again turning away from simply introducing gymnastics to school-aged children, Gulick pioneered the use of competitive games as a means to instill physical fitness and moral instruction while encouraging high academic marks among school-aged participants. This plan would eventually be endorsed by the city's school system, local authorities, and a handful of industrial giants and powerful political figures including, but certainly not limited to, J.P. Morgan, Andrew Carnegie, and John D. Rockefeller, all of whom contributed generously to the cause. Then-President Theodore Roosevelt lent even further legitimacy to this unique partnership when he agreed to serve as the PSAL's honorary vice president in 1905.[90]

Though it remained a separate entity altogether from the public school system — the PSAL worked in conjunction with the school system and maintained separate funding and leadership — they shared a common interest in the matter of youth and delinquency. But what set this particular organization apart from others was its targeting of local immigrant children whose morals and physical deterioration were thought to be in dire need of attention. As Rader notes:

> Underlying the enthusiastic reception of the league was a manifest fear of the city's foreign-born population ... [Immigrant] schoolboys often joined street gangs and defied the authority of their teachers. Above all, the ethnic youngsters exhibited a lack of understanding of American values and institutions. A carefully managed sport program, the founders believed, would reduce juvenile delinquency and "Americanize" the ethnic youth of the ghettos.[91]

Thus, what transpired was a tightly focused plan for hastening the Americanization of immigrant children, at a time of increased scrutiny of alien behaviors, through a very YMCA-like approach to implementing social instruction through competition. This plan would then be imitated in large cities around the country by the end of the first decade. It was also a matter that would serve the nation practically, as war in Europe threatened to pull America closer to having to choose sides.[92]

The Playground Movement too served in an important capacity in terms of further solidifying competitive sport as a recreational pursuit integral to proper development in children. Peripherally aligned with the churches, as well as with other era progressives and organizations, including wealthy philanthropists and even organized labor, this so-called movement accelerated a trend in the construction of outdoor and in some cases indoor recreation facilities for underprivileged urban youth.

Their legacy of providing venues for youth play led to the crafting of an extensive array of urban parks in cities that typically offered aspiring young athletes little more than the most minimal of play space and equipment. The impetus behind the move toward park construction can be traced back to Boston's Sand Gardens, built in 1885, but most insist that the turning point that brought national exposure to the movement's aims took place in 1903 when a South Chicago district approved five million dollars in support of the construction of ten area parks, including field houses with gymnasiums for both boys and girls. They also provided funding for a management system, which included a director and year-round instructors who would organize games and tournaments, that grew to resemble a more secular version of the YMCA.[93]

Other cities would soon follow, and by the 1920s, a separate organization, the Playground and Recreation Association of America, funded by the Laura Spelman Rockefeller Memorial Foundation, would serve to further professionalize the movement to the extent that they began publishing their own monthly periodical, *Playground Magazine*.[94] In all, between the years 1906 and 1917 the number of cities that could boast of managed playground facilities for urban youth would increase from 41 to 504,[95] all of which were constructed in order to lend to an urban population the opportunity to experience fresh air and a place to participate in wholesome and properly governed sporting activities and to further promote the increasingly nationalized cause for character building in youth through athletic competition.[96] Still, the move that would mark the final American embrace of the sporting model as outlined by nineteenth century reformers and their twentieth century allies was the ascension of athletic competition into the realm of public education.

Although competitive sport had become a highly visible feature of collegiate life since Reconstruction, the public schools seemed capable of resisting its spread until well into the 1880s. By then, a craze for sport, exacerbated by a middle-class embrace of college football and the enormous popularity of baseball nationwide, and the rhetoric associated with sport had become an increasingly more omnipresent feature of the cultural landscape. Given such wide-ranging models for change, school leadership was poised to rethink its position and adopt many of the features of reform-inspired physical education that in many ways would serve to reinvent the role that school played in the continued development of America's competitive culture.[97]

Arriving during a period of staggering drop-out rates and general apathy among students and their parents, both of which groups saw little demonstrable reward in American-styled education, school-sanctioned sport provided a trusted means to convince whole communities of the importance of a public education where other basic curricula and site-based adjustments had failed.[98] Furthermore, sport offered to school administration a host of measures designed to bolster its authority over the large, diverse, and often unruly student bodies during a period in which extracurricular activities were just starting to find favor among them. School dances, drama clubs, and sanctioned sporting activities were equally capable of injecting elements of social matters into a setting normally devoid of such merriment and were thought to have the potential to quell student boredom and stem the tide of indifference and chronic absenteeism. More importantly, competitive sports presented schools the same potentially effective means for social controls and behavior modification that could be found on local playgrounds, in church-sponsored athletic competitions, and within YMCA buildings. As education historian Joel Spring notes, the objectives of the American school were rapidly transforming to reflect the changing values of the nation and the changing needs of school administrators, and by entering into the realm of the social, schools were simply trying to keep up with the times while also attempting to find alternative methods for maintaining order.[99]

School-sanctioned sport also presented some less abstract advantages to administrators, including a link to a more practical, hands-on, and activity-based methodology for instruction. This idea had grown more fashionable by the 1920s, especially in the face of industrial needs that would continue to dominate the job market.[100] This design would find further resonance in schools following the 1918 publication of the Commission on the Reorganization of

Secondary Education's *Cardinal Principles of Secondary Education*, a set of guidelines for reinterpreting the role of the public school in the lives of middle- and working-class youth. These directives called for, among other things, modifications of existing curriculum that would incorporate clearer instructional objectives in order to increase the focus on preparing students for adult vocations while urging a renewed commitment to providing students with a solid grounding in contemporary character education.[101]

With its focus on the physical as well as the typical emphases on such Muscular Christian ideals as teamwork, devotion to duty, and subordination of the individual, competitive sport was certainly capable of assisting the schools in their renewed quest. It is interesting to note, however, that while these goals seem reminiscent of the types of religious- or cultural-based behaviors sought in the charters of YMCAs, PSALs, and other such manifestations, the publishing of the 1918 report coincides with a period in America's history when the public schools were self-consciously transforming themselves into epicenters of non-sectarianism as a means to incorporate a constant flux of immigrant cultures into their mix. The result appears to have been a much more modern approach to wielding sport as a mechanism for character development that was capable of shielding its targets from its more traditionally religious roots without actually disrupting the heretofore successful methodology.[102]

Unlike the colleges that often treated their athletic programs as if they were separate entities altogether, a matter that has historically made for some rather peculiar and certainly suspect relationships that continue to haunt collegiate sport into the 21st century, the public schools governed sport much in the manner that boy workers and playground philanthropists oversaw their athletic programs—with complete and often unyielding authority. In acquiescing to student requests that schools offer participatory sport on campus, school administrators were able to turn student interest in sport into a powerful tool for control over the school environment itself.[103]

Control through competitive sport was a matter that could stretch from the individual to the student body as a whole. Many felt that by tying the disparate cultures in attendance into a support system for the school's teams, the student body could be driven toward a rallying point that could provide the appearance of harmony among the often hostile students and had the potential to spill over into the community at-large. As Rader observes:

> High school sports helped give an identity and common purpose to many neighborhoods, towns, and cities which were otherwise divided by class, race, ethnicity, or religion. Geographic entities, like the schools without interscholastic games, might lack collective goals. Varsity sport could coalesce them into a united front. High school sport could become a community enterprise; the entire community might celebrate victories or mourn losses in concert.[104]

Thus, because school administrators wielded full control over scholastic athletics, they not only had in competitive sport a means to curb interethnic hostilities within the school environment, but, once in place, they could then control the population by virtue of their authority over the athletic agenda itself.

Control over individuals through institutionalized school sport held a particular fascination for school administrators. One of the more important and lasting advantages school authority held over their student-athletes was the issue of eligibility, which many saw as a way of encouraging (or demanding) higher levels of performance and acceptable behavior on the part of student-athletes. As initially broached by the PSAL, student-athletes were required to maintain an acceptable performance level in the classroom as they were on the field of play, providing tacit acceptance of the contemporary image of athletics at the forefront of a truly well rounded individual. Of course, the will to victory often trumped the notion of academic excellence, something colleges had learned early on in their initial attempts to bridge the gap between academics and athletics. This matter had in turn often led public school officials to stray toward behaviors that seemed contrary to their own stated objectives, causing more than one critic to sneer at the idea of athletic departments fostering generations of "dumb jocks."[105] Nevertheless, while school sport could offer some relief to overextended school administrators and staff, the more compelling evidence behind the decision to adopt competitive sport as part of the overall school environment rested upon the demonstrations of sport's efficacy elsewhere that supported the use of sport in the traditional model as a means to engineer desired behavior in youth.[106]

There was also a much less public feature of the move toward implementing the emergent competitive ideology in the public schools. In addition to meeting the specific needs of industrialists, schools were also faced with matters pertaining to public service in general. With war in Europe thought to be threatening (or at the least piquing) American interests, the outcry calling for schools to incorporate physical fitness training into their curriculums grew louder and more emphatic. If a fighting force were to emerge from somewhere, it would almost assuredly have to have some connection to the public schools. Hence, as war approached, the need to prepare young men for battle provided school sport with yet another challenge, a challenge that was met not with extracurricular war games or explicit military training, which would have run contrary to accepted morality, but through a strict regimen of healthful pursuits including calisthenics and team sport that could also promote the spirit of unity and cooperation integral to troops in battle.[107] As cultural historian Timothy O'Hanlon would discover:

> Educators frequently offered physical education as an alternative to military drill. They argued that a sound program of physical education (which in most cases included a prominent role for sports) offered a means of preparedness training in that it developed soldierly attributes without encouraging a lockstep military mentality.[108]

And indeed, in 1917 the National Education Association would issue its own guidelines for physical training in public institutions to promote military readiness in a report that held its distance from strictly military training and favored instead a more athletically defined methodology.[109]

The successful implementation of the sporting ideal in schools would also prove invaluable to the so-called Americanization effort at a time when disparate immigrant cultures threatened American resolve elsewhere. The problematic nature of having to incorporate the wealth of disparate cultures, customs, and even languages into the power base of Anglo-Saxon Protestant virtues would have been nearly impossible without the formation of sociocultural reference points with which to demonstrate the necessity and importance of solidarity among citizens. In schools, where they were being encouraged to breakaway from the customs and folkways of their parents, immigrant children were also being introduced to the full spectrum of Anglo-Saxon virtues through sport and other such inducements designed to reinforce Americanist ideals. This served a dual purpose by helping to speed up the assimilation process and at the same time encouraging the adoption of more group-friendly solidarity among classmates and within communities. As *Journal of Sport History* editor Steven W. Pope explains, "Symbolically, sport provided a dual identity for millions of ethnic Americans. However, embracing the strenuous life was not without conflict."[110]

The ability to control for the disparity in culture, and in some cases language, by encouraging the student body to adopt the team as its common ground was key to this process. The importance of securing rallying points associated with team sport at a time when interethnic antagonisms ran deeply within neighborhoods and certainly within the schools was not to go unnoticed in circles beyond the educational apparatus, where matters such as convincing Irish immigrants to fight alongside British soldiers or appealing to German immigrants that they should take up arms against their own were essential to American success in the pursuit of victory during World War I.[111] As Spring would argue,

> the local reorganization of the high school, state laws, and the avalanche of reports and codes on character education were providing a design for educating loyal and obedient citizens who would be go-getters and live wires in the corporate world. The world of football teams, pledges to the flag, student government, and school clubs was to produce the democratic citizen.[112]

Twentieth Century Sport Abounds

> *Reconciled to the specialization required by industrialism, the new middle classes increasingly located their hopes for an egalitarian realm of social life in leisure, rather than in work.... That perspective made the organization of leisure a central task in the drive to construct a national culture.*[113]

> *Training and competition in sport were understood to create a pattern of conduct and to shape a habit of success, and the conscious pursuit of sport had the effect of producing an unconscious but deep commitment to victory. The process worked not through a ritualistic appeal but by the practical governance of behavior, introducing physical order and discipline into the actual experience of young men fated to serve their country.*[114]

Competitive sport's twentieth century ascent into the public schools in many ways marks the final frontier in terms of its being able to assume an active role in the shaping of the nation's character. What this proliferation of sporting activities and accompanying theories accomplishes is to reinforce the twentieth century public's acceptance of competition as a contributing factor in terms of its emphasis on morality and character building. The idea that morality was tied to the dual concept of thought and action fit seamlessly within the constraints of this model and became a sort of mediator between acceptable and unacceptable behavior, especially as it related to children.[115] As Miracle and Rees maintain, by the 1920s the so-called sport-builds-character motif was firmly entrenched within the framework of national identity and national consciousness, leading many to believe that competitiveness was much too important an element of national concern to be left in the hands of amateurs and those whose agendas appeared somewhat less than proper. In short, competitive sport had become a most vital means for cultural diffusion, and it was finding itself as equally entrenched within community life as well as in the more structured world of the public schools. Furthermore, with America's entry into World War I on the horizon, it would help serve as a common feature from which the nation might draw its fighting forces and prepare for its entry into the international arena.[116]

Following the war, however, dramatic changes would take shape that would lead some to fear that America's moral compass was becoming appreciably distorted. Sport would travel alongside the extended celebration of American faculty and enter into its first golden age in the 1920s, reaffirming sport's place in American culture but this time with a highly visible entertainment dynamic that seemed destined to replace (or at the very least erode) the work of previous generations of sport-minded reformers. Like so many other elements of post-war America, sport offered puzzling contradictions that left many confounded and had some convinced that the nation as a whole was becoming too dependent on a hydra's head of consumption and unregulated leisure.[117]

American sport in an age of heroes, such as Babe Ruth and Jack Dempsey, tennis' Bill Tilden and Helen Wills Moody, football's Red Grange, and Gertrude Ederle, whose swim across the English Channel had captivated the country as never before imagined, would have shed its last remaining vestige of community interest and sedate American pastime and enter into the more substantive world of highly commercial enterprise and national spectacle. Those who had devoted the time and energy to create something wholesome through sport would find themselves in effect unable to recognize the cultural foundations they had built, causing many to grow suspicious regarding the role that sport might play in modern society.[118] A burgeoning sport consciousness may have once tamed the urban populations, served as a source of physical and moral development, enhanced the productivity of laborers, and helped make dedicated soldiers out of once-competing civilian immigrants, but the types of behaviors more commonly associated with sport in Scott Fitzgerald's Jazz Age had little in common with character building and accepted behavioral principles of previous eras. At least that was how some critics viewed it.

The pre–World War I values of virtuousness through competitive sport would remain a feature of the discussion of sport's place in American society in spite of the apparent surface changes. And yet, the glamour of the age made it increasingly difficult for the overseers of the character-through-sport paradigm to keep the general public focused in that particular direction. There were genuine concerns that the character-building measures designed by sport reformers were being destroyed by a new cultural attitude that stood poised to erase the old standards and develop newer and less conventional criteria for conduct and decorum, though in actuality the old ways were not being replaced but rather tempered by a national embrace of victory that may in fact have been a by-product of victory in Europe. As Miracle and Rees point out, the dogged pursuit of victory was something that has long been recognized as unique to the American character and problematic to the first wave of Victorian reformers, and its reemergence in the 1920s troubled critics.[119]

That sport would get caught up in this struggle is not unusual considering the role it played in shaping the early twentieth century, but faced with new challenges, many reformers found themselves torn between the idea that sport could still be useful and wholesome in the proper context while they started to look much more critically at the lessons that an emerging victory-first ethos might generate within the nation's collective moral character, a thread that we will see continue on throughout much of the century. The critical backlash that would form in the face of spectacle-laden sport would be aimed at an increasingly hedonistic 1920s-era society and stretch well into the middle decades. This rather abrupt fall from grace was indeed spearheaded by many of the same self-appointed reformers who were perhaps disillusioned by the carnage in Europe but probably more so by the increasingly ill-mannered behavior of more typically reserved middle Americans caught up in the frenzy of consumerism and mass culture.[120]

Throughout the 1920s and into the Depression era, at a time when professional educators and social critics were starting to withdraw their support for athletics and physical education in schools, the popularity of sport gave rise to a proliferation of youth-centered sporting endeavors that seemed to be designed less around the notions of character building and geared more toward celebrity, victory, and the discovery of additional gifted young athletes. Celebrity in the inter-war period would grow to become a much more essential feature of popular sport, leading to a further embrace of spectatorship over actual participation, a matter that would horrify reformers and social critics alike, many of whom would grow to detest sport in its evolving form in spite of the perceived benefits it once may have represented.[121] Historian Mark Dyerson posits that supporters of sport's more traditional conceptions were "horrified by the change in physical culture."[122] He contends further that in the eyes of many of the day's social critics

> ... sport had become an opiate which allowed the average person to cope with Big Society. It offered an arena in which the masses could turn their eyes away, if only briefly, from the grim political and economic realities of the modern world.[123]

Irrespective of these changes, athletes and administrators of the period for the most part continued to demonstrate a regard for the older notions of teamwork and virtue, the cornerstone for so much of what transpired in sporting environments before the war. Still, there were clear indications that the older traditions as they existed prior to the war were in serious jeopardy. Through technology and an increasingly widespread media presence, the stage was set for an emphasis on individual pursuits that threatened one of the central tenets of reformist aims—the team. This new focus on celebrity athletes who were heralded for their individual exploits and acumen may have rewarded excellence but also rewarded eccentricity, a matter that troubled sport's critics who viewed with disdain Babe Ruth's excesses and the effect that this would have on his younger admirers. Furthermore, the promotion of athletic excellence over behavioral and moral concerns seemed equally poised to erase the structural gains of the previous generations, threatening to take sport deeper into the abyss of post-war nonconformity. In this climate, the support of moral excellence as espoused by the traditional sport model appeared almost obsolete and seemed incapable of holding sway over the nation as a whole without the focus on the skill component. Americans reveled alongside athletic success and the tag of winner, and as winning continued to take precedence over once perceived indispensable behavioral ideals, sport reformers found it increasingly difficult to stay the course and maintain their allegiance to sport in any context regardless of how imbedded into the framework of sport character and propriety really were.[124]

One institution thought to be a major contributor to America's evolving fascination with modern sport was the increasingly pervasive sport media. Sport had been championed in the American press since the initial appearance of baseball circuits in the late 1860s, but with the proliferation of high-profile professional sport in the post–World War I era (see figure 2.3), sport and media would grow even more inseparable.[125] As newspapers competed among themselves for features, and with the birth of sports radio broadcasting in 1921, the

Figure 2.3. North American Professional Sport Franchise Growth

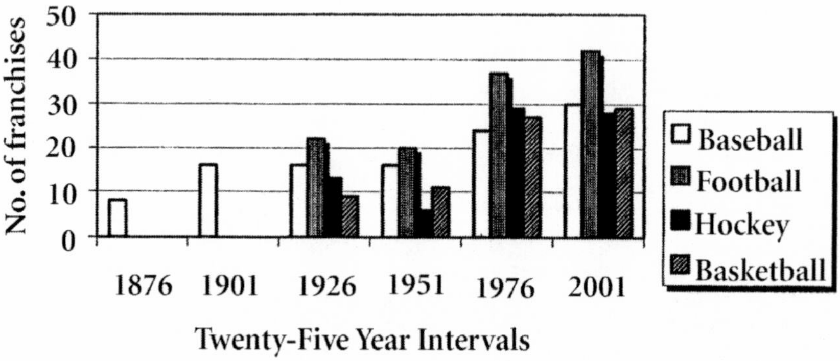

The most prominent of the North American professional sport circuits, baseball, football, hockey, and basketball, have shown remarkable franchise growth throughout the twentieth century and remain at the leading edge of the continent's mass culture.[126]

nation was replete with news from the world of sport that helped elevate it to its perceptibly over-ambitious pose while reaffirming the more traditional ideology in spite of its dramatic and sometimes blatant fade from view. With the spread of syndicated columns, the rise of nationally embraced college teams and professional franchises, and the enormous growth in audience that followed, sport appeared even more alluring and more compelling. In the pages of dailies and tabloids, a team's quirkiness, its position in the standings, and an athlete's on-field performance took precedence over nearly every other matter in sport reporting. In fact, it became a common feature of sport reporting that reporters rarely explored such reformist issues as the psychosocial effectiveness of sport, let alone the sort of negative topics regarding player behavior and such in order to remain in good stead with team management. Ironically, this had the effect of permitting athletes to be seen as infallible when they clearly were not, allowing the illusion of athletic excellence and propriety to remain linked and seemingly beyond reproach in spite of critical remonstrations to the contrary.[127] Furthermore, organizations covered by enthusiastic and particularly compliant sports reporters were able to parlay media depictions of a wholesome athleticism and benefited from the exposure in both image and at the box office at a time when the behaviors of athletes might have actually warranted public scrutiny, but very few in the general public were ever made aware of such matters.[128]

Post–World War I sport had become caught up in a frenzy of popular fiction as complicit journalists romanticized tales of athletic prowess that often constituted an absurd degree of misinformation. Moreover, the reluctance of sport's reporters to hold sport up to a more critical analysis allowed the general public to conceive of sport as having remained one of the nation's most wholesome and moral institutions at a time when these things mattered the least and in spite of critical objections being lodged elsewhere. The result is that professional and otherwise high-profile athletes came to embody the perfect blend of physical and mental competence, and through the diligence of era reporters, this depiction would serve to reinforce sport as an agent for character building while reserving for the athlete a place among the most admired contributors in American society.[129] As noted *New York Times* columnist Robert Lipsyte explained, "The role of the journalist in all this has been as steward of the mansion, preserving the status quo, parroting the owners, the mayor's, or the government's line."[130]

Of course, the more genuine concerns regarding the perceived changes in sport were aimed at its effects on youth participants. That competitive youth sport had become increasingly prone to the similar rush to spectacle, as demonstrated by the more high-profile undertakings, ultimately rendered many of the aforementioned advocates of the sporting life disquieted and beleaguered. By the 1920s and into the 1930s, many of the same voices that had unconditionally promoted youth sport primarily due to its character-building potential had begun to call for its elimination from the school curriculum altogether. Furthermore, it had become increasingly obvious that many of the emergent youth sport leagues once thought capable of relieving schools of their sport burden were being organized not around the more traditional values but more than ever around the emphasis on crowning champions, a matter than often resulted in a chorus of protest about what was regarded as a noxious blend of blatant commercialism and potentially damaging cultural practices that threatened young athletes.[131] In parallel to the rise of city leagues and community-sponsored youth sport circuits, most of which were thought to center chiefly around competitive designs aimed at making better athletes out of children, organizations intent on keeping youth sport free from such corruptive elements sprang back into prominence to denounce highly competitive sport, a position that was clearly in contrast to previous discussions.[132] As Wiggins notes, this backlash was due in no small part to a perceived shift in the nation's general perception of sport as both entertainment and a potentially lucrative commercial enterprise rather than a means to a much loftier end as expressed in the reformist model.[133]

In an attempt to retard the flood of changes taking shape within American sport, YMCAs, Boys' (and later Girls') Clubs, and a host of other, more established organizations would form community outlets for youth sport under the old guidelines of moral-based and carefully crafted physical practices. In the meantime, new organizations with decidedly older values, such as Pop Warner Football and Carl Stotz's Little League Baseball, would leave lasting marks on the nation's sporting habits in the years to come.[134] Still, while these and others may have entered into the picture out of a genuine belief in their cause, they too would eventually succumb to the public's perception that it was no longer necessary or even preferable to attempt to keep a competitive and technique-oriented design outside the realm of character training through sport.

These outcomes led to a general reassessment of the role that competitive sport might play in children's lives and the once critical demand for youth-centered sport circuits that espoused a similar value system as promoted by the pre–World War I reformers. Sport seemed to be progressing beyond an age of character building while being transformed into a type of boosterism that threatened core American values.[135] Few critics gave the older methods much of a chance to regain their once prominent place in American society and were quick to point out that the nature of professional and high-profile sport had always been tinted by a very powerful market-driven forces that even the most civic-minded and passionate reformer would be powerless to thwart. Nevertheless, what many critics overlooked was that while the old ways may have been cast aside for the newer emphases on commercial exploits and spectacular feats of athleticism that could both mesmerize crowds and turn great profits, the old standards never did fully disappear. Rather, they were altered and incorporated within the emergent treatment of sport, leading to a reaffirmation of the role of character and deportment through athletics as a matter of nationwide importance, a matter that would not be worked out easily.

To be sure, sport throughout the interwar years and on into the postwar period would remain a proving ground for the governance of established behaviors, but a creeping consumer-driven ethos and an increasing focus on outcome would begin to hover about sport and serve as a dividing line between an established old guard intent on maintaining sport's place within the culture and a nascent new guard not so convinced. While the new guard would similarly embrace the traditional values instilled into the sporting life, more modern-appearing emphases would displace some of the older ideals, and a resulting clash of ideologies would prove to have major implications on the future of the American competitive ethos, implications that will be developed in much greater detail in the next chapter.

3

Cold War Era Sport and the Countercultural Shift

The values expressed through competitive sport in the earliest days of the twentieth century would change little through its first half. Neither a paralyzing depression nor two rounds of global warfare would materially threaten its bond with the American public, but the growth of a Cold War apparatus following World War II, one that would inextricably link physical strength to national unity, would serve to both alter and strengthen sport's place as an influential albeit controversial feature within the culture.

Cold War era rhetoric did not necessarily change sport as much as it amended the more traditional ideals surrounding its presence while offering political currency for the promotion of virtue and potency in the face of persistent adversity. In the Cold War climate, fitness represented a physiological phenomenon while toughness came to be defined as a matter of attitude and personal conduct. Thus, as Americans were being reminded to stand tall in the face of the perceived communist threat, the lessons learned through athletic competition became a source for illustrating more effectively what was expected of a resolute, strong, and united nation. As sport historian Donald Mrozek observed, "Physical fitness was the price to pay for guaranteeing peace and the continuation of American civilization and celebrations of physical culture were even more convincingly the components of nationalistic ritual."[1] Or as iconoclastic journalist Matt Labash later noted, albeit mockingly:

> By the mid-twentieth century, Americans not only had copped the British system of teaching motor skills and fitness through competitive sports, but also saw physical education as a chance to perpetuate the Brits' towel-snapping vigor ... the President's Council on Youth Fitness had been created to encourage kids to stay fit in the event Communists needed to be killed.[2]

In sharp contrast to the patriotic ideal, an ideal that Mrozek refers to as a "cult of toughness,"[3] was an evolving ethos whose presence was predicated upon a hostility toward contemporary values and an opposition to state conduct both at home and abroad. In an age that featured the House Un-American Activities Committee (HUAC), as well as similar such anti-communism

77

initiatives and political assassinations, the discussion of core American values relating to such sport-friendly concepts as competitiveness and stoic self-sacrifice were to be met by a relatively small but nonetheless significant back-lash by the early to middle 1960s, an counter-offensive that seems to have emerged out of a general cynicism normally associated with 1950s era conformity. This decidedly countercultural conceptualization of modern life hinged upon a youth-driven disillusionment with the status quo and a disavowal of traditional social institutions in an attempt to expose a wellspring of contradictions within American society. It would be under these conditions that competitive sport would find itself under intense scrutiny.

Thus, this chapter will serve as an exploration of the emergence of the countercultural critique of competitive sport by looking specifically at developments within both Cold War era society at large and those taking shape within the competitive dynamic itself. Additionally, I will also try to establish a foundation within the more far-reaching sociopolitical and cultural debates pertaining to period society and sport that will have left their varied imprints on the times while proving as well to be far more influential in the decades to follow.

Sport and Cold War Era Developments

While athletics was promoted as a cure to technological society, that very society turned it into a commercial enterprise. Athletics became big business. The naiveté that led to the belief that athletics could cure society's problems overlooked the fact that without any fundamental change in the social and economic structure, athletics would be turned into a business enterprise. This occurred in public school and college athletics as well as professional sports.[4]

Winning isn't everything, but striving to win is. Striving to win is the essence of sports.[5]

Systematically rejected by the mainstream for their depictions of contemporary life as well as their tendency toward unconventional appearance and social conventions, the era's counterculture stood for the rejection of virtually all features of contemporary society that might in any way threaten the well-being and happiness of the individual. They embraced the centrality of the human subject in such a way as to champion individuality and highly personal expression over accepted group identity so ingrained within Cold War conformity, a conformity they denounced as either an acceptance of or an acquiescence to the current order. Toward this end, they often looked to traditional European thinkers, such as Nietzsche, Marx, and Freud, as well as an increasingly fashionable emergent stream of more modern philosophers and philosophical constructs for their theoretical grounding and intellectual support.[6]

As countercultural historian Theodore Roszak describes in his seminal *The Making of a Counter Culture: Reflections on the Technocratic Society and Its Youthful Opposition*, at its most basic, the Cold War era counterculture was poised to deny the efficacy of established social and cultural practices during a period of increasing social unrest. The twentieth century had been for a younger generation a distressing symbol of the consequences of a technologically advanced yet corrupted order, and in an attempt to discard elements of established practices, a countercultural wave offered critiques of nearly every facet of the contemporary world. What they sought was a more critical analysis of capitalist society and capitalism's role in international affairs, but they also expressed themselves in terms of the national culture, which is specifically how competition and competitive sport become entangled within these nascent countercultural discussions.[7]

Countercultural sport critics were well aware of the unsettling elements within sport that reflected the mood and the culture of Cold War America and built their critiques accordingly. Posing themselves as modern day muckrakers, these commentators enthusiastically sought to devalue the traditional American competitive ethos that existed within the sporting establishment by posing it as antithetical to the lives of right-thinking people. Many acted as if this tactic would be enough to help erode the veneer that once kept sport relatively free of controversy outside the boundaries of play. In the face of countless social changes relative to a seemingly constant barrage of hostility regarding warfare, hot or cold, and the civil rights struggles in the American South, circumstances that were often reflected within the sporting establishment in the most traditional sense became fodder for the countercultural struggle.

While the overwhelming majority of these debates were being aimed at anti-Vietnam War initiatives and the ongoing crisis as expressed in the American civil rights struggle, a handful of critics would emerge from within the ranks to offer up forthright and notably frank assessments of competitive sport and its role in maintaining civil obedience and conformity. Interestingly, among this first wave of highly critical sport commentators were former collegiate and professional athletes who for the first time were offering to the outside world highly personal, lurid, and often times polemical appraisals of life within the sporting establishment. Their accounts of social exclusion, exploitation, social injustice, and outright sadism served as valuable contributions to a developing countercultural critique of sport and were heartily received by sympathetic counterculturalists who saw sport as an arm of U.S. militarism that reflected the interests of both state power and ruling elites.

Feminists, anti-racists, secular humanists, and even a handful of critical mainstream journalists inspired by the momentum of the various movements joined in on the debate and offered various perspectives on the role of sport, its place, and its relevance to an increasingly discordant society. Those involved openly voiced their disapproval of sport's goal-oriented behaviors, its hierarchical and role-specific relationships, and its place within organizational schemes. From this platform, they could forge an even more spirited argument that would move sport away from its perceived tangential place within the contemporary culture toward a critique that sought to position it as a central player that served as a blatant tool of oppression that reinforced the state's hegemony over its citizens.[8] In this context, the rejection of contemporary sport and its resultant competitive spirit reinforces the central tenets of a movement designed in such a way as to find little favor with competitiveness regardless of design or intent.[9] As sociologist Walter Schafer was to note in a 1971 address pertaining to sport and social deviancy at a conference held at the State University of New York at Brockport:

> Except when carried out in fun, competition is usually abhorred by those in the counterculture, while it is inherent in sport. Those in the counterculture believe that intense competition generates conditional self-worth, role-specific relationships, goal-orientation, excellence based on competitive merit, self as a means, and subjection of self to external control — all of which are to be avoided. Certainly there is an aversion to the kind of intense winning-is-everything sport practiced in most schools and colleges.[10]

Ironically, the counterculture's position on sport was remarkably Victorian in its reach. Similar to the Victorians, counterculturalists were leery of an institution that advocated unchecked competitiveness alongside built-in mechanisms for aggression and individual accomplishment. Inherent to this critique was the promotion of a victory aesthetic best summed up by the now infamous Lombardi dictum that "winning isn't everything; it's the only thing,"[11] a position that came into prominence in the midst of the challenge to traditional competitive sport. In general, countercultural critics viewed matters relating to a stanch competitive model as anathema to human progress and argued that competitiveness at any level was inherently divisive and potentially injurious to a civilized order. In their view, promoting sport was tantamount to advocating warfare, a matter that was especially poignant in an age in which college athletic departments and Reserve Officers' Training Corps (ROTC) centers were growing conspicuously closer to one another, reinforcing for many the notion that sport and militarism had become all the more linked within the mainstream culture and something that football coaches often played upon in their remonstrations that dedicated players would gladly "take one for the team" while reminding them to win for "God and country."[12]

This emergent Left demonstrated a different sort of Victorianism in that they saw little value in sport regardless of organizational structure or a specified managerial process. The countercultural position on such matters emphasized that any institution that vigorously promoted the types of belligerent and aggressive behavior often found in competitive sport placed the individual in a position where his or her basic well-being could be compromised, which they could claim was inherently antithetical to the search for human decency. Moreover, they viewed those who participated in such spectacles as serving to rein-force the current order, rendering athletes as either complicit in the mainte-nance of status quo values or at the very least victims of their own excesses. Generally speaking, the counterculturalists treated athletes, regardless of age or ethnic makeup, as either the enemy or at the very least as unwitting dupes in a power struggle bent on social maintenance. As sport columnist Glenn Dickey offered in the foreword to his 1974 polemic, "There are rotten spots in the sports apple wherever you look."[13]

The Reevaluation of Cold War Era Sport

By the late 1960's, the revolt in the athletic world had escalated to the extent that some coaches, only half-jokingly, talked about asking for combat pay.[14]

We're trying to show that ground games such as football are crypto-fascist metaphors for nuclear war.[15]

The handful of collegians and radical youths who offered scathing critics of American institutions cannot be considered primary forces in terms of changing values and outlooks throughout the Cold War period. Their num-bers were relatively small and their behavior was often challenging to the point of absurdity in the eyes of most mainstream Americans, leaving much of what they had to say relatively unchallenged. Still, their presence was effective in a much less obvious way, as their assessment often served to stretch the param-eters of the debate just enough to allow for the development of a much larger middle ground.

In terms of sport, the self-consciously polemical approach to undercut-ting the national passion was indeed direct and steadfast, but it was also easily overlooked (or simply ignored) by most in the general population, though the subjects of many of these works, that is, owners, administrators, and broadcast sponsors, were careful to tread lightly around such analyses, and with very good reason.[16] Politicians and celebrities alike had regularly trumpeted the impor-tance of sport, and television was quick to capitalize on sport's popularity as well as aid in furthering its widespread acceptance.[17] Much as was the case fol-lowing World War I, the athletes and the games were revered, and attempts were made to place sport above the fray of typical sociopolitical debate. But, unlike previous eras, the sociopolitical climate of the age left sport exposed and vul-nerable to harsh criticism. Simply put, while athletes could once be held in high esteem and their images manipulated into metaphors for honor and cour-age throughout the middle decades of the twentieth century, this was not always the case during what would become the more volatile years of the Cold War era. This rather abrupt loss of both standing and, seemingly, innocence was regularly played upon by the sport-conscious countercultural dissenters. What would evolve was a more general analysis of America's competitive culture from both within and around the margin the competitive environment, an analysis that eventually began to find a semi-attentive audience within more typically mainstream circles. According to former track coach Jack Scott, who would become a noted academic and countercultural critic, once Americans started to recognize that the previously inviolate sports world had been rendered vulnerable by such caustic representations, the tension between the various sides would set in motion a further weakening of sport's traditional place in the social order, offering the countercultural critique the momentum to engender even stronger mainstream support.[18]

Addressing such controversial topics as increased opportunities for minorities and women while seeking an end to the increasingly brutal treatment of athletes, reports of which were beginning to alarm even traditional cultural critics, countercultural appraisals drew liberally from a well-spring of contradictions within American culture. In turn, they began to chronicle the extent to which sport had grown to resemble elements of the repressive establishment, an image that offered them the opportunity to seek considerable changes within the nation's sporting posture while at the same time demanding an end to traditional injustices found within American life. Period critics could, for example, easily pose team owners and university athletic programs as existing within a discriminatory frame and had numerous examples from which to draw, including recruiting scandals, pay disparity, and carryovers from Jim Crow issues such as access to housing and dining facilities for minority participants.[19]

Also, amid a growing trend toward the publication of bland biographical and autobiographical accounts of retired stars and countless other post-Brown and post-Merriwell type works,[20] countercultural exposés went to great — often disquieting — lengths to present another side of the American sport story, prompting such controversial works as Pete Gent's *North Dallas Forty*[21] and the late University of Texas scholar-athlete Gary Shaw's ambitious yet disturbing *Meat on the Hoof: The Hidden World of Texas Football.*[22] These types of accounts and other such lurid works presented images of sport that some found had little in keeping with the American sporting ideal, either in myth or in fact, and led to further assaults on the American sporting culture.

Gent's thinly veiled assault on his brief but stormy tenure with the famed Dallas Cowboys of the National Football League (NFL) in the mid-1960s depicts overly libidinous, drug-induced deviants governed and pampered by astonishingly sadistic thrill-seekers who seem to embody the worst elements of the vaunted Lombardi dictum. Gent's consciously vulgar and grotesquely exaggerated narrative presents an alternative impression to what many traditionally thought of as the playful antics of grown men by fusing powerful images of physical cruelty with a shocking disregard for the most basic sense of decorum, most of which was nimbly enveloped in a swath of humor whose effectiveness as social commentary was exacerbated in part by the celebrated release of the film version of the novel in 1979.[23]

Gent's portrayal of competitors being plied with promises of celebrity and sexual conquest while being saturated with potent pharmaceutical compounds displayed amid scenes of unparalleled brutality both disturbed and captivated the public at a time when football had begun to seriously erode baseball's once insurmountable monopoly over the American public's sporting imagination. As protagonist/narrator Phil Elliot, Gent's presumed alter-ego, describes in a pre-game custom:

> Because of serious injuries and the complexity of their treatment, nine players, myself included, were required to arrive at the stadium early so the trainers and team doctors could have enough time to effect repairs. A tenth player, Gino Machado, recently acquired from the [then Los Angeles] Rams, came out early just to take his amphetamines and "get ready to kick ass." Machado would sit by his locker, his legs shaking uncontrollably from the speed surging through his brain, and talk like a top-forty disc jockey to anyone within earshot. I spent hours listening to him describe sex acts, fist fights, and ball games. His lips were white from constant nervous licking, his mouth stretched open from time to time in a grotesque, compulsive yawn, and his eyes rolled while he clenched and unclenched his fists. Every now and then, gripping his shoulders with his hands, he would hug himself and bend double as if trying to slow himself down. In the early season Texas heat, the trainers often had to pack Machado in ice after a game to cool down his incredibly overheated body.[24]

For some, Gent's illustrations provided the first inkling that the games were anything but benign struggles and helped reinvigorate football's more vocal critics to gaze once again much more seriously upon the dual concerns relative to brutality and deviancy in sport.[25] What many discovered was that a book written by a former player who refused to offer more than the typically self-aggrandizing images so common in period literature offered a great deal of political capital, contributing both vigor and thrust to an age in which scrutiny was poised to replace adulation in the once impenetrable environs of American sport. It is also worth mentioning here that baseball's version of *North Dallas Forty*, Jim Bouton's controversial *Ball Four*,[26] published some three years earlier, took similar liberties by chronicling "the game within the game," that is, drugs, promiscuity, self-indulgence, in such a way that it threatened to erode public and private support of the nation's pastime and drew predictably harsh responses from both within and without the baseball establishment.[27]

Shaw's contribution, with its cover admonition, "They raise cattle and football players in Texas. The cattle are treated better,"[28] garnered little more than critical acclaim (and some death threats from Texas football zealots), but it struck deeply, nonetheless. By looking at the brutality of sport through what were supposedly less commercial enterprises, high school and collegiate football, Shaw was able to steer clear of the expected popular counterattack and present the callousness of the sport as it pertained to student athletes, a state of affairs that would be certain to inflame passions while raising questions regarding the roles of both youth participants and sport administrators. By Shaw's estimation, football in the context of a high-profile college program such as that at the University of Texas, had become a peculiar right of manhood, rendering winning and losing a matter of much more grave importance than simply basic competitiveness itself.

As the title suggests, Shaw presents university athletes as commodities, their education a remote concern at best. Shaw notes that by the end of their eligibility, players once so coveted could be easily discarded in favor of the next generation of potential stars poised to bring the program further success and celebrity. In an excerpt from his review of the text, Dave Meggyesy, himself a former collegiate and professional player turned outspoken critic, author, and later a staff representative with the National Football League Players' Association, asserts:

> In my book *Out of Their League*,[29] I pointed out the most evident elements of hypocrisy inherent in big-time college and professional football. Gary has gone much further in that he explains in vivid detail what is and what is meant by the dehumanizing and frighteningly inhumane way college football players are used....[30]

But the brutality and contradictions within sport in general were merely components of a much broader deconstruction of the sporting milieu that era critics seized upon in their analyses, informing a new line of inquiry that would develop throughout the Cold War era and beyond in spite of traditional rejoinders.

Race Impacts the Modern Discussion

Sport was a legitimate lever to bring about changes relative to race. [It would be] a battle for dignity and respect.[31]

As a nation, I think we needed the evocation of Jackie Robinson to save us from the nihilistic fires of race: from the trials of O.J. Simpson (the failed black athletic hero who seems nothing more than a symbol of self-centered consumption), from the Rodney King trial and subsequent riot in Los Angeles and, most significantly, from the turmoil over affirmative action.[32]

The issue of racial discrimination, which once had virtually no place in the discussion of American sport beyond particularist interests due largely to the enforced segregation of America's playing fields dating back to the late 19th century, also found a much more receptive audience in the highly charged climate of early Cold War era politics and fused within the more radical circles.[33] In the wake of the groundbreaking signing of rising Negro League baseball star Jackie Robinson, a move that would indicate the final stages of nearly fifty years of Jim Crow era segregation in professional baseball, racial antagonisms continued to grip sport, albeit in an altered state, and became something of a cause célèbre of countercultural critics. Whereas on the one hand, the Robinson-Rickey collaborative that initially broke baseball's color barrier in 1946 became an issue that was, and remains still today, a matter of major importance, the fact was that regardless of whatever opportunities may have existed for minority athletes, there would remain considerable obstacles in place before anything close to equality would and could exist within sporting circles.[34]

That black athletes would continue to operate well outside of the institutional walls surrounding sport in the earliest days of desegregated sport is well-chronicled in both the recent and historical literature. Though some athletes would indeed excel and be revered for their contributions to the athletic sphere, there were few occasions in which they were afforded anything close to active roles in their own lives and careers. In fact many of the same biases and contradictions that haunted black America at-large, such as a supposed natural physical excellence mixed with lethargy or prodigious strength combined with a tendency to succumb to minor injury, would find a new home in the post-Robinson era, relegating a black presence once again to a distinctly prone and secondary position. As filmmaker Ken Burns would note throughout his exhaustive nineteen part documentary *Baseball*,[35] even the most innocuous seeming remarks taken in context suggested that Major League Baseball's traditional racist pose would not simply vanish overnight. For example, when the celebrated New York Yankees, among the last to integrate, finally added a black player to their roster in 1955, managing general partner George Weiss was reported to have observed that the signing reflected the young man's status as a "gentleman," causing one modern analyst to raise the question, "Since when did being a gentleman have anything to do with a player's ability to make the team?"[36] As career homerun record holder Hank Aaron, among the second wave of African American athletes to play Major League Baseball, would later acknowledge, "In order to survive in the league, we just had to be better than our white teammates,"[37] a sentiment that permeated minority participation regardless of the sheer numbers of athletes involved.

Discriminatory exclusion from sport and/or sport's governance would serve as a central theme in the discussion of American sport in the decades to follow. Those who would attempt to sway public sentiment or speak freely on either social or racial matters, subtle or otherwise, such as renowned heavyweight boxing champion Muhammad Ali, basketball's Bill Russell, or even the handful of white critics who would offer their support, often found themselves either banished under questionable circumstances or psychically deflated from the experience. As Russell acknowledged in his autobiography, "As a rookie I was the only black player on the Boston Celtics, and I was excluded from almost everything except practice and the games."[38] Nevertheless, with the so-called invisible barrier broken, race would boldly re-enter the discussion and would prove to be a fertile direction for contemporary commentary in the face of enormous obstacles and vitriolic rhetoric.

Both white and black commentators would contribute to this debate, which by the late 1960s instigated a backlash throughout the sporting industry. As historian Benjamin Rader notes, at a time when white Northern college students were heading southward to join black Southerners in the era's socalled Freedom Rides and voter registration drives, handfuls of commentators from across the continent influenced by countercultural critiques took up the issue of the black presence in American sport. What they found was that the shift from the pre-Robinson to the post-Robinson era was fraught with many of the same contradictions and impediments to progress as before, but in slightly altered forms.[39] In fact early on into the new debates surrounding black participation, there were those who saw an alarming swing toward notably overwhelming numbers of black athletes plying their trade in front of largely white audiences that gave rise to much older themes involving Negro physical prowess and its perceived entertainment niche that favored mainstream audiences, a condition that esteemed sport sociologist Harry Edwards contends reeks of a sort of modern day minstrelsy, a matter often taken up by the era's countercultural critics.[40] For instance, writing on collegiate basketball in 1972, Canadian Marxist Paul Hoch, a frequent though controversial contributor to countercultural debates regarding sport, observed:

> In one generation the situation has gone from one of virtual exclusion of blacks from American sports to what is today sometimes called the "plantation system." The contemporary situation resembles a plantation in that almost all of the overseers are white (except for the now-standard black *assistant* [his italics] coach in basketball) and almost all of the top players are black. Moreover, when the professional basketball playoff games roll into town, we are faced with the odd situation of predominantly black teams playing before predominantly white suburbanite audiences.[41]

Edwards, a former collegiate track and basketball star turned sociologist, grew to become a significant force in this debate and regularly offered frank assessments of American racism as it pertained to the American sporting milieu. His attempt to organize a boycott of black athletes prior to the 1968 Summer Olympics in Mexico City, a matter that led in part to the infamous twin blackgloved salute by American sprinters Tommie Smith and John Carlos on the winners' podium, one of the century's most controversial yet lasting images of the racial divide that often overwhelmed American sport, thrust him into the center of the increasingly rancorous debate over the nature of sport and race. Nonetheless, Edwards's more lasting legacy would surface in the form of volumes of scholarly work on the subject of black sport participation, its consequence, and its place within the debate on racial equality in America.[42]

In his earliest works such as *The Sociology of Sport*[43] and the decidedly more trenchant *The Revolt of the Black Athlete*,[44] Edwards posed the issue of race and sport within the modern infrastructure as a characteristic more typical to issues relating to power and powerlessness that showed deliberate echoes of the sort of hierarchy of discrimination found throughout American society. He worked primarily from the assumption that for Americans along the periphery, the lure of sport served as a mirage leading down a path that would offer little substantive gain beyond immediate gratification, though conceding that for a select few, sport could and should provide a platform for inciting social transformation.[45] Writing in *The Revolt of the Black Athlete*, for example, Edwards considers the inconsistency in terms of opportunities for would-be student-athletes. What had been billed as a liberalizing and more relaxed social order as evidenced through growing black participation in sport was perceived by Edwards to be little more than a breeding ground for the exploitation of skilled black youth lured by the supposed glory to be found through success in sport:

> A black athlete generally fares well in athletic competition relative to other incoming athletes at a white-dominated college. The cards are somewhat stacked for him, however, because few black high school athletes get what are typically classified as second-and-third string athletic grants-in-aid. One simply does not find black athletes on "full-rides" at predominantly white schools riding the bench or playing second-or-third team positions.[46]

Or as he would later assert, sport had become for many minority participants caught up in the lure a mirage with very real consequences:

> [Organized sport is] a trap leading nowhere for most black youngsters, and the failure, the disillusionment, leads to social unrest and subsequent crime.[47]

Race would remain a discussion that would follow sport throughout the remainder of the century as critics continued to debate the meaning of sport and its value to black America both within and outside the sporting environment. Still, it would be in the aftermath of the Supreme Court case of *Flood v. Kuhn* (1972) that the once mutually exclusive notions of race and sport would find themselves summarily conjoined alongside class interests within a decidedly modern context.

Curt Flood and the Reserve Clause

While Flood's story generally remained confined to the sports page, as Flood and [team owner August] Busch note, the suit quite accurately mirrored the social movements of the day. This, indeed, was no coincidence. Flood's suit of baseball not only reflected the prevailing attitudes of the day but can serve as a crowning example of the 1960s social change paradigm of reformer against establishment.[48]

This is America, and I'm a human being. I'm not a piece of property. I'm not a consignment of goods.[49]

Amid the upheaval surrounding race and sport comes a watershed moment that would leave its lasting imprint on modern professional sport. Curt Flood, an established star outfielder for Major League Baseball's St. Louis Cardinals, was caught in the vise between the traditional and the emergent customs in the period's sporting establishment. A black man, Flood spent eleven years enduring the taunts and slights associated with performing in baseball's southern-most major league city, but he did so admirably, fashioning an outstanding career over an eleven year period that many agree deserves consideration for enshrinement in baseball's Hall of Fame. Following the 1969 season in which his service contract had expired, however, Flood was in the midst of renegotiating with the team when he was unexpectedly traded to the Philadelphia Phillies, a perennially hapless franchise widely known for its tradition of losing and its indifferent treatment of black players.[50]

Stating guaranteed protection under the law and backed by a seasoned labor organizer and lawyer named Marvin Miller, whom the players had voted to the newly created post of Executive Director of the Major League Baseball Player's Association, Flood refused to report to the Philadelphia franchise. As a result, he became a reluctant but committed adversary of the game, taking on baseball's infamous *reserve clause*, a standard interpretation of professional service contracts adopted by most professional sport circuits that tied a player to a particular franchise until that franchise deemed the player dispensable. It also made him something of an anomaly in the post-Robinson era in sport: a black man daring to speak out on a labor matter long held in disdain by white professional athletes as well.[51]

A controversial topic from professional sport's earliest days, and the cause of a player revolt that nearly toppled professional baseball in 1886, the reserve clause, which existed amid baseball's congressionally sanctioned anti-trust status, had been challenged only infrequently throughout the twentieth century but always by white players and never by such an established and well-compensated star. Flood's role in this dispute, however, proved to be a much different one than his predecessors.' Whereas disgruntled athletes had in the past based their appeals on the constitutional provisions that protected free movement in the workplace denied to them under baseball's accepted labor practices, few outside the sport were willing to offer up more than bemused smirks for a decidedly white workforce claiming foul while collecting salaries once estimated at seven times that of working-class America and growing larger with each passing decade (Figure 3.1).[52] That this stemmed from Flood's interpretation of the events also served to ignite a passion within race and class conscious circles that left this struggle with obstacles that had never touched previous challenges.

While Americans struggled with the unfamiliar mix of race, sport, and labor in this context, Flood found himself caught in the middle of an increasingly nationalized conflict. As *New York Times* sportswriter Robert Lipsyte would observe, amid the prevailing racial climate of the period, many Ameri-

Figure 3.1. MLB Average Salaries

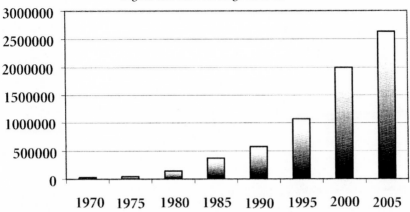

The trajectory of Major League Baseball salaries has changed dramatically in the years following Curt Flood's decision not to report to Philadelphia.[53]

cans refused to understand that Curt Flood, who stood to earn over 93,000 dollars the year he was traded, could be so dissatisfied with his arrangement when in fact the basic language of the reserve clause clearly called for workplace conditions that left athletes well-compensated yet powerless to affect changes in their professional lives.[54]

Though most Americans would have bristled at such impediments in their own employment arrangements, the power of the ubiquitous myths surrounding athletes and duty split American sentiment primarily along the color line and fueled public sentiment against such protests regarding free agency and player salaries. Even Jackie Robinson, whose politics often ran the gamut between the traditional Left and Right,[55] was initially ambivalent about the looming threat to what he maintained was the competitive balance of the game, though he eventually came to support the cause as a matter of civil rights, which he maintained trumped any other concerns.[56]

Primary to this split was the long accepted position that playing what was conceived of as children's games for money was a privilege that deserved to remain beyond the grasp of such unseemly conflicts as salary demands and contract disputes. There was also the matter of team unity, loyalty, and commitment, issues that the general sport-conscious population felt would be threatened under a new arrangement that allowed for free negotiation and movement between clubs and players.[57]

Flood, who was regularly pilloried in the mainstream American media throughout his crusade, was often reminded that as a black man in what was still considered to be a white world, he was threatening to upset an already delicate balance between race and American sport. It was also widely assumed that in other, less visible circles his daring to stand up to the baseball establishment under these circumstances, which held so much significance to the future of sport, was both reprehensible as well as considered to be "uppity" in the most traditional sense. In some cases even the language used to describe Flood's case against Major League Baseball mirrored both the language and the sentiment bandied about during Jackie Robinson's struggle in the 1940s and 1950s. As Flood himself would later acknowledge, "If the newspaper was typical, it lied that a victory for Flood would mean the collapse of our national pastime. God profaned! Flag desecrated! Motherhood defiled! Apple pie blasphemed!"[58]

Attempting to bring a sense of order to an increasingly chaotic situation, Flood maintained that his position was irrespective of race, though he would later draw upon the analogy of slavery in noting that "a well paid slave is ... still a slave."[59] In a well documented letter to then baseball commissioner Bowie Kuhn, Flood offered a simple yet poignant response to the league's unwillingness to meet his terms:

> Dear Mr. Kuhn:
> After twelve years in the major leagues, I do not feel that I am piece of property to be bought and sold irrespective of my wishes. I believe that any system that produces that result violates my standing as a citizen and is inconsistent with the law of the United States.
> It is my desire to play baseball in 1970, and I am capable of playing. I received a contract from the Philadelphia club, but I believe that I have the right to consider offers from other clubs before making any decisions. I, therefore, request that you make known to major league clubs my feelings on this matter and advise them of my availability for the 1970 season.
> Sincerely,
> Curt Flood[60]

The controversy and acrimony displayed during Curt Flood's refusal to report to Philadelphia cost him the rest of his career and his legacy as a player, though he is considered, posthumously, an important and effective social activist both within the sporting environment and without.[61] Moreover, his efforts would eventually lead to the dismantling of the reserve clause, culminating in players' winning the right to free agency by 1975. By attacking the reserve clause as if it were the embodiment of a holdover from slavery, Flood, under Miller's extraordinary counsel, was able to help initiate further support, though it may have eluded him in his personal quest, by illustrating in a most glaring fashion that ballplayers were indeed commodities and that sport franchises were systematically being operated under many of the same rules as antebellum plantations and ultimately rewriting the rules of engagement.

Flood's case against Major League Baseball would serve as a watershed moment in modern American sport. Beyond the candor and blunt honesty Flood and his representatives harnessed to their fight in an obviously rancorous atmosphere, Flood's sacrifice provided impetus for more impassioned and certainly more emboldened athletes who found strength through increasingly staggering financial arrangements and the public exposure it would bring them. On the other hand, Flood's struggle would also give rise to another phenomenon of contemporary American sport: a popular and critical backlash that methodically seeks to explore the merits of paying staggering amounts of money to athletes, which some see as merely a growing number of non-white, non-U.S.-born athletes (see figure 3.2). By adding race to this mix, free agency and the enormous salaries to follow would provide further impetus to those who feared that a black presence in sport underscored by enormous compensation would afford black America a place in the culture that few seemed willing to concede.

Figure 3.2. Top Ten Salaries MLB 2006[62]

A. Rodriguez (Yankees)	$21,680,727
D. Jeter (Yankees)	$20,600,000
J. Giambi (Yankees)	$20,428,571
J. Bagwell (Astros)	$19,369,019
B. Bonds (Giants)	$19,331,470
M. Mussina (Yankees)	$19,000,000
M. Ramirez (Red Sox)	$18,279,238
T. Helton (Rockies)	$16,600,000
A. Pettitte (Astros)	$16,428,416
M. Ordonez (Tigers)	$16,200,000

The Emergence of Women's Sport

Before the end of the nineteenth century, most women felt athletic activity to be irrelevant, if not antithetical to their concept of their role as women. But even for the first three-quarters of the twentieth century, few observers remarked on or questioned women's lack of participation in most organized sports.[63]

On both sides of the Atlantic, the Cult of Domesticity and the Doctrine of Separate Spheres kept Victorian women in the home rather than on the playing field. The virtues of strenuous athletic competition were extolled as a means to prepare the male animal for the breadwinner's struggle, but the female of the species was destined to comfort and to nurture.[64]

The appearance of women in the modern sporting landscape also corresponds to the many changes taking shape due in part to many of the countercultural debates inherent to the Cold War era. With the reinvigoration of feminist thought, spearheaded in part by the 1963 publication of Betty Friedan's *The Feminist Mystique*[65] and the subsequent birth of feminism's second wave, women, who had generally been excluded from the more traditional competitive environs, found themselves in the same situation as minorities in the previous decade, looking to establish themselves within the confines of previously inaccessible areas of American life including America's sporting culture. As sportswriters Mary Carillo and Frank Deford acknowledge in their introductory commentary to a 1999 documentary on women's athletics:

> Sport is a right of passage that has always been a privilege of gender, and although girls and women have been playing sports for over a century, it's only recently that they've been accepted as true athletes—competitive, aggressive, and bold.[66]

Though odd by today's scientific standards, the case against women participating in competitive sport dates back to nineteenth century Victorianism at a time when women were afforded only minor outlets for developing their physical abilities. By the 1830s, for example, women were encouraged to take up calisthenics, or *athletics* as they were then called, in order to keep up their strength for reproduction and to reduce bouts of nervousness thought to be common among women of all classes. But as far as anything of a competitive nature, it would remain strictly taboo for women to participate in anything so decidedly masculine.[67]

As competitive sport continued to grab hold of the nation's collective imagination, and especially in the immediate aftermath of the Civil War, more outlets for participation allowed women, and especially women of means, to explore other avenues of physical congress such as croquet, tennis, golf, all highly competitive in their own way, and even bicycling, which though controversial became something of a craze in the 1890s.[68] Brief forays into the more masculine sporting terrain, such as baseball and basketball, which for a time were being played by women in the more exclusive private colleges such as Vassar and Smith, were quickly quashed due in part to some untimely injuries and the persistent fear that women who competed too strenuously were in danger of damaging, if not outright losing, their reproductive organs.[69] As British sport researcher Jennifer Hargreaves reveals in the influential *Sporting Females*:

> Nineteenth-century attitudes to women's participation in sports were consolidated by attitudes to women that were pervasive throughout society. By the second half of the nineteenth century science was characteristically applied to social situations and, when women were characterized as a "problem" in response to changes in their lives with the growth of industrial capitalism, they became the subject matter of investigation.[70]

On the other hand, noted American sport historian Allen Guttman explains:

> While some feminist historians have suggested that men encouraged female frailty in order to consolidate the power of patriarchal society, it seems improbable that many nineteenth-century husbands were so insecure in their patriarchal roles that they needed the additional reassurance of physically debilitated wives and daughters.[71]

In practice, however, women's competitive sports were generally perceived to be unbecoming and inherently unladylike, and the ways in which some women operated within their competitive sphere often gave rise to assumptions that it was both unnatural and unhealthy for a women to even want to compete, let alone to do so successfully. As sport historians Elliott Gorn and Warren Goldstein report in their *A Brief History of American Sports*, "if [women] had begun showing up en masse, their presence would probably have puzzled — even enraged — male and female spectators."[72] Still, the common misconception that until the modern era women rarely if at all participated in competitive and even strenuous sport is just as fallacious. In fact, what most women faced in those early participatory days in addition to outright discrimination was an appearance standard that often left them competing not only against each other but with standards of femininity that often clashed with athletic performance, including the restrictive and inelegant attire in which they were expected to compete.[73]

From the onset, the twentieth century bore witness to a number of noteworthy and talented female athletes who either resisted established feminine competitive doctrines or transcended them. Tennis stars such as France's glamorous Suzanne Lenglen and her American counterpart, the more reticent and certainly less outwardly sexual Helen Wills, seemed to pave the way for a bevy of female athletic champions, including swimmers Gertrude Ederle and Sybil Bauer (who once held both the men's and women's record in the backstroke) and the multi-talented and electrifying multi-sport celebrity Mildred "Babe" Didrikson, arguably the most highly regarded female athlete of the first half of the century. While it was apparent that some women did and could compete successfully in the athletic sphere, the ways in which their participation would be interpreted by the general populace showed that their performances and skills often cut across the boundaries of acceptable female propriety and were often met with a frontal assault on the individual's lifestyle and propriety. Lenglen, for example, often skirted the sexual mores of her day by choosing to compete in flamboyant and short silk dresses while preening off-court adorned in colorful make-up, expensive clothes, and glittering jewelry with her hair bobbed into the more fashionable and certainly less pristine fashions of the day. A rebel by every account, though hardly naturally attractive in the conventional sense, Lenglen's appearance was inherently and uniquely sexual. It was also well-established that she would drink brandy from a flask between sets, which in Prohibition-era America was positively scandalous. These matters caused quite a stir among the more staid and conservative tennis audiences and period critics who genuinely demanded a more stately and refined elegance in their feminine athletes. Consequently, many of these same moral guardians were notably relieved when her reign on the courts gave way to the more conventional and understated Wills, who was, nonetheless, forced by the conventions of the day to enhance her modestly feminine image both on and off the court.[74]

Didrikson's illustrious and even legendary career was generally dogged by a host of allegations, many of which were as creative as they were inaccurate. Accusations ranging from her suffering from an abnormally significant hormonal imbalance to outright innuendo that she was really a man cleverly concealed, Didrikson was never really accepted among America's more cherished athletes until well after her death.

As researchers have found, her departures from accepted femininity, though certainly in a direction different than Lenglen's *Jazz Age*-inspired experimentation, placed Didrikson in such a position that she was often seen, as noted sport historian Benjamin Rader explains, as a sort of "bogeywoman by mothers who wished to prevent their budding tomboy daughters from pursuing sports."[75] She was also largely considered to be a lesbian, which was the general depiction assigned to many other similarly and notably talented female athletes and a genuine concern among both the general public aghast with such notions and the athletes themselves who recognized correctly that such an accusation could be career threatening. Subsequently, Didrikson's handlers managed to convince her to soften her rough-edged disposition in favor of a more traditionally feminine pretense. This softening included a total overhaul of her outward appearance and a marriage to the once-popular wrestler "Gorgeous" George Zaharias, though this did little to alter public perception until she was near death. Once outside of the more critical spotlight, however, Didrikson made few attempts to temper her competitive edges. Stories of a boastful and brash personality rising far above decidedly less talented opposition suggested that once on the field, she could be as aggressive and as unrelenting as any male athlete and perhaps even more so. As many of her contemporaries have reminded various researchers and biographers alike, whenever Didrikson entered a locker room, she was likely to announce to all other competitors, without typically feminine decorum or even the hint of modesty, that now that she had arrived, everyone else in attendance would be playing for the second place trophy![76]

While women would continue to compete in a variety of sports throughout the twentieth century, the real advances in women's participation in the American sporting milieu would ultimately be driven by the renewed awareness in women's rights in the 1960s. Amid the turmoil of anti-war and civil rights activities, women's liberation movements also sought to disrupt mainstream society's general disregard for equality between the sexes by flaunting sexual convention while assigning culpability to a patriarchal order that was thought to preside over the far reaches of American cultural spaces. In some circles, advocates for across-the-board equality sought to demonstrate in the face of centuries old posturing that women could compete in the mainstream world. By infiltrating competitive sport, considered to be among the most hegemonic dimension of the patriarchy, some women were convinced that the empirical capital that might result from athletic competition would prove invaluable. As author and former athlete Mariah Burton Nelson poses it in a more modern context:

> The female challenge to men's sports is not just, "We want to play, too," We want to play in a neither ladylike nor manlike fashion. We want men to relinquish their

treehouse mentality — No Girls Allowed — but we also want them to stop using sports to justify brutish behavior. To stop using sports to define maleness and thus femaleness.[77]

The most typically cited turning point in the recent history of contemporary American women's sport was the passage of the 1972 Education Amendments Act with its section 106.41 that went largely unnoticed by the athletic establishment. This provision, known more popularly as Title IX, stipulates:

No person in the United States shall, on the basis of sex, be excluded from participation in, be denied the benefits of, or be subjected to discrimination under any educational program or activity receiving federal financial assistance.[78]

Figure 3.3. Participation in High School
Athletic Programs by Sex (since Title IX)

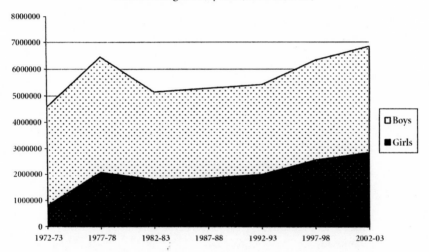

While the sheer numbers lag in comparison to their male counterparts, there has been a steady rise in the number of females participating in sport since the passage of Title IX.[79]

The passage of Title IX would indeed pave the way for unprecedented opportunities for women to participate more freely in sport underwritten by federal considerations, such as is the case with colleges, universities, and various public schools. Women raised in the aftermath of the legislation, often called Title IX Babies (see figure 3.3), have seen enormous increases in scholarship money and in participation in the international theater, where once communist bloc nations, unrestricted by the traditional language of the male-female divide in competition, dominated women's athletics in the post–World War II era. Free to explore the competitive arena more legitimately, female athletes prospered, though the old taboos regarding femininity, lesbianism, and masculine hegemony have continued to hover about the athletic sphere. But as scholar, critic, and publisher Rainer Martens has argued on behalf of further developments within American women's competitive attitudes:

> It is quite clear that in the past girls were more frequently placed into environments that directed their undifferentiated motive to be competent into channels other than sport. But as we have seen more recently, if society wants to direct girls into sport, evidence suggests that for competitiveness to develop, girls need experiences similar to boys. Young girls need opportunity, encouragement, challenge, praise, and a reasonable degree of success for competitiveness to develop.[80]

Katherine Switzer, the female distance runner whose controversial entry into the traditionally all-male Boston Marathon in 1967 made her both a hero to women and an outlaw in the mainstream of American sport, came of age just as the modern perspectives on women's sport were beginning to take shape. As she explained in an interview for a televised documentary on the evolution of women's sport:

> My generation grew up on the myths that if a woman ran, she'd get big legs, she'd grow a mustache, she'd never have babies, her uterus would fall out, she'd never attract men, she'd probably have something dangerous happen to her in terms of her attractiveness.[81]

The basic premise that women had become unwelcome intruders in the masculine sphere of athletic competition paralleled the changes brought about by Title IX, leaving many to either defend the language of equality cited in the law or to maintain that its underlying effect has been to subvert both men's and women's opportunities, leading some to depict Title IX as an abject failure. For example, Guttmann notes that while Title IX has paved the way for some remarkable gains in terms of women's participation, the human cost of bringing about social equity between the sexes has been muted. This notion has in turn led some in the predominantly male-ordered world of athletic governance to close its ranks and, in the words of former National Collegiate Athletic Association (NCAA) President Walter Byers, himself ardently opposed to the statute, "resist full implementation of the law."[82] Indeed, it would seem that by the turn of the twenty-first century, neither side of the debate seems overly satisfied with Title IX's place in sport. While advocates have been forced to assume a defensive posture by asserting that the statutes are intended to advance the cause of women's participation, opponents cite the demise of what are known as minor men's sports, that is, wrestling, swimming, lacrosse, soccer, as the real casualties of Title IX-induced equity (see figure 3.4).[83] For instance, a report circulated by the Feminist Majority Foundation's Task Force on Women and Girls in Sports in 1995 seems to refute what some have deemed the spurious notion that gender equity eliminates opportunities for male participation while citing practical obstacles to genuine enforcement of the statutes. They affirm:

> Despite persistent inequities between men and women in sports, the federal government has been very reluctant to enforce the law. The Department of Education's office of Civil Rights, charged with enforcing Title IX, is underfunded and, despite

Figure 3.4. Male Participation in NCAA Sport —
Major vs. Minor Sports (2004)

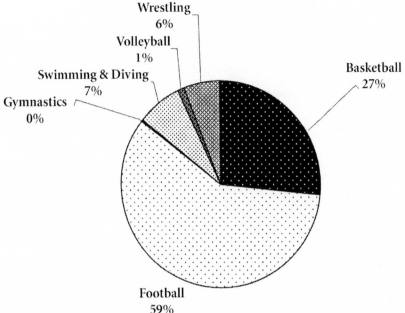

Wrestling
6%

Volleyball
1%

Swimming & Diving
7%

Gymnastics
0%

Basketball
27%

Football
59%

The thought that NCAA men's so-called "minor sports," such as gymnastics and wrestling, are finding their numbers altered in the wake of Title IX gender equity initiatives has merit when juxtaposed to football's continually high participation figures as shown in this figure. Still, critics disagree as to whether or not football or gender equity itself is to blame for the dramatic drop in numbers, which by 2004 shows football still exceedingly well out in front of the others.[84]

> the reluctance of schools to comply with gender equity, has never pulled federal funding from schools or colleges that discriminate against women and girls.[85]

The persistent posturing of both sides notwithstanding, the ascension of women into the competitive milieu suggests that further encroachment into what had long been determined was both a masculine and exclusive domain would hamper the objectivity necessary to the ongoing debate. As women's sport continued to grow outward from underneath the umbrella of Title IX and into the more mainstream and consumer-based spaces of contemporary sport, the consequences may result in a more vigorous and hotly contested discussion of supremacy within the competitive discourse, with the bulk of the discussion aimed not at whether or not women belong in the athletic sphere but how traditional gender roles and the contemporary engagement with gender within the overall debate are to be played out on the increasingly public stages of the athletic establishment.

Subtle Changes in the
Popular Depiction of Sport

It has been a custom for sports columnists and editors to be to the right of Genghis Khan, and to be behind Spiro Agnew in insight ... [but] in the past few years, things have begun to change in the sports section.[86]

The only people who had trouble with [a loosening of traditional behaviors among modern athletes] were newspapermen — old newspapermen![87]

While much of the debate regarding brutality, discrimination, and other aspects of 1960s era sport criticism had been taking place largely in academic circles driven by countercultural critiques, popular treatments of matters such as the controversy over the 1968 Summer Olympics and the debates surrounding free agency and other notable yet modern trends in sport had become regular features in the mainstream press. The popular press, having long proven to be a valuable ally of the sporting establishment, provided a voice for popular criticism but also found itself caught somewhere between Middle American values and mounting countercultural antipathy. This development of the countercultural wedge in America's sport-consciousness often forced period commentators to either adapt to the changing environs or face the risk of a more hostile response from an increasingly more socially aware public whose drift to the left is most often associated with the radical elements. As veteran sport columnist Sidney Zion reflects:

> The old sportswriters were hardly investigative reporters. They didn't go after owners ... and they were far more protective of the ballplayers. But they had style and *joie* and didn't pretend to be moral magistrates.[88]

Nevertheless, while mainstream journalism was changing with the times, albeit in measured steps, period sportswriters often seemed to be caught unaware by what was taking shape in sport and the emergent trends in analysis, but a handful of sport reporters, palpably influenced by countercultural critiques, would break with tradition and take up the challenges of the day by refusing to present sport with impunity while often recognizing their complicity with the past.[89] As noted sport journalist Red Smith would acknowledge late in his life:

> Unlike the normal pattern, I know I have grown more liberal as I've grown older. I have become more convinced that there is room for improvement in the world. I seem to be finding this a much less pretty world than it seemed when I was younger, and I feel things should be done about it and that sports are part of this world.[90]

Though mainstream sport reports were often tempered by what appeared to be a marked degree of balance that seemed to render them complicit in the eyes of more modern movements,[91] some writers broke with accepted practice and demonstrated the sort of sensitivity to the modern zeitgeist that the more militant critics had expressed both inside and outside the sports world. Most remained tied to some extent to the earlier trends in sport journalism, which included heavy doses of partisanship and uncritical commercial appeals to fan support, but some of the work of the more spirited commentators managed to steer clear of typical analyses. These mavericks of sorts often offered up more objective assessments and critical interpretations of industry phenomena that seemed to inspire a focus on developing a better understanding of the role that sport plays in modern society, a condition that Robert McChesney, then associate professor of journalism and mass communications at the University of Wisconsin-Madison, claims amounts to an adoption of newsroom-like adversarial tactics complete with real world analyses, something that few had much experience with.[92] Thus, while a young Brent Musburger at the *Chicago American* could make an overtly racial reference to the banished American sprinters from the 1968 Olympic site in Mexico City as "black-skinned stormtroopers"[93] with relative impunity, others, such as famed *New York Times* sport columnist Robert Lipsyte, could take a less traditional stand on issues of the day. As he notes in his critically acclaimed opus *SportsWorld: An American Dreamland*:

> My age-group counterparts on other papers seemed pleased when I started covering [older writers'] sins of omission — the growing discontent of athletes, racism, sexism, distorted nationalism, the sports-politics interface. By appearing in *The Times*, these stories got instant credibility. It became easier for other writers to get such stories past their own editors.[94]

One of the more noteworthy shifts in the popular analysis came at the level of the traditional image of the athlete as a cultural hero, which by the late 1960s and on into the coming decades could no longer be held up uncritically as the clean-cut American ideal. The composite image of the hero-athlete existing above the fray and subject to across-the-board reverence was being redrawn in part as a result of the ongoing debates to represent the face of the decidedly controversial and certainly more prurient image of the anti-hero, as ubiquitous an image as would exist since the Cold War years. Seemingly infallible sporting figures included baseball's erstwhile outfield trilogy of Babe Ruth, Joe DiMaggio, and Mickey Mantle, flawed though they might prove to be in later evaluations, evaluations which in and of themselves reflect countercultural-aided shifts, and revered black athletes who displayed forced obsequiousness, such as former heavyweight champion Joe Louis, the first black athlete to be wholly embraced by the American mainstream,[95] and baseball's Willie Mays, all figures of immense importance to the general public. However, the public rise of such contentious figures as the outspoken Ali, the candid feminist and openly gay star of women's tennis, Billie Jean King, and football's "Broadway Joe" Namath, the embodiment of the more modern image of the playboy hustler in professional sport, would move some to wonder aloud about the nature of heroism and propriety and their continued relevance in a rapidly evolving sporting milieu.[96] As the notably liberal and controversial sport journalist and broadcaster Howard Cosell would observe, the reaction of the sporting establishment was quite candidly stupefying:

> The shock of the establishment at such people stems, of course, from its careful adherence to the grade-school notion that no matter what happens in the society around them, no matter how habits change, no matter how much more sophisticatedly young people grow up, no matter how the social patterns of life advance, nothing that happens in real life can ever happen with athletes. Naïve, isn't it? But true.[97]

By the end of the 1960s, the once gray and predictable sporting world, often referred to in industry terms as the "toy department,"[98] with its altar boy façade, was hastily being transformed into a colorful panorama of modern life and times that included contemporary hairstyles, mustaches and beards, Nehru jackets, Pan-African styles, and heavy doses of sexuality, threatening both the traditional image of the athlete as the epitome of decorum and the aforementioned "Sunday School"[99] atmosphere that sport had long promoted as its most essential contribution. As Namath would respond amid the criticism over his frequently reported late night carousing, "It seems almost un-American to me for a bachelor not to go around for a drink with a lady now and then."[100]

By the 1970s, the age of the sport hero seemed antiquated, even quaint by modern standards. The sort of time-honored imagery found in pre-war popular songs such as Les Brown's 1941 hit "Joltin' Joe DiMaggio"[101] may have once depicted great stars who had embodied the spirit of staid yet solid masculinity amid throngs of enthusiastic fans, but these embraceable bonds were being summarily replaced by such ominous sounding laments as heard in Paul Simon's "Mrs. Robinson" with its celebrated search for a DiMaggio-like figure to actually celebrate.[102] This noted rise in public skepticism, promoted in part by evolving trends in journalistic standards by typically banal and decidedly uncritical sports writers, leads directly down a path toward a much more introspective approach to interpreting sport-related phenomena with the advent of an increasingly more applicable oppositional culture and its embrace of popular antiheroes. As Rader suggests, the clean-cut jock image fueled by traditional images of masculine and dutiful young athletes was being rendered moot by what had appeared to be an age of disobedient rowdies with flamboyant lifestyles motivated by increasingly high salaries at a time when social upheaval and a distrust of traditional social markers had reached a zenith:

> In the 1970s, the continuing war in Vietnam, the Watergate scandal, the inability of the federal government to solve such problems as inflation, unemployment, energy shortages, and pollution, the propensity of post-Watergate journalism to revel in the sordid lives of would-be heroes all contributed to a decline in public

confidence. Decisions by committees of experts, bureaucracies, and computers, some suggested, made the individual hero obsolete.[103]

Alongside this harder journalistic edge, the critical success garnered by celebrated countercultural commentators such as Edwards, Gent, Shaw, Meggyesy, and others would persist throughout the remaining decades of the Cold War period, as disenchantment continued its slow ascent from the periphery of modern thought and entered into more mainstream environments. Thus, in spite of the initial reluctance on the part of those traditionally caught in the grip of era conformity and the powerful forces that would continue to hold sway over them, the countercultural movements of the day had indeed begun to both affect their own times and lay a foundation that would shape future commentary toward the promotion of a increasingly modern outlook with a decidedly more acclaimed egalitarian pose.

4

Moral Tensions within Contemporary American Sport

Several years ago, while our then eleven-year-old son and I rode our bicycles around our neighborhood, we began informally discussing his involvement with local recreational baseball and soccer. I wanted to know what he thought of his experiences in youth league sport, and since we had just recently watched together a couple of the aforementioned video exposés concerning the current state of youth sport, this would give me the opportunity to see things from the point of view of a presumed subject of these examinations.

Initially, he offered that his biggest disappointment thus far had been what he deemed "mean coaches," though he was hard pressed to actually give me a name or an incident that conjured up a real life event. I suspected then that he was responding to the images and commentary he had seen in the televised reports, which as it turned out was a fairly accurate assessment. After he thought about it for a while longer, however, he seemed to come back with a much broader view of his own brief experiences and began to ask questions concerning the televised critiques. His more critical view of his own involvement in sport was that he was disappointed that too few of his teammates took a genuine enough interest in the sports they played. He lamented what he believed to be a sweeping apathy among his peers and wondered what it would take to motivate more of them to play harder and try to learn more of the skills and strategies it would take to play better. He also added that he could not imagine that anyone who consistently played badly would be having that much fun knowing that his or her teammates were probably annoyed by such consistently shoddy performances. And when I asked why he thought so many of his peers were dropping out of sport by the time they reached the twelve- and thirteen-year-old range, he felt it was a combination of factors that steered them away, including desire, fear, and probably a simple matter of a lack of interest. Indeed, he saw little alarm in these numbers, though many critics point to these results as evidence of the overwhelming failure of sport to nurture future generations accordingly.[1]

Something else he asked me regarding those videos struck me as interesting. He wanted to know why one of the discussants prefaced his remarks by claiming that the overwhelming majority of adults who participate directly or indirectly with youth sport behave appropriately at such functions but then go on to claim that something has to be done to reclaim youth sport for children's sake, hinting that in this arrangement children were the only ones to act in an adult-like fashion.[2] To be frank, I was hard-pressed to find an answer to that particular query.

I preface the above here in order to segue into our next point of analysis—the more recent and impacting attacks on sport at the level of their presumed moral failings. The overriding concern that sport has gotten out of hand to the point of becoming a menace of some sort or another has become a major element of concern in these earliest days of the twenty-first century. Critics cite dozens of examples of incidents involving high-profile athletes as well as others connected to sport as evidence that the perceived overall decline of values in America has struck sport with a vengeance. As one respondent noted with some alarm during a Fox Sports exposé on sport and civility, "It's going to get worse before it gets better."[3] Indeed, that HBO saw fit to title its contribution to the national chorus "Parental Rage" further indicates that the show's producers were of the opinion that incidents in which adults have crossed the line while attending youth sport events suggested an epidemic of such behaviors, rendering them commonplace and even expected in a way much more reminiscent of what sociologist Stanley Cohen has deemed a "moral panic."[4]

While it may be true that episodes of disquieting behaviors have occurred at sporting events around the country, they remain just that—episodes with very little evidence to support a growing trend irrespective of the mass of commentary to the contrary. Still, there is a much more generalized sense that the combination of financial high stakes and the promotion of aggression in the more high-profile athletic endeavors have led to a trickling down effect that is altering the nature of competitive sport in the most typically innocent of environments. The perception is that what takes place among professionals and big time college sport is dramatically changing the face of local recreational leagues to the point that everyone involved is bent on acting more like the fallen idols than as responsible, reasonable people. And as Fred Engh, the founder of the National Alliance of Youth Sport, contends, "the ugly people are growing and growing."[5]

This chapter will explore some of the more predominate themes in contemporary American sport criticism relative to the growing inclination toward treating competitiveness as either an ill-conceived plan for cultural diffusion or as part of a much larger discussion of social pathology. Among those matters to be discussed will be the more modern developmental constructs pertaining to issues such as sportsmanship, hypercompetitiveness, the role of violence in the discussion of sport, the contemporary absorption with the role model question, and the more recent fall-out over allegations of doping among some of sport's most revered celebrities.

Sportsmanship

Sports are over because they no longer have any moral resonance. They are merely entertainment, the bread and circuses of a New Rome.[6]

Let me win. But if I cannot win, let me be brave in the attempt.[7]

Anthropologist Clifford Geertz's oft-cited assessment of American sport, that it is part of a story Americans tell about themselves,[8] gives salience to the notion that competition's cultural significance can be viewed through a prism of both decorum and expectation as expressed in the modern world through a contemporary reading of Cold War era countercultural values. In that spirit, the hint that something as omnipresent as competitive sport could be subject to a loosening of standards is sure to elicit an assortment of responses relative to its ability to affect American society in any sort of notable and certainly progressive fashion. As the aforementioned Shields and Bredemeier remind, "contemporary sport is rarely just sport,"[9] a point to which others are quick to seize upon and has become even more of a mantra spoken within both philosophical as well as public spaces.

One key toward understanding the breadth of the contemporary misgivings linked to competitive sport can be found within the boundaries of the more modern discussion of sportsmanship. Within the modern theoretical interpretations of the once inviolate sportsmanship paradigm, the notions of overly competitive conduct, increasingly referred to as hypercompetitiveness (see below), the lack of proper guidance on the part of sport's overseers, and many other elements of behavior associated with competitive sport find resonance in today's interpretation of matters relating to on-field restraint and its effect both within the sporting environment and within the larger social environment.[10] As Engh declares in his general assessment of sportsmanship within youth sport today, "The lack of appropriate philosophy on our playing fields, as well as the other negative factors ... make it clear that we need to change the system."[11]

That sportsmanship has become one of the more fundamental themes of the contemporary discussion of sport can be attributed in some fashion to the notion that the whole of competitive sport's supposed degradation can be found within its consequence. In the traditional logic, sportsmanship marked both a desire to excel and a rationale for cooperation within the confines of a given set of rules and principles. On this point, nineteenth century British sportsmen were quite explicit, demanding that to be anything less than cooperative in the sporting arena demonstrated a lack of moral substance that often translated into a lack of masculine virtue as it was then conceived. For example, in his well-respected analysis of British sport, James A. Mangan would note that the paradox between Christian gentility and Social Darwinism found within nineteenth century British Muscular Christianity was indeed distinctive, but at the end of that line of consideration was the ideal of the sportsman who would ultimately "play up and play the game,"[12] in the parlance of the day.

That sportsmanship was, conceptually speaking, a major topic of discussion during America's so-called Muscular Christian period is certainly worth restating here, but in terms of the modern construct, it has taken on an added significance away from the nation building ideology so prominent during that critical period in the development of early American sport. In the contemporary discussion, what seems to predominate shows little in common with a sense of a shared collective character, with the exception being the quest to allow competitive sport to in one way or another return to its perceived golden age, a time in which competition could be looked upon as a instrument for teaching, substantiating, and reproducing social authority. In other words, what seems so striking about today's debate is not so much the search for a definition of what sportsmanship is but rather the blanket assertion that sportsmanship in its traditional sense no longer exists with any constancy for what are conceived to be a host of causes, most of which are often streamlined into a discussion of the ramifications of unsportsmanlike behavior on children. As sport psychologist Daniel Gould has observed:

> Sportsmanship is a term about which everyone seems to have an opinion but many have difficulty defining precisely. Phrases such as having a good attitude, being a good winner and loser, respecting the official's decisions, playing by the rules and giving maximum effort are common definitions. Because sportsmanship is so generally defined, however, children often have difficulty in determining the exact qualities of good and poor sportsmanship.[13]

In terms of a more modern paradigm, sportsmanship retains elements of its Victorian definition and is still considered a force for the synthesis of character and civility as described in chapter two of this work. Its primary function then, of course, involved bringing the children of various immigrant groups and subordinate classes into line with modern virtues and, hence, hastening the assimilation process. A more modern interpretation, far removed from its nineteenth century moorings, is, nonetheless, remarkably similar in that it is understood that the types of behaviors normally associated with sportsmanship are a necessary and valued feature of the competitive landscape. Where things differ, however, is the assumption that sportsmanship in the traditional sense has become a product of a bygone era and that its notable absence from the contemporary terrain is both problematic and emblematic of a culture in flux, and detrimentally so. As Clifford and Feezell contend in their treatise on contemporary trends in sportsmanship entitled *Coaching for Character*:

> ... it is important to understand that sportsmanship is not just a matter of acceptable behavior but of *excellence of character*— or, in the language of the classical tra-

dition —*sportsmanship is a virtue.* It is not altogether coincidental that there has been a return to the classical understanding of virtue right at a time when so many of our athletic superstars in professional and big-time college sports have become models of anything and everything but good character. It is particularly sad, because sport has long provided an arena in which the central ethical concept has been excellence of character.[14]

The notion that a resumption of inquiry into the modern understanding of sportsmanship has been resurrected due to its supposed absence from the sporting terrain in part informs the discussion of contemporary sport and has cast further suspicion regarding competitive sport's continued place in contemporary society, primarily at the level of teaching virtues. In many assessments, both modern and traditional, competitive sport is assumed to be a particularly useful and ostensibly palpable place for the diffusion of cultural ideals, though imbedded within those same discussions is the caveat that within the competitive framework of contemporary sport, lessons are either buried beneath the gathering notoriety surrounding spectacle or by the changing parameters of what constitutes ethical behavior. As popular child psychologist and frequent youth sport commentator Dr. Darrell J. Burnett observes:

> We're living in a age where the preservation of traditional values can no longer be taken for granted. It seems we need to have reminders to maintain our awareness of the importance of preserving the basic human values which are essential to the survival of a community.[15]

Still, the baseline for this discussion can best be marked through a more narrow interpretation as expressed in the work of sport researcher Marty Ewing of Michigan State University's Youth Sport Institute, who asserts that physical interaction "serves as a strong regulator in the developmental process,"[16] which thereby assigns to the competitive model an added incentive to recreate a desired social effect, which recalls Mangan's "play up and play the game"[17] motif as noted above.

With enormous public and critical acclaim, this notion of competitive sport as an extension of an increasingly failing moral authority, as well as a markedly more impractical tool for character building within the traditional boundaries of the accepted sporting culture, hovers candidly about this aspect of the contemporary sportsmanship debate. For example, a University of Rhode Island survey of 500 respondents led both the researchers and the National Collegiate Athletic Association (NCAA) itself, collegiate sport's governing body and in whose newsletter the results were published, to conclude that sportsmanship in America was on a sobering and perhaps irreparable decline. The results, that 79% of those queried responded affirmatively when asked if sportsmanship in the professional ranks was at an all-time low and that 73% felt similarly about collegiate sport, were widely publicized and seen as indicative of a general weakening of traditional moral and cultural values across the board as expressed in an extremely popular and important cultural institution.[18] As one anxious league commissioner posed it in relation to similar such NCAA investigations, "We are aware and concerned over the negative trends in sportsmanship and how they are becoming more visible in collegiate athletics."[19]

In a more popular forum, Brian Anderson and Peter Reinharz, writing in the self-consciously conservative monthly *City Journal*, cover similar ground in their assertion that the sportsman, as they deemed him (or her), once presented the standard from which the cultural ideal could be expressed. But in so doing, they are also wont to point out that in the contemporary construct, while he has not disappeared from view, he may be "an endangered species."[20] Standing on more solid academic footing, however, Glyn Roberts, a professor of sport psychology at the University of Illinois and who in this case is being quoted in the popular and notably apologetic monthly *Sports Illustrated*, is just as equally apt to point toward a similar and clearly as fashionable appraisal:

> Increasingly the prevailing morality on display in sports is that anything is O.K. if it works and you don't get caught. There are other things in modern society that teach this, but for kids, sports is now the major activity that drives home the point that being successful, not being good in the conventional moral sense, is what counts.[21]

Indeed, examples of this sort of rejoinder have become much more common in regards to this debate, though most tend to conclude in a similar fashion that competitive sport's governors and participants both in general ought to be more conscious of sport's place in diffusing cultural ideals. For instance, in their executive summary for 1999, the particularly omnipresent civic organization known as the Citizenship through Sports Alliance took note of the importance of implementing instructive designs in today's sportive milieu by asserting that youth participation in competitive sport is an essential feature of a wholesome and rewarding childhood experience.[22] Additionally, they declare:

> The power of sport can be harnessed as a vehicle for teaching lessons of citizenship by focusing on the importance of teamwork, integrity, fair play, personal responsibility, and media emphasis on the positive aspects of sport and individual athletes. There should be less coverage on acts of glory and more coverage on acts of sportsmanship and community service. The media needs to recognize its role in promoting citizenship, its influence over it, and that it can become a partner in the effort of envisioning entertainment and sport as almost separate entities.[23]

Similarly, Gould adds that while the debate endures as to whether or not competitive sport really is beneficial for character building in children, he cites what he contends to be a "number of personal accounts, media stories and popular books [suggesting] that participation in competitive athletics does little to develop sportsmanship in young athletes and may actually lead to unsportsmanlike attitudes and values."[24]

Indeed, the diffusive nature of the approach that competitive sport could and should serve as an incubation center for virtue is often couched under a variety of corollaries. According to kinesiologist Lori Gano-Overway, athletes are asked to make choices regarding their behaviors, but she maintains that their options are often clouded by a broadening range of mismanagement and the demands inherent to crafting competitive athletes and the pressures therein.[25] She reasons that attempts to foster more virtuous behaviors in athletes, behaviors that Engh maintains have the capacity to trickle down into youth settings,[26] is unlikely as long as the emphasis remains on product rather than process.[27] Or as physical education professor Karin Volkwein simply puts it, the sports world is "in need of a new ethics."[28]

Working from the more traditional pose that "[s]portsmanship and ethics turn out to be two sides of the same coin,"[29] Pepperdine University philosophy professor Russell W. Gough, whose interest in sportsmanship subsists along the discussion of ethics relative to sport behavior, builds on this notion of the decline (or absence) of conventional sportsmanship in his work but in a much less harried fashion than in more typical academic circles. In a chapter entitled "Avoiding Extremes,"[30] Gough purposefully cites fashionable modern appraisals of unsportsmanlike conduct but refuses to simply acknowledge their efficacy uncritically. He reports the following conditions often cited by others:

- Sportsmanship is dead.
- Sport no longer builds character.
- Athletes are not good role models.
- "Sport ethics" is a contradiction in terms.
- These days sports and sportsmanship are nothing but oil and water.[31]

Contending that such modern assessments are both cynical and extreme, he nevertheless notes:

> The big problem is that we can fall into a trap of focusing so much on our disagreements that we lose sight of just how much we actually agree on when it comes to ethics and sportsmanship. Maybe it's cynicism and negativity at work again. Maybe it's something else. But the fact is, most of the time we're in the same ballpark when it comes to basic issues of character and action.[32]

In this regard, Gough chides his contemporaries for jumping toward more extreme views regarding the basic weakening of sport-related morality when viewed anachronistically through more traditional notion of sportsmanship. Nevertheless, Gough, though certainly more moderate than others on this point, still manages to take exception to the external dynamic of contemporary competitive sport, citing, among other matters, the loss of consistency in terms of character building and a decisively resolute sense of extending what he counters should be a strong moral foundation within the dynamic itself. In his view, the sportsmanship debate revolves not so much around matters outside competition but rather those factors that inform competitive behaviors, most of which are expressed in the contemporary perception that the modern spirit of competition may be spinning out of control as typified by such time-honored indicators as the resurgence of the Lombardi dictum and the rising stakes surrounding high-profile athletic affairs. As Gough asserts, the biggest obstacle facing a grounded and legitimate sport ethic in America today is a condition that he refers to simply as the "No Place for Second Place"[33] standard, the discussion of which is generally depicted in terms of a hypercompetitive goal-orientation.

Hypercompetitiveness

Competition within sport isn't unbounded. It functions within certain rules and conventions.[34]

It's about ferocity, carnage, balancing human intelligence with animal diligence. Knowing exactly what you want, and how far you're willing to go to get it.[35]

The often emotional debates surrounding sportsmanship are certainly afforded a great deal of focus in modern debate. Alongside these challenges, however, exists an equally informative and much more recent thread of inquiry that seeks to explore the nature of competition through a more modern appraisal of competitiveness considered to border on the pathological, a behavioral model often identified in terms of a marked degree of *hypercompetitiveness*. That an expression such as hypercompetitiveness even exists in this discussion owes as much to the increased confusion surrounding the range of interpretations of competitiveness in the modern age as to the more modern anxieties often associated with a climate that appears to be ill at ease with such enthusiastically demonstrative ideals. Indeed, in an age reminiscent of countercultural ideals that had at once challenged the very existence of universal standards and the rejection of traditional means of establishing and maintaining cohesive social relationships, the more modern-seeming bandying about of terms attached to such conspicuous- and portentous-seeming prefixes as *hyper-* or even *meta-*, *inter-*, and *post-* has become a much more common feature of contemporary criticism.[36] Consequently, this corner of the discussion often appears to give rise to a perceptibly self-conscious rejection of the more customary use of language to describe various socially constructed phenomena. For example, and simply as a matter of explanation, in a work entitled *An Introductory Guide to Post-Structuralism and Postmodernism*, Madan Sarup of the South Bank University in London contends that in the context of modern theoretical constructs, the use of the prefix hyper- in this case suggests something that is "in excess of itself."[37] Sarup notes that the prefix in its modern (or postmodern) context suggests a disbanding rather than a transcendence of theoretical antagonisms. In the case of a hypercompetitive condition, thus, the use of the term itself would seem to indicate a competitive frame of reference that extends beyond conventional markers while moving unfavorably away from an acceptable staging of competitive character.[38]

For some theorists, the development of a hypercompetitive pose is both problematic in its own right and emblematic of a competitive culture that has violated its own principles and has become, perhaps, invasive, exclusive, and certainly overly aggressive in the most disreputable sense.[39] As Pennsylvania State University psychologist Carolyn Sherif was to remark, albeit somewhat mockingly, on a perceptible rise in overly competitive conduct being addressed by some academics as far back as the late 1970s:

> I leave the creation of superordinate goal structures to those who know much more than I about sports and recreation. I am convinced, however, that their planning requires not sheer individual genius but cooperation and competition among those charged with such planning to produce the most effective and viable programs.[40]

On this point, it is important to note the relative ease with which the theorist can draw the line between competitiveness and the manifestation of an overtly hypercompetitive display, which is predictably tempered by the comparatively tranquil space he or she occupies. For the athlete involved in a competitive challenge or a series of competitive challenges, such as would mark an athletic season or career, this line is not so easily recognized. This is not to suggest that detached critical investigations of competitive environments are ill-conceived — quite the contrary. Still, there is a tendency on the part of contemporary sport commentators to overstate the degree of fervor often demonstrated on the field of play. As many highly skilled athletes have indicated, while athletes are intuitively aware of the expectations and even obligations regarded as essential to on-field decorum, a fine line exists between acceptable and unacceptable behavior, especially when dealing with the passion of the moment. As one professional American football player attempts to explain:

> ... when we are engaged in an endeavor that is hostile and aggressive ... to go from being gentlemanly and following the rules of society to people who play violently and aggressively for two or three hours on Sunday.... It's not easy to do, especially when people across the line of scrimmage are literally the enemy.[41]

Doubtless there are those for whom the expression of competitiveness is the driving force of their collective existences. The annals of sport are replete with tales of athletes (and some in management) recognized by various industry expressions such as *gamer* or *hard-nosed competitor* while many more are variously described as "playing with reckless abandon" or "willing to give 110%."[42] All of these rather hackneyed references, most of which draw compelling links to sport and are what Steven Overman explores in his work regarding American sport and the Weberian Protestant ethic,[43] are nonetheless used in the more traditional sense to support an admixture of the many ways to voice one's refusal to submit to defeat, a condition that was once routinely and actively supported within the culture. In one particularly moving and relevant tribute, a journalist speaking in a documentary film once referred to baseball's incomparable Pete Rose, who garnered the sobriquet "Charlie Hustle" early on in his career as a paean to his observably frenzied style of play, as a man so driven by success and love for the game that to participate he would "walk through Hell in a gasoline suit!"[44] Moreover, these were the sorts of individuals to whom all Americans were urged to take pride in and seek to emulate given that they were perceived to embody the very spirit of success while they also demonstrated a passionate embrace of excellence. And yet, where these descriptive and certainly hyperbolic sentiments veer from contemporary analyses seems to be at a level of psychological impairment that have in many cases eroded the line between so-deemed safe levels of competitiveness and those that are demonstrably pathological.

It has become more commonly acknowledged within the contemporary frame of reference that behaviors that exhibit an overemphasis on product or skirt what are deemed to be a modest degree of restraint, run the risk of being labeled obsessive, compulsive, or even both, though certainly at the least they could be deemed precarious. Furthermore, the tendency to perceive such behaviors as intrinsically harmful redresses these sorts of matters into medical terms, giving rise to sociologist James Nolan's thesis that modern life is increasingly being informed by a medicalized and therapeutic-driven impulse, which in this particular sphere is marked by the tendency to define human activity in relation to its potential to result in pathological outcomes, a condition that is also regularly depicted in popular idioms.[45] As editor Mick Hume of the notably contentious (and since defunct) British monthly *LM* once noted:

> Where once we could look up to top international sportsmen as towers of strength and achievement, now they spend much of their time lying down while we are asked to "relate" to them as victims of the same emotional weaknesses and vulnerability that the rest of us are meant to suffer.[46]

The well-chronicled case of baseball's aforementioned Pete Rose provides an excellent example of this sort of treatment and how events operating within the context of a hypercompetitive condition are often addressed. Rose, who holds baseball's all-time career mark for base hits, has been banned for life by baseball's governing body for purportedly betting on games, a ban that has ultimately cost him his place alongside other greats in the game's Hall of Fame. To clarify, Rose was not banned because he was a known gambler akin to those who profited from such widespread endeavors up to and including those who conspired to purposefully lose the 1919 World Series. Rather, it had been contended, and since verified by Rose himself, that after his playing career ended, Rose bet on games that he was managing, which based on well-publicized and controversial reactions to other betting scandals that have in the past endangered baseball's place within the culture, Rose's actions were clearly a violation of league policy and certainly worthy of the penalty as assessed.[47]

What is remarkable in the Rose case, however, is the language often employed by the varying sides who have debated the issue of whether or not Rose deserves to have his punishment and subsequent enshrinement in the Hall of Fame revisited. On the one hand there are those who express a tendency to view Rose as a victim of an addictive medical condition that suggests that he could benefit from some level of intervention, much in the manner of a program such as Alcoholics Anonymous. The other side, however, maintains that the same sort of behaviors that drove Rose on the playing field, namely his intense drive, became manifest in his post-playing days as a sort of fixation on gambling, which indicates a latent form of the hypercompetitive condition lurking deeply beneath his otherwise scarred psyche. In other words, Rose's circumstances stem from the same obsessions that drove him to greatness as a player, which seems to say more about the thinning of the line that separates achievement from pathology than it does about the Rose case as a matter of individual responsibility and the consequences of skirting established league policy. Moreover, that neither side seems convinced that Rose was ultimately responsible for his actions further gives rise to the notion that Rose is a victim of behaviors beyond his own control.[48]

To further underscore the relationship between contemporary sport criticism and the role that hypercompetitiveness is thought to play in this debate, it is interesting (and probably helpful) to note the range of definitions for competition that are in evidence today. Indeed, there has been a great deal of movement on this question since the middle 1970s when physical education researcher and publisher Rainer Martens[49] and psychologist Carolyn Sherif[50] first began to address the topic of athletic competition theoretically and in much greater detail, sparking a renewed interest in the nature of competition and the birth of concerned sport activism in both popular and academic circles alike.[51] As humanist sociologist Michael Schwalbe of North Carolina State University notes, competition, up to that stage, though not completely ignored in the social sciences, remained notably "undertheorized"[52] and often rendered vague and inconclusive by what he identifies as folk definitions and the nature of popular ritual. These opening doors, however, seem to have produced a fount of ideas and subsequent discussions leading toward an accumulation of philosophical constructs and a mass of speculation and conjecture from many different ideological corners.

In the traditional sense, and a point generally embraced by a right-leaning orientation, the notion of breeding character through a focused and goal-oriented structure such as competitive sport is conceived of as a logical, reasonable, and appreciatively creditable path in part because sport, whose own inner dynamic is certainly capable of capturing the public's collective imagination, can also be employed to correspond to such time-honored and respected behaviors as trust, loyalty, and an individual's acceptance of authority. This is not to suggest that competitive sport is only esteemed by the Right because it is professed to have the power to subordinate. Rather, this aspect of the competitive construct has allowed competition, in a variety of guises, to remain venerated in spite of perceived breakdowns and failures in both the traditional as well as the modern assessment.[53] Furthermore, it is a point taken up collectively and quite openly by American presidents, captains of industry, some more conservative-minded childrearing experts, and others as cited throughout this work and exemplified in the words of former President Gerald Ford, himself an avid sportsman, who once noted:

> Broadly speaking, outside of a national character and an educated society, there are few things more important to a country's growth and well-being than competitive athletics. If it is cliché to say athletics build character as well as muscle, then I subscribe to the cliché.[54]

Where this debate becomes less clear is on the Left, where clusters of paradigmatic interpretations and theoretical models have become embroiled in a struggle for the most applicable definition of both the traditional and contemporary rationalization behind the competitive ideal. Though discernibly offset by more customary readings, these clusters share in common carryovers from countercultural convictions, and if these convictions are left unchecked and ill-maintained, competition can be a decidedly destructive force in modern society.

On this point, self-proclaimed humanists, whose work often marks the cutting edge of left-leaning sport criticism, provide an excellent baseline for this discussion. Humanists view competition as a matter relative to human suffering and the extent to which a so-conceived elitist and adversarial process has the potential to subvert human dignity while providing a challenge to acceptable behavior. According to Schwalbe, for example, competition can be neither unilateral nor mutually exclusive. In this sense the only conclusion that can be plausibly rendered is that competition inherently promotes stratification irrespective of what Schwalbe contends marks liberal attempts to revise the impulse through calculated measures, some of which might include Gano-Overway's admonishment that coaches should turn moral dilemmas into teachable moments while they teach individual athletes to view opponents as vehicles to personal challenges rather than impediments to success.[55] Schwalbe asserts:

> Perhaps the foremost point of criticism is that [competition] encourages purely instrumental social relations rather than encouraging relationships in which people are valued as ends in themselves.[56]

Consequently:

> The humanist critique sees that in elitist competition people thus become objectified. Competitors come to see others not as people but as obstacles to winning. Purely self-gratifying impulses are amplified to the point of drowning out impulses to respond to the needs of others.[57]

Humanists in general have a great deal to say about competition and its consequences, establishing along the way a sort of baseline for corresponding commentary. Overall, their critique establishes the competitive mystique as debasing, groundless, and divisive, and many offer assessments of competitive sport that border on a studied cynicism. For instance, psychologist Vera Elleson maintains that competitive sport with its emphasis on winning at all costs, a construct considered by some to serve as a marker for hypercompetitive behavior, openly rejects sportsmanship and may be a contributing factor thought to exist at the root of poor socialization strategies in children. Citing evidence suggesting that competitive environments decrease a child's likelihood for altruistic, if not empathetic, behavior, Elleson concludes that although competition may be part of a normal cultural development, she also maintains that its "negative effects are widespread and damaging to the health of our society as well as to its individual citizens."[58]

Perhaps the most adamant of the humanist-oriented critics of competition is the extremely popular education lecturer Alfie Kohn. For Kohn, competition at any level and under any set of circumstances serves the opposite of its intended effect. Weighing heavily on self-reflective themes, Kohn has determined that the presence of competition negates the attempt to foster cooperation, and he withdraws from efforts to presuppose that the two can ever function in harmony.[59]

In his seminal work *No Contest*,[60] Kohn, who was educated at both Brown and the University of Chicago but claims no academic affiliation, guides his readers through a maze of complex issues resulting from what he deems the American preoccupation with competitiveness, contending that it is both "the common denominator of American life"[61] and America's "number one obsession."[62] His position is one in which he identifies the various elements under which a decidedly pro-competition lobby may operate while preparing to counter arguments to challenge unconditionally what he contends to be a widespread competitive agenda.

By Kohn's estimation, notions of human nature, productivity, and character building, bulwarks of the traditional discussion of competitiveness, are anything but. He lambastes what he identifies to be contemporary strains of Social Darwinism that he claims offer salience to the myth that competitiveness is merely a part of human nature, and then he sets out to expunge the impression that competition aids productivity by any modern measurement. Moreover, Kohn's stated goal is to implode the notion of a productivity feature of competition by emphasizing the extent to which manufacturers and competitors eschew more creative means to improve or invent newer means of production in favor of trusted techniques for fear of failure in a competitive marketplace, asserting that the "enormous potential in mutual benefit (cooperative) strategies will not be tapped — or even understood — until we broaden our perspective beyond the narrow prejudice that we always do our best by trying to beat others."[63]

Insisting, that competition is an impediment to success, Kohn reasons that contrary to popular mythology, there is nothing either progressive or productive about competitiveness or a competitive society.[64] He asserts:

To the proponent of competition who insists that differences in ability will always exist, then, we may reply that it is the significance invested in these differences and not the differences themselves that constitutes competition. The inability to observe discrepant abilities without turning the situation into a contest is a learned disposition. The degree of an individual's competitiveness can be expressed as a function of how *frequently* this happens and how *strongly* one feels the need to be better. But there is not a shred of evidence that this inclination is an unavoidable feature of human life [italics in original].[65]

In terms of competition's effect on individuals, Kohn is further convinced that human beings are inherently too fragile and poorly designed when it comes to withstanding the rigors of a competitive environment. For him, the act of measuring skills in a challenging environment in order to evaluate one's aptitude or performance objectives ultimately diminishes one's chances of success regardless of standards. In an earlier work published in *The Humanist*, Kohn claims:

The cost of any kind of competition in human terms is incalculable. When my success depends on other people's failure, the prospects for a real human community are considerably diminished. This consequence speaks to the profoundly anti-humanistic quality of competitive activity, and it is abundantly evident in American society.[66]

Kohn charges that American life is steeped in a endless cycle of defeat and anxiety and counters that since the number of losers far outweighs the number of winners, society has learned to accept and expect failure. Still, it would seem that for Kohn, failure in competition may be far less problematic than success within the competitive structure itself. Though he contends that enduring the effects of having unsuccessfully competed has the potential to be both personally and publicly devastating, Kohn further maintains that it is often the victors who are left with the insufferable burden of having to protect their newly gained successes in a condition akin to a pariah status. Therefore, in addition to a culture of losing, Kohn identifies winning as similarly part of a complex cultural arrangement that leads inescapably toward an aggressive and confrontational social order constructed in no small part by a fictitious and ill-conceived ethos.[67] He notes:

The proof for this argument lies in the ephemerality of victory's thrill. We may be giddy with delight for a time, but we soon come back to earth. In fact, those who compete on a regular basis report that both the intensity of the pleasure and its duration decline sharply over time — precisely as one develops a tolerance to a drug.[68]

Moreover:

Instead of contributing to our self-esteem, then, beating other people contributes only to the need to continue trying to beat other people. The consequence of com-

petition and the cause of competition are reciprocally related, just as the consequence and cause of drinking salt water. When we talk about competition, we are
talking a vicious circle....[69]

To be sure, there are other commentators who share many of Kohn's attitudes toward competition but extend his critique to include hypercompetitiveness as a logical manifestation of the competitive model established in American
life as well as an indication of societal wide moral decay exacerbated in part by
an overarching competitive frame. For example, Finnish Olympic researcher
Juhu Heikkala, writing in the academic journal *The International Review for the
Sociology of Sport*, asserts that contemporary issues in sport, such as the use of
performance enhancing drugs or doping (see below), reflect an ever-increas-
ing awareness (problematic though it may be) on the part of athletes that their
work is meaningful, fulfilling, and important, driving them toward performance enhancement based strictly on self-absorption. Citing the atomizing effect
of high-profile and highly competitive sport as the baseline for her study,
Heikkala says further that the issue of performance enhancement and other
means toward circumventing established rules and standards indicates that
athleticism has been stripped of its purity and usurped by self-interest. She
advances the notion that given the modern social and political climate, traditional regulatory means, such as appealing to one's conscience, are no longer
applicable, and all that can be done is to call for more challenging and potentially coercive means for regulating what she contends is a growing propensity
toward unfettered competition in sport.[70]

Heikkala's claims of a lack of moral structure in athletics are wholly in
common with the works of popular sport critics such as Robert Lipsyte, the
oft-cited and highly regarded sports columnist for the *New York Times* and
whose views are widely disseminated throughout the more pedestrian reaches
of the sporting industry. In terms of the competitive element of sport, Lipsyte
claims that while on the one hand competitive sport can have an electrifying
effect on all involved and across widening social and cultural lines, he cites as
inherently problematic the identification feature that creates a class-based
hierarchy centered on athletic talent, which in turn has the power to spawn
unwelcome, if not unintended, consequences. For Lipsyte, the *SportsWorld*,[71]
as he has dubbed it, glances backward into a semi-feudal past that separates
the classes in terms of physical dimensions and athletic ability into what he
has identified as "a varsity syndrome,"[72] a not-so-subtle reference to America's scholastic sporting culture and its supposed tendency to elevate athletic
success above academic pursuits. In its willingness to deny participation to all
competitors, he maintains that this syndrome reflects both the latent possibilities and the inherent contradictions that lie within competitive circumstances:

> Sport has the potential to bring us together but the evidence suggests it rarely
> does. In fact, it often further divides communities by promoting overzealous com-

petition, violence, specialization, professionalization and an attitude of "win at all costs" that spills over into other aspects of daily life.[73]

Lipsyte's assessment combines both a romantic and a dispirited view of the potential for positive change through competitive sport. Others, however, demonstrate a much less idealistic position in their critiques. For example, Volkwein cites a host of causal factors responsible for what she deems the crisis in contemporary sport.[74] By identifying a changing moral structure framed in a historical and cultural context, she attempts to further the analysis of an increasingly problematic sport ethos by de-emphasizing the human centered activity of sport rooted in play and holding up commodified sport as prima facie evidence that ethics are incompatible with competition. She contends further that in terms of high-profile sport, the dollar amounts alone are enough to skew the perception that competitive sport has any relevancy to earlier claims to character building, faithfulness, and issues of self-esteem. For her it is the rise of commercial interests that operate alongside the character-building mythology that places competition at such a lofty level that athletes and those along the periphery of sport can no longer afford to be fair, gentle, and even conscientious in regards to their actions either on or off the playing surface. She maintains:

> ... sport is a paradox ... because on one hand competitive sport calls for actions leading to the disadvantage for others, and on the other hand, it cries out for fairness and equal chances for all competitors. The two rules of top-level sport, to overcome the opponent by any means that are legal or appear to be legal and to act fairly and morally sound at the same time, are contradicting each other.[75]

This decidedly jaundiced view of both competition and competitive sport today is echoed in other left-leaning assessments. University of Missouri sociologists John Galliher and Richard Hessler perceive the extreme competitiveness in American sport to be an obstacle to mass participation, and cite scholastic sport as the progenitor of this dynamic. Their appraisal differs in that they acknowledge that the media-derived images of elitism found within contemporary sport have emerged from school-centered athletics rather than the inverse, claiming instead that the media learned to seize upon the prototypical image of the school-yard jock and began building upon notions of puerile physical excellence as it moved into the modern era. They contend that oversimplifying the role that media plays in presenting images of sport and athleticism misses the point. For them, definitions of sport are "generated and supported by early socialization in both high schools and colleges,"[76] and are likewise disseminated throughout the population by various media outlets.

Similarly, Kohn-influenced journalist Bil [*sic*] Gilbert, writing in *Sports Illustrated* but surrounded by a large group of highly esteemed academic commentators, reflects an increasingly popular vision that stresses that in a society where results supersede all other values, the competitive ethos has no chance of being anything short of corrupted. Gilbert, noting that life should be about "avoiding competition"[77] rather than openly participating in it, argues that while the act of competing should determine the successful challenge, victory is only reflected in terms of the final score. The lack of intangible reward in contemporary society negates whatever value competition has to the participant, and by denying the intangibles, sport, athletes, and spectators all become commodities and hence corrupted. He argues:

> Nowadays, the rewards for winning and the costs of losing are becoming more substantial.... The worth of inner rewards declines in comparison with the magnificence of prizes distributed. Raising the material stakes in contests tends to move competition out of the traditional realm of sport — safe excitement and imaginary risk — and into the real world, a world that frequently seems so scary and so stressful that we invented games as a means of escaping it.[78]

The notion of risk that Gilbert stresses relates to the oft-criticized duality of high profile sport and its consequence on society as a whole and especially in matters affecting youth. It is not merely a matter of broken bones and scarred bodies but rather scarred and shattered psyches that drive this aspect of the debate, but the element of the potential for hazardous outcome is, nevertheless, omnipresent in many differing critiques irrespective of the social or political orientation of the commentator. Journalist and former athlete Teri Bostian, for example, writing in the since defunct online monthly *SportsJones*, makes this point exceedingly clear in her assessment of the relationship between competitive sport and the spate of school shootings in the United States at the end of the twentieth century:

> As a lifelong jock, I believe in the athletes' creed of sportsmanlike conduct, fairness, goodwill, teamwork, respect, and personal integrity. I know that many coaches and parents teach these ideals, and many athletes try to live by them everyday, on and off the playing field. But there is another set of values bred in jock culture: aggression, hypercompetitiveness, survival of the fittest, strict conformity of thought and action, and a sense of superiority over the "losers" whose talents are deemed less valuable.[79]

For many left-leaning critics cited in the above, the issue of competition and the move toward the recognition of a hypercompetitive component in sport are much more insidious forces in the contemporary debate, with grave implications if left unchallenged. In this respect, the desire to impede a perceived overemphasis on product and outcome in the competitive scope lends an urgency to these discussions as well as presenting untold challenges to an emergent advocacy. Thus, and merely to illustrate the effect, the 1989 suicide of former baseball pitcher Donnie Moore, who was thought to be despondent over his failure to drive his team to victory in the waning moments of the deciding game of the 1986 American League Championship Series, is often incorporated into this rather unenthusiastic assessment of competition to demonstrate in perhaps a most egregious sense that the consequences of competition have the potential to extend beyond the normally acceptable psychological domain into a realm of human existence increasingly at odds with the more modern outlook.[80] Furthermore, this assessment exposes competition in the guise of some sort of addictive and destructive substance while stressing the importance of immediate intervention in order to prevent further damage to the individual caught in the middle. As sport psychologist Stuart Walker once conceded:

> The greater the investment, the greater will be the grief when we fail. [When] emphasis is placed not upon what is accomplished but upon what is publicly recognized, not upon the demonstration of competence but upon winning, [the competitor] comes to believe that he is defective and deserves to fail.[81]

Hypermasculinity, Aggression, and Violence in Sport

> *Sports have always been a repository of a culture's values, mirroring and shaping society. At least since the time of* The Iliad, *sports have been a kind of ritual with a meaning. They have simultaneously celebrated male (and today even female) aggression and competitiveness along with civilization's triumph of channeling and containing that aggression within elaborate rules and ceremonies.*[82]

> *Violence is targeted, marketed and tolerated in our society. Violence is targeted in media reports. Violence is marketed by the media, e.g., television shows and movie advertisements. Violence is an increasingly common theme in many computer games and toys. Violence apparently sells!*[83]

Another factor thought to exist outside the margins in contemporary sport criticism is the perception of a dramatic upsurge in both on- and off-field violence resulting in part from a hypercompetitive pose exacerbated by an overly dramatic manifestation of the traditional masculine posture. For example, in his review of Susan Faludi's *Stiffed: The Betrayal of the American Man*,[84] distinguished professor of American literature and culture and former professional football player Michael Oriard of Oregon State University notes:

> Since the 1890's, [football] has represented various ways to be male, all of them related to the nature of the game (as a collision sport), and to its nearly exclusively male and hyper-masculine participants. The sport's coaches and players have traditionally represented different ways to be masculine. Individual coaching styles (kindly father, screaming tyrant, efficient technocrat) and the assorted player positions (offensive linemen who "toil in the trenches," the razzle-dazzle of running backs, the linebacker as destroyer) provide various models of masculinity to which football's diverse audience has responded in diverse ways.[85]

Again, the prefix hyper- assumes a primary role in this depiction of a behavioral construct that is believed to have ventured beyond what one might consider to be an acceptable dimension, which in this case suggests an exces-

sively masculine course that stands poised to offer latent and potentially problematic consequences. As sociologist Karen Pyke at the University of California at Riverside explains, hypermasculinity, as a theoretical construct, owes as
much to the frustration of an externally enforced subordination of working-
class men as it does to the recognition that a certain degree of physical prowess
offers the opportunity to express at least a portion of that frustration through
a heightened physical presence.[86] She contends:

> The hypermasculinity found in certain lower-status male locales, such as shop
> floors, in pool halls, motorcycle clubs, and urban gangs, can be understood as both
> a response to ascendant masculinity and its unintentional booster. With their mas-
> culine identity and self-esteem undermined by their subordinate order-taking
> position in relation to higher-status males (which potentially delegates them to the
> role of "wimps"), men on the shop floor reconstruct their position as embodying
> true masculinity.[87]

Pyke's assessment that subordination plays a role in male-sponsored
aggressive behavior marks another prominent theme in modern sport discourse,
though quite often the focus of sport-related aggression tends to be off-field.
Location notwithstanding, thoughts that sport's varied terrain has become even
more conspicuously fueled by overly aggressive behavior to the point of advancing or even sanctioning outright violence has indeed darted to the top of a
rather expansive list of themes operating within the contemporary frame of
reference. Consequently, this emergent profile has served to bring sport under
further scrutiny at the level of gender-related criticism. As Ann Hall of the
University of Alberta matter-of-factly asserts in her assessment of gender discourse in sport through what she considers to be an explosion in feminist theory over the last third of the twentieth century, "masculinity is culture,"[88]
leaving whatever descriptive means one might want to employ in order to
attempt a critique of sport to ultimately be obliged to a male-dominated ana-
lytical premise.

That a certain measure of aggressive activity remains a feature of the on-
field activities of virtually every major American sport is certainly well documented.[89] Moving deftly through some of America's more notably popular
contests, one can rather easily make the case that football and ice hockey are
indeed collision sports and inherently more aggressive whereas baseball and basketball, which by convention are not collision oriented, also allow for an apparent degree of physical jousting over the course of a given contest. For instance,
there are the bone-jarring collisions that have a tendency to occur periodically
at home plate in baseball, which are in fact legal (and encouraged as evidence
of gamesmanship),[90] and, of course, the threat of being hit by either a pitched
or batted ball is pervasive. Similarly in terms of basketball, which is popularly,
though erroneously, thought to allow no contact between players, the painted
area of the floor surrounding the basket area is notorious for attracting rough
play while the ball is in flight, increasing the likelihood of some sort of contact

on nearly every trip down the court. In fact, in the early days of both amateur and professional basketball, the courts were often surrounded by a mesh wire in order to protect the spectators seated extraordinarily close to the floor as well as to keep the ball in play without interruption. The inevitable cuts and abrasions from players being entangled in the wiring led to basketball players being dubbed *cagers*, a term that has held on through the years though few can actually recall specifically why in an age of modern palatial basketball facilities.[91]

The bulk of the controversy surrounding the contention that violence has become a more omnipresent feature of contemporary sport is often supported by the notion that a hypothetical coupling of masculinity and violence operates freely within sport, a matter that is not necessarily aimed at what may occur during competition but rather the cause and effect relationship thought to emanate outside the playing surface. To be certain, overtly hostile acts do in fact occur and quickly become fodder for intense scrutiny. Recent examples of this would include a well-publicized high-sticking of a National Hockey League (NHL) player in February 2000, the infamous 2004 brawl in Detroit when members of the National Basketball Association's (NBA) Indiana Pacers went into the stands in reaction to the taunts and debris flung on to the floor at them by fans reacting to an on-court melee, and the rather bizarre encounter between a baseball player and a series of cameramen during a pre-game workout in the summer of 2005. All of these and similar such events were extraordinarily well-publicized and drew swift and resolute condemnation from many different corners of the sporting and non-sporting world, which suggests that these breaches are anything but tolerated.

These flashes of episodic violence, while clearly not the norm in high-profile sport, are increasingly thought to occur without constraints within the more modern competitive culture and are also often linked to what some maintain is a dramatic reworking of the extrinsic motivators that drive athletic excellence. For example, as Volkwein has argued, these violent states of affair are thought to confuse and redefine contemporary sport ethics in terms of a reward system that appears to value and in some cases encourage this sort of deviant display,[92] a point to which Notre Dame University's David Shields, co-founder of the school's Center for Sport, Character, and Culture, and his associates add:

> A nearly endless stream of media reports detail instances of rule violation and aggression by athletes. While there are no reliable statistics to indicate whether the problems of cheating and aggression are any more frequent now than in times past, there is certainly a perception on the part of many that unfair and harmful behaviors are widely endorsed, openly or surreptitiously, in the sport world.[93]

Similarly, as amplified in the work of sport ethicists Angela Lumpkin, Sharon Kay Stoll, and Jennifer Beller, overly aggressive behavior that may occur in sport is often the result of an unwritten and, nevertheless, ill-conceived non-enforcement policy among officials and administrators. They maintain that a lack of initiative on the part of key enforcement personnel in turn serves to encourage and even perpetuate further violations as a sort of learned response among what they intimate are those competitors already prone to such displays. Moreover, they also contend that regardless of practice or intent, the effect of overly aggressive displays that skirt agreed-upon standards impairs whatever potential value that sport may generate, including cooperation and self-discipline.[94]

Canadian sport researcher Varda Burstyn positions what she deems overly aggressive structures within sport as part of an elaborate and largely ceremonial process operating as a lever for both reproducing and redefining a male-dominant order:

> The initiation into manhood through violence is not the only purpose or effect of the core men's sports and sports culture. But it is one of the most important of their effects, and deserves critical examination. The ideology of coercive entitlement is central to gender, race, class, and biotic hierarchies. However complex, the cultures of these stratified systems may be, all of them are based on the *force majeure* accorded to males of specific groups, and are physically policed by organized groups of armed and violently instrumental men. Linked to the cult of the warrior, the template of this ideology has been actively constructed in the ritual formations of men's culture as well as in military and paramilitary structures, above all in the bastions of men's professional sports.[95]

In the popular realm, however, the most readily conveyed explanation for the perceived escalation of violence in sport points toward a media-driven desire for ratings, but this alone is incapable of explaining the perception, though it does indeed seem to exist. It is true that television only airs what it believes will encourage a rise in viewership that will then allow broadcasters to up the ante in terms of advertising revenues.[96] On the other hand, popular spectacles such as theatrically-inclined professional wrestling circuits are widely known to be stage-managed, and highlight reels that depict overly aggressive athletes violating league rules are also more likely to be followed by commentary that dwells on rather than omits the contentious aftermath. As Mitch Albom of the *Detroit Free Press*, also a frequent guest on ESPN's critically-acclaimed round-table series "The Sports Reporters," would note, "[a]nger is a commodity,"[97] one that operates both on the field of play and in the grandstands. Still, what is both apparent and interesting to note is that references emanating from within the public sphere will rarely identify masculinity as having a causal relationship to sport-related violent activity beyond the more banal observations that a man or men have committed some offense, though this tendency has started to shift in the early days of the new century, especially on the matter of domestic violence among athletes. On the contrary, academic discussion regularly references the role that masculine comportment plays in informing this sort of overly aggressive behavior.[98]

Many theorists expand the theoretical position that competitive sport itself is the leading component in the reproduction of hegemonic behavior into a debate regarding the role that traditional masculine behavior plays in laying the foundation for contemporary sport ethics. In this model, violent activities are thought to be an essential ingredient of competitiveness.[99] For example, historian Donald Mrozek draws upon the lingering effects of the Cold War era treatment of physical prowess in his assessment. He maintains that overly aggressive acts that evince themselves as a regular feature in modern sport reflect America's previous adherence to a "cult of toughness" regimen formulated through tradition and characterized by a take-charge attitude often expressed in physical training.[100] As he notes, while this standard for physicality was rooted in mid-twentieth century conduct, its "ritualistic practice grew strong"[101] and continues to reproduce itself in the decades to follow.

Sociologist Timothy J. Curry asserts that some athletes are encouraged to participate in outrageous conduct in order to gain both the favor and the respect of coaches and teammates in a sort of fraternal bonding experience. These behaviors often entail some type of aggressive act, including the virtually clichéd athlete-inspired bar fight, as a demonstration of one's toughness. Interestingly, Curry's work was largely ethnographic in nature and relied heavily on interviews conducted in an often staged environment. Still, as a faculty member at Ohio State University, whose athletes are notorious for their off-field antics, he had ample opportunity to observe some of these behaviors in a variety of more spontaneous settings. Indeed, one legend (perhaps apocryphal) that remains popular around the university's campus asserts that former All-American football star Jack Tatum, the blueprint for the hard-hitting, even notorious defensive player, readied himself for Saturday afternoon contests by traveling from bar to bar on Friday nights in the hopes of participating in as many fights as possible.[102]

The intimation that a sort of hyperaggressive sport ethic or subculture has developed over time is often explained as an essential part of an extraordinarily hypermasculine model that champions aggressive behaviors in the hopes of drawing out even more impressive displays of athletic performance in the competitive environment. The modern conclusion that masculinity is best expressed through virility gives rise to the belief that there is a developing — or perhaps developed — violence ethic in sport, and that its fundamental nature is built on the basis of an exceedingly palpable and overtly masculine archetype.[103] This image, which is thought to operate within sport's inner dynamic, is also thought to carry over into off-field behavior as well as provide a model for a more commonplace acceptance of violent activity along the periphery of sport, and nowhere is this more evident than the varied treatment given sexual and domestic abuse relative to sport. For instance, in their collaborative effort regarding what they term the "Morality/Manhood Paradox," Shari Lee Dworkin and Faye Wachs attempt to explain the role of masculine privilege as depicted in the media in relation to male athletes and their sexual conduct. They contend that the media serves to emphasize, and offer tacit approval through a notable silence, an underlying assumption of instant gratification and submissiveness when it comes to male athletes and their pursuit of sexual liaisons. And yet, given the intolerance shown by the media for misbehaving athletes, this assessment seems hardly defensible in this context. Nevertheless, they assert that a contradiction exists when an athlete's profile intersects with the perpetuation of highly undesirable sexual comportment while noting the complexity within the arrangement. Furthermore, and perhaps ironically when we take into account modern trends, they offer that this thread of sport criticism marks an often overlooked field of inquiry. As they propose in their study, "[g]iven that sport is one of the most powerful socializing institutions for masculinity that privileges male heterosexual bodies, it provides an interesting forum for exploring norms of sexual behavior.[104]

In *Athletes and Acquaintance Rape*,[105] Jeffrey Benedict of Northeastern University's prestigious Center for the Study of Sport in Society, assesses what he claims to be an epidemic in sexual abuse cases among athletes. In his paradigmatic explanation of sexual violence in the athletic environment, he argues that the hegemonic hypermasculine culture regularly on parade in the high-profile domain of competitive sport predisposes self-obsessed, albeit physically gifted specimens, to gravitate toward promiscuity through a combination of entitlement and celebrity. Arguing that "[m]uch of the casual sex engaged in by athletes is seldom the result of affirmatively expressed consent or vocally conveyed resistance,"[106] Benedict presupposes that the poorly concealed sexual appetites thought to exist among contemporary athletes narrow their ability to interpret sexual aggression toward women as a violent act. In addition, Benedict claims that the evidence supports his contention that within the competitive arena exists a subculture that encourages sexual conquest as a means toward furthering an athlete's career goals while reaffirming the role that virility plays within the elite world of high-caliber sport. This, he argues, allows athletes in many cases to act criminally but be portrayed as archetypally masculine. He notes:

> Whereas the subculture fosters images of women as sexually compliant, and simultaneously facilitates opportunities for players who may posses proclivities toward sexual abuse to be pursued by women, sport also offers a final factor that fuels the perception that athletes are not accountable, regardless of how they treat women.[107]

Though advocative in tone, Benedict's thesis is, nonetheless, often replicated in other assessments of the link between athletes and sexual aggression. Burstyn, for instance, noting a controversial 1995 *Sports Illustrated* report that proclaimed that batterers are being exposed more often in sport than they had been previously,[108] offers that "[t]he sexual validation athletes get for their athletic violence is an important factor in this phenomenon, part of the eroticization of coercive entitlement."[109]

Similarly, other theorists have looked for a connection between domestic violence and televised sport. The implication is that male viewers can be turned aggressive by virtue of being too caught up in the frenzy of a particular sport telecast. The position here is that the draw of sport violence has the potential to transcend into peripheral elements of the sporting terrain, including the realm of spectator. The image captured in this debate suggests that the potential for violence is increased when a viewer, perhaps cajoled by the frustration of watching one's team (or perhaps wager) suffer through a progression of losing, reacts in a manner similar to what is being modeled by the athletes on display. Citing psychological assessments that have outlined such behaviors in male sports fans, some have taken to note a causal relationship triggered by the pose proffered by athletes that serves to encourage violent reactions in spectators.[110]

In *The Stronger Women Get, the More Men Love Football: Sexism and the American Culture of Sports*, former collegiate and professional basketball star Mariah Burton Nelson, whose largely anecdotal work has been well-received among academics in the field, explains that hypermasculine violence between and among competitors has become so ingrained within the institutionalized constituency of American culture that it has become both "attractive and graceful"[111] both inside and irrespective of the competitive milieu. She says:

> Strength and violence are the province of men. Televised hockey, baseball, basketball, and football define men to men and to impressionable boys, equating thuggery with masculinity and depicting men as dangerous, combative creatures with uncontrollable tempers (but, inexplicably, infinitely controllable jump shots). The sports media also defines male violence and male domination as natural.[112]

Accusations and explanations aside, what emanates from these often tapered assessments is a supposition that refuses to assign to competitive sport any other underlying feature except for a marked aggressive nature. Furthermore, by describing the presumed escalation of violence as a component of a masculine or hypermasculine culture, the inverse of these analyses suggests that in the hands of female competitors, the violent ethic is muted if not extinguished altogether, thereby consigning a notably feminized ethos to the progressive response to a male-dominated competitive aesthetic. Thus, whereas one team of academic commentators may contend that critical feminist scholarship on men's issues in sport tends to be weighted toward "negative outcomes such as pain and injury, misogyny, homophobia, and violence against women by men,"[113] this approach is often immune to criticism primarily because it is often assumed that the healthier competitive ethic exists within the feminine expression.[114] Still, as anyone who has ever witnessed women performing at the highest level of sport can attest, aggression on the playing surfaces is not necessarily a strictly male province.

Role Modeling and
Mentoring through Sport

One of the most ghastly miscontributions of sociology to social life is the concept of "role model"— a dimwitted scoutmaster's notion of the link between perceived accomplishment and motivating the young.[115]

If professionals continue to be the most important model for childhood sport, it will eventually destroy sports as we know them.[116]

As long as footballers are fit and able to deliver the goods on the pitch, I couldn't care less what they do in their free time, and neither should anybody else.[117]

Where the modern ideals relative to an inflated competitive infrastructure traverse the most sacred element of the traditional sporting motif, namely the molding of young actors into a responsible citizenry, is another well-traveled avenue of exploration in contemporary sport criticism — the role model. Indeed, many have formed a connection between the behavior of athletes and the messages thought to reach young minds. As a nation founded on certain underlying principles of both action and contemplation, Americans have grown quite sensitive to the notion that it is the responsibility of older generations to both instruct and reproduce accepted and acceptable behavior in virtually every conceivable fashion, a conceptual rendering that has been expanded into the modern construct of the role model, which is often bounded to the similar precept of mentoring.

At the root of this issue is the notion that turn-of-the-century youth live in increasingly untenable surroundings and are exposed to dangers and temptations more so now than at any other time in modern memory. That these assessments often belie statistical representation is supported in most cases,[118] but what remains in spite of the numbers is the impulse to equate the modern world as an incubator for hazard and childhood with an increasingly pathological stage in the life cycle, a phase thought to be exceedingly vulnerable to a rash of contemporary maladies of both physical and psychological significance. As psychologist Peter Marsh of the Social Issues Research Centre insists, the modern tendency toward moral panics is not supported statistically.[119] Or as British sociologist Frank Füredi states:

> During the past twenty years, concern with the safety of children has become a constant subject of discussion. Children are portrayed as permanently at risk from danger. Even a relatively balanced account of "children at risk" regards childhood as a "uniquely dangerous time of life." In Britain and the USA, concern for the security of children has led to a major reorganization of the childhood experience.[120]

This tendency to equate childhood and risk seems to have given rise to the role model construct as more than simply a matter of children latching onto heroic figures and holding them up as standard bearers of performance or behavioral excellence. Rather, the fascination with role models has grown into a sort of cottage industry by which society is given license to assign high or low marks to both public figures and private citizens in relation to their perceived social worth and potential for steering children down appropriate behavioral paths. As expressed in the mission statement of the heavily endowed Arthur Agee Role Model Foundation, "Children need others to emulate, and they will follow the example of role models if they are available on a consistent basis."[121] Or as sport-oriented psychologist Daniel Gould substantiates, "One of the primary means by which children acquire attitudes and values is by observing others whom they respect or idolize. In youth sports settings, important role models for children include parents, coaches, officials, and professional athletes."[122] To further this assessment into the realm of the sportsmanship debate, Gould also suggests:

> Adult leaders can and do have an enormous effect on some children, but it is not always apparent which children they are influencing. For this reason every adult leader involved in youth sports programs should structure practices and games to allow children the greatest opportunity to learn good sportsmanship. Repeated modeling, reinforcement, and explanations of sportsmanlike behavior are absolutely necessary if sportsmanship is to be developed.[123]

That this line of inquiry has the potential to place adults on rather uneven footing seems wholly beside the point here. To be sure, adult behavior in this climate is increasingly on display and exposed for scrutiny by a mass of external sources. Nevertheless, the investment in this approach is inestimable, and, in many ways, sport's perceived inability to keep pace with modern virtues has impacted the burgeoning role model debate in such a way as to both hasten and widen the gap between contemporary sport and other such hot-button yet related ideals.

Indeed, matters such as the reevaluation of coaching techniques, the emphasis on self-esteem, or the importance placed on providing positive experiences through sport, or the aforementioned anxieties concerning on- and off-field violence and the so-called demise of sportsmanship, can all be viewed with equal clarity through the role model construct. In this context, misbehavior within the framework of competitive sport further indicates that behaviors expressed within the athletic domain are no longer compatible with contemporary values and that sport must either be reformed through the efforts of activists wielding reasonable demands or removed from its pedestal as one of America's most esteemed institutions. For instance, writing in the *Marquette Sports Law Journal*, Troy Cross asserts:

> Americans, as a whole, watch many hours of television. They create heroes out of movie stars and sports figures. This is especially true with young children. By the time they become adults, many children have watched numerous hours of television and have dreamed about being like their heroes. Often these children choose

sports stars as their heroes. As the Gatorade commercial promotes, they want to grow up and "be like Mike" … [but they] also want be like Ray Lewis, Rae Carruth, Dennis Rodman, Roberto Alomar, Bryan Cox, Latrell Sprewell.[124]

To clarify, "Mike" would be former NBA star Michael Jordan, as ubiquitous a figure as there is in contemporary American sport, while the others are all athletes who have at one time or another run afoul of either the law or public favor. That none of those mentioned are white also presents a challenging dilemma, especially given the higher profile afforded the non-white athlete and the supposed predisposition to unfortunate and even criminal behavior (see chapter seven). Nevertheless, what is often overlooked is that the public backlash concerning those who defy expectations is often swift and quite harsh, leaving some to wonder how it is that a child could be confused about the differences between acceptable and unacceptable conduct. As *Scouting Magazine* editor Robert W. Peterson reminds, "If a child idolizes a sports superstar whose behavior is undesirable, it's important for parents to point out that people may be fantastically talented in one thing and bad in something else."[125] That the inverse is not so readily obvious—that children watching their heroes raked over the coals of public condemnation is rarely if ever deemed a lesson learned—is equally as telling.

The persistence of the role model debate runs purposefully through the contemporary sport environment, but oftentimes the discussions seem to run in completely contradictory directions. On the one hand, there are those who vociferously condemn the thought that someone as distant as an athlete, or for that matter a celebrity of any renown, should have any tangible influence over one's child at all. This contention often stems from the belief that a role model should be both accessible and credible beyond his or her celebrity, which might ensure that the lessons gleaned from such a relationship can be supervised and shaped to fit a particular child and that child's circumstances. As the Agee Foundation insists, "Athletes and movie stars are heroes [while] parents and adults are role models."[126] On the other hand, there are those who maintain that anyone, and most notably any public figure by virtue of his or her status, must be willing to accept the responsibility for and the ramifications of his or her behavior in the public eye. In other words, this point of view supports the notion that anyone can be, should be, and quite candidly is a role model whether he or she accepts the assignment or not, a contention that is no longer simply a matter of celebrity but indeed subsists within the general population itself.

Whether or not children are actually in need of some sort of advisory or guiding force in relation to the dangers of an increasingly problematic social order is also rarely addressed in this line of inquiry, though it may seem to be a more palpable and certainly even a more provocative question than who is up for the job. Moreover, the assumption that the role model designation is a legitimate feature of an enlightened society also reaffirms the position that in spite of evidence to the contrary, the modern world is a place to be feared. As

Russell Gough concedes, "If we're using the term *role model* [his italics] — as we so often use it — to mean a person who sets an example for others, who influences others, whom other people learn from and imitate then ... [we] simply don't have a choice in the matter.[127]

Indeed, for Gough and those who also support this contention, the only remaining point is whether or not the individual is worthy of the selection. In this respect, athletes are not offered the opportunity to refuse the assignment. Rather, they are expected to conform to such societal expectations and assume the role gracefully or face scrutiny, censure, and disapproval, which in today's sports world has potentially dire consequences in terms of endorsements and the other available fruits of athletic celebrity. As he notes, "If it's a question of *being* [his italics] a role model, the answer will follow along these lines: I am a role model, so I should do my best to be a good role model."[128]

Or as Gould asserts:

> Competitive sport is a particularly important setting in which social learning takes place. Sport sociologists have indicated that competitive youth sports are important today because they are one of the few activities in which children are intensely involved. In organized sports, children have a degree of control over their own fate and their actions are viewed as important by a large segment of the culture.[129]

That athletes, and, quite frankly, anyone connected to sport, have persistently been expected to uphold the image of wholesomeness and piety while publicly displaying acceptable behavior is an article of faith that many Americans have long since accepted. It has also become more readily apparent that many in the industry, and the athletes particularly, given their growing recognition of class struggle within the professional dynamic, act as if they are no longer convinced that it is their responsibility to uphold societal norms and behavioral constructs, especially in light of the changes manifest in the relationship between the athlete and the media. As salaries continue to rise alongside the financial stakes of ownership, and as sport media outlets flourish to the extent that the twenty-four-hour-a-day sporting news cycle has become the standard, the changing nature of the relationship between the press and the athlete has seemingly hastened attitudinal adjustments on both sides of this equation. Furthermore, now that there are no longer limits to the types of stories sport media outlets report, athletes have found that their lives both on and off the field are no longer cloistered but, rather, fodder for public scrutiny. This transformation has indeed led to some interesting, if not dramatic, exchanges among athletes, sport administrators, and the public.[130] As the aforementioned Mitch Albom muses in defense of the shift toward what some have deemed the rise of *infotainment* as a legitimate line of inquiry in sport reporting, "Sport without personality is calisthenics,"[131] a point echoed almost verbatim a year earlier by John Andrews in *The Economist* and with virtually the same sentiment.[132]

Interestingly, in order to maintain the semblance of a so-called fan-friendly environment, many professional franchises, and even some colleges, have set aside additional funds for a position akin to a press liaison or some variation thereof whose responsibility is to instruct the staff on public decorum or to otherwise ferret out the hint of potential controversy through a preemptive damage control mechanism. Still, in many appraisals, the attempt at damage control is viewed as both cynical and ineffective. For example, in their assessment of the controversy swirling about baseball's John Rocker, whose inflammatory comments regarding New York City's sports fans in 1999 have continued to swirl about popular sport commentary, Anderson and Reinharz, again writing in *City Journal*, appear unimpressed with both the pitcher and the collective responses of league authorities to the scandal. They note:

> Sports bosses' ... ham-handed response to Atlanta Braves pitcher John Rocker's rant against New York's wealth of homosexuals, felons, welfare moms, and immigrants shows how far they are from remembering what those values are. After yawning over violence and felonies, they impose a 73-day suspension and a $20,000 fine over this?[133]

Or as *Washington Post* columnist Michael Wilbon pronounced following Rocker's own attempt at damage control through granting interviews to various media outlets, "The apology was bogus. It was about self-promotion. They just don't get it."[134]

Similar such responses to on- and off-field indiscretions have prompted comparable responses from both the academic and popular realms, as evidenced by discussions of the O.J. Simpson murder trial, the Mike Tyson rape conviction, and the various scandals related to doping and other forms of cheating in sport enterprises. What these popular responses suggest is the extent to which the question of decorum is an understood feature of contemporary sport, but what these responses also seem to ignore is that when sport was enjoying its most heralded run within American culture, some of its most cherished figures, though protested by a cooperative media, were, nonetheless, more likely to engage in conduct that today would leave them targeted for scrutiny and ridicule within the contemporary outlook. In that respect, the return to a golden age so cherished by purists and pundits alike existed only in fiction rather than in fact, with the difference being that few ever knew what really took place behind the scenes.

One exchange that many point to as a defining moment in the modern relationship between the role modeling debate and sport was a Nike Sports commercial aired in 1993 that featured outspoken NBA star Charles Barkley. In what was then considered to be a scathing denouncement of modern expectations, Barkley foreswore much to the chagrin of his public:

> I am not a role model. I am not paid to be a role model. I am paid to wreak havoc on the basketball court. Parents should be role models. Just because I can dunk a basketball doesn't mean I should raise your kids.[135]

The public and private rebuke for Barkley's position on the role model question was indeed abundant and was repeated following his 2006 pronouncement of his gambling troubles, but in relatively few of these retorts were there references to whether or not the issue of role modeling itself is even relevant to the discussion at all. Furthermore, Barkley's position, one that assumes the salience and import of children having role models and mentors in the first place, really is in line with what many of his detractors were saying all along. That he was so willing to blatantly disregard the scope of the general vision of celebrities serving in this public fashion predominated the responses in spite of Barkley's rather obvious acquiescence. Still, as Gough reported, "While Barkley — and Nike — certainly took some heat for it — and some of that heat was understandable — in the long run the commercial served a good purpose,"[136] that purpose being to open up a dialogue between celebrities and the general public regarding modern societal expectations and the nature of public personas while establishing guidelines for both on- and off-field behavior.

To the contrary, the increasingly omnipresent Fred Engh shows himself to be decidedly against the notion of the contemporary athlete serving in such a leadership role but with a caveat. He points out that with a generation of lawless athletes being arrested and then hurrying to prepare for the next contest, why anyone would consciously choose athletes as role models is something of a modern mystery.[137] He contends:

> Today's athletes have shoved their way into the public's consciousness and hyped their way to fame and riches beyond their wildest dreams. Individualism in sports, which was frowned upon years ago, is now heartily embraced.... It's reached the point where we actually expect players to misbehave, and we go home disappointed if they don't live up to these ridiculous expectations.[138]

Similarly, journalist Kevin Baker, writing in the normally sport-unfriendly *Wall Street Journal*, assesses modern professional football in America by referring to the NFL as the "National Felons League," deeming it a "curious mix of socialism and social Darwinism"[139] that would certainly ill-befit a model for youth.

In contrast to the Barkely-inspired debate, another Nike ad aired in 1999 that would also raise the collective ire of America's more sport-conscious populace, though it was deliberately geared toward a more hip-hop oriented demographic. It featured NBA bad boy Latrell Sprewell, who two years prior had been suspended (and nearly expelled) from the league for a series of violent attacks upon his then-coach P.J. Carlesimo in the middle of the 1997 season when both men were employed by the Golden State Warriors.[140] Amid a backdrop of Jimi Hendrix's raucous and controversial 1969 Woodstock rendition of "The Star Spangled Banner,"[141] Sprewell is shown having his hair braided into the then-stylish (and notably African American) corn rows while making several statements regarding his controversial place in professional sport:

> People say I'm what's wrong with sports today. I say I'm the American dream. I've

made mistakes, but I don't let them keep me down. People say I'm what's wrong with sports. I say I'm a three-time NBA All-Star. People say I'm America's worst nightmare. I say I'm the American dream.[142]

The reaction to the since re-dubbed "American Dream" commercial was one of outrage,[143] outrage that was overwhelmingly aimed at the very notion that in attempting to defuse the circumstances that led to both his suspension and his subsequent label as one of sport's most notorious figures, Sprewell was asserting his place in sport irrespective of public censure and much in the way that Barkley had in his aforementioned spot. But as media researcher Todd Boyd of the University of Southern California contends, the reaction to Sprewell's attempt at *anti*-role modeling, while tinged with racial connotations, was every bit as pointed as Barkely's earlier refusal to admit celebrity accountability but much more explosively challenging.[144]

In Sprewell's case, his rejection of the role model dogma coincided with some obviously indefensible behavior, which certainly exacerbated matters and led to the often vitriolic exchanges drawn out by the ad. In terms of the more substantive discussion that ensued, however, others were less moved by the moral climate swirling about Sprewell's situation and used these debates as a platform to reflect upon racial matters within sport. For instance, basketball commentator Scoop Jackson, writing in *SportsJones*, whose editorial bent once gave its writers free reign to explore at a decidedly more popular level such very unpopular issues as the underlying implications of, for example, race and sport and masculine comportment and violence, notes that while Sprewell's actions toward his erstwhile coach were indefensible, a similar situation perpetrated by a white NFL linebacker on a game day before a nationally televised audience was all but ignored in the American press.[145] Similarly Boyd submits that the reaction to the commercial failed to address the more pressing concern, which he contends is a role model discussion not merely tinged and outwardly marked by racism:

> America loves Black entertainers when they behave "properly" and stay in their place. These entertainers are socialized at an early age, live under a microscope, and are constantly held to the expectations of a mainstream society that has no understanding for the fact that not everyone shares the same worldview. When the players realize their value, their significance to the game, and try to capitalize on this, they are held guilty in the highest court of contempt.[146]

In this regard, the principal obstacle that a Charles Barkley or a Latrell Spewell or anyone else would have to hurdle in his or her drive for public acceptance, let alone embrace, is the knowledge that while one's career path may run parallel to the traditional athlete-as-hero leitmotif, one has to be much more cautious in order to fully realize its benefits.

The Steroid Controversy
in Its Moral Context

*Drugs that make sport exotic drain it of its exemplary power by mak-
ing it a display of chemistry rather than character — actually, a display of chemistry and bad character.*[147]

They cheat, and I feel cheated.[148]

If you're not cheating, you're not trying.[149]

A postscript to the role modeling debate as well as a most salient link for
all of the above topics can be found in the contemporary discussions of athletes who either use or are suspected of using performance enhancers, or
steroids, as they are more commonly known. This heralded issue, one that had
a brief airing in American sport in the 1980s and early 1990s while seemingly
hovering about world sport for some time, came rocketing back into the American sport scene midway through the first decade of the new century as a string
of doping allegations thrust sport initially into the headlines and ultimately into
Congress's purview, with a flurry of wild assertions and theories about the
nature of sport, athletes, and modern governance. Moreover, it provides a
remarkably fertile ground for analysis that seems to encompass a wide range
of topics relative to modern sport and morality as it is broadly defined in the
competitive terrain.

To be sure, the list of athletes who have run afoul of public sentiment by
virtue of their having been caught with, admitted to, or simply rumored to have
subverted the rules by chemically enhancing their performances is staggering,
to say the least, but what is equally as extraordinary is the depth to which these
discussions lead us away from sport as a competitive endeavor and toward more
broadly disseminated discussions regarding everything from the consequences
of subverting the rules to the demise of human decency itself. Moreover, it has
created within the American sporting environment, once thought to be relatively immune to such allegations, the notion that its athletic arena is no longer
exceptional. As one seemingly delighted BBC print commentator noted, "America is slowly waking up to the fact that, after years of criticizing the rest of the
world, the worst offender in the anti-doping war may be itself."[150] But the external ramifications of America's turn in the doping hot seat barely scratch the
surface of the internal struggles that have resulted, spawning a number of controversial and certainly contentious disputes.

The most obvious area of contention brought forth by the reinvigoration
of the doping debate can be found in the arena of health. Though scientists
agree that they have substantiated links between the use of performance
enhancers and short-term health effects, complete with a range of emotional
disturbances, such as the much ballyhooed "roid rage," the fact is that there has
never been a full-fledged study of the long-term health effects of anabolic

steroids, human growth hormone (HGH), or many of the other more popular substances found in the athletic sphere, a matter that seems to lead much of the scientific work in this particular field toward conclusions that are both speculative and heavy-laden with supposition.[151] Thus, for all the discussions of athletes who have either died young or had their careers prematurely ended under the cloud of suspicion or even an admission of drug use, the evidence that their drug use hastened their demise is for all intents and purposes purely anecdotal. In reality, much of the so-called evidence of a link between athletes and their steroid use leading to premature death can be traced back to a 1991 interview in *Sports Illustrated* in which a dying Lyle Alzado, a former All-Pro defensive lineman in the NFL, blamed his impending death from a malignant brain tumor on his use of HGH, though there has never been a definitive causal link between HGH and cancer.[152] As ESPN.com's Mike Puma suggests in his biographical essay of Alzado's career, Alzado's fear of his impending death convinced him to speak out on behalf of future NFL players prone to use steroids, but in actuality he had no definitive information as to the cause of his cancer.[153]

When one traces the steps this regard taken by many who operate in the medical sphere, the concerns, while steeped in the language of science, often come out as cultural. For example, in their admonishment to young athletes, the American Academy of Pediatricians concludes that in spite of the supposed health effects, the more impacting impetus behind staying clean is what they deem "play safe, play fair."[154] They further this notion by pointing out that "[s]uccess in sports takes talent, skill, and most of all, [sic] practice and hard work. Using steroids is a form of cheating and interferes with fair competition."[155] In this respect, what begins as a discussion of health fluently shifts into a discussion that drips with moral indignation. As noted in a 2003 polemic published by members of the American College of Sports Medicine:

> [We] today condemned the development and use of new "designer" steroids. ACSM considers chemicals, such as the recently identified Tetrahydrogestrinone, or THG, developed and cloaked to avoid detection by doping tests as serious threats to the health and safety of athletes, as well as detriments to the principle of fair play in sports. Any effort to veil or disguise steroid use in sports through stealth, designer or precursor means, puts elite, amateur and even recreational athletes at risk.[156]

Though this rejoinder is prefaced with the acknowledgement that "[n]o one knows the extent of this yet,"[157] reminiscent of the more trendy "precautionary principle"[158] as adopted by some in science as well as science critics emerging from both the popular and academic spheres, its message is unmistakable. Moreover, that these sorts of interpretations point to health risks only in a general sense, while highlighting the matter of fair play, suggests that cultural concerns are as much at the root of the controversy — if not more so — than the former. Or as MLB Commissioner Bud Selig couches it, albeit awkwardly and amid an air of confusion, "This is about health. This is about fairness, this is about integrity, this is about social responsibility."[159] In fact what this discussion is about seems to become even less clear as the tension that surrounds it continues to build.

Candidly, it is more than a bit problematic, not to mention contradictory, to tell an athlete that it is perfectly acceptable to stand in front of a pitched ball hurtling toward him at nearly 100 miles per hour, or that one's job security hinges upon one's ability to redirect the path of a 300+ pound behemoth in full stride while at the same time citing health concerns as the rationale for banning drug use. Moreover, the recent flurry of drug-related activity also seems to underscore the fact that drugs of all types can be easily lumped into a single category, one that gives nearly equal weight to a player caught using synthetic testosterone and to one using marijuana, cocaine, or any of the other so-called recreational drugs. In fact some sport fans have seemingly caught on to this oddly linked phenomenon between steroid use and health, as was the case of a fan in Philadelphia who comically responded to Barry Bonds' approach of baseball's once hallowed mark of 714 career homeruns in the spring of 2006 by noting that "Ruth did it on hot dogs and beer,"[160] a dietary combination that is itself under fire in a more health-conscious era!

The case of Barry Bonds, Major League Baseball's enigmatic, even petulant, superstar, in many ways epitomizes the degree to which moral posturing has come to inform the doping debate in contemporary American sport. A celebrity from the time he first arrived in the big leagues with the Pittsburgh franchise in 1986 (his father Bobby had been a serviceable if not sometimes spectacular player a generation prior), he exploded into the most feared hitter in the game in the early 2000s. Always a difficult athlete by media standards, the whispers, often aided by reporters who had been shunned by Bonds, grew into a much louder chorus of righteous anger as his body began to change dramatically, most notably the size and shape of his head. Before long, his record-setting offensive prowess had been eclipsed by a cacophony of accusations that escalated to a frenzy once the United States Congress, perhaps taking its cues from President Bush's acknowledgement of a growing steroid problem in sport during his 2004 State of the Union Address, intervened with hearings in 2005.

From there, however, and in a most bizarre set of circumstances, Bonds, who has never been caught nor ever admitted to purposefully using drugs,[161] has come to be regarded as the face of what can easily be described as the perception of a rampant disease sweeping across the landscape of modern American sport, with his every move scrutinized, his every word deconstructed, and before and after photos of him dissected by media pundits and medical experts alike. In addition, the allegations and commentary that swirl about him, and in turn American sport itself, move the process forward to the point where in many ways he has become the most notable and emblematic figure in contemporary American sport, the anti-hero thought to have been lurking in sport but now taking a central role, which in and of itself served to reinforce the aforementioned illusion linking sport to spectacle and spectacle to detrimental out-comes. Bonds' decision to star in his own so-called (and short-lived) reality show on ESPN Television in early 2006 certainly did little to mitigate the cir-cus atmosphere that sprang up around him, but by then the link between Bonds and infamy had long since been established. Furthermore, the message was clear: Bonds, who represents the modern athlete, is not a worthy candidate for a mass adulation, and his place in sport should be forever obscured while his accomplishments, similar to those of Pete Rose and Joe Jackson before him, should be allowed to fade quickly from view. But, as Ohio State University lec-turer Jessica A. Johnson notes in her defense of Bonds, these messages were themselves not conceived of as fluidly as some have presented them:

> Bonds has never been a favorite of the media, mainly for his surliness toward sports reporters, and he has often waved them away in the locker room with a manner akin to one shooing away flies. As a result of his moodiness in refusing numerous interviews throughout his career, the press has depicted Bonds as a nar-cissistic act flying solo in a team sport Americans hold sacrosanct. Thus, no one should be surprised that in the wake of [numerous doping scandals], the media would not give him the benefit of the doubt.[162]

Others have run headlong into the backlash of an increasingly steroid-obsessed public, especially in the aftermath of the 2005 release of a memoir by another (this time former) superstar, José Canseco, whose aptly entitled book, *Juiced: Wild Times, Rampant 'Roids, Smash Hits, and How Baseball Got Big*, candidly and in painstaking detail highlights the unchecked use of perform-ance enhancement on virtually every team for which Canseco played over the course of his seventeen year career.[163] Canseco's book, in which he lambastes baseball management for turning its back on steroid use and then rending its clothes over the allegations of steroid use, did little to take the pressure off the anti-player backlash, though it would be Bonds— not Canseco, perceived by former teammates as a cad and a coward, nor any of the other men Canseco would accuse in his book — who would continue to serve as the face of the ongoing debate, leading some to question whether or not there is a racial dimen-sion to this particular issue lurking beneath the vitriol.

On the specter of a racialized feature attached to the escalation of the anti-Bonds sentiment, there is an improbably aligned division made particularly challenging by the presence of Henry Aaron, baseball's reigning career home-run champion at 755 and who, like Bonds, once found himself in the midst of a maelstrom as he approached Ruth's once cherished career homerun mark in 1974. In the popular realm, the contention that the controversy that swirls around Bonds is motivated by race is seen as absurd. Fingers point to the pre-dominance of African Americans in the athletic sphere, though baseball has witnessed a significant decline in that particular area (see figure 7.1). Further-more, there is the pervasive sense that Bonds brought the negative publicity on himself, which in the eyes of some mitigates any racial connotations associated with this thread. In this regard, what makes this story racial is, ironically, that so few in a position to do so are willing to examine its racial dimension, preferring instead to remain safely tucked away behind the controversy while leading the charge from the rear. As veteran commentator Michelle Tafoya candidly announced to a panel on ESPN's "The Sports Reporters," "Who would want to celebrate Barry Bonds with all the clouds hanging over his achievements?"[164]

Further obscuring any racial dimension to the Bonds saga is Aaron's own rise, one that was clearly informed by a racial climate that added further pressure to his pursuit of Ruth's venerable mark. With Jim Crow still hovering about baseball and America both, Aaron's race with Ruth's ghost rekindled a racial tension that caught many flat-footed. But in something of a re-creation of that climate, as Bonds drew closer to Ruth in the spring of 2006, hobbled as he was by then with debilitating knee and elbow injuries and haunted by the press, a second front developed that helped remind Americans of the obstacles in Aaron's path while doing little to shield Bonds from the mounting acrimony.

Aaron, himself an outspoken critic of Bonds and others caught up in the steroids controversy, was subsequently thrust into the role of the *anti*-Bonds while becoming, oddly, the champion of many of the same demographic who might have rooted against him in his playing days. Surprisingly, a man of color in the public's eye had found redemption for his having eclipsed the most cherished name in sport because, for better or worse, he was not perceived as brash, outspoken, temperamental, or simply "did not get it," in the parlance of modern sport criticism. Not since perhaps the great Joe Louis would an African American athlete be so embraced by mainstream America in spite of his blackness because he could palpably represent the archetypical symbol for heroism in the face of an imminent threat. In the words of one media pundit, up against the backdrop of Bonds, the shy, often reticent Aaron, who would find his voice only after he retired, had grown "elegant."[165]

Another side of this controversy is the moral indignation it arouses. For example, in one ten-minute segment of a March 12, 2006, broadcast of the aforementioned ESPN weekly series "The Sports Reporters," the guests and the normally reserved host of the show could be heard discussing Bonds using terms such as "exposed as a cheat and a fake"[166] while calling for the convening of "an honors council,"[167] similar to those used in grade schools, with the *Boston Globe*'s Bob Ryan resoundingly declaring that "Barry Bonds must be eliminated in the best interest of the game."[168] But beyond the obvious gaps in, for example, due process and the presence of collective bargaining agreements, the more apparent ramifications of such commentary is that these types of assessments were being aired regularly without the bother of actual evidence. In this regard the hint of impropriety is enough to ignite a firestorm of controversy, the likes of which has brought American sport out of its comfortable home in the sport sections and into the front pages and national news broadcasts, while shoving it even more closely to a political sphere that once embraced competitive sport wholeheartedly but has learned to reject it due to its perceived excesses. Thus while one incredulous blogger can note with more than a hint of sarcasm that "[p]oliticians grab headlines like baseball players grab crotches,"[169] in response to the congressional inquiries that captivated the nation in 2005, or while conservative commentator George Will, a noted baseball aficionado, can query "Would you cross the street to see Bonds hit number 755?"[170] competition is left looking from the top down like a cause of rather than an unwitting spectator to this version of the behind-the-scenes drama that has become American sport. As Dayn Perry of the more typically libertarian monthly *Reason* was to note:

> The use of steroids and other substances to enhance performance robs sports competition of any semblance of fairness. Fans, athletes and sports governing bodies need to defend the integrity of sports. They should hold accountable the athletes who use performance-enhancing substances as well as those who help them cheat.[171]

That athletes who cheat and get caught are punished, or that the frenzy surrounding the more recent round of allegations has led to increased scrutiny of athletes on many levels seems lost in translation amid this type of increasingly popular approach to steroid-in-sport commentary.

Yet another aspect to this debate can be traced to the role of management itself. The fact is that as long as there have been athletic competitions, those in charge have looked for ways to increase both the nature of the competition itself and the way competition was used within the constraints of the traditions of a given society. As Kenan Malik notes in a Radio 4 roundtable convened to explore the doping phenomena:

> [Sport] has never been clean and fair. For as long as sports have existed, sportsmen have taken drugs. Ancient Greek athletes used magic mushrooms to fortify themselves. In the 1904 Olympic Marathon, Thomas Hicks ran to victory thanks to injections of strychnine and doses of brandy administered to him during the race. It was the Cold War which turned sport — and drugs — into an ideological weapon[172]

This is particularly true in terms of the historic rise of the culture of American sport, where it has long since been established that part of the logic surrounding sport was that if one pushed the envelope enough or if one could get away with it long enough, inflexible rules could be changed to fit the times. It was not that long ago that American sport outlawed the curve ball, the dunk, and the forward pass, all staples of their respective sport. Indeed, management has historically been at the root of this phenomenon, though generally it was with an eye toward increasing revenue streams. In the case of the steroid frenzy, however, it is the athletes themselves, laborers in the scheme of things, who have taken it upon themselves to strengthen their position and forge their own revolution of sorts through chemical enhancement, which in many ways marks new ground in the evolution of sport. And irrespective of the contemporary debate, there too will come a time when this matter of doping in sport will find itself resigned to the rearview mirror. Even Frank Deford, as ardent a defender of morality within competitive sport as there has ever been, reluctantly concedes that in due time, chemical performance enhancing will become part of the training regimen of every world-class athlete, organization, or facility, much in the way that nutrition, weight training, and even sport psychology have paved the way toward performance already. As he notes, "Usually, over time, what was controversial has become accepted."[173] Even the enigmatic columnist Charles Krauthammer posits, "[p]erformance enhancement turns out to be disturbing only in the narrow context of competition, most commonly in sports. And the objection is not cheating nature, but cheating competitors. It's basically a fairness issue."[174] He further notes that "[w]hen technology is enhancing the equipment, fans become quickly reconciled to the transformation."[175]

The gist of all this is that doping in sport is a concern for reasons that seem to fly beneath the radar of competition or health or most any of the conceived rationales. Rather, they are steeped in much of the same moral posturing as can be found in all of the above-mentioned categories of moral debates in sport. Indeed, when it comes to the duality of sport and decorum or morality or however one wishes to describe it, most onlookers respond in a fashion more reminiscent of the type of nostalgic lament as expressed in the February 2006 commentary of an ESPN "SportsCenter" anchor who noted:

> There are times when we ask an awful lot of our sports, times where in addition to a final score and fun, we want sports to teach values: hard work, fair play, to install pride, and self-esteem. We want sports to amaze and inspire, and on occasion it delivers on all fronts, but rarely, curiously, through our richest, most glamorous, or most famous athletes.[176]

The end product that results from these images points toward a general assessment of competitive sport that suggests that in relation to a vision of a changing social order, the mechanisms thought to drive competitive sport appear to be at odds with the more contemporary means being offered to propel society toward a more egalitarian, fit, and perhaps even more forward-thinking future. By underscoring the potentially corrosive aspects of competitive sport, such as an epidemic of masculine violence and similar such conduct disparities, including the use of performance enhancing drugs and how these matters might impact future generations in terms of moral guidance and the like, sport's contemporary critics are able to preserve the more commonly conceived perception that the traditional measures that once sustained competitive sport have either run their course or, in some circles, were considered to have been ineffective in the first place. Furthermore, by claiming that the very nature of competition itself can be held responsible for a vast array of behavioral breakdowns, sport's critics may also maintain a genuinely anti-humanist, even Romantic, vision of human efficacy that comes wrapped in a fairly translucent modern language that implies that human beings are generally incapable of navigating the rigors of such passionately contested environments nor should they be expected or perhaps even allowed to do without the proper supervision.

5

Youth Sport in America

Some of the more influential work in the contemporary field of sport criticism exists in the realm of youth sport and the implications for children and their developmental futures. The prevailing attitude that sport and proper child development are inextricably allied has long operated, and often efficiently, within the framework of American culture, but thus far attempts to display a causal link have yet to manifest beyond the anecdotal, which leaves the debate wide open and subject to a great deal of free interpretation on all sides of the issue.

In the traditional interpretation, this coupling remains tied to the accepted wisdom that if governed properly, sport can serve as an effective deterrent to misconduct and a legitimate partner in the quest to shape youth behavior and future development, but what constitutes proper governance often remains in doubt. Emerging from less traditional circles, however, is a much more muted appraisal of competitive sport as an agent for character building as expressed in the traditional ideal, exposing it rather as anathema to progress while ranking it an anachronistic feature of an ever-changing social landscape. In this analysis, many are quick to point fingers at transgressions and transgressors, but what most hold in common is that when it comes to youth and their involvement in sport, something is amiss and something must be done to correct it. As Miracle and Rees have posed it in their seminal work on youth sport in America, sport's supposed effect on character and moral development may not be based on fact but perhaps on a spurious mix of tradition and nationalist sentiment, a coupling that appears to be remarkably resilient and seemingly resistant to even the heightened criticism of American sport today.[1]

In a climate of increasing dismay and distrust concerning such traditional institutions as sport, the evidence suggests that the grave misgivings of professionals regarding the presence of sport in children's lives have trickled down into the popular world and are evident in an overall discussion of the way that sport is governed today. Thus, the supposition that sport has become antithetical to the development of healthy young individuals as expressed in academic circles has filtered into the popular settings, and the result has been a predictable yet methodical reevaluation of the nature of competitive sport.

This chapter will consist of an exploration of this discussion of youth sport in America today resulting from changes in the social landscape relative to the overall discourse surrounding youth and sport and their respective places in contemporary American society. Additionally, I will attempt to underscore this more modern discussion of the role that sport plays in children's lives through a corresponding examination of the emergent attitudes about modern child-rearing in general while looking at ways in which these discussions as a whole seem poised to align competition with latent forms of physical and emotional abuse as outlined in the more contemporary literature.

Childhood and the Nature of Childrearing Today

Babies are not, he argued (against the prevailing wisdom of the times), little savages who must be broken to adult schedules as quickly as possible. Don't rush them, he urged; cherish them.[2]

Children won't wait for us to solve the world's problems before they grow up. While we debate solutions, they're learning. While we sit in meetings, they're experiencing life, hoping that we find a way to help them; hoping that we make their world safe; hoping that they will be loved today.[3]

Though statistical analyses of the end of the twentieth century and the start of the twenty-first bear out that children are being raised in environments safer and more favorable in their conditions than at any other time in modern history, parenting and childrearing in America have never seemed more problematic or unstable.[4] While on the one hand children seem to be growing up more quickly than ever before, the speed with which the maturation process manifests itself has left many alarmed and at a loss as to what this suggests and how this bodes for the future. Under these inauspicious conditions, adults are finding it increasingly difficult to accept the contemporary nature of childhood, and, as a result, American society wrestles with the nuances of parenting and childrearing mired in what some have described in terms of a seemingly endless torrent of ambiguity and fear comparable to other modern societal trends.[5] As one critic defines it, when it comes to the matter of children in modern America, apprehension and panic supersede most other components of the discussion.[6]

Modern society seems haunted by expectations both of and for its children. These concerns range from thoughts that children today will grow up without liberties and lacking in highly desirable life-affirming experiences, or that they will be defenseless victims unable to protect themselves from harm and perhaps a slew of unforeseen aggressors once out of parental reach. Regardless, what seems to mark common ground in this discussion is that these concerns are perceived as legitimate and that the evidence for these claims is considered by many to be both lucid and irrefutable given the climate of contemporary social commentary. As Füredi notes:

> During the past twenty years, concern with the safety of children has become a constant subject of discussion. Children are portrayed as permanently at risk from danger. Even a relatively balanced account of "children at risk" regards childhood as a "uniquely dangerous time of life." In Britain and the USA, concern for the security of children has led to a major reorganization of the childhood experience.[7]

And as if to reaffirm this particular stand, culture critic Carrie Loranger Gaska, in an article displaying the latest in high-tech parenting tools, acknowledges:

> One of the main facets of parenting has always been safety, and we live in a world where it's a top concern. Take it down the parental fear meter to everyday safety issues: latchkey kids alone for a few hours before parents get home, toddlers wandering off in the mall, trashy television, teens out with friends on Saturday night, safety on the internet.[8]

In contrast to a general concern for children and their safety, there is also considerable fear of children that presents another principal theme in modern discourse. Sensational tales of disobedient teens operating in mobs and presumably spurred on by countless forays into drug and alcohol use are thought to be at the root of crime, both petty and violent. Heinous acts, such as what was once conceived to be a rash of school shootings that reached its zenith with the 1999 Columbine shootings, have led many Americans to perceive childhood as an inescapably dangerous time while they search within themselves to uncover their personal failures and responsibilities for what seems to mark a dramatic turn of events.[9] What becomes increasingly obvious is that regardless of political or social orientation, twenty-first century American parents are more likely to agree that childhood has somehow assumed a different, more precarious, character than in previous times in America's history, with the standard bearer of difference being the debate surrounding parenting skills, an argument that develops between those who advocate a firm and resolute approach to childrearing, sometimes known as "tough love," an approach that harkens back to pre–World War II childrearing methodologies, versus those who seek to instill within the home environment the sort of nurturing and warmth that can be best described in the language of 1960s era countercultural rhetoric.[10] Notably missing from this debate, however, is what noted parenting critic John Rosemond points to as a rational middle-ground inspired approach, one that seeks to bridge the chasm between overzealous discipline, which has lost a good portion of its audience due in part to a rash of child abuse fears, and the accepted wisdom of love, nurturing, and self-esteem that seem to spark Baby Boom era parents who were themselves among the first to be brought up in an atmosphere that encouraged individuality among children and sought to replace traditional notions of child discipline with the more humanist-inspired approach.[11] Indeed, modern parents often seem wedged between the old ways and the new, which may account for the morass of confusion that exists in many sectors of the population.

The uncertainty that manifests when regarding the nature of modern childhood emanates from the overall assumption that parenting, once thought to exist in a sort of grand, almost noble light, has come under intense scrutiny, seemingly from the dawning of the age of Dr. Spock, but this hardly serves to illustrate the depth of the changes that have come to dominate this discussion in the new century. A prevailing sentiment seems to be that while children may be in need of stricter guidelines, presumably to shield them from an increasingly chaotic culture, often described in terms of its toxicity,[12] the adults in charge are generally (and seemingly genuinely) presumed to be ill-suited to the task and are themselves in need of some sort of supervision, a condition that many contend marks a notable degree of anxiety and bewilderment when it comes to knowing what's best for one's children.[13] Thus, what had once been a discussion surrounding the question of how best to raise a child has been transformed into a startling debate as to whether or not children can be raised properly at all in an increasingly untenable environment and furthered by an even more alarming exchange that ponders the question of how long society will have to endure such purportedly shoddy childrearing practices and at what cost.[14]

The idea that society has arrived at a point in time that it has come under siege by recalcitrant youth raised by ineffective parents, be it due to the pressures of modern childrearing or the climate of apprehension and distrust engendered by an ostensible fear of marauding teens and a lapse in the nation's overall moral posture, has become widespread and indicative of an unstable if not confused cultural climate. In that spirit, the modern child is portrayed as falling further and further behind emotionally, spiritually, academically, and even physically. In an age of Ritalin, Adderol, and widespread use of antidepressants, increasing scrutiny of and by public and private social service organizations, and a surge in suspicions regarding the potential for abuse, children are routinely conceived of as being at-risk while their parents have become subject to a heightened degree of scorn, skepticism, and even ridicule. As one critic has framed it, "Many human moral systems and discipline strategies are in flux, religion holds less sway, extended families in disarray, nuclear families are broken, schools are overwhelmed."[15]

As expressed herein, the so-called crisis in childhood and childrearing extends across a wide spectrum and is sullied by both doubt and cynicism. And yet, these tell-tale images, popular and effective as they have become, are anything but conclusive and have raised concern among those who refuse to indict modern parenting on what often appears to some as knee-jerk responses. Males, for instance, refers to the tendency toward "wild exaggeration and just making things up,"[16] while Glassner claims that the blanket notion that children today are more at-risk than ever before has been exacerbated less by empirical evidence and more so by media-induced overstatement. He contends:

> The misbelief that every child is in imminent risk of becoming a victim has as its corollary a still darker delusion: *Any kid might become a victimizer* (his italics). Beneath such headlines as "Life Means Nothing," "Wild in the Streets," and "Superpredators Arrive," the nation's news media have relayed tale upon blood-soaked tale of twelve- and fourteen-year-olds pumping bullets into toddlers, retirees, parents, and one another. Armed with quotes from experts who assert, often in so many words, "everyone's kids are at risk," journalists stress that violent kids live not just in the South Bronx or South Central L.A. but in safe-seeming suburbs and small towns.[17]

Füredi, on the other hand, while unconvinced that the media alone is to blame, considers that if there is a failure in modern parenting, it coincides with a breakdown of what he deems adult solidarity, which, he argues, is engendered by high level intervention and often leads to adults regarding one another as adversaries rather than allies, exacerbating the creeping tensions that already exist in modern communities.[18]

With parenting so much on the minds of professional experts, lay critics, and parents themselves, the ambiguity and the discontent regarding modern childrearing practices seem far from resolved. What is not in dispute, however, is that like so many other features of the modern world, a problem is assumed to exist, and it is believed that something has to be done to correct it. As child psychologist/advocate John Breeding reminds in his admonishment to parents, it is the lack of proper parenting that is thought to be at the root of contemporary child advocacy, noting that "[c]hildren are born with an expectation that caring adults will respond to their needs in a good, loving and thoughtful way. Please do not allow this trust to be violated!"[19]

A survey of modern parenting books found in libraries or bookstores underscores this trend and reveals considerable anxiety on matters relating to children and childrearing today. Titles such as *Good Kids, Bad Behavior*,[20] *Smart Parents, Safe Kids*,[21] *Don't Be Afraid of Discipline*,[22] *Good Parents for Hard Times*,[23] and the portentous sounding *Raising Good Kids in Tough Times*[24] are noteworthy for their provocative language alone, but beyond their attention-grabbing titles, they all seem to point to the notion that contemporary parenting exists in a state of muddled confusion. Coupled with televised and written reports of turmoil in the schools and in the streets, parenting in America seems comparable to the most hazardous of modern functions. As one convinced expert warns:

> Times are tough for raising kids. Parents of every generation feel that way, but parents in the nineties have had special problems and the problems are likely to continue in the future. Dangerous examples and attitudes that tempt children are everywhere. Along with the ever-present power of peer influence, we have the media — TV, talk shows, movies, music, videos, and the internet. Parent influence is also challenged and shared with teachers, soccer coaches, scout leaders, gymnastic and music instructors — all vying for family time.[25]

Kay Hymowitz, a senior fellow at the decidedly conservative Manhattan Institute, is convinced that modern fears are directly linked to ineffective parenting brought about by modern parenting schemes as espoused primarily by post–World War II baby boomers heavily influenced by 1960s era countercultural rhetoric. She contends that at the root of social pathology in America's young is the modern climate of parental over-permissiveness, echoing the concerns of similarly minded adults, more traditional-minded professional educators, and political conservatives.

In the ominously titled "Parenting: The Lost Art,"[26] Hymowitz implicates by design the sorts of contemporary childrearing initiatives that she perceives exacerbate increasingly anomic behavior in America's young. She maintains that modern parents, often hamstrung by popular sentiment and a maze of legal hurdles, are not being guided by rational and structured tactics but by an overemphasis on the emotional well-being of both their children and their families as a whole. She restates growing concerns that modern families are being negligent in their responsibilities to provide basic needs to their children along with behavioral guidelines that might instill both limits and civility in school-aged children, primarily in the name of spearheading self-enhancement initiatives such as building self-esteem and placating ego development, modern constructs that she argues have left the American home virtually devoid of leadership.[27]

Hymowitz poses the tenor of the modern American household as a sort of collegial dormitory setting in which a more tolerant democratic spirit exists at the expense of invaluable life lessons. Obviously unmoved by what she deems liberal childrearing practices, she writes:

> As their children gobble down their own microwaved dinners, then go on to watch their own televisions or surf the Internet on their own computers in wired bedrooms where they set their own bedtimes, these parents and their children seem more like housemates and friends than experienced adults guiding and shaping the young. Such parent-peers may be warm companions and in the short run effective advocates for their children, but they remain deeply uncertain about how to teach them to lead meaningful lives.[28]

By her estimation, it is this climate of permissiveness coupled with an omnipresent breach of decorum emanating from modern media outlets that has fostered an explosion of disrespect and disrepute in America's young, leading her to question the effectiveness of the modern parent while drumming up support for the notion that children are out of control and lack even the most basic needs in terms of adult supervision. By citing a list of grievances ranging from parents hosting co-ed sleepovers to students attending school dressed in lavish and risqué attire, Hymowitz has touched upon yet another pervasive theme in the discussion of modern parenting: It is the children — not the adults— who may actually be in charge of the American home, and given the contemporary climate, the adults may be powerless to intervene anytime soon, a notion bandied about by other critics who fear a further erosion of the traditional American family structure.[29] As one concerned parent posed it in a letter to the editor of a local newspaper, "children rule the roost"[30] while "parents are hostages in their own homes."[31]

While some voices in dissent attempt to steer the course of what often appears as contemporary paranoia, when it comes to childrearing today most parents are generally afforded little more than the nightmarish scenarios as expressed in the works of concerned advocates and major media outlets rather than the more learned and contemplative breakthroughs. Attempting to accentuate this point, Rosemond acknowledges:

> Raising children is not fundamentally difficult, but the "experts" made it sound difficult, and we made the mistake of believing them. After all, they have their fancy degrees, didn't they? In fact, their rhetoric often concealed more than it revealed. If you strip away all that fancy, intellectual language, however, you'll discover some basic, timeless truths that serve to make childrearing quite simple. The problem with these truths is that they are neither romantic or sentimental. They are realistic, pragmatic, and hard-headed. For example: The Ultimate Purpose of Parenting is to help our children out of our lives.[32]

That parenting has become a much more pronounced balancing act is an increasingly common concern today and is reflected quite readily in the literature and often expanded to corroborate a strong sense of uneasiness within the relationship between children and adults in a wide range of social environments. In the United States, this would include longstanding suspicions and contemporary analyses that regard a wide range of cultural institutions that rely on the coalescence of young and old as contributing factors to the increasingly ubiquitous discussion of children as being inherently at-risk due in part to a combination of ineffective adult governance and participation in mainstream childhood activities that lack the structure or the values that might deflect the sorts of behaviors called into question today. Among the many features of the modern world currently undergoing reevaluation in this area is the venerable institution of youth sport, whose criticism seems directed predominantly at the adults who govern it.

The Nature of Kids' Sports

[Sport] can be a powerful tool for the general instruction of youth. [It] can be used to teach a great number of desirable things: how to master skills and the satisfaction that follows; good general work habits and cooperation; how to break down racial and class prejudices; how to build respect for and the responsibility toward other people.[33]

Watching the crazy culture of kids' sports in America today, a cynic might marvel at how the world has changed. The good news is that the cold war is over. The bad news is that the East Germans won.[34]

*A standing gag claims that kid baseball is a very good thing because it
keeps the parents off the street.*[35]

Whether painted with a hypermasculine brush or typified in an unrelenting achievement ethos reminiscent of a nearly obsolete social environment,
youth sport today is increasingly thought of as being inconsistent with the values of a presumably modernizing order. In spite of the dramatic rise in the
popularity of competitive sport nationwide (see figure I.1 in the Introduction),
hastened in part by an explosion in media outlets as well as in other realms of
the popular imagination, the ongoing debates surrounding the changes in sport-
oriented behavior are being waged and continue to address and in some cases
redress the scope of the discussion. This is particularly so when it comes to the
effect that modern sport is thought to have on youth and their overall development amid the backdrop of dramatic changes taking shape within the context of the nation's collective self-image.

The prevailing attitude that competition and proper child development are
inextricably allied has long operated efficiently within the framework of American culture, but thus far attempts to display a causal link have yet to manifest
beyond the anecdotal. This manifestation often leaves the debate wide open
and subject to a great deal of free interpretation along the various sides of the
issue.

To recap previous analyses herein, in the traditional construct, the discussion of competition remains tied to the accepted wisdom that if governed
properly, participation in competitive sport can serve as an effective deterrent
to misconduct and a legitimate partner in the quest to shape youth behavior
and future development, but what constitutes proper governance often remains
in doubt. Emerging from more modern spaces is a murkier appraisal of competitive sport as an agent for character building as expressed in the traditional
ideal. This theme poses competition as anathema to progress while ranking it
an anachronistic feature of an ever-changing social landscape. In this analysis,
critics are quick to point fingers at transgressions and transgressors, but what
ties this particular thread together is that when it comes to youth and their
involvement in sport, something is amiss and something must be done to correct it. As Miracle and Rees have posed it in their seminal work on youth sport
in America entitled *Lessons of the Locker Room*, sport's supposed effect on character and moral development may not be based on fact but perhaps on a spurious mix of tradition and nationalist sentiment, a coupling that appears to be
remarkably resilient and seemingly resistant to even the heightened criticism
inherent to the contemporary discussion. They note:

> Americans' beliefs about sport seemingly require no proof. Certainly if we look for
> scientific evidence to support popular, cherished beliefs about sport, we shall be
> disappointed. Studies purporting to demonstrate proof for the sport myth either
> have examined small, special populations or they have used flawed methodologies.

No studies capable of withstanding rigorous scientific scrutiny offer much support for any tenets of the myth. If the sport myth is to be supported with convincing scientific evidence, the research has yet to be done.[36]

In a climate of increasing dismay that often intersects concerns regarding similar such traditional institutions, the evidence suggests that the grave misgivings regarding the presence of athletic competition in children's lives have trickled down into the popular world and are evident in an overall discussion of the way that sport is governed. The notion that competition has become, or in this particular construct, has always been, antithetical to healthy and positively developed individuals has filtered into the popular settings, and the result has been a predictable yet methodical reevaluation of youth sport.

By the end of the twentieth century on into the first decade of the twenty-first, the extraordinary increase in American youth sport participation, (see figure 5.1), which Fred Engh, the director of The National Alliance for Youth Sports (NAYS), places at well above twenty million,[37] corresponds to changes in the realm of youth development taking shape in the aftermath of World War II when the post-war generation of so-called baby boomers received more widespread attention and focus than any other generation in America's relatively

Figure 5.1. US Youth Sport Participation, 2002

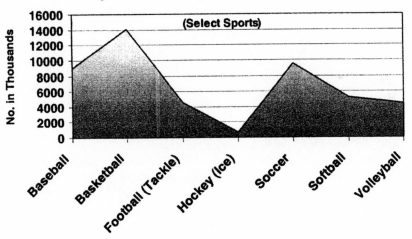

This breakdown offers a glimpse of the types of sports that youth participants gravitate (or are pushed) toward. Of particular interest is how far football, arguably America's most popular sport, lags behind not just baseball/softball and basketball but soccer, which often has little fanfare beyond youth participation.[38]

brief history. Their nurturing and development were of primary importance, Cold War fears notwithstanding, and in many ways the emergent breed of post-war parents took the notion of childrearing to heart much more significantly than had the previous generations. Toward this end, they actively sought a variety of avenues for their children to explore in the hopes of providing them with the most rewarding and successful upbringing possible.[39]

That avenues for youth sport participation were already in existence prior to the war years has already been chronicled elsewhere in this work, but as respected sport sociologist Jay Coakley of the University of Colorado at Colorado Springs notes, the boom in post-war youth sport was driven in part by a combination of creative funding schemes and the ideological carryovers relative to sport and character building assessments already in place in the nation's consciousness.[40] Coakley notes that though "[f]athers became coaches,"[41] and "[m]others became chauffeurs and short-order cooks,"[42] this is less a reflection of traditional gender roles than it is a glimpse of the rationalized organizational principles inherent to the changes within family dynamics based on the reaffirmation of the importance of athletics and athleticism in the lives of young men and later in young women. Still, the concern that youth sport was becoming too widespread and subsequently too competitive is also rooted in that expansionist arena. American novelist James Michener, for example, a noted sports enthusiast who chronicled America's growing obsession with sport both in terms of participation and spectatorship, notes in his work *Sports in America* that by the 1970s, the sorts of drama perceived to be commonplace in today's youth sporting arenas were starting to manifest even in those presumably more reflective times:

> Parents with ordinary common sense began looking with a critical eye at what was happening to their sons. They started going to games and saw the paranoia, the coaches screaming at twelve-year-olds, fathers belting their sons for striking out, little boys ruining their arms trying to pitch like big leaguers before their bone ends hardened. They saw mothers behaving insanely, and boys falling into despair because of an error for which their parents abused them.[43]

Coakley also concludes that the primary differences between post-war youth sport developments and the more substantive changes that mark the aftermath of the post–Cold War era stem in part from increasing privatization that may have exacerbated the tensions developing both within and outside the ranks of youth sport in what he deems to be an emphasis on a "performance principle,"[44] noting:

> The performance principle has become increasingly important in many organized youth sport programs. With some exceptions, programs have put more and more emphasis on progressive skill development and competitive success.[45]

Additionally, what Coakley, as well as other researchers,[46] infer from these arrangements is that by promoting themselves as performance centers, privately owned athletic establishments set aside for youth participation stood poised to reap the benefits of an achievement ethos that was a potential windfall for profiteering through youth sport. This assessment, however valid, nonetheless fails to explain the depth to which the continued importance placed on performance and aptitude is often expressed within the contemporary American competitive philosophy, marking a recurrent theme within the many criticisms of youth sports today.

The Perception of Abuse

Many reasons could be given to explain this increased interest of parents [in youth sport during the 1960's], but three major causes were believed to be the increasing awareness of the athlete as a viable professional endeavor, overly competitive mothers and fathers, and parents' desire of "sure victory" for their children.[47]

After a game adults ask questions like, "Who won? Who scored?" Kids ask questions like, "Who was there? How were the snacks?"[48]

Bearing the brunt of these sorts of concerns as well as the lion's share of the responsibility for what had been and is now taking shape in contemporary youth sport are those who have historically served as the keepers of the nation's sporting heritage—committed adults, most of whom serve in the capacity of volunteers. This ideal alone marks a radically different view of American sport's traditional image. Whereas previous generations sought to involve their children in competitive sport for a host of reasons ranging from psychosocial concerns to issues pertaining to physical fitness and sheer enjoyment, modern critics, and even some proponents of traditional sport motifs, are finding it increasingly difficult to endorse competition for youth participants without stated caveats and stipulations well beyond the established traditional boundaries, though the numbers of participants continue to grow in proportion to the national population. As sport historian Allen Guttmann was to note in the late 1980s:

> The bill of indictment against adult-organized children's sports is lengthy. Empirical studies have shown that children enter Little League with a preference for the pleasures of participation — or, in their words, for having fun rather than for winning, [and] critics of children's leagues have blamed parents for their refusal to accept the children's priorities. The trouble is that fathers and mothers are vicariously involved in their sons' and daughters' performances. Through the psychological mechanisms of identification and projection, middle-aged men and women relive their own childhood triumphs and expunge the memory of their own athletic failure.[49]

Remarkably, this is a strain of thought that resonates just as loudly several decades later but even more so within popular discourse.

More than at any other time in modern American history, youth sport's governors—coaches, league administrators, and even the parents themselves—are looked upon both in an academic and in the more popular context as being the representatives of a debased and perhaps moribund institution whose motives and tendencies are being subjected to increased scrutiny as never before. The work first undertaken during the earlier stages of the twentieth century by professional child care workers and a handful of child psychologists is often sustained in part by laypeople and professional child advocates whose most common position stems from the thought that whenever children and adults find their collective interests thrust together, it is invariably the children who suffer the consequences of these arrangements. As expressed, for example, by the American Academy of Child and Adolescent Psychiatry, a vital source for policy setting among childrearing professionals:

> Sports help children develop physical skills, get exercise, make friends, have fun, learn to play as a member of a team, learn to play fair, and improve self-esteem.... The highly stressful, competitive, "win-at-all-costs" attitude prevalent at colleges and with professional athletes affects the world of children's sports and athletics, creating an unhealthy environment. It is important to remember that the attitudes and behaviors taught to children in sports carry over to adult life.[50]

What fuels this sentiment is a steady proliferation of books, pamphlets, editorials, and even highly structured video-enhanced guides that easily leave one with the impression that competitive youth sport today can no longer measure up as a useful and functioning feature of American culture as long as the current order remains unchallenged. That parental involvement is thought to exacerbate this fall further reflects the extent to which modern standards place more traditional institutions such as competitive sport in a precarious yet indeterminate state. The popular image of the unreasonable and presumably ill-tempered "Little League parents," as they are sometimes termed, have left many with the impression that when it comes to the relationship between youth and sport, adult involvement can be seen as an extension of the perceived crisis in modern parenting.[51] As Lumpkin, Stoll, and Beller reference in their academic treatise on ethics within the contemporary sport paradigm:

> Most youth sport programs are loosely organized and rely on voluntary compliance with a philosophy of fun-filled athletic programs for children and adolescents. Yet the actions of some parents indicate a willingness to do whatever it takes to get and keep their children playing on the best teams.[52]

Thus, the chaotic and often lurid tales associated with the contemporary youth sport environment have become less the extreme expression of the institution and more a sort of litmus test by which youth sport today is evaluated.

The aforementioned Fred Engh, who is among the more influential youth sport critics, charges that youth sport has grown to serve as a reflection of dramatic changes taking shape within America's own distinctive normative outlook. Often expressing his concern and dismay in a language of falling expectations and rising disillusionment, he explains to a *Time* magazine reporter:

> We Americans are a competitive bunch. It was probably inevitable that the striving impulse would sooner or later reshape kids' sports. But the trend has been abetted

by other, less predictable changes in American life: the ascendancy of the automobile, the shrinking of open spaces, the ubiquity of the two-earner family and the pervasive fear of crime. Baby-boomer parents may look back wistfully at their own childhood, when playing sports was a matter of heading to the corner sandlot or the neighborhood park after school for a pick-up game. But the sandlot's been filled in by a four-bedroom Cape Cod with a two-story atrium. To pay for the Cape Cod, Mom and Dad are both working, and with Mom and Dad both working, the kids are signed up for extended-day sessions at school. And by the time extended-day is over, it's dusk. And even if Mom and Dad were home, they'd never let the kids wander alone to the neighborhood park. You never know who they'll find at the neighborhood park.[53]

Engh's *Why Johnny Hates Sports*[54] has become a principal component in popular youth sport criticism since its initial release in 1999. Its theme suggests that lying at the root of what he deems the crisis in youth sport is adult action (or inaction) that has potentially catastrophic consequences. Engh is convinced that youth sport has lost step with the changing times, and that the desperation and confusion inherent to contemporary life exposes such child-centered activities as youth sport to grave peril due in large part to the injudicious mishandling by the adults in charge. By his own estimation, what he claims to be the "bleak picture of organized sports in America today"[55] results from a shift in focus owing to a combustible mix of overzealous parents, ineffective administrators, and win-at-all-cost coaches who have distorted the once vaunted American competitive ethos while reflecting the worst elements of modernity. He addresses popular claims that adults have removed the elements of fun and sportsmanship from athletic competition by virtue of infusing within children's sport the element of vicarious thrill that harkens back to an adult's own perhaps inadequate childhood, and he restates these claims as an impulsive desire to push one's progeny toward excellence or shield one's offspring from either physical or psychological harm. Presenting this thesis before an HBO Sports reporter during what was billed as an exposé on youth sport in America, Engh explains:

> As a parent, I have a tremendous fear today — more than ever — that my child will not be number one. "It's just not going to happen the second time around. I didn't make my little league team, didn't make the high school team." They're living through their kids. "My child is going to make some of that big money." And that's where it crosses the line.[56]

Beyond the perceived boorishness of the parents in question, of whom Engh freely admits mark only a fraction of those who actively participate in their children's activities,[57] Engh nonetheless expresses a fear that the growing instances of misbehavior and misdeeds associated with youth sport parallel other relationships that have been labeled abusive, leaving him to not only question the direction of youth sport today but also to no longer separate actions exacerbated solely by the heat of competition. In his assessment, a vocal parent at a youth sport event walks a thin line similar to that of any other abusive parent in any similar context. Thus, by his estimation, this potentially damaging relationship is marked by increasing unpredictability that is unlikely to cease without dramatic interventions by outside authority. He claims:

> When an adult places unrealistic expectations on a child, such as winning every game, scoring the most points, or playing without making any errors, that is emotional abuse. While this type of abuse is often more subtle than the others, it is equally devastating. When emotional abuse is delivered during growth periods, the expectations and the standards may haunt the children for a lifetime. These are the ones who are going to be chronically unhappy because they never did quite enough. Failure will dominate their existence and devastate their spirits.[58]

Openly embittered by his assessments, Engh nonetheless demonstrates a remarkable sensitivity to the situation as it pertains to the so-called abusive parent in question:

> It's really no big mystery why so many parents lose perspective while watching their children participate. Athletic competition places their children in a vulnerable position, and the natural impulse is to try and control things, to insure that nothing bad happens. This is an extremely difficult position to be in, wanting to control something — the competition — that by its very nature is uncontrollable. However, this is what happens when the impulse of the love toward their children becomes transformed into the types of irrational behaviors discussed.[59]

Or as a similarly concerned writer/mother acknowledges regarding her own experiences in the youth sport environment:

> I tend to scoff at parents who get overly invested in their children's athletic endeavors, assuming these armchair quarterbacks and benchwarming first base coaches are attempting to relive real or imagined glory days through their offspring. Yet even I, who claim that my football-playing brothers got all the competitive genes while I got the do-gooder ones, have found myself caught up in this parent trap. I sometime struggle to detach my self-image as a parent from my child's prowess on the field.[60]

What these commentators are reacting to is an increasingly modernized notion that rather than serving as an aid in a child's overall developmental processes, sport participation, as overseen by ineffective adults armed with ill-conceived strategies, has demonstrated the potential to negatively impact child development. As youth sport researcher Marty Ewing of Michigan State University's Youth Sport Institute reminds:

> The learning of social competence is continuous as we expand our social arena and learn about different cultures [and] in addition to the development of social competence, sport participation can help youth develop other forms of self-competence. Paramount among these self-competencies is self-esteem.[61]

On this point, we can also surmise that because youth sport has eschewed its more traditional ideological promise as established by previous generations of youth sport advocates, sport's efficacy should be waning considerably under the weight of such accusations. Still, while some continue to cling to the more conventional belief that competitive sport can be productive in the most traditional sense, assuming proper governance and such, disenchantment among a range of commentators, increasingly supported by the general population, serves to remind that American society is far removed from such a time when sport and proper child development were inextricably linked. As nationally syndicated columnist Shepherd Smith notes, "We have to stop rationalizing this stuff away, convincing ourselves that there's nothing terribly wrong with our approach to children's sports."[62]

With incompetent adults perceived to be at the helm, youth sport is thought to represent the antithesis of its once valued place in American culture. Still, while critics debate the particulars of an increasingly ill-conceived sporting ethos and contemplate reforms that may stem the flow of perceived negative outcomes, few academics or laypeople openly support a comprehensive dismantling of the competitive athletic frame itself. The effect of the criticism has certainly stimulated a maelstrom of discussion with regards to what can be done to redefine youth sport's place within the culture, the discussion of which demonstrates notable parallels to much older debates, though in a decidedly different context. But if there has been a persistent cord throughout the discussion of youth sport in America, the matter of shaping behavior, whether the focus is on character building, teaching patriotism, or hastening assimilation, continues to cut across a wide range of agendas, connecting, among other features, nineteenth century Victorian interests to today's more contemporary ideologies. For example, in his assessment of similar shifts taking shape within the British sport model, British football researcher Carlton Brick, writing in a popular context, notes themes that reflect a more reactionary approach within the debate regarding youth and competition:

> In the late twentieth century, the new social missionaries are revamping football in their own image. The mission of the government's task force is to transform stadiums into arenas of social and moral education.... Football today is less of a sport and more like a Sunday school [or] a morality play for the millennium; and in this respect, it is going back to its roots in the last century.[62]

And as if to accentuate Brick's point, Engh weighs in with his own thoughts surrounding today's fear of ill-conceived and certainly ill-advised youth sport with what appears to be a very Victorian-sounding position:

> I believe that competition, instilled with the values of fair play, sportsmanship, and ethics, can help build character traits in young people that will last a lifetime. These are the traits we admire in the people with whom we want to work, play, and spend quality time. People with a competitive spirit are usually the leaders in every aspect of our society. So competition can be a positive thing, but if adults do not keep it in perspective, they can make children miserable and drive them away from sports.[64]

Variance within the
Modern Youth Sport Environment

Today, most adults believe that if their children are involved in organized sports, then they must be at play. However, that might not be the case. With organized sports, we have simply taken play, put it into an organized form, and added factors like skill development and discipline. But in doing so, we have changed the fundamental nature of play; now it is competition.[65]

The primary importance of fun — of sport pursued for sheer exhilaration — is a credo repeated, and often honored, by coaches, kids, and parents. At the same time, though, the pushy parent, red-faced and screaming from the sidelines or bleachers at a hapless preteen fumbling on the field, has become an American archetype and a symbol of the unmeasured cost of kids' sports.[66]

American youth sport has come under attack and been reprimanded both publicly and privately for its foibles while at the same time hastening its own radical reevaluation through the efforts of an exceedingly controversial, yet convincing, lobby that has found itself at the forefront of these debates. By presenting itself as the caretakers and moral arbiters of youth development through sport, this contemporary wave of what had once been labeled *boy workers* (see chapter two) has insinuated itself within the presumed inviolate spaces where American youth sport once thrived. As urban historian Mark Rosentraub of Cleveland State University has observed, "in recent years we have become all too keenly aware of some of the negative psychological factors that sport can impart,"[67] a point often echoed throughout the modern discussion and one that also seems to imply that preceding generations may not have understood the full scope of the psychosocial ramifications of building such an pervasive youth sport apparatus.

Modern depictions of and expectations for youth sport are thought to be burdened with such contradictions that one can no longer simply acknowledge the contemporary American sporting landscape without conjuring associative images of disorder, pretense, and other objectionable behaviors, matters that sport psychologist Daniel Gould first began to notice in the early 1980s:

> ... mere participation in youth sports does not guarantee positive psychological effects on the children. Rather, participation is viewed as a double-edged sword that may have either positive or negative effects on the child. The outcome depends on who wield the sword — the parents, adult leaders, and coaches supervising young athletes.[68]

In this sense, the presence of adults in the youth sporting environment has been perceived as deleterious rather than constructive. Thus, whereas sport may have been once hailed as the very definition of Americana in terms of its perceived value in buttressing and strengthening family relations, this paradigmatic shift has redirected matters into a decidedly contradictory course.

Indeed, even once-cherished images such as those captured in the paintings of Norman Rockwell, whose earliest work contained myriad images of middle-class American boys and their fathers amid various sport-related backdrops, and in Gilbert Patton's Frank Merriwell books, which were the American equivalent of Thomas Hughes' remarkably successful yet decidedly British *Tom Brown's Schooldays*, have been found lacking in the more recent assessment.[69] As child sport psychologist Darrell J. Burnett, an increasingly dynamic and respected contributor to such discussions, reminds, "Adults remove the fun of childhood activities."[70] Or as Vernon Seefeldt of Michigan State University's Youth Sport Institute muses, "Proponents contend that any organizational event involving children in which the activity is largely conducted by adults who serve as volunteers is likely to have some problems,"[71] Both sentiments share notable thematic unity with other decidedly modern constructs, and while other critics at times have pondered these themes prior to this modern departure, it is the expansion of this discussion, one that often connects sport to other debates, that allows this transformation to lodge itself along the forefront of contemporary criticism.

Though many youth sport critics maintain vestiges of the conventional belief that sport can and should be governed in such a way as to help promote a comprehensive and wholesome maturation process, the overall skepticism relative to more modern discussions often shows this particular thread to be fraught with uncertainty.[72] For instance, Gould contends that irrespective of the older claims concerning competition and its relationship to childrearing, competitive sport can no longer be considered a given when it comes to matters of character development in youth.[73] Moreover, others maintain that given the historical character of competition itself, the line that once separated national myth from a perhaps unsympathetic reality has been forever breeched, rendering the national embrace of sport little more than groundless folly. As Rosentraub assesses it:

> The romanticized view that many people have of sports has two primary threads. First, people are fond of telling one another that there are a number of positive values that can be taught (or taught more easily) only through sports. These values include the merits and payoffs from hard work and practice; the importance of leadership; the meaning and benefits of team efforts to accomplish or reach a group's goal; and the value of individual sacrifice for group achievement. If these worthy attributes are not sufficient to create a sympathetic environment in which to discuss a sports subsidy, the second thread of the romanticized ideal of sports can be touted: Sports provide a complete set of activities in which parents and children can play together. As a result, for many people a number of their memories of parents and childhood are intertwined with these shared activities. Whether it is attending a game together, playing games together, or watching other family members play in their games, family life is not only interwoven with many dimensions of sports but is at least partially defined by sports.
>
> To be sure, in recent years we have become all too keenly aware of some of the negative psychological factors that sports can impart. Many male athletes, exposed

to levels of violence that are integral parts of certain sports, have had little difficulty finding the appropriate boundaries for this physical violence in their lives. From excessive drug abuse to rape and spousal abuse to inappropriate risk-taking, promiscuity, and gambling, there is ample evidence that sports have contributed to several of society's pathologies.[74]

On this point, modern commentary, popular or otherwise, is more likely to point toward the incongruity of the once sport-friendly consensus that had long since developed in American culture, contending, among other things, that more traditional assessments of sport can at best be linked to cluttered, even agenda-based analyses. These more recent and dramatic shifts in the discussion further support the appearance of an organized resistance aimed at what many feel is a markedly divisive institution that is often regarded, rightly or wrongly, as a reinforcer of the traditional order that continues to obstruct social transformation while being directed by an irresolute and indifferent populace. As oft-cited University of California at Los Angeles (UCLA) sport psychologist Tara Scanlon laments in a once-heralded *Sports Illustrated* exposé on youth sport:

> Kids [today] see athletes threatening each other and intentionally trying to cause injuries, virtually bragging about cheating and not getting caught. Coaches slug players, intimidate officials, throw chairs, lie about recruiting. The main message is that just about any means you can use is justified by the end of winning. Once sport encouraged ethical behavior, what used to be called sportsmanship. In many instances it is now teaching violence, greed, selfishness, disrespect for others.[75]

In many such accounts, today's discussion of youth sport pits adult misbehavior against what remains of childhood innocence, suggesting that in today's frenetic sport environment, once cherished ideals of fun, play, and managed competitiveness are being thwarted by overzealous and overly involved adults unable to control their competitive urges or contain their lust for athletic excellence and the prestige it offers, all at the expense of their own children. Indeed, one of the chief criticisms of contemporary youth sport is that its structure is often thought to be too reflective of work and workplace productivity that serves to sacrifice the internal dynamic of play and enjoyment, which critics contend is what is supposed to draw youth toward participation in the first place. Those who assume this position maintain that youth sport's overseers discourage fun by overemphasizing achievement, a matter that has fallen dramatically out of favor in the contemporary imagination and is subject to a considerable degree of public scrutiny, especially as commentators delve more deeply into matters relating to scarred psyches and the psychological cost of children participating in events geared toward zero-sum outcomes.[76] As science critic Bryant Furlow challenges in the monthly *New Science*:

> Organized sports are too structured to emulate spontaneous play, and there's often so much pressure involved that [such activities] aren't even fun. With schooling

beginning earlier and becoming increasingly exam-oriented, play is likely to get even less of a look-in. We have basically become a playless society.[77]

It is also apparent that few commentators on either side of the youth sport debate reference the leisure and enjoyment components of sport participation as addressed above. Critics seem more comfortable when reflecting upon concerns such as psychological as well as physical risk, poor socialization schemes, the unhealthy aspects of an overdeveloped sense of hypercompetitiveness, and even the maintenance of traditional social inequality, anxieties drawn out from sport participation that are often mirrored in popular thought and expressed through the social science literature. As highly respected sport sociologist George Sage was to note:

> ... organized sport has nothing to do with playfulness—fun, joy, self-satisfaction — but is, instead, a social agent for the deliberate socialization of people into the prevailing social structure.[78]

Certainly this statement would hold true for schemes relating to youth sport as much today as it would have in previous generations. Still, as one seemingly beguiled observer comments, sport may retain its play motif for children in spite of the best efforts of adults who may work to degrade this impulse:

> Youth sport becomes so regimented and work-like that distinctly identifiable elements of "play" are noted to appear spontaneously—and [in] contrast to the game itself, e.g., throwing dirt, playing with water balloons, chasing one another, playing soccer with a rock in the dugout, tossing hats in the air on a windy day....[79]

These claims are often made in the face of some fairly overt reminders to the contrary. For example, Coakley notes:

> When talking to children about their sport involvement and watching them play informal sports, it is clear that they are not interested in the socialization implications of their activities. In fact, character building is irrelevant to their games. However, one explanation for why action, involvement, close scores, and friendships are so important in children's informal sports is that children are basically interested in expressing themselves, learning new things about their own capabilities, and being recognized for demonstrating skills. They set up their own sports so that these things don't happen very frequently.[80]

Or as the narrator of an aforementioned HBO Sports segment on youth sport poses it:

> It's the parents who put up the scoreboards, the all-star team, the [league] standings, the championships. You ask the kids if they want that: "nah!" What they want is to have fun.[81]

It is also interesting to note that in the midst of this debate regarding fun and leisure and an adult's propensity to degrade these elements of youth sport, Steven Overman, a professor in the Department of Health, Physical Education, and Recreation at Jackson (Mississippi) State University and author of *The Influence of the Protestant Ethic on Sport and Recreation*, seems less apprehensive with the notions of a sporting experience caught between the traditional and the modern construct and places it rather in the context of American values themselves. He maintains that sport, and for that matter most of what amounts to American culture in general, remains cloaked in the time-honored convention of the uniquely American work ethic. Reminding that American culture has always celebrated success conceptually while hailing upward mobility among its people, Overman argues that the sporting milieu has long since been shaped to serve as a ready-made laboratory for both children and adults to learn the most salient principles of American life.[82] Furthermore, he places the achievement ethic and the continued presence of structure in youth sport so caught up in controversy today in the context of that particular model:

> The national emphasis on youth sport programs is a testament to Americans' discomfort with play. Adults have interdicted children's free play in favor of a prophylactic of organized sport and recreation. In the final reckoning, play has been deemed too important to leave to children.[83]

Nonetheless, the stage has been set for assigning the responsibility for what has thought to have occurred within the tradition of youth sport to the adults who have failed to acknowledge either the changing expectations surrounding youth sport participation or the emergent orthodoxy poised to oversee these changes.

Coaching and Winning in the Contemporary Climate

Every child in whom we instill these [win-at-all-cost] attitudes is one more person we're sending out into the world who will contribute to the moral decay of our society. We must not allow that to happen.[84]

Ideally, all coaches should be required to take courses in interpersonal relations, child development, and human values.[85]

What do you call it when you almost win? Oh yeah — losing![86]

The perception of pathology that frequently results from modern discussions of the nature of competitive sport oftentime falls squarely upon the shoulders of sport's on-field authority or coach. In contrast to the once fêted prototype of the forceful, no-nonsense, authoritarian patriarch that predominated the American consciousness, and saddled with the burden of preserving experiential splendor as well as the preservation of sport for future generations, the modern coach is no longer merely an uncompromising military-type vociferously barking out instructions to his athletes in the pursuit of victory. To the contrary, he, or she, as is increasingly the case, is obliged to weigh matters of on-field competency with off-field expectations as never before. As California State University at Los Angeles kinesiologist Daniel Frankl admonishes, "Coaches that angrily shout criticism from the sidelines are not appreciated or liked as are relaxed, supportive, knowledgeable coaches who emphasize the improvement and learning of new skills."[87] Or as Kathleen Vail, the associate editor of the *American School Board Journal*, observes:

> The most successful coaches are those who show they care about all their players. Strong-arm tactics often don't produce winning seasons. The players can tell if a coach is using them; some players react to that pressure by quitting the team. Winning and teaching are not mutually exclusive.[88]

On the one hand there is the omnipresence of the Lombardi dictum swirling about the conventional coaching paradigm that in effect mandates the pursuit of excellence while insisting upon a performance ethic. Gradually more in the modern pretext, however, a coach's assumed role, and especially in a more hotly contested youth sport environment, is to serve in an exceedingly more byzantine capacity, one that in effect demands balancing the teaching of modern values with the rigors of extracting athletic performance from participants while presupposing psychic injury in addition to the potential for physical harm.

The modern coach is no longer to be viewed as a competitor in his or her own right, preparing athletes for a stated performance standard on the field of play. Rather, contemporary expressions relative to coaching suggest an amalgam of duties that might include therapist, nurturer, confidant, and even cleric, followed finally by some nod toward field management, but only after the other matters have been suitably tackled. To be sure, many of the more traditional-minded coaches have found this arrangement quite foreign to them, which may account in part for some of the turmoil radiating about contemporary youth sport. For example, writing in the early 1970s, noted sport psychologists Bruce Ogilvie and Thomas Tutko, anticipating then that America was on the verge of great change in its athletic culture, had already begun to identify a clash between old and new ideologies in coaching:

> We find most coaches uncertain and anxious about changes taking place in sport. They have shown an overwhelming positive response to our efforts to bring the tools of psychology into their careers. They're crying for new methods, new information. They know that they are not fully prepared for their tasks.[89]

As they would later conclude:

> Many coaches won't be able to stand the strain. Eventually, the world of sport is going to take the emphasis off winning-at-any-cost. The new direction will be toward the joyous pursuit of [aesthetic] experiences toward wide variety of personality types and values. Inevitably these changes are going to force the least flexible coaches out of the business— perhaps as many as a third of them.[90]

By adding to this mix the more recent societal condemnation of the traditional coaching posture as viewed through the prism of an increasingly suspect competitive ethos, it would seem that for most coaches what occurs on the playing surface is often secondary to what is taking place in the stands and along the periphery of modern society. As University of Northern Colorado's Jerold Strong has noted in the *Journal of Sport Behavior*, an overemphasis on winning and a lack of emphasis on ethics has manifested itself both on the field of play as well as off it, leading him to conclude that the answer lies in the de-emphasizing of product in order to a ensure a positive experience for all participants.[91] But while the search continues outside the field for the proper mix of skill and empathy to take the place of the conventional methodology, the coach on the field is often left to search for his or her own acceptable deportment. Moreover, as psychologists Ronald Smith and Frank Smoll remind, in the more modern context, the role of the coach cannot be underestimated:

> Coaches influence the effects that youth sport participation has on children through the interpersonal behaviors they engage in, the values and attitudes they transmit both verbally and through example, and the goal priorities they establish (for example winning versus equal participation and fun). Coaches not only occupy a central and influential position in the athletic setting but their influence can extend into other areas of the child's life as well.[92]

It has indeed become notably more evident that today's coach is held to a performance standard that seems remarkably foreign when juxtaposed to the conventional coaching pose. While society's collective gaze appears fixed and poised on coaching behavior well beyond matters of wins and losses, except in the more high-profiled environment where these matters still predominate, the coach's role within the youth sport paradigm exists in a state of flux bordering on ambiguity that leaves it exposed to criticism and open to condemnation as never before. This scrutiny often results in myriad restrictions and regulations being implemented in order to serve as a barrier to improper technique. As Engh explains:

> ... youth coaches have the power to turn children off to sports forever, or to make sports a life-long passion. With the proper training, knowledge, and skills, a coach can improve the quality of his children's life [*sic*] immensely and help prepare them for the future. Yet coaches who operate from ignorance can do enormous harm with the same activity. We can't insure that every coach will do what's best for children in every case, but we can adopt policies requiring that every coach has at least been exposed to a good training program before he coaches a child.[93]

The premise that coaches have the power to spread prevailing attitudes regarding conduct while emitting a general transference of cultural ideals through sport is certainly not a new feature of American sport. To be precise, the coach has long been expected to participate in this arrangement, though historically there have been a wide range of difficult challenges posed by these arrangements. As Overman has observed, nineteenth century sport ideals, the diffusion of those ideals, and the coach's role in circulating those ideals were as contradictory then as they often appear in today's discussion:

> [The] noble sounding goals employed to justify sport soon were subordinated to more pragmatic ones. Many athletic coaches showed less interest in sports' poten-

tial to mold character and save the world than in the development of players who could win athletic contests. By the close of the nineteenth century, school officials began to realize that they had an "athletic tiger by the tail," and admonished overly competitive coaches for stressing the goal of "winning at any cost" and for ignoring the character-building goals of sport. Yet, the goal of victory on the athletic fields was consistent with an ethic which equated winning at any endeavor with personal salvation. Thus, the goal of winning carried strong moral overtones in a Protestant ethic society.[94]

The baseline for that commitment to diffusion remained whether or not the coach was capable of winning games and, generally speaking, fit for the assignment itself. The thinking here was that a clearly inferior or otherwise ill-prepared coach would never command the type of respect and authority necessary to hold the interests of young athletes or spectators alike. In the modern vision, by contrast, the matter of winning or losing seems to no longer be a marker of coaching success, at least beyond that of high-profile sport where this principle still manages to cling to the more traditional ideal, and much to the dismay of contemporary youth sport critics. As Frankl laments, "A casual observer of any little league game site will notice the excessive seriousness and tension exhibited by coaches on the sidelines,"[95] a condition to which he and others contend is a nod toward more high-profile competition.

Certainly, the presence of heavy-handed, often irrepressible figures from a bygone era, such as the oft-mentioned Vince Lombardi, or other coaching stalwarts such as Woody Hayes,[96] Frank Kush,[97] or even John J. McGraw,[98] once juxtaposed to today's coaching expectations, are hard to fathom in the modern framework. It is unlikely that any one of these highly regarded coaching figures, whose collective track records suggest on-field success accompanied by reputations for aggression bordering on boorishness, would have survived in the modern athletic environment, though in truth many of these same individuals have managed to retain a certain level of admiration and reverence within the sporting community in spite of their more notorious reputations and in the face of today's rhetoric.[99]

The case of college basketball's Bobby Knight, one of the sport's most respected strategists infamous for his temper, boorish outbursts, and propensity for hard-nosed and aggressive discipline, illustrates this point more clearly. Prior to the 2000–2001 basketball season amid his storied run as coach of the Indiana University Hoosiers and following a series of well-publicized displays aimed primarily at the university's administration and members of the press who had been openly lobbying for his dismissal, Knight was relieved of his duties. Unlike Hayes and Kush, whose careers overlapped the initial period of change, allowing them to retain their distinctly traditional autocratic bearing, Knight found himself in the midst of an untenable situation, though he was able to continue his coaching career — much to the dismay of his detractors — primarily due to his reputation as a winner and as someone who typically runs what is generally referred to as a "clean program."[100] That the university seemed to have been looking for a reason to remove him was commonly noted, but his coaching record all but ensured that he would be a difficult employee to dismiss from a public relations standpoint, a matter that was rehashed for some time following his formal dismissal. Still, and equally telling in this particular case, given the current climate surrounding sport, and moving beyond the boorishness of Knight's often indefensible behavior, it is highly unlikely that a budding Bobby Knight–type coach working his way through the ranks of college basketball but without an established reputation in hand would stand much of a chance of landing a position or even surviving such public scrutiny in spite of his potential for competitive success. In other words, a coach who does not pay the requisite obeisance to modern sensibilities, as Knight most certainly would not, seems unlikely to be able to withstand the scrutiny of an increasingly skeptical and progressively more sensitive public rebuke.[101]

Where this modern construction of acceptable coaching behaviors comes into focus most notably is on the matter of winning and the contemporary fascination with the win-at-all-cost coaching ethic, a component of the so-called hypercompetitive condition. There is certainly a strong surge of condemnation emanating from both popular and academic circles alike that claims the destruction of the competitive ethos can be traced back to adults, and namely the admixture of coaches and parents, who undermine the process as well as the potential for competitive sport to keep pace with modern expectations by misrepresenting competition as a "win or go home" state of affairs. As Ewing observes:

> Most coaches and parents espouse the virtue of fair play until they perceive that the opponent is gaining an advantage or winning unfairly. Parents may even chastise the coach who abides by the rules and does not win, which sends a mixed message to youth about the importance of fair play. Journalists and broadcasters have fallen into the same trap of believing that the only worthy performance was that given by the winning team regardless of whether they abided by the rules or not.[102]

Or as Engh concludes, "when the focus shifts from what's best for the young participants to what's best for others, that's where problems begin."[103]

For Engh, and other popular critics at the forefront of this debate, the effect of placing winning above teaching, self-fulfillment, safety, or even enjoyment places young athletes in a precarious situation. It not only encourages children to adopt similar ideals, but as Engh asserts, lends further evidence of the degeneration of the modern order.[104] In this respect the coach seems the most logical choice to present behavioral models of an affective sort, but it is also apparent that there is an undercurrent of skepticism that such an individual, irreparably torn between the competition at hand and a sense of being duty-bound in order to meet modern expectations, actually exists.

Examples of this sort of treatment can be found in both academic and popular criticism of modern competitiveness. For instance, while commenting on the relationship between coaching and on-field violence, Lumpkin et al. note that a "too-common scenario finds parents and coaches maneuvering and pressuring young athletes, as if they were pawns on a chessboard, to achieve adult satisfaction and status."[105] Marquette University law professor Troy Cross, in turn, writing on behalf of the National Association of Sports Officials (NASO), questions whether or not modern day coaches will ever be made to understand their responsibilities as presented by the emergent focus on coaching decorum. He notes:

> ... coaches watch or read about one attack on a sports official and see that nothing of consequence happens to the perpetrator. As a result, they are less apt to control themselves in a similar situation. After all, they will likely be back coaching in a short period of time, while the official whom they attacked will probably never work another one of their games because assignors and league officials might fear another incident.[106]

Similarly, in her advice to aspiring coaches, Lori Gano-Overway of Michigan State's Youth Sports Institute asserts:

> ... the key to improving the quality of sport experiences for young athletes is to emphasize the totality of the sport experience rather than just playing the game. This concept means structuring a program philosophy for sportsmanship, being prepared to teach moral reasoning when situations occur, and monitoring your own behavioral (verbal and nonverbal) responses to situations.[107]

She further notes that the ramifications of an ill-conceived focus on competitiveness within the sporting milieu has the potential to breed dire consequences while hinting that the effects may be irreversible and potentially devastating:

> An overemphasis on winning in a sport may also cloud perceptions of moral behavior.... [It could be] concluded that an emphasis on winning in organized sport may lead children to become rivalrous in social interactions with other children, which may in turn lead to a decline in helping others. Overemphasis on winning can also lead individuals (athletes and parents alike) to engage in antisocial or delinquent behaviors aimed at trying to gain an advantage to win.[108]

Thus, the emphasis on coaching behavior and the importance placed on the diffusion of contemporary values through the emergent competitive environment suggests that in today's moral vision, one in which all cultural spheres are expected to serve as a sort of preternatural classroom for ethics, the coach serving in the capacity of facilitator becomes a logical extension of the modern ideal.

The Wussification Debate

We are all winners if we leave this event with a new friend and a little more knowledge and experience than we brought with us.[109]

When I step out on the field, it's a war zone out there.[110]

Another challenge facing those who continue to advocate competitive sport as both part of a learning process and a key component of a character building program is the more contemporary notion that suggests that the possibility for psychic scarring negates any perceived benefits derived from athletic participation. Referred to in some popular circles as "the *wussification* of America,"[111] the idea that physical and emotional upheaval are the chief risks inherent to the competitive process have left the youth-sport coupling prone to further criticism in the modern construct on the basis of what are judged to be medical concerns.

Used in arguments more likely to be assumed within popular assessments, the pejorative term *wuss* refers to one for whom mental or physical toughness is unattainable and is used in this context to denote weak and even effeminate children unable to withstand the effects of overly (and overtly) aggressive behavior. The overtures toward identifying a sort of softened youth order are also to be understood in this context and are often weighed against the perceived benefits of competition, including enjoyment and leisure.

Juxtaposed to the spirited, goal-oriented activities formally associated with competitive sport, the image of passive and even reluctant athletes attempting to hurdle the not-so-subtle nuances of athletic competition seems in opposition to the competitive ideal while prohibitively at odds with emergent ones as well. Thus, Tutko and Bruns' assertion that Americans play their games "against the backdrop of an intensely competitive culture"[112] takes on a more meaningful guise once this benchmark of American life is examined more closely, especially in the context of the shadow of male-female orientations so much a part of contemporary sport criticism.

In a popular context, some have addressed this issue in relation to one of America's favorite schoolyard games, dodgeball, which is also known in some circles as murder ball or killer ball or some variation thereof.[113] According to a report in the popular magazine *Time*, some states, including Texas, Massachusetts, Virginia, and Maine, have begun to equate the muted violence associated with "dodging and throwing balls at one another"[114] with the chilling effects of the types of school violence that had occurred in places ranging from Columbine High School in suburban Denver, Colorado, to Santana High School in suburban San Diego, California. Fearing the spread of such aberrant behaviors on the part of a handful of disaffected youth, whose run-ins with school athletes are thought to have accelerated the urge to attack classmates and faculty in many of these situations,[115] advocacy groups have emerged that have encouraged school officials to ban rougher physical displays from physical education curricula in order to mitigate the effects of tension between the less athletic outsiders and the more notoriously indecorous jock/bullies. Also under reconsideration is the convention of playing such contests in less restrictive environments such as recess, moves that in turn have served to generate a rationale for further review of similar such games that skirt the contemporary ideal of peaceful and harmonious activity. As Dr. Neil Williams, a physical education professor at Eastern Connecticut State University, bemoans, "[Dodge ball] allows the stronger kids to pick on and target the weaker kids.... It's like *Lord of the Flies* with adults encouraging it."[116] Or as *Education World* co-editor Ellen Delisio contends:

> The words dodge ball still can cause some adults to shudder, even though it might have been decades since a ball beaned them in a physical education class. Though some adults thrived on the competition in their school physical education classes, others remember the experience as humiliating, with the operative word being last — picked last for a team or coming in last in the mile run.[117]

Still, others are not so readily convinced, taking the position that if the aggressive aims of dodge ball are to be reexamined, then the whole of American sports should be targeted as well. As one apprehensive school administrator in Utah contends, "If we are going to ban dodge ball for aggressiveness, we would have to look at the whole gamut of sports such as football, kickball, and wrestling.[118]

Other critics of this particular shift are even more leery in regards to further attempts at rewriting the rules for physical engagement among children, a standard that some have identified in terms of a "New PE."[119] Whereas proponents of introducing non-competitive games in order to foster an appreciation for life-long fitness among America's increasingly overweight youth are buoyed by such manifest changes in methodology,[120] others contend that these new directions stand to retard both physical and psychological growth in their targeted populations, threatening to create future generations of ill-prepared and ill-defined youth actors. As laconic social critic Matt Labash dismissively tells HBO Sports:

> It seems like we are more and more raising our kids like little veal chops, tenderized little medallions that we need to guard.... We need to sort of plane all the hard edges off of life. We can't let our kids go to school and get hit in the side of the face with a hard red rubber ball.[121]

Thus, in spite of the rhetoric from both sides of this particular dispute, what stands out is the implication that if competition among youth participants cannot exist without conflict amid a firestorm of uncertainty, then the most obvious solution is to continue the trend toward removing the ambiguity from competition before it results in further damage.

Gender analysts are also contributors to this particular debate. Some maintain that because contemporary sport has emerged from within a masculine or even hypermasculine construct, the logical conclusion is that in a world that seeks to discount traditional masculinity on the basis of its divisive and violent tendencies, competition remains at odds with a rejection of such qualities.[122] Therefore, competitive sport in its present form, because it oftentimes requires a degree of aggression, or at the very least self-assuredness, not only skirts modern behavioral norms but openly defies them. In this respect, youth sport can be seen as abusive if not perplexing, especially when children are asked to compete in ways that they have been taught are antithetical to proper comportment. As Canadian sport researcher Varda Burstyn reflects in her acclaimed *The Rites of Men: Manhood, Politics, and the Culture of Sport*:

> The problem ... is that sport [divides] people in ways that are often destructive and antisocial. Sport divides people against themselves. It separates children from children, men from women, men from men, and community from community. Sport models and exacerbates social conflict and encourages antisocial and antidemocratic values. And it does this most centrally through its inflection of gender, particularly its offering of ideal types and behaviours for men.[123]

That sport may be viewed as threatening to stability in individuals as well as in social relations is certainly at odds with many of the emergent orthodoxies. While there is no way to predict the outcomes of athletic competition short of stage-managing the results, sport continues to remain a realistic option for those seeking physical outlets and camaraderie though sport participation for their young, and these participants also seem compelled to require such non-threatening outcomes that echo these sorts of sentiments. The result is often a dialogue concerning competition that begins with discussions of skill acquisition, intrinsic rewards, self-knowledge, and the value of cooperation while concluding with such disparate matters as the impact of peer evaluation and threats to an individual child's esteem that may occur when a child is faced with having to measure up athletically. When combined with more contemporary concerns ranging from conflict- and anger-management to bridging the social divide, reading youth sport as simply a component of a child's overall experience base seems to no longer be a viable alternative. As Scanlon reminds:

> ... the competition process must be placed within the larger socialization process to be adequately understood. Although competition is an important process, it cannot be isolated from the child's greater social context. The role of significant others and competence in other situations must be considered as they influence the positive, negative, or neutral long-term consequences of competition.[124]

On the other hand there is the popular syndicated columnist William Raspberry who counters, "One of the reasons we tout athletics and urge our children to participate is our belief that athletic competition helps prepare them for success in the rest of their lives."[125]

Parental Disturbances in the Youth Sport Environment

[Disturbances at youth sporting events] can happen anywhere. If things are getting out of hand in your ballpark, stand by and keep your eyes open because things like this will happen. They'll come out of nowhere, and they'll come out of nowhere in your town.[126]

Listen to what the kids are telling us. The parents don't know how to behave themselves. We must change the culture. Parents need to listen to their kids. [127]

Some of the most common forms of child abuse take place on athletic fields. [128]

A subplot to the uncertainty surrounding the discussion of youth sport in America is the issue of on- and off-field violence perpetrated primarily by adults in attendance. A panic regarding such incidents, since termed *parental rage*, sometimes *sports rage*, and even *sideline rage*, has left many feeling that as never before the atmosphere surrounding youth sport has become even more untenable and potentially even more dangerous for children, officials, and innocent bystanders alike.[129] As Barry Mano, the founder of the National Association of Sports Officials, implores:

> ... the health of our games is being attacked by a cancer of bad behavior, much of it occurring in full view of our young people who participate in organized sports. We must do something to send a clear signal that such behavior will not be tolerated....[130]

The depth to which the American public has been exposed to such concerns is not to be underestimated. Between 1999 and 2001, no fewer than four national networks devoted entire programming segments to the issue of adult-inspired violence in youth sport environments,[131] and countless local and regional television and radio stations, newspapers, town meetings, informal discussions, and even fictional accounts of such events have followed suit in order to reaffirm the daunting nature of the challenges that lie ahead in terms of adult misconduct in and around youth sport venues. Furthermore, since the mid-1990s there have been countless youth sport advocacy organizations, some of which have emerged as nationally renowned, such as NAYS, that have been founded precisely to organize against those adults whose actions have been deemed unacceptable while they are judged to be inevitable. In no small fashion the cries of indignation once reserved for images of European and South American football rioting have been thrust aside in favor of concerns that what had once seemed impossible in the United States has indeed manifest itself. As noted sport psychologist Daniel Wann asserts in an assessment for the NAYS web site:

> My take is that if you have one person in one million that acts abusively toward a player, coach, spectator or official, then it's a huge problem.... One of anything bad is a huge problem. Let's not forget the fact that most parents are good, but the fact that most people behave appropriately does not allow those that don't to be dismissed.[132]

There is simply no denying that some horrific instances of violence have taken place over the past few years, some examples of which I will list below:

- A man in Reading, Massachusetts, was beaten to death by a rival's father following a disagreement at a youth league hockey game.[133]
- A referee was assaulted by a disgruntled coach in Port St. Lucie, Florida, following the suspension of a youth soccer match that left the referee with numerous facial fractures and lacerations.[134]
- A baseball umpire in Hollywood, Florida, had his jaw broken by a Pony League (14–16 year old) coach following a disputed call.[135]
- Eight members of a 12 to 14 year old youth football team were poisoned in Las Vegas, Nevada, for allegedly picking on the child of the assailant.[136]
- A police officer in Pennsylvania was convicted and sentenced to twenty-three months in jail for bribing a ten year old youth league baseball pitcher with two dollars to purposely throw at the head of another ten year old to whom the officer was not related.[137]
- A dentist in Albuquerque, New Mexico, received two days in jail and mandatory community service hours for allegedly sharpening the face guard on his son's football helmet, an act that resulted in injury to five players and a referee.[138]
- A T-ball coach near Pittsburgh, Pennsylvania, was under investigation for allegedly offering up a $25 bounty for a team member who would injure an autistic teammate in order to keep him from participating in a presumably important game.[139]

Incidents such as these certainly reach beyond the limits and can doubtlessly leave society apprehensive, especially when the safety of one's child lay in the balance. Isolated as they are, these incidents have, nonetheless, served to galvanize a more recent counterattack aimed at ridding youth sport of its perceived abusive and otherwise negative influences and have become the subject of great consternation in both academic and popular circles. As Wann suggests in the above, this rash of violence is thought to have reached epidemic status and is considered to be sweeping across the youth sport landscape, and the topic of what to do to prevent further disruption has grown to become a major point of contention within the modern culture. As one syndicated reporter notes:

> Coaches are being threatened, referees assaulted and kids hurt more than ever by the hostile parents of an estimated 30 million young players in organized sports. From parents brawling at a T-ball game in Florida while 4- and 5-year-old children watched to a father being beaten to death at a hockey game in Massachusetts, anger is growing. Leagues are responding by banning rowdy parents from the stands, holding silent games and trying to teach coaches and parents how to behave. When that fails, authorities are putting the worst offenders in jail.[140]

Furthermore, as if to emphasize the modern nature of the construct as one mired in clinical explanations, Engh declares, "From road rage to airplane rage to cell phone rage, children in sports aren't immune to all of this."[141]

Others share this particular stance while they seek to uncover the hidden causality responsible for this supposed rash of behavior. Dr. Richard Lapchick, for example, founder of Northeastern University's influential Center for the Study of Sport in Society, draws a line between modern sport-related violence and the perhaps unsettling childhoods of today's parental offenders. He contends that excesses brought to youth playing fields are a "reflection of when parents grew up in recent years with violence in their childhood being the norm. It would be unrealistic to think all of them have matured enough so that this violence didn't carry over."[142] Psychologist Darrell Burnett, on the other hand, maintains that the causal effect is more a matter of the clash between good intentions and the proximity of wealth in today's modern sport world:

> I think there's an increase in emotional over-involvement with parents because, in some instances, the stakes are higher in youth sports than in the past. Some parents are dreaming of "catching the brass ring," getting a scholarship for their kids through sports, or even a professional contract someday. Consequently, parents may tend to react a little more emotionally at a game or even a practice if there's a chance that a "scout" or a potential coach may be watching.[143]

Echoing Burnett, Shepherd Smith asserts that this particular dynamic is the result of the hypersensitivity inherent in today's connection between parents and children, asserting that "the athletic field is where children's skills or lack thereof are on display for the world to see."[144] Furthermore, he maintains:

> At every youth game you see them the parents who over-identify with their children's performance on the field, who can't draw the boundary between themselves and their children, and who forget that the game is about their kids, not about themselves.[145]

And Gano-Overway simply offers that a perceived increase in immoral behavior in and around sport may be the result of an "overemphasis on winning."[146]

Regardless of rationale, however, what is apparent is that in the estimation of today's commentators, the rash of violent incidents perpetrated at youth sporting events is enough to warn offenders and non-offenders alike that these disturbing developments denote a trend that materially threatens the future of youth sport, and the reactions have been direct and in some instances severe. As Smith laments, "It's a sad commentary on modern-day life if legislation is needed to remind adults to act like adults in the presence of youngsters,"[147] though this has increasingly become the case. Indeed, by the turn of the twenty-first century many states, including Illinois, Arkansas, and Massachusetts, had either enacted or had been considering legislation aimed at curbing assaults against youth league officials, which in some cases leave prosecutors with the option of extending the penalties for particularly heinous offenses beyond the maximum penalties because the crimes were committed at youth sports events.[148] While various local organizations have worked within communities to shore up sagging behavioral norms through typical word-of-mouth policing, others have taken more dramatic steps to ensure that the sorts of behavior bizarre enough to warrant national attention are dealt with in a much more concrete and structured fashion through the implementation of formally conceived adult training sessions. Moreover, Lumpkin et al. reassert that while these acts continue to grab America's collective attention, the real culprit in all this may indeed be the contemporary culture itself, which seems to tolerate, if not encourage, abusive behaviors:

> A too-common scenario finds parents and coaches maneuvering and pressuring young athletes, as if they were pawns on a chessboard, to achieve adult ego satisfaction and status. Violence in school sports has escalated because of overzealous fans, too much pressure to win, and the desire to capture media attention.[149]

The notion of offering training for improving coaching skills or administrative support has long been a part of the youth league experience, but the idea of training youth coaches and administrators specifically at a behavioral level was first introduced in 1985 by the National Youth Sport Coaches Association (NYSCA) when it began offering mandatory courses for those seeking to volunteer their services. By the turn of the twenty-first century, community leagues around the country, with assistance from NAYS (whose mission statement reads "The goal of the National Alliance for Youth Sport is to make sports safe and positive for America's youth"[150]), are requiring volunteer coaches to submit to a two-hour NYSCA training session that involves an hour-long video presentation, a question-and-answer session conducted by a certified member, a post-discussion quiz, and a pledge first read aloud by each member of the class and then signed by each attendee, requiring the newly inducted members to uphold the organization's Coaches' Code of Ethics. As explained in their course manual published by NAYS:

> Being an NYSCA certified coach does not indicate that you are qualified in the sense of a paid coach on the high school, college, or professional level. By virtue of your attending the NYSCA Training/Certification Program conducted by a qualified Clinician, NYSCA Headquarters certifies that you have been trained in your responsibilities to children in sports. Specifically:
>   1. Responsibility for being aware of the psychological and emotional needs of children while participating in sports
>   2. Responsibility for knowing that safety and first-aid care are the most important factors in the well-being of children and that at all times a person of authority (physician, paramedic, etc.) should be called to treat any kind of injury
>   3. Responsibility for being aware that conditioning, nutrition, flexibility, and strength development are important factors in children playing sports.
>   4. Responsibility that to the best of your ability you will teach the proper sports techniques
>   5. Finally, by signing the NYSCA Coaches' Code of Ethics Pledge, you are reminded that in youth sports the consideration of the children should be placed above all and that as an NYSCA volunteer coach you are held accountable to a Code of Conduct[151]

Among the first to formally structure adult training for parents who are not officially connected to a youth sports league through coaching or administration was Florida's Jupiter-Tequesta Athletic Association (JTAA), who in February of 2000, along with the Parents Alliance of Youth Sports (PAYS), another subsidiary of NAYS, offered the adults of the nearly 6,000 registered athletes a mandatory training session developed to reinforce the organization's behavioral expectations. The course, which consisted of a nineteen minute video presentation and a code of ethics that each parent in attendance was asked to read and sign, was created in the aftermath of a number of incidents involving adults in attendance, including the assault in nearby Port St. Lucie (see above). Moreover, it was decreed at the beginning of the 2000 season that any child who did not have at least one parent in attendance at the seminar would be deemed ineligible and barred from competition, resulting in a minor wave of discontent from some in the community who felt coerced.[152] Still, when asked to respond to the criticism, the association president cited both a concern regarding a lack of moral structure among parents in attendance and a fear that an influx of outsiders would somehow change their overall competitive climate. He charged, "We want to communicate with them that this is the kind of organization we are, and this is what we expect."[153]

In an interview conducted by a NAYS volunteer, the JTAA President, Jeff Leslie (JL), further elaborated his community's concerns, matters that have ultimately spawned the training process, which appears in hindsight to have been more proactive than reactive:

NAYS: Why did you decide that parents needed training?

JL: We have been training our coaches with the NYSCA program for the past fifteen years, and it seemed like a natural progression when the National Alliance for Youth Sports came out with the parents' program. While we have been fortunate not to have a situation in which an adult has physically confronted or attacked another adult, we have been close to that situation occurring, and we have also experienced extreme negative parent pressure on children. Additionally, we have had problems with scholarship fever at young ages and have had, although very infrequently, physical skirmishes between participants that we believe parents have contributed to.

With all the parents going through the PAYS program, we feel that positive peer pressure will take over in the stands, and they will help each other keep it in perspective and remind each other that this is only kids playing games, and it is meant to be fun.

NAYS: Do you really think it will make a difference?

JL: Is it a cure all? No. Is it a great way to get your message to the parents? Absolutely! Look. You can't change a person's personality, but you can expect them to behave themselves and be held accountable for their behavior if they don't. We figure that if you don't tell parents what you expect out of them, how can you expect them to know? The PAYS program does that for us with a clear, concise, and consistent message.[154]

In the spring of 2001, El Paso, Texas, joined with the JTAA by making a similar training session mandatory for the parents of their youth sport participants, while other community organizations in places such as Cleveland, Ohio,

Figure 5.2

According to NASO's *Special Report: The National Association of Sports Officials. Officials under Assault: Update 2002,* a NAYS survey of 500 youth sport parents cited the following:

- 82% of those surveyed believed that parents behave aggressively at youth sporting events
- 50% of those surveyed stated that they had witnessed aggressive adult behavior during a youth sporting events
- 72% of those surveyed agreed that aggressive behavior by adults at youth sporting events should be banned[155]

and Scarsdale, New York, have taken steps to further police off-field behavior through initiatives such as moratoriums on parental attendance, a notable increase in on-site security presence, and proposals such as "Silent Sundays," a practice that allows parents to attend competitions but say nothing aloud for the entire length of the contest, a notion that Fred Engh refers to mockingly as "the greatest time-out in American sports."[156]

By the middle of the decade, there were well over than 175 cities in the United States that required parents to participate in some form or another of spectator training,[157] and NAYS, NASO (see figure 5.2), and PAYS can boast of more than 2,200 chapters nationwide combined, all of whom share the concern that adult misconduct in the youth sport arena has crossed the line from bizarre to criminal in too many cases.[158] Still, while it would be difficult for those who disagree with these types of responses to adult on- and off-field incidents, there are those who find that mandatory training sessions and oaths and pledges are over the top and in some ways insulting to the population, the overwhelming majority of whom do not play a part in such misbehavior.

For example, during the summer of 2001, and in the midst of the more commonplace images of out-of-control parents and degraded youth sport organizations, ESPN television aired as part of its weekly program "Outside the Lines" a debate on the issue of parental abuse and youth sport.[159] Calling this segment "Parental Guidance Is Suggested," the show's producers allowed for open debate between Fred Engh, who as expected staunchly supports the rigorous methods for curbing adult behavior at youth sport events, and Cliff McCrath, a highly successful soccer coach at Pacific University in Seattle, who deems these measures to be both Machiavellian and ineffective. Though both agreed that there were indeed some who overstepped the boundaries of civility and debased such ideals as fair play and common decency, McCrath also maintained that by making training sessions and other assorted measures aimed at mitigating these incidents contingent upon a child's participation served to both punish children unfairly and lump the overwhelming majority of well-managed and reasonable parents with the minority in question. Countering Engh's claims that the so-called sideline rage phenomenon was a matter that had reached epidemic proportions in the United States, McCrath argued that measures that stifle supportive parents are neither productive nor necessary in this case, maintaining that young players "need to hear their parents screaming out for them."[160] Furthermore, on the matter of video presentations, codes, pledges, and coursework, McCrath offered that the trend toward over-policing the issue seemed more indicative of placating the public's media-induced biases while allowing some of sport's seamier elements to remain clear of public scorn and Madison Avenue's image of sport could be left wholesome and pure and still worthy of the public's continued adulation, a point that echoes Overman's contention that American sport has long been saddled by a rather undeserved and often limiting "Sunday School" demeanor.[161] As one viewer would later offer in response to the broadcast:

> Requiring parents "who get it" to publicly recite "good conduct pledges" as a condition of their child's participation is beyond unfair — it's insulting and demeaning. Implementing simplistic "feel-good" solutions to complex social problems is not likely to change parents' attitudes or behavior.[162]

What was most fascinating about the program's various exchanges, however, was the extent to which McCrath's concerns were routinely pushed aside by Engh, Jim Thompson, an executive member of PAYS, and Steve Ferranoci, the referee who was attacked in Port St. Lucie. Their collective insistence that the violent incidents referred to in this debate did indeed constitute an epidemic, and their persistent claims that mandatory education and stronger security measures were the only means to rid society of the scourge were handled equally proficiently by McCrath, who maintained his position in spite of the backlash. But in the end, the commentators, show hosts, the handful of at-large respondents, and even the follow-up responses aired during the next week's telecast continued to stress the urgency of the matter irrespective of disagreements while some went so far as to maintain that those who are not convinced of the seriousness of the situation are either naïve or complicit. Thus, to be quite candid, the phenomenon of the over-enthusiastic parent besotted with his or her child's athletic performances but articulated through a medicalized language as suffering from some form of a disorder is no longer considered to be a mere feature of the national landscape but its very definition. Accordingly, this character, enveloped in the swath of moral panic and considered to mark the stark reality of modern life, stands poised to remain a part of the setting of youth sport for some time to come.

Perhaps the best indicator of the mechanical acceptance of the issue of adult-induced violence in and around youth sport is its absorption into the popular culture itself. As a means to further illustrate this point, I refer to an episode of the popular crime drama *Law & Order*[163] that originally aired in the spring of 2001. Co-written by Bernard Goldberg, the narrator of HBO's "Real Sports" segment on parental rage that first aired in October 2000,[164] and entitled "Thin Ice," this particular episode presented a situation in which the father of a potentially talented young hockey player beat his son's coach to death presumably because the coach refused to play the team's stars, which the father perceived might have lessened the boy's chances of being discovered by either college recruiters or professional scouts. Given the nature of the crime and the lack of any substantive defense, the defendant's attorney sought to mitigate his client's guilt by claiming that the motivation for the crime was an insatiable psychological drive to protect one's progeny from the pressures of high-profile sport, what he would go on to deem a form of incontrollable rage. In turn, in his closing arguments before the jury, the prosecuting attorney acknowledges the depth to which American society has become consumed with brutality while commenting on the increasing tendency to medicalize issues through what he terms the "rage defense":

> Road rage, airport rage, sports rage. Add to that parent rage, office rage, employee rage. It might be nice to think of all this as some new mental illness, but the truth is that this kind of behavior has become ordinary, and to ask you to excuse it through the fiction of a new mental illness is just that — a fiction, because it certainly is not the law.
> The law says that your right to rage stops at the other guy's nose. The defendant's right to be angry stopped the moment he raised his fists. It stopped the moment he struck [the victim], beat him, and left him for dead.[165]

And then, as if to reinforce the substantive issue of adults and their effects on children, he levies one last shot before asking the jury to convict:

> Are we really prepared to create a society in which no one is responsible for controlling their anger and teach those lessons to their children?[166]

The resonance of such an episode, and many other similarly larded depictions in television, film, literature, and even talk radio, lends further credence to this notion that the once inviolate and traditionally respectable environs of youth sport have indeed been penetrated by a most unseemly and conceivably pernicious disease brought about through a noxious concoction of hypercompetitive adults and a steadily degraded culture that encourages such displays. As Darrell Burnett would claim, somewhat ironically, "We're living in an age where the preservation of traditional values can no longer be taken for granted."[167]

What becomes glaringly apparent regarding this discussion of youth sport and its relationship to children and their development, be it psychosocial, physiological, or otherwise, is that inherent to this equation is the supposition that competition in the modern context is wholly incapable of falling into line with acceptable standards. Here again the drift from what constitutes propriety within the traditional construct clashes with a modern interpretation that anticipates that any activity that forces children to be goal-oriented and challenging to be potentially harmful and in opposition to a nascent worldview that seeks to redress notions of manifest or latent aggression with a more introspective and egalitarian pose that is by and large presented as incontrovertible and rarely subject to further inspection.

6

Self-Esteem and Youth in Competitive Sport

One perceptible shift in the way many Americans conceive of contemporary sport can be found in the various discussions pertaining to the psychosocial and developmental implications of competition, especially as it pertains to youth. As competitive sport is increasingly thought of as potentially damaging to the child, the measured withdrawal from the once vaunted embrace of competition appears in part to be the result of sport's inability to reconcile recent reevaluations relative to such matters as the acquisition and recognition of the self in both child-aged participants and observers alike.[1]

Discussions pertaining to matters of self-actualization and how cultural contributions inform the acquisition of healthy self-concepts have indeed shifted toward a more bleak depiction of humanity on the brink. How this more recent shift toward the introspective operates often serves to underscore the seriousness with which those committed to the promotion of more favorable self-concepts pursue their aims. Adding children to this mix certainly ratchets up an already volatile and emotionally driven discourse. Still, given the increasingly more noxious portrayal of competitive athletics, this continued pairing of sport and youth, especially when viewed through the prism of the self, reaffirms the growing consensus that when put to this test, sport fails to deliver on its more traditional promise.

This chapter marks an attempt to examine and in some cases reexamine these changes in the discussion by exploring more deeply the trend toward interpreting culture through the prism of the self. Inherent to this analysis are the ramifications of such critiques, and how the recent shift toward a more self-reflexive consciousness in turn informs the discussion of contemporary sport.

Self-Esteem in America

Self-esteem is essential for psychological survival. It is an emotional sine qua non — without some measure of self-worth, life can be enormously

*painful, with many basic needs going unmet ... Judging and rejecting
yourself causes enormous pain. And in the same way that you would
favor and protect a physical wound, you find yourself avoiding anything that might aggravate the pain of self-rejection in any way.* [2]

*Welcome to the High Self-Esteem Program. You have just entered the
world of self ... self-awareness, self-discovery, and self-actualization.
You are about to begin your greatest journey ... the search for a higher
self-image.... Our quest for High Self-Esteem never ends ... it is a life-
long journey ... an incredible adventure....* [3]

If there is a single concept that galvanizes the many critics of modern
American sport, it is the effect that sport has on the development of the self
and how these developments translate into the acquisition of the self in youth
participants. The explosion in awareness of the self, introduced initially through
a growing acceptance of pop psychology and legitimated further by recent
developments in talk show programming and self-help literature, has created
a ground swell of public support for what once had been academic positions
regarding healthy self-concepts and other issues relative to both adults and
children alike. The key element of this repositioning of the self at the center of
modern discourse is self-esteem, and as Western society continues to grasp for
some element of cohesiveness and solidarity in the wake of post–Cold War
adjustments and, less abstractly, the 9/11 attacks and continued instability in
the Middle East, an abundance of constituents, professionals, and laypeople
alike have latched onto an emergent ethos that places the acquisition of self-
esteem as the more enlightened path for a modern and presumably progressive society.

To be sure, the pairing of the self and sport marks a dramatic shift from
the more traditional analyses associated with American sport, but as widespread
awareness of the psychosocial ramifications of daily life continues to fundamentally alter public perception, few existing institutions have been able to
escape this sort of scrutiny, and sport is no exception. In this regard, a modern sport-related discussion seeks to replace the more traditional aggressive,
success-driven, and morality-based sport model with one that values positive
experiences for all participants. Thus, by welding psychology-based critiques
of the self-concept to contemporary sport criticism, critics have exposed a pattern within the sphere of competitive athletics that highlights a more pronounced and problematic nature, especially as it pertains to the role that the
acquisition of healthy self-esteem plays in this sphere.

By the late twentieth century, self-esteem had indeed become a fêted social
and psychological construct that oftentimes offers up the impression of a soci-
etal-wide yearning to find something in which to believe during a period of
mounting turmoil and skepticism. Its evolution into the American consciousness springs predominantly from late nineteenth and early twentieth century
attempts to bring psychology down to more popular levels, but it also displays

deep antecedental roots dating back to Puritan era self-help literature that chronicled that population's search for what one modern commentator refers to as "Christian goodness."[4] Twentieth century Americans, however, have since managed to turn what can be described as a pedestrian fascination for self-reflection into its present day incarnation, a complex and lucrative industry that has served to rewrite the rules for social and political engagement by the promotion of a new value system that acknowledges the self as the primary point of context and esteem as the triumph of the human spirit.

This open embrace of self-awareness expresses itself through an ambiguously aligned, almost spiritual mission that has adopted an ethos that places feeling good over achievement, self-consciousness over public scrutiny, and the pursuit of internal recognition over once vaunted external markers that informed previous societal trends, a development that corresponds to an overall pattern that runs alongside a gamut of physical as well as mental health–related concerns. As explained on the popular self-help web page SOLO Lifestyles for Singles:

> Self-esteem is not the way others see you; it is the way you see yourself. You are the only source of your self-esteem, [and] the only things keeping you from enjoying the gifts of self-confidence and self-respect are your thoughts and self-talk.

They continue:

> Self-esteem requires a respect for your inner worth — your feelings and values — and your outer worth — how you behave and fit into the world around you. Don't listen to an inner critic.[5]

The more modern discussion of the nature of self-esteem is one that elicits a great deal of attention in contemporary academic and popular literature and cuts a wide swath across the sociopolitical spectrum. While many are in agreement that identifiable levels of positive regard are necessary to ensure healthy actualized selves, commentators have also been quick to draw their own conclusions away from the actual synthesis of esteem within the individual and toward an analysis of the means with which the individual may obtain the properly prescribed levels. What makes this issue so contentious is not so much self-esteem's efficacy or value in the human experience but rather whether or not self-esteem can be effectively and consciously implanted within individuals through prescribed intervention processes, and what this shift toward esteem-based intervention represents for the future of good mental health, especially as it pertains to youth. As sociologist Steven Ward notes in the *Canadian Journal of Sociology*:

> During the period from the late 1960's until the early 1990's, we see the concept of self-esteem retranslated for the self-help and parenting literature. No longer was the concept merely part of the specialized jargon of psychologists but a real tool for changing one's life. The alliance between self-esteem and self-help parenting literature allowed the concept to move into new areas and develop a larger, more

encompassing, network of support. As the self-esteem literature became more popular and was integrated into TV discourse and everyday talk, the concept became much stronger than before.[6]

A Brief History of Self-Esteem

Self-esteem is the emotion or feeling a person has with regard to his/her self-worth which is composed of his/her self-competence and self-respect. It is the limiting factor on a person's performance.[7]

Self-esteem development must become part of the explicit, not hidden, agenda of our instructional practices by leading us to focus on strategies targeted to enhance self-esteem and consequently motivation and achievement.[8]

Self-esteem's evolution from the academic spheres of counseling and psychotherapy lent it considerable legitimacy by an increasingly therapy-conscious populace. To be quite candid here, America has always seemed ripe for such rabid pop-cultural adoptions as the contemporary awareness of the self suggests. And yet, while previous so-called crazes delivered the requisite passionate embrace followed by the inevitable fade from public view, this particular fascination with self-reflection has shown a remarkable resiliency. Indeed, the modern fascination with self-esteem can lay claim to a considerable amount of social, political, and cultural capital in spite of the more recent assessments by some critics that its cohesive value may have begun to wane, albeit slightly. Nonetheless, by the 1990s, post–Cold War American society seemed primed to accept the self-help literature with a sense of purpose as well as an urgency to reevaluate itself in relation to all facets of contemporary life.[9]

The awareness of self-esteem as an integral component of contemporary life emerged in its modern form primarily through the pioneering work of William James and other so-called pioneers in social psychology, including Gordon Allport, Abraham Maslow, Carl Rogers, and symbolic interactionists such George Herbert Mead and Charles Horton Cooley. In contrast to the behaviorists who routinely turned away from such abstractions as the self, these scholars worked through the analyses offered by the likes of Descartes, Rousseau, Hume,[10] and Freud in order to gain further insight into human behavior while defining elements within the individual that allowed for feelings of general self-worth in spite of one's circumstances or conditions.[11]

It would be James who first gave rise to the notion that within the human psyche exists a complex set of coping mechanisms that were to fall under the broader heading of what he would later term *esteem*. James posed the self as an extraordinarily affective building block whose worth is determined through the very act of awareness, leading to James' initial discovery of the concept itself. As one observer notes:

James claimed a person's level of self-esteem arises from an aggregation of the number of life's successes divided by the number of pretensions (and priori claims/beliefs of impending success). Thus, not surprisingly, according to James a high self-esteem person is one who can make good on her claims regarding her capabilities. On the other hand, a low self-esteem person is an individual who consistently fails to live up to her aspirations.[12]

Advocates of what critics claim to be the more fashionable trend toward offering education through a self-esteem-driven ethos often turned to some of James' younger cohorts for further understanding of these developments. One such was Gordon Allport, who theorized alongside James that self-esteem functioned as a sort of deceptive measure to perpetuate individual self-worth in the face of adversity. While he recognized that it was possible that these measures might breed a false sense of accomplishment or even bravado in the individual, he maintained, nonetheless, that they would also provide that same individual with the fundamental mechanisms for coping with whatever hardships that may arise. In his judgment, "[self-esteem] enables one for the time being to put off the admission of unpleasant truths until one is ready to receive them."[13] Or as Neilands concedes, "from the perspectives of Allport and James, self-deception carried out in the service of self-esteem protection is of adaptive value."[14]

While most of the earlier theorists placed the majority of their focus on self-esteem in adults, by the 1960s some began to take up the issue as it pertained to childhood. Writing in an age of baby boomers, social upheaval, and Benjamin Spock, noted psychologists Morris Rosenberg and Stanley Coopersmith forged new ground in this particular field. They agreed that the most likely source of high self-esteem in children came from proper parenting along with the requisite backing from local schools, which at that time remained in good standing with the general population as opposed to the much more hostile perception of the modern American educational infrastructure that has become the standard fare of early twenty-first century observers. Regardless, Rosenberg's primary position was to maintain the notion that effective levels of self-esteem in adolescents were predicated on such life experiences as family dynamics, class, ethnicity, and religious orientation, and he tied low self-esteem to a wide range of pathologies traceable to poor parenting and reinforced in part by a similar lack of affective stability in the schools.[15]

While much of Coopersmith's work echoed Rosenberg, he furthered the analysis by maintaining that the levels of self-esteem found in parents themselves are what often translated into better parenting. This might, in turn, according to Ward's assessment of Coopersmith's work, maximize the potential for similarly high levels of individual esteem in their offspring, thus affirming the importance of proper parenting in the modern interpretation of constructive child development.[16] Deeming self-esteem "the evaluation which the individual makes and customarily maintains with regard to himself"[17] as well as serving as the "personal judgment of worthiness that is expressed in the attitudes the individual conveys to others by verbal reports and other expressive behaviors,"[18] Coopersmith broadened his analysis by predicting that self-esteem would continue to be a primary focus in educational contexts because "it is considered to be a major factor influencing such processes as motivation, persistence, standards of success, and causal attributions for success and failure outcomes.[19]

The driving mechanism behind the emerging commentary continued to be the ability or the inability of the individual to cope with whatever hardships life might advance. As long as self-esteem could be posed as a coherent mediator in the face of disappointment or other unpleasant circumstances in order to ward off the effects of a potentially serious psychic breakdown, then its place among the exalted features of a more humanely structured contemporary order would be vindicated. For those increasingly captivated with its role in human development, self-esteem, though variable and subject to fluctuations dependent upon myriad life circumstances, became thought of as the link between surviving and thriving in the modern world, and the interest placed in discovering further links to these sorts of psychic coping mechanisms led to a steady advance of the concept from the periphery of psychotherapy into the more mainstream currents of modern thought.

In the modern context, child development professionals, as well as a growing number of laypersons, share the position that self-esteem represents such an integral feature of human existence that its presence, or lack thereof, is crucial in terms of all human interaction. Many draw parallels between low levels of self-esteem and a variety of social maladies facing policy-makers and social critics alike, including, but certainly not limited to, crime, suicide, and substance abuse as well as a variety of other disorders as described in the vast social science literature. This awareness has in turn succeeded in creating a notable shift in the way many Americans perceive events in our time in such a way as to affect nearly every perception of existing institutions and their continued legitimacy in contemporary life. As sociologist James Nolan would assert in his discussion of the self in relation to politically motivated reactions to contemporary life, this internalization of what was once inherently external stimuli has led to wide-reaching reevaluations and reforms in the function of a variety of hallowed conventions, including the system of jurisprudence in United States courts.[20]

Definitions aside, it is not the concept itself that is viewed in such conflicted terms but rather it is the embrace and the agendas thought to be behind the advocacy that lie at the center of the debate. To clarify, no one is specifically an opponent arguing against self-esteem in and of itself. Rather, the sides are drawn in terms of how one acquires it — if one can actually acquire self-esteem — under what set of conditions self-esteem finds its way into the public's consciousness, and, ultimately, how these discussions manifest in actual human behavior.

The Debate

Real self-esteem doesn't come from a bumper sticker proclaiming your child to be a superstar at his or her elementary school. It comes from solid academic achievement based on high standards and hard work, including plenty of reading and homework.[21]

... the importance that an individual attaches to a particular domain or activity will determine the extent to which a successful or unsuccessful outcome will affect the individual's self-esteem. For example, a child's low perceived competence in physical skills may not have a negative effect on total self-esteem because he or she does not value physical competence as important for being successful.[22]

An emergent contemporary self-esteem advocacy has become increasingly recognizable for the enthusiasm and ardor with which it expresses itself in defense of its aims. For example, there is John Vasconcellos, principal organizer of the California Task Force to Promote Self-Esteem and Personal and Social Responsibility. In his estimation, the more recent awareness of the consequences of low self-esteem is comparable to such timeless human concerns as unlocking the secrets of the atom and the unraveling of the mysteries of the universe.[23] Others, such as British sociologist Frank Füredi, are not so moved by this trend, claiming instead that this shift marks less an embrace of human efficacy and more a retreat from a human-centered discussion. He notes:

Today's emphasis on feeling good reflects the fact that the individual self has become the central focus of social, moral and cultural life. And since feeling happy is regarded as something like a state of virtue, things that distract the individual from attending to his emotional needs are devalued: hard work, sacrifice, altruism and commitment are presented as being antithetical to the individual quest for happiness.[24]

Regardless of where one is situated in terms of this debate, however, the rhetoric concerning self-esteem is emotionally charged, prone to polemics, and is, generally speaking, predictably controversial. Moreover, its most vocal promoters are those who approach the issue with an eye cast toward children and child development, which in turn has transformed the American school into the issue's primary staging ground. As oft-cited researcher Maureen R. Weiss, the director of Sport and Exercise Psychology at the University of Virginia's Curry School of Education, has posed it, "the self-concept has been a central construct in education for years."[25]

A jumping-off point for understanding the context of this more recent development and its place within contemporary social discourse is James Nolan's *The Therapeutic State.*[26] Nolan, whose work traces the link between the modern criminal justice system and contemporary education methodology through what he deems the contemporary absorption with self-related initiatives, posits that for many Americans therapy, with its implications for further self-actualization, has become the standard for much of what we know about our world and ourselves.[27]

By Nolan's estimation, contemporary society is marked by a notable departure away from shared cultural ideals toward a more modern construct that repositions the self as a sort of intermediary force while looking to psychotherapy to serve as the backdrop for a healthier and much more effective social order. Correspondingly, Nolan argues that an emerging therapeutic ethos offers a complex and challenging world a ready set of plausible explanations for modern injustices and hardships by reinterpreting life as a process of navigating diseased minds and scarred psyches through spaces in which either successful healing or the trauma of denial or relapse dictates the means by which a modern society conducts its daily affairs. And in Nolan's estimation, the most central feature that affects this change toward a therapeutic ethos is the exaltation of self-esteem.

For Nolan and other scholars who seem to share his particular bias, the focus on the construction of individual self-esteem marks the departure of the more traditional human-centered liberation project away from the collective and on to the realm of the individual.[28] Throughout his analysis, Nolan traces the evolution of an increasingly passionate and driven self-esteem advocacy that Nolan admits identifies itself in such a way that it takes on the guise of a massive social movement.[29] This embracing advocacy has in turn charged itself with the daunting task of bringing the joys and benefits of increased self-esteem into the public domain even in the face of mounting scientific skepticism, resulting in what Nolan deems a conspicuous arrival of the emotive self in the contemporary discussion.[30] As Nolan poses it:

> Clearly, the self-esteem philosophy sees itself as a cushion to the harshness of life in the machine.... Thus it is clear that the self-esteem movement views the nature of our rationalized society as repressive, disempowering, mechanistic, and hostile to our natural humanness. Yet, in spite of this evident disapproval of the bureaucratic nature of the modern rationalized world, self-esteem advocates wholly endorse the capitalist order.[31]

In this model, Nolan argues, an orthodoxy emerges that seems poised to affect much of society's day-to-day existence in virtually every social milieu. As self-reflective emotionality takes precedence over the more objectively defined constructs of achievement, ambition, and success, it can insinuate itself into a wide range of modern institutions. Among the many that stand out in this case, and one that has become an extraordinarily effective point for its further dissemination into the culture, is America's schools. As columnist Janet Daley was to note:

> Educational ideology for the past thirty years has been devoted to the encouragement of self-esteem: if you feel good about yourself, then what you can do or accomplish in an "artificial" setting is of little importance. The aim was to make all children feel valued and confident rather than giving 'disproportionate' approval to

the able few. School was a form of therapy, intended to equip the "whole child" for life, not just for academic achievement.[32]

According to those who champion this particular perspective, both scholarly and along the more popular fronts, little of what transpires in a given school day occurs beyond the reach of the self-reflective ideology. Boasting a strong character development component and acting in conjunction with the enthusiastic support of school administrators and contemporary educational theorists, the self-esteem advocacy operates most freely within the context of modern education, affecting decisions on both curriculum matters and along the periphery through enrichment and otherwise extracurricular activities. Here, in an environment that is often depicted as increasingly angst-ridden and stressful, most contend that they are attempting to foster healthier self-concepts in school-aged children by promoting creative measures drawn toward furthering the development of self-esteem in youth. It is in this environment that such dramatic seeming measures such as *creative spelling*,[33] *social (or peer) promotion*,[34] and any number of self-directed student activities thought to remove the stress of skill mastery and performance are utilized in order to make students feel better about themselves, their deficiencies, and their futures. In this respect, teachers, some of whom resent the implications of a number of these actions, are nonetheless finding themselves and their roles rewritten to fit the growing advocacy's aims. As teacher increasingly becomes analogous to counselor (in parallel to the transformation of the modern coach — see chapter five), and as students find themselves the focus of emotive concerns rather than performance matters, it becomes apparent that school, with its artificially enhanced gloss of esteem, has become a radically different place.

In her ethnographic study of curriculum shifts in American schools in the 1990s, American education researcher Rita Kramer noted what she contends was an alarming incursion of the self-esteem ideology to the detriment of both the children and the educational process:

> Wherever I went ... I found a striking degree of conformity about what is considered to be the business of school and the job of teachers. Everywhere I visited ... I heard the same things over and over again ... I found idealistic people eager to do good. And everywhere, I found them being told that the way to do good was to prepare themselves to cure a sick society. To become therapists, as it were, specializing in the pathology of education.... What matters is not to teach any particular subject or skill, not to preserve past accomplishments or stimulate future achievements, but to give to all that stamp of approval that will make them "feel good about themselves" ... Self-esteem has replaced understanding as the goal of education."[35]

In other words, the primary means by which teachers are to perhaps cure their students of whatever negative feelings or other such issues that may manifest in their young lives is through the promotion of self-esteem. Furthermore, this position is continually being presented and defended as the most effective means to insure proper child development. But as University of California at Berkeley psychology professor Martin V. Covington, a staunch proponent of the advocacy's work, defends it:

> To most Americans, achievement is everything; it is our badge, our national identity. As a people, we are known for our ability to get the job done, and done on time. We have always been more committed to the *product* than comfortable with the *process*, and when productivity suffers we become uneasy and troubled. But there is much more to educational achievement than a test score, a course grade, or a report card. As virtues, effort and accomplishment will flourish only to the extent that we consider the *reasons* that students strive. This is the essential message of the self-esteem perspective. When we fail to consider motives and feelings, individuals may strive successfully, but for the wrong reasons—with the consequence that the benefits of these successes are illusory.[36]

To be sure, this debate is often sparked by flurries of accusations depicting pro-esteem advocates sacrificing success through actual achievement by applying synthetic successes through stage-managed and otherwise artificially enhanced environments, leaving some to fear a calamitous purging of a traditional achievement ethic from cherished traditional institutions. Such accusations pose self-esteem without tangible external context as anathema to the very progress that the advocacy seeks to instill in individuals. These critics argue that the shift toward what they depict as an artificial implementation of esteem serves rather to degrade the self-concept as well as whatever sense of accomplishment that may develop. They view these measures as impediments to the once vaunted achievement ethos and fear that what will result will reflect Covington's embrace of internal indicators by defining success solely in terms of what the advocacy will defend on humanitarian and democratic grounds.[37]

It is on this last point that the questions abound: How is it possible to first reconcile the divide between those with high levels of self-esteem and those who suffer in its absence? Furthermore, in terms of the adaptive value of self-esteem serving as a coping mechanism, what happens to the nature of success and achievement in the traditional construct when today's focus has fallen clearly in favor of increasing esteem society-wide by any means necessary?[38] Writing in a 1992 article in *The New Republic*, for instance, Christopher Lasch observed, candidly:

> Democracy once meant opposition to every kind of double standard. Today we accept double standards—as always, a recipe for second-class citizenship—in the name of humanitarian concern. We hand out awards indiscriminately, hoping to give the recipients the illusion of accomplishment. Having given up attempts to raise the general level of competence, we are content to restrict it to the caring class, which arrogates to itself the job of looking out for everybody else. The professionalization of compassion does not make us a kinder, gentler nation. Instead it institutionalizes inequality under the pretense that everyone is "special" in his own way.[39]

Others share Lasch's position that the failure of self-esteem without context has the potential to subvert the more substantive aims of the movement, and this concern is voiced once again in the case of education and child development. Dr. John Rosemond, an enormously popular syndicated child development specialist, places this move toward the more self-esteem-laden objective by looking at the types of individuals who tend to score highly on self-esteem measurements. For example, Rosemond cites a Case Western Reserve University and University of Virginia joint study that contends that high self-esteem scores seem to correlate with a propensity for high levels of violence and the potential for criminal behaviors. He notes further that gang members, career criminals, and wife abusers tend to score highest on such measures of self-esteem, whereas high academic achievers tend to be much more self-critical and unpretentious in their individual self-assessments. Voicing his disagreement and displeasure with those who espouse the modern self-reflective construct without first offering limits, Rosemond submits:

> Humility and modesty are timeless virtues that shore up character, make for good citizenship, and promote higher achievement. In fact, if everyone had slightly "low" self-esteem, the world would be a more peaceful place.[40]

Nina H. Shokraii-Rees, an officer in the conservative Center for Equal Opportunity in Washington, D.C., questions the motives of those who espouse the conscious acquisition of self-esteem in schools. She claims that a self-esteem-based methodology for education often ignores the importance of teaching children how to perform and cope in real life circumstances through the experiences of disappointment and conflict.

Shokraii-Rees builds upon what she deems the more globalized notion of true self-esteem. She claims that not only does achievement precede self-esteem, an ideal echoed throughout the self-esteem lobby's position, but that in the more fashionable current models, "self-esteem theory threatens to deny children the tools they will need in order to experience true success in school and as adults."[41] Calling for schools to abandon what she considers the mindless pursuit of empty self-esteem, she warns:

> Traditionally, public schools have thought that students' satisfaction will follow on the heels of their academic success. In other words, children who perform well in class will consequently feel good about themselves. But more recent educational theories have reversed this logic. They say that students must secure high self-esteem before they can hope to achieve. In other words, they must feel good about themselves before they can perform well in class....[42]

Shokraii-Rees further maintains that while some children may be ambivalent toward, reluctant about, or even terrified of school, it is certainly not a new concern nor does she contend that it can be so easily phased out by artificially infusing measures that lead to increased self-esteem in children without a reasonable context. Similar to the more advocative corners of this debate, she also acknowledges that the impetus behind this so-called self-esteem movement is rooted in what many have judged the unacceptable diminishment of academic success as evidenced by lowered test scores and a subsequently perceived rise in juvenile delinquency along with a general belief that society has grown impossibly apathetic to the education of its young. Still, she asserts that the run toward embracing esteem measures, while understandable amid the backdrop of modern sociopolitical developments, remains a desperate attempt to reverse the trends in a manner that she declares is "fundamentally wrongheaded."[43] And clearly she is not alone in her appraisal. As New York University humanities professor Herbert London echoed in a syndicated editorial, "Kids may be happy about a school because the classes are easy, or the basketball team is having a winning season, or they've discovered puppy love. But none of these conditions enhance what children know.[44]

At times even those in the general population are compelled to weigh in on the subject as evinced by the following remark found in an editorial in Reno's *Nevada Appeal*:

> Of course a child who is never challenged academically and does little or no homework, but still moves easily from one grade to the next, feels pretty good about him or herself. School is easy. Hey, I'm having fun! And why shouldn't they be having fun if they spend far more time watching television than doing homework?[45]

Onkar Ghate of the ultra-conservative Ayn Rand Institute offers a most impassioned rejection of the self-esteem advocacy, harnessing issues of morality alongside the self-esteem conundrum. Ghate foresees a stifling commonality behind the self-esteem movement, one that in his estimation is to blame for the same low levels of esteem in children that they lament. He contends that by consciously minimizing activity and achievement, self-esteem advocates debase their own position by substituting actual success with a relativized definition. He claims that while there may indeed be a significant lack of self-esteem in today's youth, he is also convinced that it is the lobby itself that is not only preventing positive regard among its charges but, by virtue of its pose, may also be the source of this same despair among youth:

> Genuine self-esteem ... consists not of causeless feelings, but of certain knowledge about yourself. It rests on the conviction that you — by your choices, efforts, and actions — have made yourself into the kind of person able to deal with reality. It is the conviction — based on the evidence of your own volitional functioning — that you are fundamentally able to succeed in life and, therefore, are deserving of that success.[46]

Ghate, who lambastes those who believe that self-esteem is simply a matter of feeling good, counters that convincing students to set their own parameters for success and achievement devoid of contextual links actually impedes success— and, hence, esteem — by encouraging youth to embrace an emotional orientation to the outside world rather than affecting an objective one. He stresses that when one's reality becomes rooted in emotion rather than reason, it creates not understanding but uncertainty, and this uncertainty serves to perpetuate many of the same acknowledged enemies of self-esteem: inactivity, helplessness, anxiety, and self-doubt.

Through this construct, Ghate allows that there can be no wrong answers, no inadequate performances, no shared successes, and no tangible notion of progress outside the mind of the individual, perpetuating even further one's estrangement from the outside world by virtue of what he considers the propensity on the part of so-called progressive educators to assume that "logic is a straightjacket."[47] It is through this degree of what he deems to be a pseudo-self-esteem that Ghate accuses modern educational methodology of threatening to erase both standards of excellence and the search for meaning from the developmental equation, a position for which he fears many seem all too comfortable:

> Erase the concept of truth — these educators maintain — and the child will never discover that he is thinking or acting wrongly. If he is taught that anything he does is right because he feels it, he will always "feel good" about himself.... Today's child lacks self-esteem precisely because modern educators encourage him to dispense with his mind and to indulge his feelings.[48]

Still, others remain unconvinced and pose their positions around the singularly incontrovertible position that instilling self-esteem in children is not indicative of a move to denigrate the achievement ethic but rather exists as a step toward reconciling the gap between those who have yet to experience any measurable success in a highly stressful environment.

The lining up of these disparate sides has come at a price, and there appear to be no easy solutions, especially when the debate is charged with the emotionality inherent to any discussion involving children, their education, and their security. And yet, the polarity that exists between the sides is glaring. On the one hand there are those who view the promotion of self-esteem as an anti-depressant measure utilized in the fight to reduce external pressures but without actual and tangible longstanding effect. As Nolan notes, "Educators who eliminate grades and encourage self-esteem are seeking to assuage the stress of an overcompetitive environment."[49] The other side, however, is marked by a litany of suggestions for across-the-board improvements in academic performances through strategies for implementing the new focus on the self by reinventing the language of education. As Covington outlines it, improvements in children's self-concepts can be made by:

- Increasing the number of meaningful rewards available so that students can learn to approach success rather than looking to simply avoid failure
- Directing a decided shift in the meaning of success and failure by targeting effort (or lack thereof) as the primary factor in achievement
- Re-directing student tendencies toward self-assessments steeped in self-loathing and self-criticism to reflect the effort component rather than the more typical success or failure paradigm

- Promoting a view that depicts ability as incremental and expansive irrespective of immediate results and performances[50]

The ideological clash outlined above affects the discussion of youth in virtually every youth-related endeavor, especially when it pertains to any child-aged activity within the reach of contemporary education. With its long and storied association with youth and especially in terms of traditional mechanisms for socialization, competitive sport has entered into this discussion, and with it have come questions pertaining to sport's continued relevancy and worth relative to children and the quest to insure healthier developmental processes.

Youth, Sport, and the Acquisition of Self-Esteem

I'm a firm believer that sport is the greatest tool we have in today's society to help children develop positive character traits and life values. But when the focus shifts from what's best for the young participants to what's best for others, that's where problems begin.[51]

To me sports are a chance to have others push us to excel.[52]

If there were no sports, life would be easier because you wouldn't have to play games every other day.[53]

When it comes to evaluating the legitimacy and the validity of competitive sport in the lives of young people today, there are distinctively competing orthodoxies at play. On the one hand the American Academy of Child and Adolescent Psychiatry can acknowledge the positive values found in sport participation in the lives of American youth by recognizing that sports "help children develop physical skills, get exercise, make friends, have fun, learn to play as a member of a team, learn to play fair, and improve self-esteem."[54] From there, however, their concerns regarding the course of sport begin to take on a more modern air:

> American sports culture has increasingly become a money-making business. The highly stressful, competitive, "win-at-all-costs" attitude prevalent at colleges and with professional athletes affects the world of children's sports and athletics, creating an unhealthy environment.[55]

That this type of debate regarding the promotion of self-esteem in youth could reach the once seemingly impenetrable environment of sport is in and of itself remarkable. And yet, the signs are unmistakable. Whereas in the past, the dual ideals of sport and the self were rarely paired directly in previous analyses, they have grown to inform one another's significance in a debate that centers around youth participation, a debate that regularly reaches into the realm of higher profile adult sport and its implications outside this particular milieu.

It was not so much a case that sport's past promoters and advocates ignored issues of self-reflection and similarly constructed self-concepts in their critiques of sport. Rather, the assumptions made by most traditional youth sport advocates were that issues relative to the self and sport participation were fundamentally self-explanatory — that a talented and successful child participant would naturally find fulfillment through participation in sport while the less talented might find that sport has taken him (and later her) down a much more disheartening course. Thus, these constructs were assumed then to be a part of the total sport experience and a by-product of the participatory nature of sport within the ebb and flow of success and failure inherent to the competitive model. Given that most estimates place participation rates as hovering in excess of twenty million children with an estimated withdrawal rate of nearly eighty-eight percent by the time children reach the age of fourteen,[56] this reconsideration of competitive sport has the potential to effect dramatic shifts in perception.

What is important to note here is that sport commentary then tended toward a more collective focus and often gravitated toward issues pertaining to socialization, transmission of ideals and values, and the importance of life lessons gleaned from a sportive environment, hard lessons though they may have been in many cases. This often left the more particularist aspects of individual behavior and the reflexive psychological ramifications of sport participation to the realm of behavioral science and child development, which in a manner most typical of academicians then, tended to regard sport as frivolous and irrelevant in spite of the importance of sport as determined by community organizations and the child advocates who had aligned themselves with the more traditional character building initiatives (see chapter two). Concern over whether or not sport could accommodate the self seemingly had no tangible place in those particular discussions. As many coaches have reminded their young charges, both then and now, "there is no 'I' in team,"[57] which contraindicates this trend toward introspection within the modern sport paradigm.

Gradually, however, the popular appeal associated with trends in the development of self-concepts and the search for a de rigueur measure of self-fulfillment through socially defined interactions, including participation in sport, have seeped into the increasingly crowded field of contemporary youth sport criticism.[58] What had once been accepted rather matter-of-factly is today looked upon as both alarming and beyond the reach of modern expectations. As one apprehensive commentator/parent has noted on the parental link of the popular web site of *Sports Illustrated for Kids*:

> Sports are supposed to be fun, healthy activities that help build self-esteem. Sports are supposed to teach kids that it is okay to make mistakes and to not always be the best. But sometimes sports are not fun. And sometimes those mistakes do not feel okay. All young athletes face moments that challenge their self-esteem. They

may be cut from a team, drop a fly ball, or overhear a stinging comment by a teammate or parent.[59]

At the forefront of this shift are researchers from both within and outside the academy whose main focus is the psychosocial ramifications of participation in youth sport, a field of inquiry that until recently only existed on the periphery of social science. This sphere of inquiry, dominated by child psychology, aims its collective spotlight on sport and seems at the very least intent on convincing a decidedly sport-driven public to reconsider its once sacred devotion to competition as a precursor to sound development by turning inward and reflecting on the images, debates, and controversies surrounding today's high-profiled sports world and its potentially harmful effects on children. And while researchers in this area tend to vary from point to point regarding the specific effects sport has on children, what most seem to agree upon is the notion that when it comes to children, sport presents an almost incalculable risk. As Marty Ewing of Michigan State University's Youth Sport Institute posits, the difference between a successful competitive experience and an unsuccessful one has the capacity to dramatically impact a child's self-perception:

> Children will feel good about themselves as long as their skills are improving. However, if children feel that their performance during a game or practice is not as good as that of others, or as good as they think mom and dad would want, they often experience shame and disappointment.[60]

A predominant feature of this developing apprehension on the part of modern commentators, and of what constitutes health and healthfulness in youth sport today, is to what extent a child's self-concept is affected through a continued association with organized sport. When viewed in this light, whether the child participant experiences success or failure in a sporting endeavor seems oddly beside the point as sport today is increasingly perceived to be antithetical to the well-being of child-aged participants irrespective of outcome. Primarily as a result of their analyses and observations, more have come to accept that links to sport have the potential to negatively affect a child's self-image, and this potential for psychic scarring leaves many to doubt sport's continued place in the lives of American youth. Through this construct, the traditional roles are reversed, leaving self-esteem as the constant while it is the nature of competition itself that becomes the variable and subject to a wide range of negatively expressed criticisms. As Ewing again notes:

> ... the development of self-esteem is critical to help youth buffer the negative influences experienced by youth in today's society, [and while] high self-esteem will not guarantee that youth will make the right decisions, it does provide a stronger basis for resisting the pressures that currently exist [and] in addition to developing a positive sense of self, involvement in sport activities can assist children in learning what is right from wrong.[61]

This manner of evaluation has become an especially familiar feature of

Figure 6.1

A preoccupation with the self can be seen in such widely disseminated images as this Georgia tae kwon do school window.[62]

the contemporary debate and has a great deal to do with the dramatic and widespread change in perception regarding high-profile sport and its sociological influences. Indeed, displayed on the large windows along the front of our son's former tae kwon do school in Savannah, Georgia (see figure 6.1) was the rather imposing reminder of the school's stated goals and objectives, objectives that make no references to fun, recreation, and camaraderie, once considered to be the most basic and cherished internal rewards of youth participation and its youthful participants. Rather, their goals called for the more reflective-friendly motifs so prominent in the contemporary and decidedly more collective sport vision: self-control, self-discipline, self-confidence, and self-esteem (with a touch of self-defense thrown in for good measure!). And yet, every time we would arrive at a function there, we were generally greeted by a fairly recognizable mix of athletic intensity along with masses of sweaty, jovial, loud, and noticeably rambunctious boys and girls working hard but obviously enjoying themselves in spite of the pedagogically enhanced atmosphere. In this sense it would appear that the only constituents of that particular group who were plunged knee-deep into the modern constructs were the organizers and the parents who saw this particular athletic pursuit and their role in the proceedings as part of a much grander scheme based on a litany of larger psychosocial concerns. The children, on the other hand, seemed rather impervious to the developmental and management concerns of

intervening adults and simply preferred to play and perform as one might
expect of youth.

Self-Esteem and the
Psychology of Modern Youth Sport

*Most discussions of competition among children do not concern the
strenuousness of activity; they concern the social-psychological effects
of competition that no amount of talk can alter. To some, competition
is regarded as natural, healthy and essential for building character. To
others competition is regarded as harmful, psychologically injurious,
and detrimental to cooperative activity, which is endowed with all manner of beneficial effects and seen as the highest state of human relations.*[63]

*Haley Joel Osment asked me backstage that since we have fifty-two
entries, can't we make this like little league where everyone gets a trophy?*[64]

In 1996 psychologist Michael Passer of the University of Washington in
Seattle prefaced a discussion on the potential for competitive sport to impact
negatively the self-concepts of youth by reminding parents:

There simply is no magic age beyond which participation in youth sport programs
can be delayed so as to guarantee that such [problematic] outcomes will not
occur.[65]

He furthered his assessment by asking rhetorically whether or not we allow our
children to participate in sport too early on in their development while he outlined a register of what he perceived to be the risks intrinsic to participation
in youth sport:

• The potential suffering of one's self-perception of physical confidence
• The onset of long- and short-term competitive anxiety
• Decreasing popularity with teammates and peers due to poor performance
• The possibility for psychic bruising (said to effect one's ability to assimilate
  into sport at an older age)
• A perceived general decrease in self-esteem levels[66]

This version of the now ubiquitous *precautionary principle,*[67] which underscores
the risks of sport participation rather than any possible benefits, has become a
much more common feature of the contemporary analysis, placing sport participation beyond the basics of play and such by regarding risk conceptually to
be a more notable characteristic of sport.

Even those who throw their support toward the maintenance of some form
of youth sport participation do so with increasingly evident reservations, drawing heavily upon the psychosocial ramifications related to participation and

how these features may negatively impact an individual's self-concept. For instance, while sport and exercise psychologist Maureen Weiss can offer her support of school sport because "physical activity and sports have tremendous potential to enhance children's self-esteem and motivation,"[68] she can also warn elsewhere that "little substantive evidence exists to support claims of heightened self evaluations [that] recur from physical competence."[69] Likewise, Ronald Jeziorski, author and co-curricular consultant for the Santa Clara (California) School District and a contributor to the State of California's embrace of esteem-related initiatives, can draw liberally on older traditions by endorsing sport based on the long-held belief that youth participation in sport equates often to higher grades and better and more manageable behavior. Still, while he emphasizes the behavioral and character building benefits of sport participation, he also indicates a concern that these benefits may in time prove themselves to be fallacious and that sport administrators have a great deal of work to do in order to keep sport a viable and worthwhile refuge for youth.[70] Additionally, while oft-cited sport psychologist Tara K. Scanlon reminds us that sport may indeed serve as an achievement arena for youth actors, she also concedes that sport's more tangible contributions to youth development may only be possible in a highly scrutinized and structured environment:

> We need to show that what they have learned on the field applies in other areas of life. Learning how to work with peers and adults and the joy of mastering skills are just a few things that can be learned in that environment if it's done right.[71]

Indeed, there is a tendency among modern-day commentators to view youth and sport as a pairing that seems to be headed on a collision course, one that threatens the self-concepts of youth while exposing the weaknesses inherent to competition as a legitimate force in the lives of children, an image that certainly represents a direction in sport studies that seems decidedly far removed from older discussions. In this respect even those who can maintain a positive regard for some aspect of the traditional sport model seem skeptical unless the requisite esteem and character issues pertaining to the self-concept can be guaranteed through professional intervention and upheld by a learned constituency. As Weiss notes:

> Physical educators and sport practitioners share the enduring belief that a positive relationship exists between the development of physical skills and the enhancement of self-esteem. In essence, those who subscribe to the beneficial outcomes of sport participation agree that motor skill improvement will result in heightened levels of self-regard. Despite these claims, however, surprisingly little empirical research exists to substantiate them.[72]

Weiss continues reemphasizing the importance of self-esteem by imploring those adults involved in youth sport, and those high-profiled athletes whose presence are said to impact the perceptions and behavior of their young admirers, to adopt proactive measures for delivering self-esteem through sport as part of an "explicit, not hidden, agenda of our instructional practices by leading us to focus on strategies targeted to enhance self-esteem and, consequently, motivation and achievement."[73]

The tendency to view the constancy of success and failure within sport as exceedingly problematic is another common feature of this discussion. Many researchers readily point to the stressors most often associated with sport as both inherently threatening to an individual's self-concept and potentially irreversible regardless of outcome, while at the same time they seem committed to the notion that some physical exercise, albeit modified to insure optimum success, is necessary to insure proper development in children. As Ewing contends:

> Physical play during infancy and early childhood is central to the development of social and emotional competence. Researchers have reported that children who engage in more physical play with their parents, particularly with parents who are sensitive and responsive to the child, exhibited greater enjoyment during the play sessions and were more popular with peers. Likewise, these early interactions with parents, siblings, and peers are more important in helping children become more aware of their emotions and to learn to monitor and regulate their own emotional responses.[74]

On the other hand, some sport psychologists, such as Bruce Ogilvie and Thomas A. Tutko, have arrived at the conclusion that competitive sport may not be the answer to a fully integrated self-concept initiative after all. Rather, they perceive that from their vantage point, "competition doesn't even require much more than a minimally integrated personality."[75] But as Scanlon observes:

> Whenever social evaluation of ability occurs, positive or negative consequences can result during any given competition ... the important point is that many children engage in intense competition over extended periods of time with similar consequences potentially being repeated over and over again. This repetition makes developmental considerations, such as self-esteem development, relevant.[76]

To be sure, there are those who see sport not as a test of acumen but as something to be coped with and endured while hoping for the fewest possible psychological consequences at the end of the contest.[77]

This particular concern over outcome in turn leads many to place a great deal of emphasis on early sport experiences and the implications of these experiences. For example, University of Ottawa kinesiologist and non-competitive games advocate Terry Orlick maintains:

> A child's early sport experiences are extremely important. Positive beginnings nourish future involvement in sport whether for pleasure or as a career. Early sport experiences have an enormous impact on how a child feels about himself or herself not only in relation to sport but also in relation to global self-esteem. Children want and need positive experiences in sport. They want to play, not watch others play; they want to achieve their own goals, not adult goals; they want less emphasis on winning and more freedom to have fun.[78]

Yet, while some look to hold on to any semblance of the notion that competition can be rescued from its inevitable fall, others remain unconvinced and are much less accepting, exhibiting instead a disdain for sport while centering much of their criticisms on what many deem to be the more detrimental effects that sport may have on the development of healthy self-concepts. As exercise scientists James Whitehead and Charles Corbin contend:

> For years physical education, organized sport, and recreation agencies have promoted a variety of forms of physical activity with a view to enhancing self-esteem of children and youth. The best evidence suggests that when properly used, physical activity can indeed provide positive benefits to physical self-esteem and at the same time facilitate the most desirable forms of motivation. However, it is also apparent that physical activity and physical education programs can be double-edged swords. Used inappropriately they can have negative effects on self-esteem and motivation.[79]

Consequently, many are unwilling to endorse competitive sport because of the potential to negatively impact a child's self-concept, opting instead for much more noticeably austere assessments of the role of sport in children's lives while questioning its continued presence. Thus, Ogilvie and Tutko can claim:

> The competitive sport experience is unique in the way it compresses the selection process into a compact time and space. There are few areas of human endeavor that can match the Olympic trials or a professional training camp for intensity of human stress. A young athlete often must face in hours or days the kind of pressure that occurs in the life of the achievement oriented man over several years. The potential for laying bare the personality structure of the individual is considerable.[80]

In terms of the issue of pressure and its effect on young participants, Fred Engh, the director of the National Alliance of Youth Sport (NAYS) and a highly visible force for reform within the youth sport environment, assumes a position similar to that of Ogilvie and Tutko. Citing legitimate concerns for the well-being of young athletes, he maintains that the pressure of performing before family, before teammates, and before coaches has the potential to place the young athlete in a position from which he or she may never be able to recover. Toward that, he implores:

> Children shouldn't be forced into stressful situations where how they perform is all that matters. It's going to be a pretty traumatic experience for children who drop a pass in front of a whole group of coaches whom they desperately want to impress. And why were they put into this position in the first place? Only because all they wanted to do was play a sport and have fun in the process.[81]

The accepted wisdom that the frailty of childhood can be exploited by the precariousness of sport participation illustrates the most basic premise of this particular analysis: that there exists in contemporary society an institution — sport — whose draw is such that its potential to victimize far outweighs whatever perceived benefits it may have once offered. Ironically, what sets this more recent analysis apart from older interpretations says less about the weaknesses inherent to the competitive process and rather remains focused on the perceived weakness of the modern individual, a mode of inquiry that places sport in a position where it must struggle to justify its presence in the face of such decidedly anti-human assumptions.

7

A Developing Gulf:
Sport, Feminism,
and Anti-Racism

The collision of sport, competition, and the confluence of modern thought expresses itself vibrantly within the contemporary athletic sphere. Free from the constraints of Cold War era conventions and driven by a dedication to a range of newly embraced ideals, a contemporary political shift has in part redirected the discussion of competition into unprecedented territory. Included among these points would be matters pertaining to self-reflection and a deeper commitment to the psychology of emotions and the politics of identity, matters that had once appeared to exist too distinctively outside the margins of American life. As sociologist James Nolan has noted, the changing nature of American culture suggests that as time-honored institutions and once-trusted social conventions continue to demonstrate that they are no longer capable of forging solidarity in their traditional guise, modern Americans are finding it increasingly necessary or at the very least expedient to embrace the new or rewrite the old either in spite of or because of the upheaval of the age.[1]

The increased scrutiny of competitive sport suggests that in order to survive, it must acquiesce to nascent values or risk further denigration from a public no longer captivated solely by national memory, and in some cases this has already occurred. Furthermore, that the once impenetrable environs of sport have been overcome by individuals historically prevented from active participation would also seem to suggest that these developments might give rise to an innovative reinterpretation of the meaning of competition. With African Americans and other ethnic minorities well ensconced within the world of American sport, and with the growth of women's professional basketball and soccer and the introduction of women's ice hockey on the world stage, and the success of such openly gay athletes as Martina Navratilova in women's tennis, Greg Louganis in men's diving, and Rudy Galindo in men's figure skating, those once denied access to the competitive arena are no longer, at least institutionally speaking, openly steered into other directions. And yet, the interpretation of these circumstances is often couched in a perception that renders such states of affairs as problematic in their own rights, creating unusual and sometimes awkward schisms within the various advocative corners once meant to mediate such concerns.

In this chapter I will attempt to depict select features of these adjustments by revisiting elements of the countercultural legacy relative to inequality and the push for a more egalitarian outlook. In addition, and perhaps even more compelling, I will trace notable developments within some of the more prominent factions central to the countercultural legacy and explore the growing schisms taking shape within these once ideologically aligned clusters relative to their positions on sport.

Contemporary Sport within the Margin

Each year "little" leagues, junior high schools, high schools, colleges, and universities draw upon American communities for talent while professional sports enterprises draw upon colleges and universities — all under the aegis of "sports creed" or ideology, which espouses, among other things, the development of socially acceptable character traits, a high value upon brotherhood, and a commitment to the American ideals of individualism, fair play, and honest competition.[2]

As long as footballers are fit and able to deliver the goods on the pitch, I couldn't care less what they do in their free time, and neither should anybody else.[3]

By the end of the Cold War, what remained of the country's fascination with countercultural ideals will have come full circle as William Jefferson Clinton, the nation's first president to have actively and unapologetically protested the war in Vietnam while embracing a wide range of countercultural themes, would assume the office and offer the nation a more formal reading of once radical politics in a more distinctively official and widely disseminated fashion. While President Clinton's stand on public affairs, both foreign and domestic, included strong doses of customary Cold War era rhetoric, his administration's positions on such sociopolitical policy matters as race, gender, sexual orientation, and other themes that have historically been exploited by powerful national figures seeking very different ends, were little short of unprecedented.[4]

Under a Clinton White House, the very notions of equality as espoused by a previous generation's left wing will have entered into the mainstream of social discourse that would in turn mark the groundwork for a new national language, one that continues on in spite of a subsequent conservative administration with supposedly differing values. At the same time, even traditional power bases, poised for an inevitable redrafting of prevailing national attitudes, have turned away from traditional American philosophies while demonstrating in a much broader sense that a host of once-cherished features of American life have developed to the point where they are simply no longer capable of arousing the public's collective imagination, not to mention its affection. This revision would most assuredly have to include newer standards more in keeping with the changing nature of American ideals while leading to an even more pronounced fragmenting of the nation's cultural moorings. Thus in hindsight, that sport would get caught up in the middle of these developing debates seems for all intents and purposes unremarkable.

As expressed in previous chapters, the more contemporary critiques of American sport indicate that the battles being waged over its continued presence within the culture are marked in part by a series of struggles involving divergent philosophies that are often informed by the legacy of 1960s era counterculture. With its continued embrace of competitiveness, its presumed hegemonic masculine posture, and its unwavering insistence upon excellence, sport and the conventions that surround it are certainly at odds with the emergent politesse of the post–Cold War period. While sport seemed able only to teach the consequences of physical excellence, strength, virility, and devotion to duty, all matters inextricably linked to what have become for many a reviled and debased set of behavioral motifs, it would be unlikely that sport could hope to re-mark its boundaries given the commitment to egalitarianism through the relativizing of human efficacy.

Without the unwavering support of the populace, sport has been summarily exposed to and found in retreat from a nation in the midst of a pervasive yet significant state of social and cultural flux with no particular end in sight. Even in the more particularist circles of advocacy, where change is afforded a certain measure of currency, the nagging suspicion that acceptance through sport or even mobility through sport rests on an exceedingly dampened landscape has left many once inextricably aligned constituencies in a state of perpetual quandary as they sort through their legacies while attempting to reconcile the ramifications of sport participation for those historically along the periphery of American life.

African Americans in the Modern Sporting Milieu

While most humanists would not hesitate to admit that this intensified role of sports is an important symptom for the understanding of contemporary societies, they would also insist that, as a symptom in this sense, sports can only be read as a symptom of cultural decadence. Such a widely institutionalized prejudice may be the reason why so few scholars — if any — have seriously asked the question of what makes sports so particularly appealing to so many of our contemporaries.[5]

America loves the Black entertainers when they behave "properly" and stay in their place. These entertainers are socialized at an early age,

> *live under a microscope, and are constantly held to the expectations of*
> *a mainstream society that has no understanding for the fact that not*
> *everyone shares the same worldview. When the players realize their*
> *value, their significance to the game, and try to capitalize on this, they*
> *are held guilty in the highest court of contempt.*[6]

The relationship between African America and sport has a long and tragic trajectory, but a more modern interpretation places it on even less solid footing than some might suppose while creating something of a fissure within the more customary elements of contemporary sport criticism. The black American athlete is certainly as omnipresent a feature in sport as ever projected in contemporary circles, though the number of those who can actually recall America's Jim Crow sport world is certainly decreasing.[7] To be sure, African Americans, as well as myriad other racial and ethnic minorities, are extremely well-represented in the modern athletic sphere — at least in terms of field participation — with the estimates of the current disparity between black and white participation in the more high-profiled world of American sport almost staggering in some cases.

Whereas there are only 39 million citizens in the United States who can claim African ancestry, a scant thirteen percent of the total population, African Americans compose eighty percent of professional basketball players, seventy percent of professional football players, and over a third of professional baseball players (see figure 7.1),[8] though these figures are often offset by the equally

Figure 7.1. Percentage of African American Athletes 2004

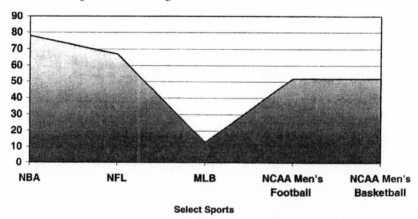

As sociologist Earl Smith notes, while African Americans make up only thirteen percent of the American population, they constitute an almost overwhelming majority in many of America's most popular sporting circuits with the exception of Major League Baseball, which he claims has shown a dramatic decline from as recently as the 1980s.[9]

Figure 7.2. Top Ten Highest Paid U.S. Based Athletes 2005

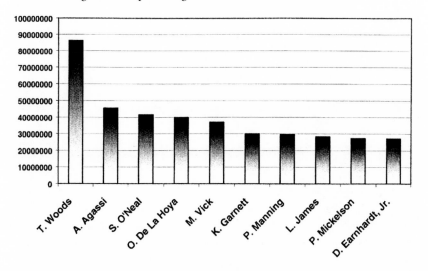

As seen in the above graph of the top ten earning athletes in American sport, five are African American and one is of Hispanic origin. Equally impressive is that the bulk of their salaries come from endorsements rather than straight salary figures. It is significant, too, that tennis' Serena Williams, ranked at #17, is the only woman to appear in the top fifty.[10]

as dramatic dearth of African Americans in leadership roles (see figure 7.2). That basketball's Michael Jordan and golf's Tiger Woods have emerged as not merely national but international phenomena also suggests that the dawning of the age of a dominant black presence in sport, at least on the playing surfaces, has left African America poised on the brink of upward mobility and social acceptance, given what had once occurred in terms of white ethnic immigrant cultures and their final stages in the assimilation process that was often marked by a group's presence in sport.[11] Still, as black athletes become more recognized as the standard bearers within the more high-profiled sporting milieu, their presence is frequently the subject of often unsettling and heated deliberations as to whether or not this element of black life is a positive gain or part and parcel of another sport-inspired myth with potentially devastating consequences.

Heralded sport sociologist Harry Edwards, a leading voice in terms of advocacy for minority rights in and around American sport, vacillates on this point over the course of his career. As he was to note in 1976, "[Organized sport is] a trap leading nowhere for most black youngsters, and the failure, the disillusionment, leads to social unrest and subsequent crime.[12] In more recent assessments, however, he seems to have reversed his stance, observing instead that the age of black dominance in high-profile American sport is coming to a close, which he deems a matter of some concern that should be monitored as well as mourned. As he declares in a 2000 interview in the publication *Color-Lines*, Edwards notes that recent history will demonstrate that through

> ... societal processes, through institutional erosion, through the degradation of the black athletic pool, through disqualification, judicial procedures and deaths, we have so emaciated the talent pool, that we are beginning to see a drop-off in performance at every level, in all sports where blacks participate in numbers. We are simply disqualifying, jailing, burying, and leaving behind our black athletes, right along with our potential black doctors, black lawyers, and so forth.[13]

To be sure, this is a controversy that continues to be played out in both scholarly and popular circles.

Counterbalancing Edwards on these points is University of Texas Germanic languages scholar John Hoberman who, in his often polemical *Darwin's Athletes: How Sport Has Damaged Black America and Preserved the Myth of Race*, offers an analysis of African American sport participation in a work that has generated a wealth of controversy within an already contentious terrain.[14] Hoberman's assessment of contemporary African American sport dominance is that it has become an inherently negative feature of black life in so much as it has offered little to the black community at large, short of a false sense, created by a fixation with the competitive domain, that it had arrived in the American mainstream, a conclusion that was once embraced by black and white intellectuals both but has seemed to have fallen out of favor in more modern appraisals.

Regardless of the black identity foci of many intellectuals working in this sphere who are quick to demonstrate that black artistry and grace, often obscured by American racism, are positively displayed in the athletic arena, Hoberman observes that there is a false illusion of black success through sport being supported by dramatic declines in black accomplishments and mobility elsewhere as evidenced by rising unemployment, further decay in urban neighborhoods, birth and death rates that decry first-world environments, and prisons overwhelmed by expanding black populations.[15] He considers that while many prized moments in popular black history are steeped in the athletic experience—for example, the successful albeit often controversial boxing careers of Jack Johnson and Muhammad Ali and the galvanizing of World War II era unity through the efforts of Joe Louis,[16] the ascension of Jackie Robinson into Major League Baseball in the aftermath of World War II, and the attention afforded younger athletic stars such as Jordan, Woods, and tennis' Williams sisters, to name a few — the success of what amounts to a minute fraction of black athletes reaffirms a deeply rooted contention regarding the black body in its physical locus while stirring yearnings within the black populace that sport is the surest way out of degraded environments. His critique offers an insistent refutation of an increasingly popular contention that sport offers black America a way out of its varied plights. He notes:

Exalting black athleticism has ... led some intellectuals to question the value of non-physical forms of cultural self-expression that supposedly do not dramatize black life with the immediacy of athletic competition. These writers believe that physical prowess represents the essence of the black experience in a way that other forms of expression cannot. Here too we see a fascination with the phenomenon of sheer physical struggle that can prompt the writer to confess his own shameful ineffectuality in comparison with the black athlete, who acts out the oppression of his people in real blood, sweat, and tears.[17]

Hoberman is notably guarded when it comes to those who seek to elevate any aspect of African American culture, whether it be through competitive sport, music, or any other element of black popular culture, into the realm of the exalted, claiming that such an embrace constitutes an unhealthy near-fetishizing of the black cultural milieu. In a chapter entitled "'Writin' Is Fightin': Sport and the Black Intellectuals," Hoberman engages a wide range of modern-day black scholars whose cultural analyses of contemporary black life have grown extremely popular among both academics and popular commentators alike.

Hoberman is particularly critical of the work of Eric Michael Dyson, among the vanguard of what he deems to be a community of African American scholars. Hoberman claims that Dyson, and others who espouse similar views, erroneously and perhaps even irrationally convert black popular cultural successes into far-reaching predictions of black advances that are unsupported either historically or through modern empirical analysis. In Dyson's essay "Be Like Mike? Michael Jordan and the Pedagogy of Desire,"[18] Hoberman observes that Dyson seeks to transform Michael Jordan into a sort of messianic figure on a par with Joe Louis and Jackie Robinson, though, by Hoberman's estimation, Jordan's era lacks anything close to the sort of social dynamics that would lead one to equate his place in sport alongside either man's historically timely emergence.[19]

Though Hoberman praises Dyson for elements of his work, including Dyson's recognition of Jordan's indifference to his role in creating marketing frenzies within impoverished communities, he is equally troubled that in Dyson's analysis, Dyson fails to acknowledge that Jordan represents not the narrowing of the racial divide but rather its reinforcement. He writes:

To be sure, Dyson is aware that black athleticism is vulnerable to exploitation. He knows, for example, that "the African-American aspects of Jordan's game [spontaneity, improvisation, deceptiveness] are indissolubly linked to the culture of consumption and the commodification of black culture,"[20] and he is candid enough to fault Jordan for his advertising appeals to young blacks. The moral force of these doubts dissolves, however, in the dazzling brilliance of Jordan's "unparalleled cultural status"[21] and the fact that his achievements "have furthered the cultural acceptance of at least the athletic black body."[22] But how can Dyson fail to understand the meagerness of this achievement, since accepting "the black athletic body"[23] has always been the path of least resistance for whites who will not recognize black people as fully human?[24]

Equally as telling in Hoberman's varied assessments are his apprehensions concerning a previous generation's lack of consistency in their analyses of transformations taking place within an emergent and notably modern black sporting ethos. With the exception of Harry Edwards, who acknowledged that sport would exert a "novocain [sic] effect"[25] upon the urban black populace, Hoberman insists that the lead roles in many critiques of black advances within sport during the height of Cold War America were assumed by more militant male critics whose position on establishing a heightened masculine presence often clashed with their female counterparts' designs on leading the African American public down a more intellectual path. He notes that "[c]ultural critics who remain confined within this legacy, held hostage by the false dichotomy between the martyred black athlete and the effete black thinker who 'acts white,' will find it difficult to assess the costs and benefits of the black athletic subculture with the dispassion this analysis requires."[26] In other words, Hoberman assumes that the spurious claims of the more recent critiques result from fallacies emanating from much older reviews that have remained as of yet unchallenged.

The debate regarding Hoberman's thesis has been significant indeed, stirring sentiment further around an already loaded and emotionally charged climate regarding the clash of race and sport. For example, in their discussion of African American athletes and the perception of assumed criminal behavior, much of which often translates into the transgressions of a sexual nature, Bonnie Berry of the Social Problems Research Group in Gig Harbor, Washington, and Earl Smith, Rubin Distinguished Professor of American Ethnic Studies at Wake Forest University, concur with Hoberman's point about a false image of mobility as expressed in media depiction of successful black athletes.[27] In addition to their results that suggest that the notion of predatory black athletes skirting established behavioral conventions for high-profiled athletes is both overplayed and perhaps indicative of a much deeper and problematic stereotypical rendering, they also note that in terms of tangible opportunities for mobility through sport for the majority of black participants, this concept is equally mythical and problematic. They emphasize, for example, that a "simplistic dichotomy"[28] of morality, as generally expressed in media portrayals of the consequences of black athlete behavior that clashes with modern standards, does not support policies offered to boost racial equality but rather hinders it. They also demonstrate similar concerns paralleling those expressed in Hoberman's analyses. Specifically, they claim that by overemphasizing sport as a means toward expanding opportunities for growth and acceptance, black youth are being socialized into accepting sport as a legitimate lever for a more genuine role within American life. They note:

> Popular culture suggests that sports are the best (and only) source of equal opportunity for African Americans. Involvement in sports is often presented as a way out of the ghetto, as though most African Americans live in ghettos or as though most African Americans from ghettos aspire to sports careers. Nevertheless, given that education and employment are not distributed equally in our society, some

African Americans may indeed see sports as an avenue to wealth and fame and as an avenue that has worked for others.[29]

University of Minnesota sociologist Douglas Hartmann also considers Hoberman's thesis in terms of the effect of increasing opportunities for African American athletes in sport. He points out that while such conclusions regarding whether or not African American sport participation has either helped or hindered black progress remain unanswered, he does suggest that at least on the popular level, the consensus is that black participation is a key element in the discussion of mobility and acceptance. In terms of the scholarly debate, however, Hartmann senses a categorical approach to this question, namely that academics, while notably convinced of sport's detrimental effect, are divided between the more commonly devised critiques of race and racism within sporting circles and what he terms the "culturalist orientation,"[30] which he claims "emphasize[s] the symbolic role in the formation of racial meanings and practices broadly conceived."[31] He contends that while it may be "rare to hear bold and unqualified statements about sport's positive racial force"[32] among the various scholarly critiques, he also advises that by highlighting such disparities while ignoring the popular consensus, critics run the risk of cynically dismissing popular conjecture that often leaves creditable scholarship one-sided to the extent that it fails to recognize or value "the complexity of sport's place in the American racial order."[33]

Though he is sympathetic to Hoberman's original thesis that challenges prevailing contentions, Hartmann also criticizes Hoberman's unwillingness to appreciate the extent to which an increasing black presence in sport helped foster the changing racial climate in American life. As he stresses:

> While it may not be perfect, sport is an unparalleled institutional site of accomplishment for African Americans and remains one of the most integrated institutions in American life ... [becoming] a crucial social space for the development of an African American identity and aesthetic. This distinctive cultural style is obviously useful in terms of its market value, but it is more significant still, in theoretical terms, for its capacity to inspire productive, creative labor among African American young people living in otherwise alienating and disadvantaged circumstances.[34]

Specifically addressing Hoberman, Hartmann then concludes:

> ... suffice it to say that if African Americans tend to see sport positively, it is not because they are fixated on sport; indeed, some evidence shows that African Americans are not any more fixated on sport than any other group of Americans. Rather, it is because sport offers African Americans opportunities and freedoms found rarely in other institutions in the society. The popular ideology, in this respect, is not simply a misguided set of ideas and beliefs.[35]

Indeed, some, including Edwards, have maintained that an assessment such as Hoberman's, though certainly effective and guided by a genuine mistrust of mainstream intentions, nonetheless denigrates black contributions to American life and ultimately denies the black athlete his rightful place among more exalted figures in the culture.[36] Washington University Merle Kling Professor of Modern Letters Gerald Early, a contemporary of Dyson writing in the monthly publication *The Nation*, notes that while Hoberman assesses the apolitical side of sport, a quarter that is often exacerbated by a collection of apologists and the overly romantic language of the sporting media, his discussion of a black obsession with sport has led his thesis away from social commentary and into the highly controversial realm of psychology, a matter that has long been held in suspicion by the African American public. He notes:

> As a critical theorist, Hoberman was never interested in proving [his overall thesis] with thorough empiricism, and, as a result, was attacked in a devastatingly effective manner by black scholars, who blew away a good number of his assertions with an unrelenting empiricism. But he has got into deep trouble with black intellectuals, in the end, not for these assertions or for the mere lack of good empiricism. Hoberman, rather, has been passionately condemned for suggesting that blacks have a "sports fixation" that is tantamount to a pathology, a word that rightly distresses African-Americans, reminiscent as it is of the arrogance of white social scientists past and present who describe blacks as some misbegotten perversion of a white middle-class norm.[37]

The general consensus, though hardly clear, suggests that Hoberman's look at the relationship between African Americans and competitive sport is admirable but flawed. The insistence that a pathological state of sport obsession threatens to drive black Americans further away from the center of American life, as Hoberman says, is steeped in reductionist and overly simplistic assessments that serve to both deny black advancement and add fuel to a mordant nihilism creeping further into black consciousness. As Early muses:

> Sports do not mask the absurdity of life but rather ritualizes it as a contest against the arbitrariness of adversity, where the pointless challenge of an equally pointless limitation, beautifully and thrillingly executed, sometimes so gorgeously as to seem a victory even in defeat, becomes the most transcendent point of all. Black people have taught all of us in the blues that to lose is to be human. Sports, on any given day, teaches the same.[38]

Race, Sport, and Sexuality as Conundrum

During [football's] grotesque Jim Crow era, for example, masculinity on the field was conceived in terms of gender — football players were fundamentally not-women, not 'sissies.' But over the past thirty years, the game has been transformed by race, by what are increasingly defined as black and white styles of masculinity.[39]

Basketball is slavery to most white folks. It's just in an advanced form. Today's slave market is open for a slave to make $100M, but look at what the slave owner gets in return! Now ask yourself: Who's the Mack?[40]

Another element of the African American incursion into the sporting milieu that has certainly caused a ripple effect within modern criticism deals with the notions of masculinity as expressed among black athletes and their supporters. Hoberman makes note of this in his brief discussion of writer Amiri Baraka, who Hoberman contends is something of a Norman Mailer-esque critic with an eye for machismo.[41] Hoberman cites a mid-1960s Baraka diatribe aimed at the racial hostility of the age in which Baraka, who was then still known as Leroi Jones and represents Hoberman's example of the sort of masculine-based black commentator, charged:

> Most American white men are trained to be fags. For this reason, it is no wonder that their faces are weak and blank.... That red flush, those silk blue faggot eyes ... Do you understand the softness of the white man, the weakness, and again the estrangement from reality?[42]

For Hoberman, this foray into sexual politics, though dated, remains nevertheless problematic in that it reflects backward on the racist depiction of the hypersexual, hypermasculine black man, which, given the contemporary climate relative to gender discourse, remains a salient criticism while speaking volumes about other, more contemporary issues operating within the once exclusive environs of white male sport. In other words, the dynamic of having black athletes so much in vogue is easily transmuted by the recurring ideology that seeks to downplay the competitive ethos as being informed by a hegemonic male-dominated and certainly heterosexual order of which the black athlete has become an active constituent while playing up to the more traditional and inherently associations of hypersexuality and the black body.[43]

To be sure, homosexuality, once seen as problematic in women's sport earlier in the twentieth century, is today looked upon as nothing less than the last frontier of men's. In a tradition whose foundation was built upon shared notions of heterosexual masculinity and bravado, the hint of male homosexuality has always and continues to remain as taboo an idea as ever existed in competitive assemblages. Though there have been inroads carved through sport's heavily macho terrain by a more recent trend toward what has been relabeled "Queer Theory" relative to sport, only in individual sports do we see openly gay athletes operating in such public space. For example, the 2005 assertion by WNBA superstar Sheryl Swoopes, possessor of the only female-branded basketball shoe in the Nike catalog, that she is a lesbian elicited almost no reaction from the sporting public as if this revelation was simply business as usual, causing several commentators to wonder when this frontier was finally conquered.[44] Nevertheless, just a hint of an openly gay man in a team sport remains a matter chock-full of intrigue, conjecture, and anxiety as witnessed by the collective response to two rather ignominious moments in early twenty-first century Major League Baseball.

In May 2001 the editor of the monthly *Out* announced in an open letter that he had been having a clandestine romance with a man he designated as a high-profile professional baseball player on the East Coast.[45] Following this revelation, the sport world grew increasingly more prickly at the suggestion that there may have been homosexuals in its midst, leading to a wealth of speculation and rumor that ultimately compelled one athlete, former New York Mets star catcher Mike Piazza, nearly a full year later to publicly state that he was not the athlete in question and to declare himself heterosexual amid the swirl of conjecture, an irony not lost on some critics.[46] That Piazza had taken such rumors so seriously as to call a press conference to announce that he was *not* coming out underscores the significance of the gay-macho continuum that exists in the locker rooms of male team sport. And though the conjecture as to who it may be continued to swirl about in popular and probably even academic discussions, the reaction alone marked an extremely interesting moment in modern sport history. Never before had homosexuality in men's sport been such an openly debated topic, though ultimately the rejection of such an idea remains the most common response. Indeed, when asked to comment on the issue of professional athletes openly declaring their homosexuality, sport commentator John "Spider" Salley, a former NBA player, was very direct in his assessment. He noted that the likelihood of a gay man being accepted in the notoriously heterosexually macho men's athletic environment despite many of the liberalizing attitudes toward homosexuality today was minute at best, offering instead that "[Major League Baseball pitcher] John Rocker would be accepted into the NAACP before a gay guy would be welcomed into a men's locker room."[47] That Salley once performed in and seems to have been shaped by his time in the conceivably hypermasculine and overwhelmingly black environment of professional basketball gives rise to an increasingly problematic debate within the notably liberalized and often self-consciously inclusive field of sport criticism.

Many critics of hegemonic masculine behavior in the sporting environment tend toward offering impacting, if not socially muted, claims that serve to indict the black athlete as culpable for continued expressions of homophobia as expressed in sport circles in spite of their typical lack of control for what happens either on or away from the playing surfaces. Whereas the once formidable trilogy of race, class, and gender, which, to clarify, typically includes discussions pertaining to sexual orientation, often paves the way for more substantive examinations of the nature of marginalized factions within both the competitive paradigm and the modern orthodoxies relative to inclusion and identity, the mounting presence of black athletes in high-profile sport has threatened to disrupt this relationship in the more scholarly treatments of competitive sport. Where this is most notable is the reemergence of gender roles in relation to previous racist claims of irrepressible black male sexual desires and the heightened awareness of sexual aggression toward women perpetrated by athletes. Assessments offered by sport researchers guided by more contemporary theoretical premises may impact the discussion of sex roles and aggression in sport, but they also do as much to reaffirm racist claims by tacitly accepting the traditional image of the black sexual predator hyped up on a combustible mix of endorphins and rage and perhaps other more controversial substances seeking to claim the prizes that celebrity might afford. As Berry and Smith argue, while hypermasculinity, intense sexism, and monosexual environments are perceived to occupy center stage in the discussions relative to athletes and crime, this expression is often geared toward a modern sounding assessment couched in much older sentiment:

> African American men, from a racist perspective, are not only considered highly sexed but dangerous.... This perspective is carried over into sports. When white athletes commit sex crimes, it is said that "boys will be boys." This is far less likely when the athletes are African American.[48]

The friction that develops, thus, in terms of the once shared recognition of similar battles previously fought by, in this case, female athletes, both black and white, and black male athletes, who were all once excluded from the mainstream of American sport, is underscored by what appears as a tacit acceptance on the part of the black man of what feminists might identify as hegemonic and certainly chauvinistic attitudes as reproduced through competitive sport. Furthermore, this tension is often exacerbated by homosexual incursions into sport that share a similar path into the more exclusive realm of competition.[49] As larger numbers of black athletes continue to enter into the sporting environment and display the more typically dominant male attitudes, another stereotype often enters into the fray, what some have alluded to as the myth of black male homophobia as expressed in the above Baraka citation as well as other rather infamous and remarkably resilient claims such as Eldridge Cleaver's contention that homosexual behavior was akin to "baby-rape."[50] Indeed, when queried as to why it seems that openly gay athletes such as figure skater Rudy Galindo and diver Greg Louganis have been accepted and even embraced in mainstream sport while the notions of team sport remain off-limits to such revelations, Eric Anderson, then a doctoral candidate at the University of California at Irvine, and the man who holds the distinction of being America's first openly gay track coach, a journey that he has chronicled in the acclaimed *Trailblazing: The True Story of America's First Openly Gay Track Coach*,[51] noted that the disparity between individual, less visible sport and the more intensely guarded environs of high-profile sport are such that it's unlikely that an openly gay man would dare to step into this particular spotlight. He notes, albeit informally:

> Because we'd expect less crap from an individual sport, which tend to be non-contact, [queer theorists] loosely theorize that an athlete is more likely to "come-out" in the artistic, individual sports and then increasingly less likely to come out through the ranks until you hit football.[52]

The discussion of race and masculinity in terms of both women and homosexuals and their relationship to the competitive domain is indeed fraught with potential schisms and vitriol that stands poised to threaten the solidarity each once championed. The notion that femininity and homosexual behavior clash with the accepted masculine expression of competitiveness marks a difficult terrain for which these groups must negotiate either together or apart, often leading to mixed analyses and subtle yet just as impacting statements that may certainly be construed as both over-generalized and excessively critical coming from all sides. For example, Brian Pronger of the University of Toronto, a self-professed queer theorist and vocal advocate for the cause of gay rights in sport, claims that the perpetuation of the masculine sport myth is about "phallic conquest and anal closure,"[53] declaring:

> So here is the hermeneutic circle: sportsmen and boys are socially legitimated by the various ways they perform masculinity, which is about degrees of the abjection of women. It's about loss. The more successful we are in competitive sport, the more we perform phallocentric masculinity, the more we are in abject difference, the more we lose.[54]

In this respect, it becomes rather apparent that in terms of presenting challenges to hegemonic male authority being reproduced through competitive sport, the alliances between feminists and homosexual advocates are hard pressed to include positive discussions of the relationship between black men and their place in the sporting culture. As Theresa Walton explains in her critical assessment of the Sprewell-Carlesimo incident (see chapter four), the line between unacceptable violence, that is, a black athlete choking his white coach, and acceptable violence, that is, sexually aggressive athletes abusing women, runs deftly through the discussions circling around the competitive frame, to which the black man has become an active contributor.[55] As she argues, "The separation between workplace violence and domestic violence works to elevate the violence between Sprewell and Carlesimo above anti-woman violence committed by the same population of men (athletes and coaches)."[56] But as British writer Emmanuel Oliver of the once self-consciously iconoclastic monthly *Living Marxism* reasons, the 1992 conviction of former heavyweight champion Mike Tyson, hailed as both a victory for women's rights and a watershed moment in the advancement for equal treatment, can be read in another light:

> [A media driven advocacy] took the side of one oppressed group only because it gave them the opportunity to stick the boot into the other. Under the pretext of standing up for the rights of rape victims, they stamped all over the rights of black people.[57]

Or as Syracuse University historian Elizabeth Lasch-Quinn notes in her often scathing critique of what she has termed a new racial etiquette, this clash of black cultural behavior and the modern condemnation regarding enforced gender roles owes as much to mythically built traditional ideas of black masculinity and the continued misrepresentations of such ill-considered constructs:

The myth of hypermasculinity encouraged black men to live up to their image, as conveyed by the wider culture, in order to reject the arbitrary authority of whites. By embracing this imposed definition of their very identity, however, black men participated in their own subjugation.[58]

Female Athletes at a Crossroads

The notion of the "gentleman," or indeed any notion of masculinity attached to gentility, has almost vanished from the cultural air ... I guess you could start by observing that many areas of life that were once "gentlemanly" have simply been opened to women and thus effectively demasculinized.[59]

According to research from the Women's Sports Foundation, half of all girls who participate in some kind of athletics develop higher than average levels of self-esteem, and they experience less depression than girls who are not active in sports. Later, as teenagers, girls who have high self-esteem are less likely to become pregnant, and, as adults, are more likely to leave an abusive relationship than girls with low self-esteem. When teen-agers evaluate themselves in a positive way, they are more capable of avoiding drugs, alcohol, tobacco, gangs, and violence. Of course, high self-esteem will not guarantee that youngsters will always make responsible decisions, but it does provide a stronger basis for resisting the pressures that currently exist in society today. Now, because of Title IX, that is more likely to be the case for all the youth of America, male and female.[60]

Women competitors too face significant challenges in the new, more egalitarian sporting terrain that are often fraught with similar contradictions facing African American males. The mixed reviews often tendered in the face of women's gains in the athletic sphere often display a tension between those seeking to erase the forced obsequiousness and sensitivity frequently addressed in the female character while at the same time adopting and modeling the behaviors expressed in the new egalitarian ideology. As Mills College philosophy professor Helen Longino notes in her essay "The Ideology of Competition," the traditional rejection of competition by women had always been based on the idea that to compete was "unwomanly,"[61] which would be redressed within the modern feminist movements as "unsisterly."[62] As she reckons:

Feminist separatists have advocated withdrawal not just from the male world, but from the sphere allocated to women by patriarchy and to which women will always be restricted in a patriarchal system. Outside that system, in nonoppressive, nondistorting environments, women can develop fully as the human beings we are. Sisterhood means being supportive of one another, cooperative, nurturant, not trying to outdo one another, which is typically what men do.[63]

Walking the thin line between competitiveness and the reproduction of hegemonic masculine attitudes often presents a challenging obstacle for female athletes and their advocacy. In her review of sport commentator Mariah Burton Nelson's *Embracing Victory: Life Lessons in Competition and Compassion*, for example, Teri Bostian of the since defunct on-line monthly *SportsJones* notes that by participating in competitive sport, women have to be conscious of not upholding traditional masculine values while at the same time attempt to shed the tendency to reproduce no longer tolerable models of feminine comportment, including passivity, daintiness, pettiness, and the accepting of second place finishes as, nevertheless, satisfying. Bostian adds that in her critique, Nelson argues that by timidly approaching the sporting environment by tempering one's appearance with beauty, softness, and acquiescence, some female athletes are serving only to accommodate the interests of the hegemonic order.[64] As Nelson challenges, "It would be unhealthy for men to act passive, dainty, obsessed with their personal appearance, and dedicated to bolstering the sense of superiority in the other gender, so it's unhealthy for women too."[65]

Others have taken to suggesting that rather than being a polemically expressed and highly politicized issue, the growing ubiquity of women athletes should be a galvanizing moment in human history worthy of celebration. As Ruth Conniff writes, almost gregariously, in *The Nation*:

> It has been my generation's great good fortune to grow up in the era of Title IX. Never before has a single law made it possible for so many previously disfranchised people to have so much fun. Since Title IX of the Education Amendments Act passed in 1972, requiring publicly funded schools to offer equal opportunities to male and female athletes, the number of American high school girls who play sports has jumped from one in twenty-seven to one in three. The effects are visible everywhere: an explosion of female Olympic stars, college and professional women's teams playing to pack stadiums, new magazines aimed at female athletes. But most of all, the effect of Title IX is evident in the freedom, strength and joy of a whole generation of young women.[66]

Others, however, see this turnabout in very different terms. Outlets for women's sport are often shrouded by a distinctive fear of lesbianism, reminiscent of much older claims suggesting a repressive environment that, as one NCAA female athletic director observes, is wielded "like the McCarthyism of the 1950's."[67] Furthermore, as she adds, "The fear is paralyzing."[68] Akilah Monifa, a public relations strategist and media trainer with the Independent Media Institute's SPIN Project,[69] writing in *ColorLines* grants, "Just take a look at the WNBA's[70] promotional 'femming up' campaign to avoid even a question about the sexual orientation of the players or women coaches," which seems to suggest that while women's participation in sport is often heralded as a progressive step in the battle for inclusion and equality, it is often displayed as a sort of compromise, a compromise that some find regressive and detrimental to the cause of egalitarian ideals as engendered by the above-mentioned lack of regard for Sheryl Swoopes' declaration. As highly respected sport sociologist Howard Nixon has observed, the toughness element entrenched within the competitive sport model is bound to enter into the new age of female sport participation, which he claims will have little effect short of teaching once socially constructed passive women engaged in sport how to express aggressive behavior more easily through sport's socializing influence.[71] Or as British sport expert Jennifer Hargreaves reasons, in the case of female participation, a contemporary mainstream element has a great deal of difficulty interpreting modern change relative to a redrawing of sport's more recently accessible spaces:

> The historical focus of women's struggles in sports has been over inequalities with men; and the attempts of women to wrest power away from men and to have more equal access to resources suggests that all women share a common philosophy. But women are not a homogenous group and do not have identical needs and desires. Different women see the social world of sports in different ways and struggle amongst themselves, as well as with men, over definitions of women's sports."[72]

Another theme encompassing the discussion of a more modern and inclusive sport environment pertaining to female athletes touches upon the notion of the development of a notably feminized sporting ethos and its effect both inside the sporting world and along the margins of sport-influenced society. The notion that women have the capacity to bring to the sporting arena a softer-edged expression of competitiveness replete with a more womanly decorum, a notable respect for the authority of coaches and officials, and a healthy spirit that accepts defeat gracefully while publicly exuding modesty and humility emanates from many sides of the modern discourse and is certainly not in line with contemporary images of men's sport. Though Nixon might deflect such assessments as ill-befitting the socializing influences within sport, as noted above,[73] these claims, which are also ill-supported by empirical examination, have nonetheless become just as likely to mark a more progressive modern sport construct.[74] The suggestion is that the female — in contrast to male — athlete, was far more likely to be a good sport, unselfish, team-oriented, and, while at times tough and aggressive as befits an athlete, could generally display the wherewithal to remain in control and civil to her opponent.

British sociologist Frank Füredi's rejection of such a conclusion is best illustrated in his depiction of a highly controversial incident that took place on the last day of the 1997–1998 NCAA women's basketball regular season.[75] That season's number one ranked school, the University of Connecticut, having already qualified for the postseason tournament, apparently worked in partnership with their opponents from Villanova University and the game's officials to have their injured star forward, Nykesha Sales, her leg encased in a cast but a mere two points shy of the career scoring mark for women, stand underneath the Villanova basket while the two teams went through the pretense of an opening game tip-off. While opponents, referees, and spectators looked on, Sales' teammates gingerly slipped the ball to her, allowing Sales to score, claim her record, and subsequently hobble off the court.[76]

This obviously staged event caused a furor in and around the sporting milieu as well as within many diverse corners within sport criticism, much of which consisted of the dispute as to whether Sales' record was legitimate.

Füredi's point, however, considers neither the legitimacy of the record nor whether as a valued member of the team Sales was simply entitled to it. Rather, it was the ramifications of such an event occurring during what has always been conceived of as a spontaneous display of physical and mental acumen. As German scholar Eugen König contends in an article written in the *International Review for the Sociology of Sport*, competition exists as an a priori standard of codified equal opportunity,[77] but what transpired that evening in Connecticut certainly lacked such considerations. Thus, when one of the officials who participated in the ruse maintained later that "men compete, get along and move on with few emotions"[78] while "women break down, get emotional, get so much more out of the game"[79] relative to a statement regarding the biological and social mechanisms that drive men and women differently, Füredi's position was marked by a recognition that the contemporary inclusion model, seen here within the competitive construct and steeped in an artificially enhanced feminine gloss, suggests:

> We prefer sad men and women who openly indulge their weaknesses to those who want to get on with life, take risks, and if necessary ignore the pain. And instead of acknowledging our anxieties and trying to overcome them, we wallow in them and insist that we are actually more "aware" and more in touch with our feelings.[80]

That incidents such as the Sales matter can be perceived within some elements of society as the mark of a positive change taking shape within competitive sport indicates just how far the pendulum has swung. The celebration concerning the American women's victory in the 1999 World Cup seemed steeped in a similar tone that suggested comparable implications for the future of competitive sport while threatening to undermine the integrity as well as the very nature of athletic competition. The commonality of terms generated to reflect the significance of both the victory and the acclaim suggested that women, in contrast to their male counterparts, were far more spectator friendly, better sports, unselfish, team-oriented, and, while at times they too could be tough and aggressive, they generally displayed the wherewithal to remain in control and civil to their opponents in spite of their success, though venerable sport commentator Frank Deford has observed otherwise, noting in a recent radio commentary:

> Oh, my — we had hoped when women started coming into sports in large numbers after the passage of Title IX that they would improve the institution, investing it with the fine feminine values. Well, the results so far seem to indicate that instead sports has won and womanhood has lost.[81]

Regardless of who has won and who has lost in this case, however, what is apparent in these discussions of feminine versus masculine attributes in sport is this perception that the juxtaposition of the more refined, good-natured, hard-working, and appreciative woman with boorish, loutish — even atavistic — man suggests two very disparate views of competitiveness that when viewed in this light present a binary between the good (women) and the evil (men).

Certainly these attacks on the so-called masculine nature of contemporary sport are not new, but rarely have they enjoyed being aired on such a lofty perch. Furthermore, the suggestion that women and even homosexuals, as suggested in many descriptions of so-called gay sport,[82] could have the sporting market cornered by virtue of their more natural proclivity toward traditional sporting behavior is both illogical and potentially even more detrimental to the cause of true equality. To be candid, this brand of supposition buys into the pseudoscientific presumptions that have long haunted women and minorities in the quest for a truly egalitarian social order by naturalizing and hereby justifying treatment that cuts across the grain of progress. Thus if we are to assume that these discussions are borne of the struggle for liberation, it would seem that the logical first step is to denaturalize the process rather than putting a mere maternal face to it. As these debates occur, however, they seem prone toward accentuating human frailty rather than underscoring a sense of vibrancy born of the experiences of living and thriving in a human-centered environment. Furthermore, and perhaps the ultimate irony, as more and more heterosexual men of traditionally marginalized groups continue to enter into the mainstream through sport, they will find that collectively their position alongside others seeking to challenge the traditional status quo will continue to wear away under the weight of expectations as broadly defined by the various constituencies.

Conclusion

We found no empirical support for the tradition that sport builds character. Indeed, there is evidence that athletic competition limits growth in some areas. It seems that the personality of the ideal athlete is not the result of any molding process, but comes out of the ruthless selection process that occurs at all levels of sport. Athletic competition has no more beneficial effects than any intense endeavor in any other field. Horatio Alger success — in sport or elsewhere — comes only to those who already are mentally fit, resilient and strong.[1]

When parents push their kids, they see millions of dollars flying around from big league contracts. Their attitude is "My son will be a player whether he likes it or not."[2]

In many ways, one can point to the American fascination with competitiveness and both marvel and shudder at its various guises but still not come to terms with its place in American life. On the one hand, athletic competition, in spite of the contested terrain, remains a repository of the American cultural imagination, where it represents a most salient and spirited etching of mankind's enduring battle with both itself and the natural world. In this ideal, competition can be viewed through a trove of innovative and often artistic literary devices, the image of human beings defying natural law while achieving unimaginable levels of success and the associated splendor of celebrating the challenges themselves.[3] And yet, this oftentimes romantic image has in some manner been conjoined to a much more distressed, even churlish condemnation of the once vaunted competitive ethos.

From the suppressed undercurrent of the 1950s era to the explosive social and political confrontations of the 1960s and on into the blander periods of withdrawal and self-absorption inherent to the 1970s and 1980s, America has played host to a fairly steady breakdown in terms of its ability to define and interpret the nature of its sociocultural heritage and the meaning of what constitutes right moral thinking. No longer the stereotypical dynamic and energetic go-getter, so much a staple of America's vaunted self-image, this more traditional rendering of the conventional American character is being supplanted by an evolving caricature that places caution above action while showing a reverence for mediocrity over excellence. Moreover, as this emergent orthodoxy, built on the duality of human excess and infirmity, continues to grow even more pervasive, conventional means of instilling traditional values, such as those found in competitive sport, only appear to perpetuate the notion that American culture is steeped in a most perceptible and seemingly sustained clashing of cultural imperatives. But as sociologist Frank Füredi cautions, these developments are "underpinned by the idea that individuals are weak and fickle [and] are no longer seen as self-determining subjects capable of exercising democratic citizenship, but rather as potentially 'damaged goods' who need the support of professionals."[4]

This more recent trend assigns to the modern competitive arena a marked degree of pathos that has opened up a much more controversial view suggesting, among other things, that competition cannot always be aligned with human decency and that its place in the contemporary imagination should, and perhaps must, be challenged. As the founder of the National Alliance for Youth Sport, Fred Engh, maintains:

> I believe that competition, instilled with the values of fair play, sportsmanship, and ethics, can help build character traits in young people that will last a lifetime.
> These are the traits we admire in the people with whom we want to work, play, and spend quality time. People with a competitive spirit are usually the leaders in every aspect of our society.[5]

From there, however, Engh, an outspoken advocate for sport reform, readjusts his original position:

> So competition can be a positive thing, but if adults do not keep it in perspective, they can make children miserable and drive them away from sports.[6]

It is this last note, the suggestion that an incorrectly wielded competitive spirit evinces institutional breakdown, that underscores the tenor of this particular discussion while providing a foundation for understanding the modern reevaluation of competitive sport as being based in part on a perception that a little competition has the potential to generate challenges that could foster unacceptable consequences.

Thus, the move away from the competitive ethos as expressed throughout this project is part and parcel of a highly complex and extremely volatile mix of modern social constructionist ideology and the resiliency of traditional cultural motifs that continue to operate within American life. The boundless energy and enthusiasm generated by the varying factions functioning within the range of these discussions seem to offer their collective expressions of doubt and uncertainty with a genuine and sincere expression of social justice and decorum, but in the end what has occurred is a cluttered notion of what it means to be human and a perhaps unwitting denigration of the spirit of human achievement and the efficacy of mankind.[7]

Is Soccer the Answer?

Steering your child into soccer may have been fashionable, but it wasn't a decision to be made lightly.... As I later discovered, my parents made this sacrifice of their leisure time because they believed that soccer could be transformational.[8]

When it comes to soccer, the US has no sandlot culture.[9]

The move toward the establishment a more modern hierarchy through the introduction of particularly innovative guidelines as to what constitutes admirable social behavior, palatable interpretations of success, and the ensuring of more fashionable self-friendly mechanisms for measuring achievement has brought a renewed focus on sport as an agent for character building and social bonding, but this comes irrespective of the once seemingly exceptional American sporting tradition.[10] The remarkable growth of youth soccer in the United States (see figures C.1 above and C.2) reflects the sentiment that while on the one hand the tradition of involving oneself in competitive sport remains solidly entrenched within the American culture, its meritorious claims and public persona are in need of some extensive rehabilitation. As Engh explains:

Part of the attractiveness of soccer for parents, besides the safety factor, is that it's an ideal way to introduce a child to sports, mainly because there is not much pressure attached to playing. In baseball, on the other hand, there's a

---

Figure C.1. Growth Patterns in American Youth Soccer Participation

In their turn-of-the-century analysis of American recreation market trends, John R. Kelly, Professor Emeritus at the University of Illinois at Urbana-Champaign, and Rodney B. Warnick of the University of Massachusetts at Amherst report the following in regards to the growth of the more recently acknowledged American soccer tradition, which they claim is both "growing from the ground up"[11] "and statistically striking:

- an overall growth rate in participation of twenty percent across the board during the 1990's
- adult participation has increased from one percent in 1991 to as high as two and a half percent by 1996, which comes out to 4.5 million participants and 124 million play days
- child aged participants have shown a four percent upsurge yearly between 1990 and 1997, which puts the participation numbers as high as 13.7 million, of which they estimate that just over 4 million can be considered regular participants.
- the greatest increase in child aged participants has been generated in youth ages seven to eleven, which have shown a twenty-seven percent increase between the year 1990 and 1996, though they claim that youth ages twelve through seventeen have shown a five percent drop that they owe in part to the selection processes of more competitive interscholastic leagues and traveling youth soccer associations.
- they project continued albeit slower growth in youth participants that they attribute to a rise in female participation rates and in areas with growing Latino and European populations[12]

Figure C.2. U.S. Youth (7–17)
Soccer Participation 1994–2003

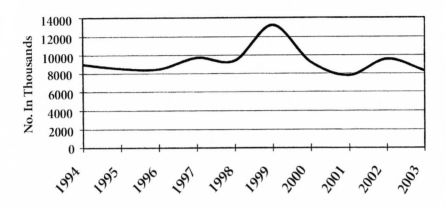

While youth soccer participation in the United States seems to have peaked in 1999, all signs point to a strengthening of the soccer tradition in the U.S. especially given the nation's more recent embrace of such world-wide affairs as the men's and women's World Cup competitions.[13]

degree of accountability built in, since each player has a turn at bat. In basketball, within just five players on the floor at a given time, there's added pressure to perform. However, in youth soccer, it's just kids running up and down the field chasing a ball. If a child goes to kick the ball and misses, it's certainly not as meaningful to parents as missing a tackle in football or striking out in baseball, for example.[14]

Or as Michigan State University youth sport researcher Michael Clark suggests, the move toward a less strenuous embrace of sport through such novice ideals as soccer, which really has little deep rooting in American life when compared to baseball, football, and basketball, satisfies a more recent attraction toward emphasizing the athlete first, the effort second, and somewhere near the bottom of the ledger is the notion of triumph or some variation of achieved success.[15] In a climate where an estimated seventy-three percent of young participants withdraw from sport because they are believed not to be enjoying themselves,[16] the move toward the less weighty demands of a nascent Americanized vision of a more sophisticated philosophy of sport, complete with stage-managed and often choreographed contests where no one knows the score and everyone takes home a trophy, seems to be a welcome respite with a calming and egalitarian influence.

What the future holds for such human endeavors is unclear, but perhaps future attempts to retrace these steps will uncover even more challenging debates yet to manifest. Amid the myriad controversies relative to hypermasculinity, violence, self-esteem, self-absorption, spectacle, and the like, competitive sport might appear to have little value left in terms of its ability to offer any contributions to modern life. As Kenan Malik has noted on several occasions, "We live in an age that is deeply pessimistic about the human condition; an age that more often than not sees human activity as a force for destruction rather than for betterment."[17]

Nevertheless, in spite of the public reproach, the scholarly and critical denouncements, and the popular sentiment that insists that the good old days when athletes performed and knew their places are gone forever, once stripped of its excesses and removed from the flurry of contemporary discourse, competitive sport as an integral feature of American life continues to demonstrate a remarkable resiliency in the face of such challenges. While it is conceivable that we someday may eschew this feature of our culture, it is equally as likely that we will someday find that we have not merely thrown the baby out with the bath water but have indeed condemned the mother for something of our own doing, bringing to mind a favorite utterance from the epic *A Man for All Seasons* when actor Paul Scofield, playing the role of a doomed Sir Thomas More, so eloquently reveals of his world:

> If we lived in a state where virtue was profitable, common sense would make us saintly. But since we see that avarice, anger, pride, and stupidity commonly profit far beyond charity, modesty, justice, and thought, perhaps we must stand fast a little, even at the risk of being heroes.[18]

How effectively we can connect the new century to More's world is yet to be determined. Nevertheless, it is imperative that we embark upon this journey in order to see for ourselves.

Appendix

Major American Sport Attendance by Sport[1]

Figure A.1. Major League Baseball Attendance

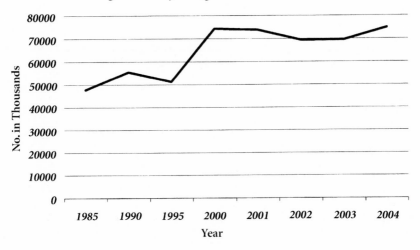

Figure A.2. NBA Attendance

NBA Attendance

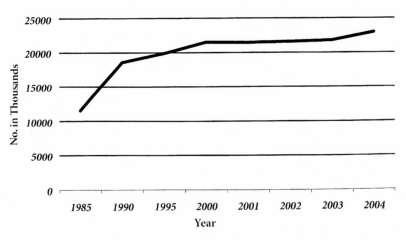

Figure A.3. NCAA Division I Men's Basketball Attendance

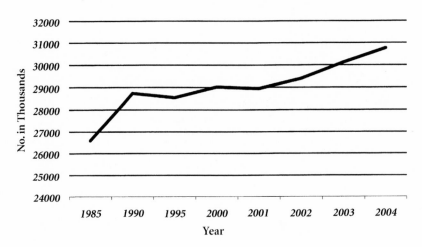

Figure A.4. NCAA Division I Women's Basketball Attendance

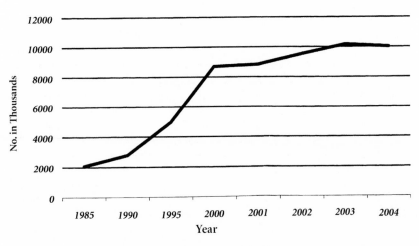

Figure A.5. NFL Football Attendance

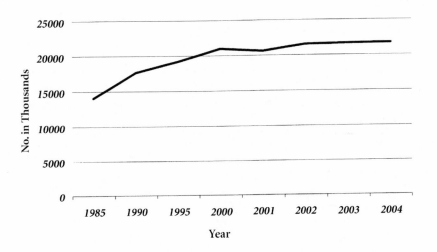

Figure A.6. NCAA Division I Football Attendance

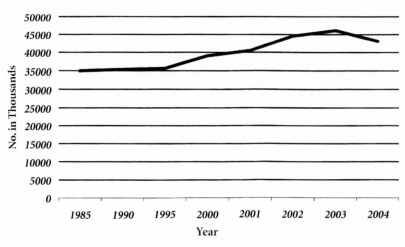

Figure A.7. NHL Attendance

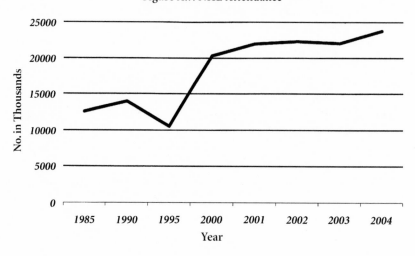

Notes

Preface

1. Benjamin Rader, *American Sports: From the Age of Folk Games to the Age of Televised Sports*, 4th ed. (Upper Saddle, NJ: Prentice Hall, 1999), 337.

2. Mark S. Rosentraub, *Major League Losers: The Real Cost of Sports and Who's Paying for It: What Governments and Taxpayers Need to Know*, rev. ed. (New York: Basic Books, 1999), 41.

3. A concerned reader offering a positive yet passionate review of Alfie Kohn's "No Contest" for Amazon.com. http://www.amazon.com. See also Alfie Kohn, *No Contest: The Case Against Competition: Why We Lose in Our Race to Win*, rev. ed. (Boston: Houghton Mifflin Company, 1992).

4. See Joel Nathan Rosen, "All-Sports Radio: The Development of an Industry Niche," *Media History Monographs* 5, no. 1 (2001–2002), http://www.elon.edu/dcopeland/mhm/mhm.htm. See also Joel Nathan Rosen, *"Your Question or Comment Please": A Sociological Study of All-Sports Radio*, Masters Thesis (University: The University of Mississippi, August 1995).

5. Reverend Jesse Jackson, Jr. narrating the short film "Citizenship through Sports." The Citizenship through Sports Alliance and the National Federation of State High Schools. Todd Erlich, prod. 2000.

6. John Bowles, *The Imperial Achievement: The Rise and Transformation of the British Empire* (London: Secker and Warburg, 1974), 290. This quote also appears in Andrew W. Miracle, Jr., and C. Roger Rees, *Lessons of the Locker Room: The Myth of School Sport* (Amherst, NY: Prometheus Books, 1994).

7. Christopher Lasch, *The Culture of Narcissism: American Life in an Age of Diminishing Expectations* (New York: W.W. Norton & Co., Inc., 1978), 109.

Introduction

1. Beverly Stoelje, "The Snake Charmer," in Colleen Ballerino Cohen et al., *Beauty Queens on the Global Stage: Gender, Contests, and Power* (New York: Routledge, 1996), 13.

2. Recurring opening lines from the HBO series "Arli$$," with Robert Wuhl.

3. See, for example, Michael Atkinson, "Fifty Million Viewers Can't Be Wrong: Professional Wrestling, Sports-Entertainment, and Mimesis" *Sociology of Sport Journal* 1, no. 19 (2002): 47–66 and David Leonard, "The Decline of the Black Athlete: An Interview with Harry Edwards," *ColorLines* 3, no. 1 (Spring 2000): 20–24. See also Scott Freeman, "John Rocker's Not Crazy: He's the Product of the Wrestlization of America," *Atlanta Magazine* (April 2000): 74–77 and 150–153. Freeman contends that the boorishness inherent to everyday American life reflects the dramatic rise in popularity of professional wrestling, which is less sport and more an entertainment spectacle consciously packaged as such.

4. Source: *Statistical Abstract of the United States: 2006. The National Data Book*, 125th ed. (Washington, D.C.: U.S. Census Bureau, 2006): 793–794.

5. See, for example, Brian Wilson, "The 'Anti-Jock' Movement: Reconsidering Youth Resistance, Masculinity, and Sport in the Age of the Internet," *Sociology of Sport Journal* 19, no. 2 (2002): 206–233. Wilson, a member of the human kinetics department at the University of British Columbia, affirms the importance of political submovements and their use of Internet technology in terms of expanding their positions. In this particular case, he looks at a web ring of anti-sport activists who maintain relatively close relationships through cyber-linking with similar such and otherwise sympathetic organizations.

6. John R. Gerdy, *Sports: The All-American Addiction* (Jackson: University Press of Mississippi, 2002), 249.

7. Allen Guttmann, *A Whole New Ballgame: An Interpretation of American Sports* (Chapel Hill: The University of North Carolina Press, 1988), 69.

8. Thomas Tutko and William Bruns, *Winning Is Everything and Other American Myths*

(New York: MacMillan Publishing Co., 1976), 4.

9. Duleep Allarajah, "Football between God and Mamon: A Review of David Conn's *The Football Business*," *LM* 116 (December 1998/January 1999): 44. See also David Conn, *The Football Business: Fair Game in the '90s?* (London: Mainstream Publishing, 1998).

10. Fred Engh, *Why Johnny Hates Sports: Why Organized Sports Are Failing Our Children and What We Can Do About It* (Garden City Park, JN: Avery Publishing Group, 1999), 191.

11. See, for example, Phil Sheridan, "Eagles, City Plot Tighter Coverage for Fan Offenses," *Philadelphia Inquirer* (November 21, 1997). The now defunct Veterans Stadium was once home to a holding center carved out of a former maintenance closet that acted as a makeshift courtroom. There, presiding judges heard indictments, conducted trials, and ultimately passed out sentences against allegedly unruly patrons in attendance, a trend that has been copied either in part or in total in other similar venues. See also Carlton Brick's polemic on Great Britain's move toward turning the sport stadium into a twenty-first century center of "social and moral education." In Carlton Brick, "Using Our Religion. A Review of Gary Armstrong's and Richard Giulanotti's *Entering the Field: New Perspectives on World Football*." *LM* 104 (October 1997): 39.

12. "Parent-Proof Baseball Field," "All Things Considered," National Public Radio, Robert Siegel, Narr. July 9, 2002.

13. See, for example, Elliot Aronson, "Look Beneath Surface of School Violence," *Savannah Morning News*, March 8, 2000. Aronson, professor emeritus in psychology at the University of California Santa Cruz, advocates the search for what he terms the classroom atmosphere without "losers," which he feels created the culture from which school violence festered.

14. David Light Shields and Brenda Light Bredemeier, "Moral Reasoning in the Context of Sport," Studies in Moral Development and Education Web page (Chicago: University of Illinois at Chicago). This paper was originally delivered at the annual meeting of The Association for Moral Education in Minneapolis, MN, October 1999. http://tigger.uic.edu/~lnucci/MoralEd /index.htm.

15. Ibid.

16. Ibid. Bockrath and Franke offer similar such assessments in their analysis of value in sport. Franz Bockrath and Elk Franke, "Is There Any Value in Sports? About the Ethical Significance of Sport Activities," *The International Review for the Sociology of Sport* 3 and 4 (1995): 287.

17. Cited in Tutko and Bruns, op. cit., 38.

18. Andrew Ferguson, "Sport: Inside the Crazy

Culture of Kids' Sports," *Time* 154, no. 2 (July 12, 1999): 5. http://www.time.com.

19. James Davison Hunter, *Culture Wars: The Struggle to Define America: Making Sense of the Battles over the Family, Art, Education, Law, and Politics* (New York: Basic Books, 1991), 34.

20. Writer Ralph Schoenstein spoofing modern psychology on "All Things Considered," National Public Radio, November 4, 2000.

21. Actor Harry Morgan as Col. Sherman T. Potter in "Letters," "M*A*S*H," Charles S. Durbin, Dir. FX Network, March 21, 2001. This episode originally aired November 24, 1980.

22. See, for example, Kohn 1992, op. cit. See also Terry D. Orlick and Louise Zitzelberger, "Enhancing Children's Sport Experiences," in Frank L. Smoll and Ronald E. Smith, eds., *Children and Youth in Sport: A Biopsychosocial Perspective* (Boston: WCB McGraw-Hill, 1996): 330–337; Terry D. Orlick, *The Cooperative Sports and Games Book: Challenge without Competition* (New York: Random House, 1978) and Terry Orlick, *The Second Cooperative Sports & Games Book* (New York: Random House, 1982). Orlick, a sort of new age guru in contemporary competition analysis, is revered for, among other things, his work in creating a line of non-competitive versions of popular games for both children and adults.

23. Thomas Keil, "Sport in Advanced Capitalism," *Arena Review* 8 (1984): 24.

24. Steven J. Overman, *The Influence of the Protestant Ethic on Sport and Recreation* (Brookfield, VT: Avebury, 1997): 200–204. Overman concedes that the connection between sport and morality was such that in some powerful circles, devotion to sport was a precursor to devotion to general obedience across the board.

Chapter 1

1. "Goin' Deep," Fox Sports Network, Chris Myers, host, Gary Foremen, dir., October 11, 2000, and "Parental Rage," "Real Sports," HBO Sports, Bryant Gumbel, Host, Bernard Goldberg, Narr, Alvin Patrick, Prod., October 12, 2000.

2. To clarify, the reference to Shinn here is a reference to George Shinn, the owner of the National Basketball Association's then Charlotte (later New Orleans) Hornets who had been embroiled in a messy sexual harassment lawsuit.

3. Brian C. Anderson and Peter Reinharz, "Bring Back Sportsmanship" *City Journal* 10, no .2 (Spring 2000): 44.

4. James Davison Hunter, *Culture Wars: The Struggle to Define America: Making Sense of the Battles over the Family, Art, Education, Law, and Politics* (New York: Basic Books, 1991), 61.

5. Morris Berman, *The Twilight of American*

Culture (New York: W.W. Norton and Co., 2000), 1.

6. John J. Mearsheimer, "Why We Will Soon Miss The Cold War," *The Atlantic Monthly* 266, no. 2 (August 1990): 35. Mearsheimer's was one of many responses to the coming end of the Cold War to reflect such uncertainties about the abrupt changes that would result. See also Francis Fukuyama, *The End of History and the Last Man* (New York: Avon Books, 1993) and Roger Kimball, "Francis Fukuyama and the End of History," *New Criterion* On-Line 10, no. 6 (February 1992): 1–11. http://www.newcriterion.com/

7. Kenan Malik, *The Meaning of Race: Race, History and Culture in Western Society* (London: MacMillan, 1996), 11. See also Frank Füredi, *Mythical Past, Elusive Future: History and Society in an Anxious Age* (London: Pluto Press, 1992). In this text Füredi points to an alarming trend toward idealizing and romanticizing in historicism, which in turn, he argues, leads often toward a revisionist interpretation of historical phenomena with potentially deleterious consequences.

8. See, for example, Martin Walker, *The Cold War: A History* (New York: Henry Holt and Company, Inc., 1993), 303–323, and Adam Burgess, *Divided Europe: The New Domination of the East* (London: Pluto Press, 1997). Both Walker, an American historian, and Burgess, a British sociologist, suggest that what have been popularly labeled as smoldering and long-standing resentments in such places as the Yugoslavian Federation and among the many African nations struggling through civil unrest have more to do with modern instabilities created by the loosening of Cold War ties and the sudden impact of local rule emanating from what can best described as a sort of political vacuum.

9. Malik, op. cit., 13.

10. James Heartfield, *The "Death of the Subject" Explained* (Sheffield, UK: Sheffield Hallam University Press, 2002), 15–21. Interestingly, Heartfield notes that Pope John Paul II is simply one of many modern figures who not only accepted but actually embraced modern nihilism through the recognition that evil rather than hope "has marked our age." In ibid., 16.

11. Anthony Giddens, *Beyond Left and Right: The Future of Radical Politics* (Stanford, CA: Stanford University Press, 1994), 4–7.

12. Ibid., 6.

13. Ibid., 6.

14. Terry Eagleton, *The Illusions of Postmodernism* (London: Blackwell, 1997), 15–17; 123–130.

15. Ibid., 15–16.

16. See Frank Füredi, *Culture of Fear: Risk-Taking and the Morality of Low Expectations* (London: Cassell, 1997), 15–44.

17. Berman, op. cit., 58–59.

18. Giddens, op. cit., 5.

19. See Hunter, op. cit.

20. Ibid., 108.

21. James L. Nolan, Jr., *The Therapeutic State: Justifying Government at Century's End* (New York: New York University Press, 1998), 45.

22. Todd Gitlin, *The Twilight of Common Dreams: Why America Is Wracked by Culture Wars* (New York: Owl Books, 1995), 39–106.

23. Giddens, op. cit., 49. Giddens' discussion of neo-conservatism and neo-liberalism marks an attempt to demonstrate that Left and Right have virtually exchanged postures, with the Left assuming the more dogmatic, even defensive, posture while the Right finds itself embracing a hybrid form of what he claims is a discernibly conservative radicalism.

24. Gitlin, op. cit., 80.

25. Füredi 1992, op. cit., 1. See also Barry Glassner, *The Culture of Fear. Why Americans Are Afraid of the Wrong Things: Crime, Drugs, Minorities, Teen Moms, Killer Kids, Mutant Microbes, Plane Crashes, Road Rage, & So Much More* (New York: Basic Books, 1999), xx–xxi.

26. Alexis de Tocqueville, *Democracy in America*, Vol. I, posted on *Democracy in America* On-Line, http://www.tocqueville.org.

27. Richard Sennett, *The Corrosion of Character: The Personal Consequences of a Work in the New Capitalism* (New York: W.W. Norton & Company, 1998), 80.

28. Host Bob Ley on "Outside the Lines," ESPN Television, April 15, 2001.

29. Junker, op. cit., 1.

30. See Eagleton, op. cit., 20–44; 123–130.

31. Gitlin, op. cit., 200.

32. Ibid., 201.

33. Ibid., 201.

34. Ibid., 200–201.

35. Joel H. Spring, *Images of American Life: A History of Ideological Management in Schools, Movies, Radio, and Television* (Albany: State University of New York Press, 1992), 31–48. Spring uses these terms as a backdrop for how immigrants were ultimately convinced to drop what remaining vestiges of Old World culture they carried with them to America and adopt the ethos of a forward-moving American Protestant ethic.

36. Cited in Steven A. Riess, "Sport and the Redefinition of Middle-Class Masculinity in Victorian America," in S.W. Pope, "American Sport History — Toward a New Paradigm," in S.W. Pope, ed., *The New American Sport History: Recent Approaches and Perspectives* (Urbana: University of Illinois Press, 1997), 186.

37. In Heartfield, op. cit., 230–234.

38. Andrew Calcutt, *Arrested Development: Pop Culture and the Erosion of Adulthood* (London: Cassell, 1998). Berman also makes this point, referring to the remnants of 1960s activism as the

dawning of the age when infantilism became an ideology. See Berman, op. cit., 58.

39. Calcutt, op. cit., 7.

40. To note, this reevaluation of childhood as a mark of purity is often offset by a remarkable fear of children in terms of both their safety and a supposed contention that children today are out of control and prone to violence as never before. See Glassner, op. cit., 51–84. See also Peter Braunstein, "Forever Young: Insurgent Youth and the Sixties Culture of Rejuvenation," in Peter Braunstein and Michael William Doyle, *Imagine Nation: The American Counterculture of the 1960s and '70s* (New York: Routledge, 2002), 243–273.

41. Glassner, op. cit., 25.

42. Füredi 1997, op. cit., 10.

43. Ibid., 10.

44. Ibid., 13.

45. I would reasonably define this as a condition of heightened empathy and an overly acute awareness of another's suffering (see chapter 4 for a brief discussion of the prefix *hyper-* in its modern context).

46. Glassner, op. cit., xviii; 3–19.

47. Hunter, op. cit., 61.

48. Kenan Malik, "What Is It to Be Human?" Paper presented at The Institute of Idea's Science, Knowledge, and Humanity Conference (New York: The New School for Social Research), October 24, 2001; article posted on http://www.kenanmalik.com.

49. Friedrich Wilhelm Nietzsche, *The Portable Nietzsche*, edited and translated by Walter Kaufmann (New York: Penguin Books, 1982), 129.

50. Mick Hume, "Whatever Happened to the Heroes?" *Living Marxism* 94 (October 1996): 5–6.

51. Füredi 1997, op. cit., 56.

52. Christopher Hitchens, "The Obligatory Proto-Capitalist Worldview: Ayn Rand," Business 2.0 Web page, August 2001; article posted on http://www.business2.com.

53. Christopher Lasch, *The Culture of Narcissism: American Life in an Age of Diminishing Expectations* (New York: W.W. Norton & Co., Inc., 1978), 11.

54. Ibid., 85–86. See also, for example, Allan Bloom, *The Closing of the American Mind* (New York: Touchstone Books, 1987) and Frank Füredi, *Culture of Fear: Risk-Taking and the Morality of Low Expectations* (London: Cassell, 1997).

55. Lasch, op. cit., 53.

56. Ibid., 108. To note, Lasch argued these points in the context of countercultural initiatives aimed at reforming (or perhaps even eradicating) American sport.

57. Berman, op. cit., 54.

58. Pat Califia, *Dick for a Day: What Would You Do If You Had One?* (New York: Villard, 1997), 96.

59. Quote attributed to feminist columnist Elizabeth Sargent in Michael P. Wright, "A Critical Look at Rape Awareness Week at the University of Oklahoma: How Accountable Is the Women's Studies Program?" *Clarion* On-Line 4, no. 4 (March/April 2000), posted on the Pope Center for Higher Education Policy Web Site, http://www.popecenter.org.

60. Katie Roiphe, *The Morning After: Sex, Fear, and Feminism* (Boston: Little, Brown and Company, 1994), 4–5.

61. Berman, op. cit., 14–70.

62. Ibid., 61.

63. Heartfield, op. cit., 232.

64. Frank Füredi, "Is It a Girl's World?" *Living Marxism* 79 (May 1995):10.

65. Betty Friedan, *The Feminist Mystique*, introduction by Anna Quindlen (New York: W.W. Norton & Co., 2001). See also, for example, Ann Hall, *Feminism and Sporting Bodies: Essays on Theory and Practice* (Champaign, IL: Human Kinetics, 1996), 1–9. Hall, a professor in physical education at the University of Alberta, offers an impassioned road map of her conversion to feminism by virtue of reading Friedan and other such writers of the period.

66. Geneviève Rai , ed. *Sport and Postmodern Times* (Albany: State University of New York Pres, 1998), xiv-xv.

67. Ibid., xiv.

68. Camille Paglia, "Feminists Must Begin to Fulfill Their Noble, Animating Ideal," *The Chronicle of Higher Education* (July 1997), posted on the Bergen University Library On-Line, http://privat.ub.uib.no/bubsy/apollon.htm. See also Varda Burstyn,. *The Rites of Men: Manhood, Politics, and the Culture of Sport* (Toronto: University of Toronto Press, 1999), 41–42. To clarify, Burstyn maintains that Paglia brought "some much-needed corrections" to the essentialist image that posed women as "cream-puffs" juxtaposed to men being "monsters."

69. Paglia, op. cit.

70. Mary Zeiss Stange, "Point of View: The Political Intolerance of Academic Feminism," *The Chronicle of Higher Education* On-Line (June 21, 2002), http://chronicle.com.

71. As an aside, Ann Hall, in a particularly telling commentary, reminds male theorists that they must "check with women" before they begin to elaborate theories relating to their own masculine experiences. In Hall, op. cit., 46.

72. Stephen Heath, "Male Feminism," in Alice Jardine and Paul Smith, eds., *Men in Feminism* (New York and London: Methuen, 1987), 1.

73. See for example, Roger Horrocks, *Masculinity in Crisis* (London: MacMillan, 1996). Horrocks, a British psychotherapist, argues vehemently that as agents of patriarchal domination, men also play a role in their own domination by virtue of being held captive by socially con-

strained and consigned behaviors that may indeed be against their very natures. See also Heartfield, op. cit., 232.

74. See, for example Fred Pfeil, *White Guys: Studies in Postmodern Domination and Difference* (London: Verso, 1996), 234.

75. See, for example Robert Bly, *Iron John: A Book about Men* (New York: Vintage Books, 1992).

76. Giddens, op. cit., 235–242.

77. Ibid., 240.

78. See Ann Beutel and Margaret Mooney Marini, "Gender and Values," *American Sociological Review* 60 (June 1995): 436–438. In preparation for their study of gender roles among high school aged subjects, Beutel and Marini forge a rather traditional portrait of masculine and feminine traits including making the distinction that men are more likely to act heroically and more chivalrously when in the midst of a crisis.

79. See Füredi 1997, op. cit., 87–88, and Burstyn, op. cit., 268–269.

80. Michael Gurian, *The Good Son: Shaping the Moral Development of Our Boys and Young Men* (New York: Jeremy P. Tarcher/Putnam, 1999), 29.

81. John MacInnes, *The End of Masculinity: The Confusion of Sexual Genesis and Sexual Difference in Modern Society* (Milton Keynes: Open University Press, 1998). See also Frank Füredi, "In Praise of Masculine Men — and Women," *LM* 112 (July/August 1998): 11.

82. Füredi 1998, op. cit., 10.

83. Roiphe, op. cit., 12.

84. Teri Bostian, "A Review of Mariah Burton Nelson's *Women and Competition: Embracing Victory*," *SportsJones* On-Line (August 24, 2001), http://www.sportsjones.com.

85. Sportswriter Frank Deford offering a defense of male sport spectators, whom he believes learn loyalty, sensitivity, and an almost mawkish sense of perspective, traits that are generally thought to be female in nature. "Morning Edition," National Public Radio, June 12, 2002.

Chapter 2

1. S.W. Pope, "American Sport History — Toward a New Paradigm," in S.W. Pope, ed., *The New American Sport History: Recent Approaches and Perspectives* (Urbana: University of Illinois Press, 1997), 8.

2. Quote attributed to former United States Vice President Spiro T. Agnew. Cited in Harry Edwards, *Sociology of Sport* (Homewood, IL: The Dorsey Press, 1973), 92.

3. Foster Rhea Dulles, *A History of Recreation: America Learns to Play*, 2nd ed. (New York: Appleton-Century-Crofts, 1965), 198–199.

4. Frederick Jackson Turner, *The Frontier in American History* (New York: Henry Holt, 1935), Chapter One, posted on http://xroads.virginia.edu/~HYPER/TURNER/.

5. In John A. Garraty, *A Short History of the American Nation*, 7th ed. (New York: Longman, 1997), 179. Quote taken from de Tocqueville's *Democracy in America*. See also Alexis de Tocqueville, *Democracy in America*, Vol. I, posted on *Democracy in America* On-Line, posted on http://www.tocqueville.org.

6. See, for example, Steven J. Overman, *The Influence of the Protestant Ethic on Sport and Recreation* (Brookfield, VT: Avebury, 1997), 158–232. See also Elliott J. Gorn, and Warren Goldstein, *A Brief History of American Sports* (New York: Hill and Wang, 1993), 47–81 and Varda Burstyn, *The Rites of Men: Manhood, Politics, and the Culture of Sport* (Toronto: University of Toronto Press, 1999), 45–75.

7. According to Gorn and Goldstein, antebellum recreations were normally construed as having been incidental to daily life, though they also note that this would change dramatically in the decades to come. Gorn, and Goldstein, op. cit., 48–49.

8. See Max Weber and Talcott Parsons, *The Protestant Ethic and the Spirit of Capitalism* 2nd ed., translated by Anthony Giddens (London: Routledge, 2001). See also Overman, op. cit. Overman's work is essentially a Weberian critique of American sport.

9. Overman, op. cit., 119–121. See also Benjamin Rader, *American Sports: From the Age of Folk Games to the Age of Televised Sports*, 4th ed. (Upper Saddle River, NJ: Prentice Hall, 1999), 19–25 and Allen Guttmann, *A Whole New Ball Game: An Interpretation of American Sports* (Chapel Hill: The University of North Carolina Press, 1988), 23–34. Guttmann provides an especially passionate critique of Puritanism, leisure, and sport in the early American colonies.

10. Dulles, op. cit., 183.

11. Peter Levine, "'Oy Such a Fighter!': Boxing and the Jewish-American Experience," in Pope, op. cit., 254.

12. See, for example, Gorn and Goldstein, op. cit., 53. Riess in tandem referred to these same participants more distinctively as "urban machine politicians, seasonal workers, Irish immigrants, dregs of society, and adventurous social elites." In Steven A Riess, "Sport and the Redefinition of Middle-Class Masculinity in Victorian America," in Pope, op. cit., 173–174.

13. Gorn and Goldstein, op. cit., 49. See also S.W. Pope, op. cit., 6–9, and Melvin L. Adelman, "The First Modern Sport in America: Harness Racing in New York City," in David K. Wiggins, ed., *Sport in America: From Wicked Amusement to National Obsession* (Champaign, IL: Human

Kinetics, 1995), 95–108, and Christopher Lasch, *The Culture of Narcissism: American Life in an Age of Diminishing Expectations* (New York: W.W. Norton & Co., Inc., 1978), 110–114.

14. Gorn and Goldstein, op. cit., 91.

15. Dyerson, op. cit., 121–122.

16. Ibid., 50. See also Rader, op. cit., 19–24; Dulles, op. cit., 84–99; and Jay J. Coakley, *Sport in Society: Issues & Controversies*, 6th ed. (Boston: Irwin McGraw-Hill, 1998), 70–79.

17. Gorn and Goldstein, op. cit., 49–52.

18. Ibid., 49–52. See also Overman, op. cit., 119–121.

19. David I. Macleod, *Building Character in the American Boy: The Boy Scouts, YMCA, and Their Forerunners, 1870–1920* (Madison: The University of Wisconsin Press, 1983), 18.

20. Ibid., 18.

21. Overman, op. cit., 119–126.

22. Ibid., 125–126.

23. Ibid., 127.

24. Burstyn, op. cit., 45.

25. Gorn and Goldstein, op. cit., 63.

26. Dulles, op. cit., 148–167, and Rader, op. cit., 19–33.

27. Rader, op. cit., 26–30.

28. Ted Vincent, *Mudville's Revenge: The Rise & Fall of American Sport* (Lincoln: University of Nebraska Press, 1981), 29.

29. Ibid., 18.

30. See Overman, op. cit., 106–132; Gorn and Goldstein, op. cit., 61–97; and Riess 1997, op. cit., 173–197.

31. Riess 1997, op. cit., 191.

32. Merely as an aside, it is important to mention here that Americans have long tried to distance themselves from British sport but have historically made little effort to hide the origins of their most cherished games. See Melvin Adelman, *A Sporting Time: New York City and the Rise of Modern Athletics, 1820–1870* (Urbana: University of Illinois Press, 1986). See also a more detailed discussion of this matter pertaining to America's relationship to world football in Andrei S. Markovits and Steven L. Hellerman, *Offside: Soccer & American Exceptionalism* (Princeton, NJ: Princeton University Press, 2001).

33. Source: George Washington University's Polling Report.com, posted on http:www.pollingreport.com/sport.htm.

34. Rader, op. cit., 50–80, and Riess 1997, op. cit., 188–189. See also Dulles, op. cit., 183.

35. Adelman, op. cit., 278–279.

36. See Guttmann, op. cit., 23–34. Guttmann, a highly respected sport historian and professor in English and American studies at Amherst College, claims that contrary to common misconception, the Puritans had a much more secular view of sport than the Victorians would show. See also Dulles, op. cit.

37. Rader, op. cit., 23. Rader's work is one of a number of texts to outline the nature of causes of Victorian influences in American sport.

38. Riess 1997, op. cit., 173–197. See also Rader, op. cit.; Guttmann, op. cit.; Gorn and Goldstein, op. cit.; and Overman, op. cit.

39. Guttmann, op. cit., 73.

40. Quote taken from John W. Elliott, "Gentlemen or Gamesmen?" *The Middle Stump* On-Line, http://www.geocities.com/middlestump1/JWE3.html. No other information available.

41. Adelman, op. cit., 279.

42. Guttmann reports that while initially the term "stung" its perceived architect, Charles Kingsley, he would eventually accepts its basic premise. Op. cit., 73.

43. Andrew W. Miracle, Jr., and C. Roger Rees, *Lessons of the Locker Room: The Myth of School Sports* (Amherst, NY: Prometheus Books, 1994), 35. See also James A. Mangan, *Athleticism in the Victorian and Edwardian Public School* (Cambridge: Cambridge University Press, 1981).

44. Miracle and Rees, op. cit., 31–39.

45. Adelman, op. cit., 279–280.

46. Burstyn, op. cit., 56.

47. Dyerson, op. cit., 121–122.

48. Pope, op. cit., 7.

49. Miracle and Rees, op. cit., 20.

50. Riess 1997, op. cit., 184.

51. While it would be inappropriate to dwell on this issue here, as a matter of clarification, note that this same reform element did not consider the masculine virtues and ruggedness of sporting activities to be consistent with period expectations for women or girls. Luther Gulick and his mentor G. Stanley Hall, as well as others, were in agreement that sport tested manliness, not womanliness, and, as Hall maintained, when it comes to women and sport, a woman "performs her best service in her true role of sympathetic spectator rather than as a fellow player." See G. Stanley Hall, *Adolescence*, Vol. I (New York: D. Appleton, 1905), 207.

52. Mark Dyerson, "Regulating the Body and the Body Politic: American Sport, Bourgeois Culture, and the Language of Progress, 1880–1920," in Pope, op. cit., 125.

53. Riess 1997, op. cit., 179.

54. Ronald Story, "The Country of the Young: The Meaning of Baseball in Early American Culture," in Wiggins 1995, op. cit., 132, and Timothy P. O'Hanlon, "School Sports as Social Training: The Case of Athletics and the Crisis of World War I," in Wiggins 1995, op. cit., 192–193.

55. Macleod, op. cit., 3. See also Rader, op. cit., 99–101.

56. Macleod, op. cit., 32.

57. Rader, op. cit., 99. See also Jack W. Berryman, "The Rise of Boys' Sports in the United States, 1900 to 1970," in Frank L. Smoll and

Ronald E. Smith, eds. *Children and Youth in Sport: A Biopsychosocial Perspective* (Boston, WCB Mc-Graw-Hill, 1996), 4, and David K. Wiggins, "A History of Highly Competitive Sport for American Children," in Smoll and Smith, op. cit., 27.

58. Rader, op. cit., 99–101.

59. Macleod, op. cit., 54.

60. Story, op. cit., 132.

61. Edwards, op. cit., 319.

62. Miracle and Rees, op. cit., 9–16.

63. Ibid., 44–50.

64. Macleod, op. cit., 189.

65. Alan Klein, "Anti-Semitism and Anti-Somatism: Seeking the Elusive Sporting Jew," *Sociology of Sport Journal* 17, no. 3 (2000): 219.

66. Macleod, op. cit., 50.

67. Macleod, op. cit., 54.

68. Ibid., 10–29.

69. Macleod, op. cit., 10.

70. Source: Research Department, YMCA of the USA, Chicago, 2000.

71. Gorn and Goldstein, op. cit., 96.

72. See Leon Chorbajian, "Toward a Marxist Sociology of Sport: An Assessment and a Preliminary Agenda," *Arena Review* 8 (1984), 55–69.

73. Wiggins 1996, op. cit., 17.

74. Macleod, op. cit., 98–99.

75. Rader, op. cit., 104–105.

76. Ibid., 27.

77. Wiggins 1996, op. cit., 16–17. See also Rader, op. cit., 101–107, and Guttmann, op. cit., 84–90.

78. See Guttmann, op. cit., 73. Guttmann's discussion of basketball places it in the context of an additional means utilized to serve the cause of the YMCA's ideology. He also points out that the game's creator, Canadian James Naismith, sought to bring young men to Christ while helping to further the process of Americanization in immigrant children.

79. Ibid., 101–106. See also Macleod, op. cit., 98–99.

80. Guttmann, op. cit., 88.

81. Cited in Joel H. Spring, "Mass Culture and School Sports," *History of Education Quarterly* 14 (Winter 1974), 492.

82. Dyerson, op. cit., 40.

83. See Burstyn, op. cit., 106.

84. Donald J. Mrozek, *Sport and American Mentality, 1880–1910* (Knoxville: University of Tennessee Press, 1983), 40. As Mrozek insists, it was an article of faith that had little chance of being rooted out scientifically.

85. Taft, a renowned baseball supporter, was personally responsible for the vaunted "Seventh Inning Stretch" and the tradition of having dignitaries toss out the ceremonial first ball.

86. Ibid., 41. See also Miracle and Rees, op. cit., 45 and Roberta J. Park, "Sport, Gender, and Society in a Transatlantic Victorian Perspective," in

James A Mangan, and Roberta J. Parks, eds., *From Fair Sex to Feminism: Sport and the Socialization of Women in the Industrial and Post-Industrial Eras* (London: Frank Cass, 1987), 74. From this point forward, the American presidency would serve as a bully pulpit for sport, often positioning itself as an erstwhile associate of winning teams and as the shining beacon of American virility through sport.

87. As Macleod would note in his discussion of Gulick's contributions to the YMCA, amid his recognition of the power of team sport to teach important values of individual subordination, moral decency, and physical fitness, Gulick also recognized that sport was exciting enough to guarantee for the organization a steady stream of consumers from subsequent generations of sport enthusiasts. Macleod, op. cit., 97.

88. Ibid., 189. See also Guttmann, op. cit., 70–75, and Gerald R. Gems, "Selling Sport and Religion in American Society," in Pope, op. cit., 300–311.

89. Rader; op. cit., 113.

90. Miracle and Rees, op. cit., 48.

91. Rader, op. cit., 107.

92. See also Cary Goodman, *Choosing Sides* (New York: Schocken Books, 1979).

93. Rader, op. cit., 108. See also Guttmann, op. cit., 83–85, and Robert Goldman, "We Make Weekends: Leisure and the Commodity Form," posted on the Lewis and Clark College Web site; originally published in *Social Text* 8 (Winter 1984).

94. Information posted on "Prosperity and Thrift: The Coolidge Era and the Consumer Economy, 1921–1929," Web page designed by the American Library of Congress, http://lcweb2.10c.gov/ammem/coolhtml/coolhome.html.

95. Rader, op. cit., 108.

96. Riess 1997, op. cit., 176.

97. Miracle and Rees, op. cit., 63.

98. See O'Hanlon, op. cit., 190. In his discussion of school sports and socialization, O'Hanlon reports that enrollments rose an impressive 711% from 1890 through 1918, though relatively few made it through high school. In Wiggins 1995, op. cit., 189–206.

99. Spring 1974, op. cit., 33, 491.

100. Goldman, a sociologist at Lewis and Clark College in Portland, Oregon, argues that *Taylorism* and various other forms of scientific management fueled the embrace of leisure activities and were thought by industrialists to be in effect highly productive. Going back to the nineteenth century, businesses often sponsored athletic events and even representative teams in the effort to improve moral and engineer satisfaction through oftentimes inhumane working conditions. See Goldman, op. cit.

101. Commission on the Reorganization of Sec-

ondary Education, *Cardinal Principles of Secondary Education* (Washington, D.C.: U.S. Bureau of Education Bulletin, 1918). Most every critic who discusses elements of twentieth century education will reference *The Cardinal Principles of Secondary Education*. Unfortunately, few can agree upon their initial publication date, which can range from 1917 to 1920 depending upon the source, though the actual date of publication is 1918. See, for example, Rader, op. cit., 109–111; Spring, op. cit., 492; and Miracle and Rees, op. cit., 63.

102. James L. Nolan, Jr., *The Therapeutic State: Justifying Government at Century's End* (New York: New York University Press, 1998), 132–137.

103. Guttmann, op. cit., 88–89.

104. Rader, op. cit., 111. See also Burstyn, op. cit., 59.

105. Miracle and Rees, op. cit., 60. Miracle and Rees note that the so-called dumb jock in many ways comes to exemplify high school life, a common thread of inquiry in the field. Still, as an aside, one has to ask how it might be possible that a highly trained athlete could in actuality be, using their parlance, dumb.

106. Rader, op. cit., 106–107. See also Guttmann, op. cit., 82–91 and Joel H. Spring, *Images of American Life: A History of Ideological Management in School, Movies, Radio, and Television* (Albany, NY: State University of New York Press, 1992), 31.

107. See O'Hanlon, op. cit., 189–190, and Spring 1992, op. cit., 31–33.

108. O'Hanlon, op. cit., 200–201.

109. Ibid., 201. This report was entitled *The National Education Association's Committee on Military Training in Public Schools*.

110. Pope, op. cit., 14.

111. O'Hanlon, op. cit., 193. See also R.A. Moore, *Sports and Mental Health* (Springfield, IL: Charles C. Thomas Publishing, 1966), 11–15. Moore referred to the matter of sport as a national display of virility that was supported by the federal government and a matter that was exploited by the American war effort.

112. Spring 1992, op. cit., 39.

113. Dyerson, op. cit., 123–124.

114. Miracle and Rees, op. cit., 42.

115. Ibid., 178–179.

116. Ibid., 48–49.

117. Goldman, op. cit.

118. Mark Dyreson, "The Emergence of Consumer Culture and the Transformation of Physical Culture: American Sport in the 1920's, in Wiggins 1995, op. cit., 207.

119. See Miracle and Rees, op. cit., 41.

120. See Goldman, op. cit. Goldman refers to the architects of the new morality as the "captains of non-industry."

121. Dyreson, op. cit., 213.

122. Ibid., 213.

123. Ibid., 213.

124. Rader, op. cit., 134–151. See also Miracle and Rees, op. cit., 49–51, and Gorn and Goldstein, op. cit., 153–221.

125. Adelman, op. cit., 270.

126. Source: K. Michael Gaschnitz, *Professional Sports Statistics: A North American Team-by-Team, and Major Non-Team Events, Year-by-Year Reference, 1876–1996* (Jefferson, NC: McFarland, 1997).

127. Edwards, op. cit., 32. Edwards reports that the sporting press was often at odds with the more traditional press regarding ethics and standards of proper journalistic practices. They were often perceived by their own colleagues as little more than extensions of the teams they covered.

128. The tendency toward non-treatments of sport by media types is what led directly to the much more common image of period reporting of sport as little more than an extension of an organization's public relations and marketing scheme while giving rise to the image of era reporters as hangers-on and "shills," to use the vernacular of the day. See Robert Lipsyte, *SportsWorld: An American Dreamland* (New York: Quadrangle, 1975).

129. Goldman, op. cit. One interesting note is that Babe Ruth's finest season, 1927, was also a year in which he was being hounded by a multitude of paternity suits, though few beyond Ruth's handlers were ever informed of this by a sporting press eager to placate management in order to retain access to the team.

130. Robert Lipsyte, "SportsWorld Revisted," in Richard E. Lapchick, *Fractured Focus: Sport as a Reflection of Society* (Lexington, MA: Lexington Books, 1986), 316.

131. Berryman, op. cit., 9. Berryman, a medical ethicist operating out of the University of Washington at Seattle, cites a number of community organizations that fit the pattern of the new emphasis on athletic prowess, including baseball tournaments for boys thirteen and under in Cincinnati, Milwaukee's "Kid's Baseball School," and twelve-and-under tackle football in Denver, Philadelphia, and Los Angeles.

132. *The Journal of Health and Physical Education* was particularly critical of school-sanctioned sport for younger students for physical reasons, though most pointed to the psychosocial ramifications. See "Two Important Resolutions," *The Journal of Health and Physical Education* 9 (1938): 488–489, and Berryman, op. cit., 4–6.

133. Wiggins 1996, op. cit., 19.

134. David K. Wiggins, "A History of Organized Play and Highly Competitive Sport for American Children," in Daniel Gould and Maureen R. Weiss, *Advances in Pediatric Sport Sciences. Vol. 2: Behavioral Issues* (Champaign, IL: Human Kinetics Publishers, Inc., 1987), 8. See also

Guttmann, op. cit., 92, and Berryman, op. cit., 9–10.

135. Spring 1974, op. cit., 496.

Chapter 3

1. Donald J. Mrozek, "The Cult and Ritual of Toughness in Cold War America," in David K. Wiggins, ed., *Sport in America: From Wicked Amusement to National Obsession* (Champaign, IL: Human Kinetics, 1995), 262.

2. Matt Labash, "What's Wrong with Dodgeball? The New Phys Ed and the Wussification of America," *Weekly Standard* 6, no. 39 (June 25, 2001): 18–19. Note: The president Labash mentions would be John F. Kennedy.

3. Mrozek, op. cit., 257–258.

4. Joel H. Spring, "Mass Culture and School Sports," *History of Education Quarterly* 14 (Winter 1974): 495.

5. Vern Seefeldt of Michigan State University's Youth Sport Institute revisiting the Lombardi dictum in such a way a to make it relevant to today's debate. In Michael A. Clark, "Winning! How Important Is It in Youth Sports?" *Spotlight on Youth Sports* On-Line 17, no. 3 (June 16, 2000), http://ed-web3.educ.msu.edu/ysi/spotlight.

6. See, for example, James Heartfield, *The "Death of the Subject" Explained* (Sheffield, UK: Sheffield Hallam University Press, 2002), 15–21. Heartfield, an often acerbic British commentator, contends that the success of countercultural rhetoric was due in part to what he deems as the growing nihilism and frustration of the age. See also Doug Rossinow, "The Revolution Is about Our Lives," in Peter Braunstein and Michael William Doyle, *Imagine Nation: The American Counterculture of the 1960s and '70s* (New York: Routledge, 2002), 99–124.

7. Theodore Roszak, *The Making of a Counter Culture: Reflections on the Technocratic Society and Its Youthful Opposition* (Garden City, NY: Anchor Books, 1969), xii-xiv.

8. See, for example, Harry Edwards, *Sociology of Sport* (Homewood, IL: The Dorsey Press, 1973) and Robert Lipsyte, *SportsWorld: An American Dreamland* (New York: Quadrangle, 1975). See also Jim Bouton, *Ball Four*, edited by Leonard Schecte (New York: Dell Publishing Co, Inc., 1970); Harry Edwards, *Revolt of the Black Athlete* (New York: Free Press, 1969); Peter Gent, *North Dallas Forty* (New York: Villard Books, 1973); Paul Hoch, *Rip Off the Big Game: The Exploitation of Sports by the Power Elite* (Garden City, NY: Anchor Books, 1972); Dave Meggyesy, *Out of Their League* (New York: Ramparts Press, 1970); and Jack Scott, *The Athletic Revolution* (New York: The Free Press, 1971).

9. See Walter E. Schafer, "Sport and Youth Counterculture: Contrasting Socialization Themes," paper Presented at the Conference on Sport and Social Deviancy, Brockport, NY: SUNY-Brockport (December 10, 1971), 1–17.

10. Ibid., 13.

11. See Glenn Dickey, *The Jock Empire: Its Rise and Deservéd Fall* (Radnor, PA: Chilton Book Co., 1974). See Thomas Tutko and William Bruns, *Winning Is Everything and Other American Myths* (New York: MacMillan Publishing Co., 1976), 4. Tutko and Bruns report that the first public utterance of the kind came from Vanderbilt University football coach Red Smith in the 1940s and echoed nearly verbatim by John Wayne who played a small college football coach in the film *Trouble along the Way* (With John Wayne, Michale Curtiz and John Wayne, Dirs., Warner Bros., 1953). To be fair, it has been widely reported that Lombardi regretted that his words were taken so fiercely out of context and given such significance, and he maintained that his point was about the competitive spirit and not one associated with the "win-at-all-cost" attitude that appears to swirl about contemporary sport still.

12. See Scott, op. cit., 50–64. These sorts of crude yet common sport-ordered expressions refer to athletes willing to sacrifice their bodies and their statistics for the good of the outfit as a whole.

13. Dickey, op. cit., vii.

14. Scott, op. cit., v.

15. Robert Downey, Jr., as Derek Lutz in the film *Back to School*, with Rodney Dangerfield, Alan Metter, Dir., Orion, 1986

16. Ibid., ix-x. Scott, in contrast, maintained that the "criticism of these outsiders was usually dismissed by people involved in sports," but empirical evidence suggests otherwise as owners and overseers began to close their ranks following the initial wave of sport-aimed polemics in the early 1960s.

17. There are numerous treatments of the relationship between sport and television. See, for example, David A. Klatell and Norman Marcus, *Inside Big Time Sports: Television, Money & the Fans* (New York: MasterMedia Limited, 1996) and Lawrence A. Wenner, ed., *Media, Sports, & Society* (Newbury Park, CA: Sage Publications, 1989).

18. Scott, op. cit., 212.

19. Note: It was widely offered that black players often had to make their own housing arrangements while on "road trips," arrangements that often placed them miles from their teammates and left gaping holes in both team schedules and moral.

20. Tom Brown and Frank Merriwell were British and American fictional characters who were portrayed as the embodiment of Western Protestant values gleaned through sport. Their

creators, England's Thomas Hughes and the American Gilbert Patton helped contribute to the climate surrounding sport and morality in the nineteenth century. See Andrew W. Miracle and C. Roger Rees, *Lessons of the Locker Room: The Myth of School Sports* (Amherst, NY: Prometheus Books, 1994), 36–40.

21. Peter Gent, *North Dallas Forty* (New York: Villard Books, 1973).

22. Gary Shaw, *Meat on the Hoof: The Hidden World of Texas Football* (New York: St. Martin's Press, 1972).

23. See *North Dallas Forty*, with Nick Nolte and Charles Durning, Ted Kotcheff, dir,. Paramount, 1979.

24. Gent, op. cit., 219.

25. It should be noted that disgust over the violence of football dates back to its advent in the 19th century and reaches its peak in 1905 when then President Theodore Roosevelt threatened to outlaw it in the wake of a number of on-field deaths. See Benjamin Rader, *American Sports: From the Age of Folk Games to the Age of Televised Sports*, 4th ed. (Upper Saddle River, NJ: Prentice Hall, 1999):180–181.

26. Jim Bouton, with Leonard Schecter, ed. *Ball Four* (New York: Dell Publishing, 1970). Leon Chorbajian refers to *Ball Four* as a "precursor" to the exposé genre, though he is very quick to point out that it is little more than a text whose popularity is based on its irreverence rather than on Bouton's critical insights. See Chorbajian, op. cit., 68.

27. To note, Bouton, an active player at the time of the book's release, made no effort to mask his disenchantment with the baseball hierarchy through these accounts and was dismissed as a traitorous crackpot by both teammates and hardened fans alike. He has since written three full books on his experiences in professional baseball and appears regularly as a sport commentator on various networks.

28. Shaw, op. cit., cover insert.

29. Dave Meggyesy, *Out of Their League* (Berkeley, CA: Ramparts Press, 1970).

30. Meggyesy quoted on the book jacket of Shaw, op. cit.

31. Harry Edwards interviewed in "Fists of Freedom: The Story of the '68 Summer Games," Executive Producer Ross Greenberg, HBO Sports, 1999.

32. Gerald Early, "Performance and Reality: Race, Sports and the Modern World," *The Nation* 267, no. 5. (August 10/17 1998):12.

33. See Chorbajian, op. cit., 62–64. Additionally, Lomax reports that in terms of the African American presence in professional football, there was relatively little coverage of this phenomenon even through the more turbulent years of the 1960s, though football had integrated a full year

before baseball's more celebrated moment. Michael E. Lomax, "The African American Experience in Pro Football," *Journal of Social History* 33, no. 1 (1999): 165–166. See also Robert W. Peterson, *Only the Ball Was White: A History of Legendary Black Players and All-Black Professional Teams* (New York: Oxford University Press, 1970) and Jules Tygiel, *Baseball's Great Experiment* (New York: Oxford University Press, 1983).

34. Rader, op. cit., 297–299. Branch Rickey, the Brooklyn General Manager who signed Robinson to a minor league affiliate of the famed National League Brooklyn Dodger franchise in 1946, proclaimed repeatedly that his motivation to sign the young Negro League star was to improve his club's on-field performance rather than to break baseball's color line carte blanche. By the end of the 1960s, franchises throughout the high-profile sporting establishment will have followed Rickey's lead. Additionally, Early noted that Robinson's athletic career at UCLA prior to his time spent playing Negro League Baseball was also a factor in Rickey's decision to sign him, as he represented a black athlete well-familiar with the white sports world. See also Early, op. cit., 14.

35. *Baseball*, nineteen parts, John Chancellor, Narr., Ken Burns, Exec. Prod., 1994.

36. Washington Post columnist George Will in *Baseball*, op. cit., "Inning Eight." The player's name was catcher Elston Howard.

37. "When It Was a Game III," HBO Sports, Ross Greenberg, Exec. Prod., 2000.

38. Bill Russell, and Taylor Branch, *Second Wind: The Memoirs of an Opinionated Man* (New York: Random House, 1979), 188.

39. See Radar, op. cit., 301–303.

40. Harry Edwards in Jon Entine, *Taboo: Why Black Athletes Dominate Sports and Why We're Afraid to Talk about It* (New York: Public Affairs, 2000), 334–35.

41. Hoch, op. cit., 170.

42. See Radar, op. cit., 301–303, and "Fists of Freedom: The Story of the '68 Summer Games," op. cit.

43. Edwards 1973, op. cit.

44. Edwards 1969, op. cit.

45. Edwards cited in Thomas Tutko and William Bruns, *Winning Is Everything and Other American Myths* (New York: MacMillan Publishing Co., Inc., 1976), 129.

46. Edwards 1969, op. cit., 9–10.

47. Quoted in Tutko and Bruns, op. cit., 129.

48. Pat Brady, "Blasphemy: Curt Flood's Suit against Baseball," December 1997, article posted on the *Crossroads* Web page, http://xroads.Virginia.edu,

49. *Baseball*, op. cit., "Inning Eight."

50. See ibid. See also William C. Kashatus, "Dick Allen, the Phillies, and Racism," in Bill Kirwin, ed., *Out of the Shadows: African American*

Baseball from the Cuban Giants to Jackie Robinson (Lincoln, NE: Bison Books, 2005), 147–193.

51. *Baseball*, op. cit., "Inning Eight." See also Charles P. Korr, *The End of Baseball As We Knew It: The Players Union, 1960–81* (Urbana: University of Illinois Press, 2005) and "Curt Flood," *ESPN's Sport Century*, Chris Fowler, Narr., ESPN2, February 27, 2001.

52. Number cited in *Baseball*, op. cit., "Inning One." 1994. See also Brady, op. cit.

53. Source: *Baseball Almanac* Online, 2006, http://www.baseball-almanac.com.

54. Lipsyte, op. cit., 37.

55. Joel Nathan Rosen, "Separating Wheat from Chaff: Looking for Jackie Robinson in an Uncritical Age," paper presented at the conference *From Jack Johnson to Marian Jones: Gains Made-Struggles Remain for African Americans in Sport* (Ithaca, NY: Ithaca College, January 2005), 5.

56. See transcript of "Meet the Press" Television and Radio Broadcast,. National Broadcasting Company, Sunday, April 14, 1957, Lawrence Spivak, Prod., Lawrence Spivak Papers, Library of Congress Manuscript Division, National Publishing Company, Washington, DC, Vol. 1, No. 15, article posted on *Baseball, the Color Line, and Jackie Robinson*, Library of Congress' American Memory Project Web page, http://memory.loc.gov/ammem/collections/robinson/meetpres.html.

57. Brady, op. cit.

58. In Brady, op. cit. This quote was taken from Curt Flood, *The Way It Is*, with Richard Carter (New York: Trident Press, 1971).

59. Ibid.

60. *Baseball*, op. cit., "Inning Eight."

61. To note, there are many in baseball circles who feel that Flood, who died in 1997, had the sort of career that under normal conditions would have made him a prime candidate for enshrinement in Major League Baseball's Hall-of-Fame.

62. Source: *USA Today* Online, Baseball Page, 2006, http://asp.usatoday.com/sports/baseball/salaries/default.aspx. Note: Ironically, none of the above cracks the list of top-ten highest paid U.S.-based athletes (see figure 7.2).

63. Elliott J. Gorn and Warren Goldstein, *A Brief History of American Sports* (New York: Hill and Wang, 1993), 197.

64. Allen Guttmann, *A Whole New Ballgame: An Interpretation of American Sports* (Chapel Hill: The University of North Carolina Press, 1988), 141.

65. See Betty Friedan, *The Feminine Mystique*, introduction by Anna Quindlen (New York: W.W. Norton & Co., 2001).

66. *Dare to Compete: The Struggle of Women in Sports*, Mary Carillo and Frank Deford, Writers, Ross Greenberg, Exec. Prod., HBO Sports, 1999.

67. See Andrew W. Miracle, Jr., and C. Roger Rees, *Lessons of the Locker Room: The Myth of School Sports* (Amherst, NY: Prometheus Books, 1994), 37–38.

68. Rader, op. cit., 208–210. To note, cycling for women was eventually disgraced due to the considerable risqué attire women riders were fashioning

69. See *Baseball*, op. cit., "Inning One." See also Guttmann, op. cit., 142; Nelson, op. cit., 14; and "Dare to Compete," op. cit.

70. Jennifer Hargreaves, *Sporting Females: Critical Issues in the History and Sociology of Women's Sports* (London: Routledge, 1994), 44.

71. Guttmann, op. cit., 139.

72. Gorn and Goldstein, op. cit., 199.

73. See "Dare to Compete," op. cit. and Margaret A. Coffey, "The Modern Sportswomen," in John T. Talamini and Charles H. Page, *Sport & Society: An Anthology* (Boston: Little, Brown and Company, 1973), 281.

74. Hargreaves, op. cit., 116. See also "Dare to Compete," op. cit.

75. Rader, op. cit., 216. Rader cites William O. Johnson and Nancy P. Williamson, "*Whatta Gal:*" *The Babe Didrikson Story* (Boston: Little, Brown & Co., 1977). See also Carolyn W. Sherif, "The Social Context of Competition," in *Social Problems in Athletics*, edited by Daniel M. Landers (Urbana: University of Illinois Press, 1976), 30.

76. Rader, op. cit., 216 and Nelson, op. cit., 24. See also "Dare to Compete," op. cit.

77. Mariah Burton Nelson, *The Stronger Women Get, the More Men Love Football: Sexism and the American Culture of Sports* (New York: Avon Books, 1994), 12–13.

78. In James A. Michener, *Sports in America* (Greenwich, CT: Fawcett Crest, 1976), 170.

79. Source: *Statistical Abstract of the United States: 2006. The National Data Book*, 125th ed. (Washington, D.C.: U.S. Census Bureau, 2006), 795.

80. Rainer Martens, "Competition: Misunderstood and Maligned," *Comparative Physical Education and Sport*, 6 (1989), 38.

81. In "Dare to Compete," op. cit.

82. In Guttmann, op. cit., 155.

83. See Mary C. Curtis and Christine H.B. Grant, "Overview of Title XI," posted at the University of Iowa Gender Equity in Sport Project, http://bailiwick.lib.uiowa.edu. Grant, an associate professor in sports administration at the University of Iowa was the university's first ever female athletic director and is among the most vocal American commentators in the quest for gender equity in sport.

84. Source: *Statistical Abstract of the United States: 2006. The National Data Book*, 125th ed. (Washington, D.C.: U.S. Census Bureau, 2006).

85. "Empowering Women in Sports," A Pub-

lication of the Feminist Majority Foundation's Task Force on Women and Girls in Sports, Series No. 4. 1995, report posted at the Feminist Majority Foundation On-Line, http://www.feminist. org.

86. Lewis Leader, Sports Editor of the University of California's *Daily Cal*, during the spring of 1970 cited in Scott, op. cit., 68–69.

87. Veteran sportswriter Robert Lipsyte in *Playing the Field: Sports and Sex in America*, Frank Deford, Writer, Rick Bernstein and Ross Greenberg, Exec. Prods., HBO Sports, 2000.

88. Sidney Zion, ""What about the Fans? Fuhgeddaboutit [*sic*]," *The Nation* 267, no. 5. (August 10/17, 1998), 34.

89. Robert Lipsyte of *The New York Times*, Los Angeles Times reporter Jim Murray, Dick Schaap of New York's now defunct *Herald Tribune*, and Phil Pepe of the *New York Post* were among the first to accept and in some cases defend countercultural positions in their sports columns. See Lipsyte, op. cit. and James A. Michener, *Sports in America* (Greenwich, CT: Fawcett Crest, 1976), 400–415. See also David Halberstam, "Schaap Was a Pioneer ... and a Good Guy," ESPN.com: Page 2, December 24, 2001.

90. In Jerome Holtzman, *No Cheering in the Press Box*, rev. ed. (New York: Henry Holt and Company, 1995), 256.

91. As an aside, reporters were still expected to report everything about a given story without a hint of subjectivity, a standard of journalism that would often lead to highly unusual circumstances, such as the seriousness of Senator McCarthy's accusations and many HUAC-related matters, though this practice would indeed fade as the Cold War era progressed. See *David Halberstam's The Fifties*, Edward Herrmann, Narr., Nancy Button, Prod., 1997.

92. Robert W. McChesney, "Media Made Sport: A History of Sport Coverage in the United States," in Wenner, ed., op. cit., 67. See also Joel Nathan Rosen, "All-Sports Radio: The Development of an Industry Niche," *Media History Monographs* On-Line, 5, no. 1 (2001–2002).

93. George Willis, "2 Raised Fists Still Breaking Down Barriers," *New York Post* On-Line, August 22, 1999, article posted at http://promotions.nypost.com. See also "Fists of Freedom: The Story of the '68 Summer Games," op. cit. Note: Brent Musburger would rise to become one of America's most noteworthy and respected sport commentators, appearing almost ubiquitously in both print and electronic formats.

94. Lipsyte, op. cit., 183.

95. The dimensions of Louis' defeat of Germany's Max Schmelling in 1938 provided a galvanizing moment that many believed spilled over into the American pursuit of World War II. The commonality of Louis being treated as a heroic figure ranks among the most notable shifts in public perceptions relative to race in the first half of the twentieth century, and in many ways Louis would become lionized and revered for his symbolic defeat of the treacherous Hun by virtue of his stunning defeat of the German champion, which offered notice to both black and white that these spurts of changes were indeed possible. See, for example, Paul Oliver's chapter on Joe Louis as American folk hero in *Screening the Blues: Aspects of the Blues Tradition* (New York: Da Capo Press, 1968), 148–163.

96. Rader, op. cit., 320.

97. Howard Cosell, *Cosell*, with Mickey Herskowitz (Chicago: Playboy Press, 1973), 241–248.

98. Halberstam, op. cit.

99. Steven J. Overman, *The Influence of the Protestant Ethic on Sport and Recreation* (Brookfield, VT: Avebury, 1997), 200.

100. "Playing the Field," op. cit.

101. Alan Courtney and Benjamin Homer, "Joltin' Joe DiMaggio," *Baseball: A Film by Ken Burns*, Original Soundtrack Recording (New York: Elektra Entertainment, 1994).

102. Paul Simon and Art Garfunkel, "Mrs. Robinson," *Bookends* (New York: Columbia Records, 1968). Note: This song was originally released on the soundtrack of *The Graduate*, with Anne Bancroft and Dustin Hoffman, directed by Mike Nichols, MGM, 1967

103. Rader, op. cit., 320.

Chapter 4

1. A recent study by the Institute for the Study of Youth Sport at Michigan State University has determined that of the twenty million young boys and girls who participate in sport every year, seventy percent will have quit by the age of thirteen. See http://ed-web3.educ.msu.edu/ysi/.

2. Fred Engh speaking in HBO's "Parental Rage," "Real Sports," HBO Sports, Bryant Gumbel, Host., Bernard Goldberg, Narr., Alvin Patrick, Prod., October 12, 2000.

3. See "Goin' Deep," "Sport and Civility," Fox Sports Network, Chris Myers, Host, Gary Foremen, Dir., October 11, 2000.

4. See, for example, Stanley Cohen, *Folk Devils and Moral Panics: Thirtieth Anniversary Edition* (London: Routledge, 2002). See also David L. Altheide, *Creating Fear: News and the Construction of Crisis* (Hawthorne, NY: Aldine de Gruyter, 2002) and Joel Best, ed., *How Claims Spread: Cross-National Diffusion of Social Problems* (Hawthorne, NY: Aldine de Gruyter, 2001).

5. In Ibid.

6. Robert Lipsyte, "The Emasculation of American Sports," *The New York Times Magazine*, April 2, 1995. This quote also appears in Craig

Clifford and Randolph M. Feezell, *Coaching for Character: Reclaiming the Principles of Sportsmanship* (Champaign, IL: Human Kinetics Publishers, Inc., 1997), vi.

7. The Special Olympics, "The Special Olympics Oath," bundled mail, November 10, 2005.

8. This is actually a paraphrase of Geertz as expressed in Miracle and Rees, op. cit., 9.

9. David Light Shields and Brenda Light Bredemeier, "Moral Reasoning in the Context of Sport," Studies in Moral Development and Education Web page (Chicago: University of Illinois at Chicago). This paper was originally delivered at the annual meeting of the Association for Moral Education in Minneapolis, MN, October, 1999, http//:tigger.uic.edu/~lnucci/MoralEd/index.htm.

10. See Karin A.E. Volkwein, "Ethics and Top-Level Sport — A Paradox?" *The International Review for the Sociology of Sport* 3&4 (1995): 317. Volkwein of West Chester (PA) University's Department of Physical Education assumes the position that revolves around what she deems to be the failure of contemporary play initiatives and other such attempts to mitigate the effects of an improper sport ethos.

11. Fred Engh, *Why Johnny Hates Sports: Why Organized Youth Sports Are Failing Our Children and What We Can Do About It. Putting the Fun Back in Sports for Boys and Girls* (Garden City Park, NJ: Avery Publishing Group, 1999), 191.

12. In Miracle and Rees, op. cit., 31–38. See also James A. Mangan, *Athleticism in the Victorian and Edwardian Public School* (Cambridge: Cambridge University Press, 1981).

13. Daniel Gould, "Sportsmanship: Building 'Character' or 'Characters'?" In Deborah Feltz, ed., *A Winning Philosophy of Youth Sports* (East Lansing, MI: Institute for the Study of Youth Sports, 1981), 29.

14. Clifford and Feezell, op. cit., 15.

15. Darrell J. Burnett, "Noticing Progress: The Key to Keeping Kids in Youth Sports," Youth Sports Instruction Web site, February 1998, http://youth-sports.com. Burnett posits that while the sporting environment may not be the end all for ethical training, it does, nonetheless, lend itself to introducing important life-lessons for children.

16. Marty Ewing, "Promoting Social and Moral Development through Sports, *Spotlight on Youth Sports On-line* (Summer and Fall 1997) http://ed-web3.educ.msu.edu.

17. In Miracle and Rees, op. cit., 38. See also Mangan, op. cit.

18. *NCAA News*, October 6, 1997.

19. Mid-Continent Conference Commissioner Jon A. Steinbrecher in *NCAA News*, September 28, 1997.

20. Brian C. Anderson and Peter Reinharz,

"Bring Back Sportsmanship," *City Journal* 10, no. 2 (Spring 2000): 44–45.

21. In Bil Gilbert, "Competition: Is It What Life's All About?" *Sports Illustrated* (May 16, 1988): 98.

22. "Sports Culture in the New Millennium," Executive Summary for the Citizenship through Sports Alliance, Leawood, KS, June 27–29, 1999, article posted on the Citizenship through Sport Alliance Web site, http://www.sportsmanship.org /main.html.

23. Ibid.

24. Gould, op. cit., 25.

25. Lori Gano-Overway, "Emphasizing Sportsmanship in Youth Sports," *Education World* On-Line, May 3, 1999, http://www.education-world.com.

26. Engh, op. cit., 23–24.

27. Gano-Overway, op. cit. See also Paul E. Dubois, "Competition in Youth Sports: Process or Product?" *Physical Educator* 37 (1980).

28. Volkwein, op. cit., 318.

29. Gough cited in *NCAA News*, July 22, 1996.

30. Russell W. Gough, *Character Is Everything: Promoting Ethical Excellence in Sports* (Fort Worth, TX: Harcourt Brace College Publishers, 1997), 3–5.

31. Ibid., 3.

32. Ibid., 25.

33. Ibid., 10.

34. Steven J. Overman, *The Influence of the Protestant Ethic on Sport and Recreation* (Brookfield, VT: Avebury, 1997), 229.

35. Victor Garber as a Harvard law professor describing competition to one of his students in the motion picture *Legally Blonde*, with Reese Witherspoon, Robert Luketic, Dir., MGM, 2001.

36. See, for example, Terry Eagleton, *The Illusions of Postmodernism* (Oxford, UK: Blackwell Publishers, 1996). Eagleton's work is discussed in much greater detail in chapter 1 of this work.

37. Madan Sarup, *An Introductory Guide to Post-Structuralism and Postmodernism*, 2nd ed. (Athens, GA: The University of Georgia Press, 1993), 166. In this particular instance, Sarup's criticism reflects the work of Jean Baudrillard and his continued insistence on a condition that Baudrillard has termed hyper-reality.

38. Ibid., 166.

39. See, for example, the brief discussion of what the authors deem the *overemphasis on negative outcomes* in Jim McKay et al., *Masculinities, Gender Relations, and Sport* (Thousand Oaks, CA: Sage Publications, Inc., 2000), 6–9. See also Dubois, op. cit., 151–154 and Kathleen Vail, "It's How You Play the Game," *The American School Board Journal* 184, no. 8 (August 1997): 16–18.

40. Carolyn Sherif, "The Social Context of Competition," in *Social Problems in Athletics*, ed-

ited by Daniel M. Landers (Urbana: University of Illinois Press, 1976): 36.

41. Frank Litsky, "Aggression Necessary, Hill Says," *New York Times*, January 22, 1987. This quote also appears in Alfie Kohn, *No Contest: The Case Against Competition: Why We Lose in Our Race to Win* (New York: The Houghton-Mifflin Co, 1992), 238.

42. These terms are industry vernacular that regularly reflects this issue.

43. See Overman, op. cit.

44. Quote attributed to Thomas Boswell, a baseball beat-writer for the *Washington Post*, in *Baseball*, "Inning Eight," John Chancellor, Narr., Ken Burns, Exec. Prod., 1994.

45. James L. Nolan, Jr., *The Therapeutic State: Justifying Government at Century's End* (New York: New York University Press, 1998), 9.

46. Mick Hume, "A Man's Game?" *LM* 111 (June 1998): 4.

47. Author's Note: For the record, while I support Major League Baseball's decision to penalize Rose, I have concerns about keeping him and another incontrovertibly exceptional player, "Shoeless" Joe Jackson, out of the Hall of Fame. It seems incomprehensible that two men who hold records that may never be approached again (Rose's mark for career hits and Jackson's post-season batting average) are not enshrined with their peers as if these accomplishments simply do not exist. In this regard, the participation ban seems justified, but the enshrinement issue seems excessive to the point of being counterproductive.

48. See, for example, Ed Mahoney, "Solving the Pete Rose Dilema [*sic*]," *Elysian Fields Quarterly* On-Line 18, no. 1 (2001), article posted on http://www.efqreview.com. See also James Reston, Jr., *Collision at Home Plate: The Lives of Pete Rose and Bart Giamatti* (Lincoln, NE: University of Nebraska Press, 1997) and George Will, *Bunts: Curt Flood, Camden Yards, Pete Rose, and Other Reflections on Baseball* (New York: Scribner, 1998). To note, Mahoney, Reston, and Wills all favor Rose's reinstatement, and each is critical of the attempts to turn Rose's situation into a means to further expand therapeutic infringements into the private sphere.

49. Rainer Martens, "Competition: In Need of a Theory," in Landers, op. cit., 9–17.

50. Sherif, op. cit., in Landers, op. cit., 18–36.

51. See Engh, op. cit., 39–41.

52. Michael L. Schwalbe, "A Humanist Conception of Competition in Sport," *Humanity & Society* 01.13, no. 1 (1989): 44.

53. See, for example, "The Sporting Life," *National Review* 46, no. 3 (February 21, 1994): 20–21.

54. Gerald Ford, "In Defense of the Competitive Urge," in David L. Vanderwerken and Spencer K. Wertz, eds., *Sport Inside Out: Read-

ings in Literature and Philosophy* (Fort Worth, TX: Texas Christian University Press, 1985), 247. This quote originally appeared in Gerald R. Ford and John Underwood, "In Defense of the Competitive Urge," *Sports Illustrated*, July 8, 1974, 17.

55. Gano-Overway, op. cit.

56. Schwalbe, op. cit., 47.

57. Ibid.

58. Vera J. Elleson, "Competition: A Cultural Imperative?" *The Personnel and Guidance Journal.* (December 1983): 197.

59. Alfie Kohn, "Why Competition?" *The Humanist* (January/February 1980): 15.

60. Kohn 1992, op. cit.

61. Ibid., 1.

62. Ibid., 1–10. This line serves as the title to his first chapter.

63. Kohn 1992, op. cit., 69.

64. Ibid., 45–78.

65. Ibid., 43.

66. Kohn 1980, op. cit., 49.

67. Kohn 1992, op. cit., 96–167; 233–245

68. Ibid., 112.

69. Ibid., 113.

70. Juhu Heikkala, "Modernity, Morality, and the Logic of Competing," *The International Review for the Sociology of Sport* 28, no. 4. (1993): 355–356.

71. See both Robert Lipsyte, *SportsWorld: An American Dreamland* (New York: Quadrangle, 1975) and Robert Lipsyte, "SportsWorld Revisted." in Richard E. Lapchick, *Fractured Focus: Sport as a Reflection of Society* (Lexington, MA: Lexington Books, 1986), 313–317.

72. Robert Lipsyte, "The Varsity Syndrome: The Unkindest Cut," *The Annals of the American Academy* 445 (1979), 15–23.

73. Ibid., 16.

74. Volkwein, op. cit., 311–321.

75. Ibid., 316.

76. John F. Galliher and Richard M Hessler, "Sports Competition and International Competition," *Journal of Sport and Social Issues* 3, no. 1 (Spring/Summer 1978): 12.

77. Gilbert, op. cit., 89.

78. Ibid., 96–97.

79. Teri Bostian, "Brutality in Our Schools: How Jock Culture Can Breed Violence," *SportsJones* On-Line, April 30, 1999, http://www.sportsjones.com.

80. See Mike Sowell, *One Pitch Away: The Players' Stories of the 1986 League Championships and World Series* (New York: MacMillan Books, 1995).

81. Stuart H. Walker, *Winning: The Psychology of Competition* (New York: W.W. Norton, 1980), 111, 250.

82. Anderson and Reinharz, op. cit., 44.

83. Robert M. Malina, "Sport, Violence, and Littleton: A Perspective," article posted on the

Youth Sport Institute Web site, (Spring 1999), http://ed-web3.educ.msu.edu,

84. Susan Faludi, *Stiffed: The Betrayal of the American Man* (New York: Harperperennial Library, 2000).

85. Michael Oriard, "A Review of Susan Faludi's *Stiffed: The Betrayal of the American Man,*" *SportsJones* On-Line, December 1999, http://www.sportsjones.com.

86. Karen D. Pyke, "Class-Based Masculinities: The Interdependence of Gender, Class, and Interpersonal Power," *Gender & Society* 10, no. 5 (October 1996): 530–531.

87. Ibid., 531.

88. M. Ann Hall, "Discourse of Gender and Sport.: From Femininity to Feminism," *Sociology of Sport Journal* 5 (1988): 332–333.

89. This quartet is understood (in no particular order) to be baseball, football, basketball, and ice hockey, though Markovits and Hellerman remind that based on television ratings and revenue, ice hockey is at best a distant fourth. Their term for identifying the popular American sport is "The Big Three and One-Half." Andrei S. Markovits and Steven L. Hellerman, *Offside: Soccer & American Exceptionalism* (Princeton, NJ: Princeton University Press, 2001), 6.

90. To note, University of Southern California sociologist Michael Messner appears troubled by this in his retelling of a home plate collision that ended up injuring one of his respondents. See Michael A. Messner, *Power at Play: Sports and the Problem of Masculinity* (Boston: Beacon Press, 1992), 70–71. Messner's work will be discussed elsewhere.

91. See, for example, Robert W. Peterson, *Cages to Jump Shots: Pro Basketball's Early Years* (New York: Oxford University Press, 1990).

92. Volkwein, op. cit., 311. See also John J. Sewart, "The Rationalization of Modern Sport: The Case of Professional Football," *Arena Review* 5 (1981), 45–51, and Lori W. Tucker and Janet B. Parks, "Effects of Gender and Sport Type on Intercollegiate Athlete's Perceptions of the Legitimacy of Aggressive Behaviors in Sport," *Sociology of Sport Journal* 18, no. 4 (2001): 403–413.

93. David Lyle Light Shields et al., "Leadership, Cohesion, and Team Norms Regarding Cheating and Aggression, *Sociology of Sport Journal* 12 (1995): 325.

94. Angela Lumpkin, et al., *Sport Ethics: Applications for Fair Play*, 2nd ed. (Boston: WCB McGraw-Hill, 1999): 68–69.

95. Varda Burstyn, *The Rites of Men: Manhood, Politics, and the Culture of Sport* (Toronto: University of Toronto Press, 1999): 164.

96. In my discussion of "Ratings and Revenue," I point out the broadcast concept of *good radio*, which drives broadcasters to air typically risqué or otherwise controversial programming in order to boost advertising revenue streams. Joel Nathan Rosen, *"Your Question or Comment Please": A Sociological Study of All-Sports Radio*, Masters Thesis (Oxford, MS: The University of Mississippi, August 1995), 108–138.

97. "The Sports Reporters," ESPN Television, March 5, 2006. See also example, Michael Atkinson, "Fifty Million Viewers Can't Be Wrong: Professional Wrestling, Sports-Entertainment, and Mimesis," *Sociology of Sport Journal* 1, no. 19 (2002): 47–66 and Scott Freeman, "John Rocker's Not Crazy: He's the Product of the Wrestlization of America," *Atlanta Magazine* (April 2000): 74–77, 150–153.

98. During the summer of 2002, a spate of domestic violence charges among athletes spawned a renewed interest in the link between sport and domestic abuse in the popular press. See, for example, "Bucks' Robinson Faces Domestic Violence Charges," CNN.com, July 24, 2002 and "Orioles Pitcher Arrested on Assault Charges," CNN.com, July 24, 2002. Both articles posted on http://www.cnn.com. See also "Flag Them for Illegal Use of the Hands," *The New York Times*, July 27, 2002. Article posted on *The International Herald Tribune Online* located at http://www.iht.com. A more scholarly treatment of this link can be found in Lisa R. Wenzel, "Position Paper: Athletes and Domestic Violence," The Program for Public Policy in Sports On-Line, University of North Carolina at Chapel Hill, May 1998, article posted on http://www.unc.edu/depts/ppps/.

99. See Don Sabo et al., "Domestic Violence and Televised Athletic Events," in Jim McKay et al., *Masculinities, Gender Relations, and Sport* (Thousand Oaks, CA: Sage Publications, Inc., 2000), 129–130. See also Michael A. Messner and Donald F. Sabo, *Sex, Violence, and Power in Sports: Rethinking Masculinity* (Freedom, CA: Crossing Press, 1994) and Timothy Jon Curry, "Booze and Bar Fights: A Journey to the Dark Side of College Athletics," in Jim McKay et al., *Masculinities, Gender Relations, and Sport* (Thousand Oaks, CA: Sage Publications, Inc., 2000), 162–175.

100. Donald J. Mrozek, "The Cult and Ritual of Toughness in Cold War America," in David K. Wiggins, ed., *Sport in America: From Wicked Amusement to National Obsession* (Champaign, IL: Human Kinetics, 1995), 257.

101. Ibid., 258.

102. Curry, op. cit., 172–174. See also Jack Tatum and Bill Kushner, *They Call Me Assassin* (New York: Morrow/Avon Reading, 1980).

103. See Suzanne Laberge and Mathieu Albert, "Conceptions of Masculinity and of Gender Transgressions in Sport among Adolescent Boys," *Men and Masculinities* 1, no. 3 (January 1999): 248–265. See also Michael A. Messner, "Sports and Male Domination: The Female Athlete as

Contested Ideological Terrain," *Sociology of Sport Journal* 5 (1988): 197–211 and Tracy Taylor and Kristine Toohey, "Sport, Gender, and Cultural Diversity: Exploring the Nexus" *Journal of Sport Management* 13 (1999): 1–13. To note, Taylor and Toohey assess the gender climate in sport by way of comparing their native Australia to that of other continents including North America, a comparison that demonstrated substantial overlap.

104. Shari Lee Dworkin and Faye Linda Wachs, "The Morality/Manhood Paradox: Masculinity, Sport, and the Media," in Jim McKay et al., *Masculinities, Gender Relations, and Sport* (Thousand Oaks, CA: Sage Publications, Inc., 2000), 50. See also Todd W. Crosset et al., "Male Student-Athletes Reported for Sexual Assault: A Survey of Campus Police Departments and Judicial Affairs Offices," *Journal of Sport and Social Issues* 19, no. 2 (May 1995): 126–140.

105. Jeffrey R. Benedict, *Athletes and Acquaintance Rape: Sage Series on Violence against Women* (Thousand Oaks, CA: Sage Publications, 1998). See also Joel Nathan Rosen, "Review of *Athletes and Acquaintance Rape*," *Reviewing Sociology* 11, no. 2 (1999), http://www.rdg.ac.uk/RevSoc/.

106. Ibid., 3.

107. Ibid., 23.

108. William Nack and Lester Munson, "Sport's Dirty Secret," *Sports Illustrated* (July 31, 1995): 62–74. Also in Burstyn, op. cit., 169.

109. Burstyn, op. cit., 170.

110. See, for example, Sabo et al., op. cit., 130. See also M. Carlson et al., "The Effects of Situational Aggressive Cues: A Quantitative Review," *Journal of Personality and Social Psychology* 58 (1990): 622–633 and Daniel L. Wann et al., *Sport Fans: The Psychology and Social Impact of Spectators* (New York: Routledge, 2001), 93–152. Wann et al. identify a stereotype of male fans consisting of references to "beer-drinking couch potatoes with a pathological obsession with a trivial and socially disruptive activity" prone to marital difficulties.

111. Mariah Burton Nelson, *The Stronger Women Get, the More Men Love Football: Sexism and the American Culture of Sports* (New York: Avon Books, 1994), 203.

112. Ibid., 202–203.

113. McKay et al., op. cit., 6.

114. See, for example, Sandra L. Hanson and Rebecca S. Kraus, "Women in Male Domains: Sport and Science," *Sociology of Sport Journal* 16, no. 2 (1999): 92–110 and Helen Longino, "The Ideology of Competition," in Valerie Miner and Helen E. Longino, eds., *Competition: A Feminist Taboo?* Foreword by Nell Irvin Painter (New York: The Feminist Press at the City University of New York, 1987), 248–249. Longino entertains a brief discussion of previous feminist research that questioned whether or not women even contained within their biological make-up enough of a competitive nature to compete within the work world, leaving them particularly unsuited to even try. See also Judith Bardwick, *Psychology of Women* (New York: Harper & Row, 1971).

115. Lionel Tiger, "Constituency Esthetics," *New York Press* On-Line 13, no. 1010 (March 2000), http://www.nypress.com.

116. Highly respected former NCAA basketball coach John Wooden in Thomas Tutko and William Bruns, *Winning Is Everything and Other American Myths* (New York: MacMillan Publishing Co., 1976), 51.

117. Duleep Allarajah, "Who Wants a Footballer for a Role Model?" *sp!ked online*, December 28, 2001.

118. See Altheide, op. cit., 17–21.

119. Peter Marsh, "In Praise of Bad Habits," Social Issues Research Centre On-Line, November 17, 2001, http://www.sirc.org/index.html.

120. Frank Füredi, *Culture of Fear: Risk-Taking and the Morality of Low Expectations* (London: Cassell, 1997), 115.

121. The Arthur Agee Role Model Foundation Web site, http://www.edgesportsintl.com/Arthur.htm. Note: Arthur Agee was one of two young men chronicled in the 1994 film *Hoop Dreams*. *Hoop Dreams*, with William Gates and Arthur Agee, Steve James, Dir., Fine Line Features, 1994.

122. Gould, op. cit., 30.

123. Ibid., 35–36.

124. Troy Cross, "Assaults on Sports Officials," *Marquette Sports Law Journal* 8, no. 2 (Spring 1998): 1–16. Article posted on the National Association of Sports Officials Web Site at http://www.naso.org.

125. Robert W. Peterson, "Helping Children Learn Positive Values," *Scouting Magazine* On-Line, January-February 2001, http://www.bsa.scouting.org/mags.

126. Ibid. See also Tipper Gore, "From the Visiting Experts: Be a Role Model," National Parent and Teacher Association (PTA) Web site, n.d., http://www.pta.org.

127. Gough, op. cit., 61.

128. Ibid., 67.

129. Gould, op. cit., 25.

130. See, for example, Paul Mitsdarfer, "The Media's Portrayal of Athletes' Lives away from the Game," Bowling Green State University Web site, n.d., article posted on http://www.bgsu.edu.

131. "The Sports Reporters," ESPN Television, May 2, 1999.

132. John Andrews, "The World of Sport: Not Just a Game," *The Economist* 347, no. 8071 (June 6, 1998): 6. Andrews, writing in an issue of *The Economist* devoted almost entirely to sport, asserted "Sport without competition is exercise."

133. Anderson and Reinharz, op. cit., 51. See

also Jeff Pearlman, "At Full Blast," *CNN-Sports Illustrated Online*, December 23, 1999. Article posted on http://sportsillustrated.cnn.com. See also chapter 3 of this work.

134. Wilbon quoted during an episode of "The Sports Reporters," ESPN Television, March 5, 2000.

135. Text found in Gough, op. cit., 57.

136. Gough, op. cit., 57.

137. Engh, op. cit., 17–20.

138. Ibid., 17.

139. Kevin Baker, "NFL: National Felons League," *Wall Street Journal*, February 4, 2000.

140. To clarify, the Golden State franchise is located in San Francisco. See Tony Kornheiser, "What Is Fair for Carlesimo?" *Washington Post*, December 11, 1997, and Theresa Walton, "The Sprewell/Carlesimo Episode: Unacceptable Violence or Unacceptable Victim?" *Sociology of Sport Journal* 18, no. 3 (2001): 345–357.

141. Jimi Hendrix, "The Star Spangled Banner," *Jimi Hendrix: Woodstock* (Universal City, CA: MCA Records, 1994).

142. In Todd Boyd, "Amerikkka's Most Hated," *SportsJones* On-Line, June 11, 1999. http://www.sportsjones.com.

143. See, for example, David Shields, "Taboo Topics, True Subjects," *Austin (TX) Chronicle*, November 19, 1999, and Rick Reilly, "Get the Message?" *CNN-Sports Illustrated Online*, August 9, 1999. Article posted on http://sportsillustrated.cnn.com. See also Philip Weiss, "Is Sprewell Still a Black Menace?" *Jewish World Review* On-Line, June 18, 1999. Article posted on http://www.jewishworldreview.com.

144. Boyd, op. cit.

145. Scoop Jackson, "White Man's Game," *SportsJones* On-Line, May 27, 2000. http://www.sportsjones.com.

146. Boyd, op. cit.

147. George Will, "Steroids Ruin Sport with Chemistry and Bad Character," *The Morning Cal*, December 8, 2004.

148. Mike Lupica of *New York Newsday* on ESPN's "The Sports Reporters," June 18, 2006.

149. Quote attributed to popular sports talk radio host Jim Rome on his syndicated program. "Jim Rome's Jungle," Premiere Radio Network, March 1, 2000.

150. Tom Fordyce, "America Wakes up to Doping Nightmare," *BBC Sport* On-line, June 9, 2004, http://newsvote.bbc.co.uk/.

151. See, for example, "The Contrarian View," "Real Sports," Bryant Gumbel, Host, HBO Sports, January 25, 2006.

152. Lyle Alzado and Shelley Smith, "I'm Sick and I'm Scared," *Sports Illustrated*, July 8, 1991, 21–27. Note: Other so-called victims of steroid-induced death or disease, including the late baseball star Ken Caminiti, who was also a heavy

recreational drug user, and football's Steve Courson, whose well-publicized heart transplant ignited the debate on drugs in football in the 1980s, are generally the other members of what has become an unholy trinity alongside Alzado, but again, the only actual links to their individual cases and their use of performance enhancers remains purely anecdotal, though it is often accepted as fact.

153. Mike Puma, "Not the Size of the Dog in the Fight," A SportsCentury Biography, ESPN. com, n.d., http://espn.go.com.

154. "Steroids: Play Safe, Play Fair," American Academy of Pediatricians home page, n.d., http://www.aap.or/family/steroids/htm.

155. Ibid.

156. "Steroids Threaten Health of Athletes and Integrity of Sport Performance: American College of Sport Medicine Calls for Increased Vigilance in Identifying Steroid Use," American College of Sports Medicine home page, October 23, 2003, http://www.acsm.org.

157. Ibid.

158. See, for example, Bill Durodié, "The Precautionary Principle Assumes That Prevention Is Better Than the Cure," *sp!ked online*, March 16, 2004, and Christine Sismondo, "Why Cigs? Why Not Beef? The Vagaries of the Precautionary Principle," *The Toronto Star* Online, May 28, 2006.

159. Don Walker, "Selig Says Steroids Plague Sport: Female Journalists Hear His Message," *Milwaukee Journal-Sentinel* Online, June 5, 2004, http://www.jsonline.com.

160. In Charles Krauthammer, "If Enhancers Are OK for Others, Why Not for Bonds?" *The Morning Call*, June 5, 2006.

161. Bonds maintains that he was an unwitting recipient of a collection of creams that he believed were legal but later learned contained banned substances. See, for example, Mark Fainaru-Wada and Lance Williams, "The Truth about Barry Bonds and Steroids," *Sports Illustrated* 104, no. 11 March 12, 2006, 44. This piece was excerpted from their *Game of Shadows: Barry Bonds, BALCO, and the Steroids Scandal That Rocked Professional Sports* (New York: Gotham, 2006).

162. Jessica A. Johnson, "Media Won't Give Bonds a Break," *The Columbus Dispatch*, December 17, 2004.

163. José Canseco, *Juiced: Wild Times, Rampant 'Roids, Smash Hits, and How Baseball Got Big* (New York: Regan Books, 2005).

164. "The Sports Reporters," ESPN Television, Weekly Series, April 30, 2006.

165. Krauthammer, op. cit.

166. "The Sports Reporters," op. cit. March 12, 2006.

167. Ibid.

168. Ibid.

169. Jim Schmaltz, "Panic Room: The Baseball-Steroid Issue Reaches the Senate, and Legal Supplements Get Smeared in the Process," *LookSmart Online*, n.d., http://www.findarticles.com/.

170. George Will, "Steroids Ruin Sport with Chemistry and Bad Character," *The Morning Call*, December 8, 2004.

171. Dayn Perry, "Are Steroids Ruining Sports, and Should Cheating Athletes Be Held Accountable?" Posted on the Hi International home page, 2006, http://hiinternational.com/.

172. In Kenan Malik et al., "Analysis: Tainted Gold: A Transcript of a Programme for a Radio 4 Analysis Strand," posted on the Kenan Malik home page, January 4, 2004, http://www.kenanmalik.com/.

173. Frank Deford, "Gene Therapy and the Future of Competition," National Public Radio, November 17, 2004.

174. Krauthammer, op. cit.

175. Ibid.

176. Sport New Anchor John Anderson on "Sports Center," ESPN Television, Daily Sport News Program, February 27, 2006.

Chapter 5

1. Andrew W. Miracle, Jr., and C. Roger Rees, *Lessons of the Locker Room: The Myth of School Sport* (Amherst, NY: Prometheus Books, 1994), 222.

2. *Time* writer Paul Gary paraphrasing the basis of Dr. Spock's philosophical construct. Paul Gary, "The Man Who Loved Children. Benjamin Spock: 1903–1998," *Time* On-Line 151, no. 12, March 30, 1998, http://www.time.com.

3. Content foreword found at the Children Today, Inc. Web site, http://www.childrentoday.org.

4. See, for example, David L. Altheide, *Creating Fear: News and the Construction of Crisis* (Hawthorne, NY: Aldine de Gruyter, 2002), 17–21.

5. See Barry Glassner, *The Culture of Fear: Why Americans Are Afraid of the Wrong Things: Crime, Drugs, Minorities, Teen Moms, Killer Kids, Mutant Microbes, Plane Crashes, Road Rage, & So Much More* (New York: Basic Books, 1999), 51–84, and Frank Füredi, *Culture of Fear: Risk-Taking and the Morality of Low Expectations* (London: Cassell, 1997). See also James L. Nolan, Jr., *The Therapeutic State: Justifying Government at Century's End* (New York: New York University Press, 1998), 150–172.

6. Mike Males, "The Culture War against Kids," *AlterNet* On-Line, June 1, 2001, http://alternet.org.

7. Füredi 1997, op. cit., 115.

8. Carrie Loranger Gaska, "Parent Tech," *American Way*, June 15, 2001, 64.

9. For a popular sample of this sort of treatment of childhood see *Time* 157, no. 11 (March 19, 2001). The stories in this particular issue are devoted to children today including "It's Only Me," "Girlhoods Interrupted," and "The Legacy of Columbine," which are all drawn together under the heading "The Columbine Effect." See also Nadya Labi, "Let Bullies Beware," *Time* 157, no. 13 (April 2, 2001), 46–47.

10. See, for example, Males, op. cit. and Kelly King Alexander, "Is Spanking Ever Okay?" *Parents* (May 2001): 90–98.

11. See John Rosemond, *John Rosemond's Six Point Plan for Raising Happy, Healthy Children* (Kansas City, MO: Andrews and McMeel, 1989), 43–79. See also "Making Sense of the Sixties," Part I, Producer, Kirk Wolfinger, Narrator, Carol Rissman, 1991. The producers of this documentary included a very balanced debate regarding the efficacy of Spock-inspired discipline and its effect on children who came of age in the 1960s. Among the criticisms were that children raised in the nurturing environment free of conformity and expectations grew to be overly self-consumed and too focused on internal rather than external pressures.

12. Males, op. cit.

13. See, for example, Helene Guldberg, "Just Another Expert," *sp!ked online*, May 23, 2001, http://www.spiked-online.com. See also Frank Füredi, "Robbing Kids of Their Childhood," *LM* 113 (September 1998): 24–26. Füredi's examination of modern parenting anxieties is also presented much more laboriously in *Paranoid Parenting: Abandon Your Anxieties and Be a Good Parent* (London: Allen Lane, 2001).

14. Benjamin Spock and Steven Parker, *Dr. Spock's Baby and Childcare: A Handbook for Parents of the Developing Child from Birth through Adolescence*, 7th ed. (New York: Dutton, 1998). Spock's work, though it remains immensely popular, is thought to be at the root of modern parenting debates.

15. Michael Gurian, *The Good Son: Shaping the Moral Development of Our Boys and Young Men* (New York: Jeremy P. Tarcher/Putnam, 1999), 11.

16. Males, op. cit.

17. Glassner, op. cit., 68.

18. Guldberg, op. cit.

19. John Breeding, *The Wildest Colts Make the Best Horses: The Truth about Ritalin, ADHD, and Other "Disruptive Behavior Disorders* 2nd ed. (Austin, TX: Bright Books, Inc, 1996), 53–54.

20. Peter Williamson, *Good Kids, Bad Behavior: Helping Children Learn Self-Discipline* (New York: Simon and Schuster, 1990).

21. Robert Stuber and Jeff Bradley, *Smart Parents, Safe Kids: Everything You Need to Protect Your Family in the Modern World* (Kansas City, MO: Andrews and McNeel, 1997).

22. Ruth Peters, *Are Your Kids Driving You Nuts? Don't Be Afraid of Discipline: The Common-sense Program for Low-Stress Parenting That Improves Kids' Behavior in a Matter of Days, Stops Nagging and Hassling, Restores the Parent-Child Relationship, Creates Lasting Results* (New York: Golden Books, 1997).

23. Joanne Barbara Koch and Linda Nancy Freeman, *Good Parents for Hard Times: Raising Responsible Kids in the Age of Drug Use and Early Sexual Activity* (New York: Simon & Schuster, 1992).

24. Roger McIntire, *Raising Good Kids in Tough Times: Seven Crucial Habits for Parent Success* (Berkeley Spring, WV: Summit Crossroads Press, 1999).

25. Ibid., vii.

26. Kay S. Hymowitz, "Parenting: The Lost Art," *American Educator* (Spring 2001): 4–9. See also Kay S. Hymowitz, "Who Killed School Discipline?" *City Journal* 10, no. 2 (Spring 2000): 34–43.

27. Ibid., 4.

28. Ibid., 6.

29. See Guldberg, op. cit. See also Kay S. Hymowitz, "Raising Children for an Uncivil Society," *City Journal* 7, no. 3 (Summer 1997): 62, and Ron Taffel, "Teaching Kids Respect," *Parents* On-Line, June 1999, http://www.parentsmagazine.com.

30. Roger W. Allen, Sr., "Begin Now to Prepare Local School Children for Their Future," *Savannah Morning News*, June 11, 2001.

31. Ibid.

32. Rosemond op. cit., 3. Rosemond, a prolific author on childrearing, is syndicated in newspapers around the country. He poses himself as something of a maverick disciplinarian, and his message is a distinctive cry to remain calm and contemplative, which given the contemporary air renders him a different sort of breed in the field. See also John Rosemond, *Parent Power! A Common Sense Approach to Parenting in the '90's and Beyond* (Kansas City, MO: Andrews and McMeel, 1990).

33. Bil Gilbert, "Competition: Is It What Life's All About?" *Sports Illustrated*, May 16, 1988, 92.

34. Andrew Ferguson, "Sport: Inside the Crazy Culture of Kids' Sports," *Time* On-Line 154, no. 2, July 12, 1999, 5, http://www.time.com.

35. Mickey Herskowitz and Steve Perkins, *The Greatest Little Game* (New York: Sheed and Ward, 1974), ix. Also cited in Rainer Martens, "Competition: Misunderstood and Maligned," *Comparative Physical Education and Sport* 6 (1989): 29–30.

36. Miracle and Rees, op. cit., 222.

37. Source: *Statistical Abstract of the United States: 2001, The National Data Book,* 124th ed. (Washington, D.C.: U.S. Census Bureau, 2004–2005): 774.

38. Fred Engh, *Why Johnny Hates Sports: Why Organized Sports Are Failing Our Children and What We Can Do About It* (Garden City Park, NJ: Avery Publishing Group, 1999), 3. Engh also claims that of that twenty million, seventeen and a half million of them will leave sport disgruntled and disillusioned with competition.

39. See, for example, *Making Sense of the Sixties*, op. cit. This aforementioned series highlights the changing landscape relative to post–World War II America by chronicling the change from what appeared to be 1950s era complacency to 1960s era discontent among America's youth. Of particular interest was the confluence of thought regarding modern child rearing, inspired by such voices as Benjamin Spock, and the importance of indulging children and their interests through a carefully crafted strategy for success.

40. Jay J. Coakley, *Sport in Society: Issues & Controversies*, 6th ed. (Boston: Irwin McGraw-Hill, 1998), 116–118.

41. Ibid., 117.

42. Ibid., 117.

43. James A. Michener, *Sports in America* (Greenwich, CT: Fawcett Crest, 1976), 137.

44. Coakley, op. cit., 120.

45. Ibid., 120.

46. See also D. Stanley Eitzen and George H. Sage, *Sociology of North American Sport*, 6th ed. (Madison, WI: Brown & Benchmark, 1997), 57–61. Drs. Eitzen and Sage have collaborated on sport-related research for nearly forty years and are responsible for helping to shape much of the contemporary focus on sport as a legitimate field of study within the social sciences.

47. Jack W. Berryman, "The Rise of Boys' Sports in the United States, 1900 to 1970," in Frank L. Smoll and Ronald E. Smith, eds., *Children and Youth in Sport: A Biopsychosocial Perspective* (Boston: WCB McGraw-Hill, 1996), 11.

48. Darrel J. Burnett, "Noticing Progress: The Key to Keeping Kids in Youth Sports," Youth Sports Instruction Web site, February, 1998, 1–4, http://youth-sports.com.

49. Allen Guttmann, *A Whole New Ball Game: An Interpretation of American Sports* (Chapel Hill: The University of North Carolina Press, 1988), 92.

50. "Children and Sports Fact Sheet No. 61," *The American Academy of Child and Adolescent Psychiatry* Web site, December 1997, http://www.aacap.org/.

51. See, for example, Guldberg, op. cit. and Füredi 1998, op. cit., 24–26.

52. Angela Lumpkin et al., *Sport Ethics: Applications for Fair Play*, 2nd ed. (Boston: WCB McGraw-Hill, 1999), 84.

53. Engh cited in Ferguson, op. cit., 11.

54. Engh, op. cit.

55. Ibid., 3–4.

56. In "Parental Rage," "Real Sports," HBO Sports, Bryant Gumbel, Host, Bernard Goldberg, Narrator, Alvin Taylor, Producer, October 12, 2000.

57. Engh typically cites 15% as the baseline for his assessments, though as few as five years ago he maintained the number probably crested near 5%. See "Parental Guidance Is Suggested," "Outside the Lines," ESPN Television, Bob Ley, Host, Shelly Smith, Narr, July 15, 2001, and Tim Dahlberg, "Youth Sport Violence Is Spreading," June 2, 2001, article posted on the ABC26 Web site, http://www.sns.abc26.com.

58. Engh, op. cit., 140–141.

59. Ibid., 71.

60. Kris Berggren, "Lombardi and Little League Make a Poor Karmic Match," National Catholic Reporter, September 5, 1997, 15. This text was also made available in Spotlight on Youth Sports On-Line, Summer and Fall 1997, http://ed-web3.educ.msu.edu/ysi/spotlight.

61. Marty Ewing, "Promoting Social and Moral Development through Sports," Spotlight on Youth Sports On-line, Summer and Fall 1997, http://ed-web3.educ.msu.edu.

62. Shepherd Smith, "Is the Choice Sportsmanship or Death?" Savannah Morning News August 1, 2000.

63. Carlton Brick, "Using Our Religion." A Review of Gary Armstrong's and Richard Giulianotti's Entering the Field: New Perspectives on World Football," LM 104 (October, 1997): 39. See also Gary Armstrong and Richard Giulianotti, Entering the Field: New Perspectives on World Football (Oxford: Berg Publishers, 1997).

64. Engh, op. cit., 128.

65. Ibid., 126.

66. Ferguson, op. cit., 4.

67. Mark S. Rosentraub, Major League Losers: The Real Cost of Sports and Who's Paying for It. What Governments and Taxpayers Need to Know, rev. ed. (New York: Basic Books, 1999), 40.

68. Daniel Gould, "Sportsmanship: Building 'Character' or 'Characters'?" in Deborah Feltz, ed., A Winning Philosophy of Youth Sports (East Lansing, MI: Institute for the Study of Youth Sports, 1981), 25.

69. See Miracle and Rees, op. cit., 39, and Christina Larson, "Reconstructing Rockwell: How an American Icon Became an Artist," The Washington Monthly Online, October 2001.

70. Burnett quoted in "Parental Rage," op. cit.

71. Vern Seefeldt, "The Future of Youth Sports in America," in Frank L. Smoll and Ronald E. Smith, Children and Youth in Sport: A Biopsychosocial Perspective (Boston: WCB McGraw-Hill, 1996), 423.

72. See, for example, Miracle and Rees, op. cit.; Coakley, op. cit.; and Alfie Kohn, No Contest: The Case Against Competition. Why We Lose in Our Race to Win, rev. ed. (Boston: Houghton Mifflin Company, 1992), and Thomas Tutko and William Bruns, Winning Is Everything and Other American Myths (New York: MacMillan Publishing Co., 1976). There are also numerous journals, organizations, and seminars devoted to this particular focus as well.

73. Gould, op. cit., 25.

74. See Rosentraub, op. cit., 39–40.

75. In Gilbert, op. cit., 97–98.

76. See Lori Gano-Overway, "Emphasizing Sportsmanship in Youth Sports," Education World On-Line, May 3, 1999, http://www.education-world.com. See also Jerald M. Strong, "A Dysfunctional and Yet Winning Youth Football Team," Journal of Sport Behavior 15, no. 4 (December 1992): 319–326.

77. Bryant Furlow, "Play's the Thing: Kids Need the Playground Just as Much as the Classroom," New Scientist On-Line, June 9, 2001, http://www.newscientist.com/features. Furlow claims that the impetus for his analysis came from Marc Bekoff, "Social Play Behavior: Cooperation, Fairness, Trust, and the Evolution of Morality," Journal of Consciousness Studies 8 (2001): 80–91.

78. In Gilbert, op. cit., 93.

79. Gary Alan Fine, "Sport as Play," The World and I, October 1988, 654.

80. Jay J. Coakley, "Children and the Socialization Process," in Daniel Gould and Maureen R. Weiss, eds., Advances in Pediatric Sport Sciences. Vol. 2: Behavioral Issues (Champaign, IL: Human Kinetics Publishers Inc., 1987), 54–55.

81. In "Parental Rage," op. cit.

82. Steven J. Overman, The Influence of the Protestant Ethic on Sport and Recreation (Brookfield, VT: Avebury, 1997), 259.

83. Ibid., 254.

84. Engh, op. cit., 27–28.

85. Tutko and Bruns, op. cit., 171.

86. Actor Robert Duvall as driven coach Buck Weston in the motion picture Kicking & Screaming, with Will Ferrell and Robert Duvall, Jesse Dylan, Dir., MCA Home Video, 2005.

87. Daniel Frankl home page, http://www.cal-statela.edu/faculty/dfrankl/dfrankl.htm.

88. Kathleen Vail, "It's How You Play the Game," The American School Board Journal 184, no. 8 (August 1997): 18.

89. Bruce C. Ogilvie and Thomas A. Tutko, "Sport: If You Want to Build Character, Try Something Else," Psychology Today, October 1971, 63.

90. Ibid., 63.

91. Strong, op. cit., 319–326.

92. Ronald E. Smith and Frank L. Smoll, "The Coach as a Focus of Research and Intervention," in Smoll and Smith, op. cit., 125. See also Ogilvie and Tutko, op. cit., 63, and Clifford and Feezell, op. cit., xi–xii.

93. Engh, op. cit., 95.

94. Overman, op. cit., 196.

95. Frankl, op. cit.

96. Hayes was thought to represent the embodiment of the heralded Ohio State University football program. His storied career was cut short following an incident on national television in which he struck an opposing player who had successfully ended an Ohio State comeback during a nationally televised game in 1978.

97. Kush was a controversial collegiate and professional football coach whose career ended following two well-publicized incidents in which he was said to have struck players during team practices. Michener claims that in some circles prior to his untimely fall from grace, Kush was hailed as the second coming of Vince Lombardi. See Michener, op. cit., 323–324.

98. McGraw, nicknamed Muggsy by the sporting press for his combative and often thuggish demeanor, was a Hall of Fame manager primarily with baseball's New York Giants franchise in the early stages of the twentieth century. He was considered by many to be baseball's most productive manager ever, but he was equally noted for his ability to bait both his own and opposing players as well as game officials. See David W. Anderson, *More Than Merkle: A History of the Best and Most Exciting Baseball Season in Human History* (Lincoln, NE: University of Nebraska Press, 2000).

99. Lombardi was able to in part rewrite some of his legacy for today's audience by retracting (and in some cases denying) his so-called dictum and claiming to have been taken out of context. See, for example, Brian C. Anderson and Peter Reinharz, "Bring Back Sportsmanship," *City Journal* 10, no 2 (Spring 2000): 48 and Ogilvie and Tutko, op. cit., 63.

100. Knight's Indiana teams were never investigated for recruiting violations and seemed to always be among the nation's leaders in player graduation rates, figures that are always scrutinized with every successive graduating class.

101. See Erik Lords, "Death Threat Spurs Critic of Bob Knight to Take Unpaid Leave from Indiana U," *The Chronicle of Higher Education* On-Line, June 15, 2000, http://chronicle.com. To note, Murray Sperber, the critic in question herein, was once a colleague of Knight's at Indiana but turned highly critical of Knight's tenure at the university, a position that was not well-received by the school's basketball faithful. His stance on the Knight question, thus, garnered him death threats and public contempt that would force him to seek refuge by going on sabbatical to deflect any further controversy during what turned out to be Knight's last year at the university. See also Murray Sperber, *Beer and Circus: How Big Time College Sports Is Crippling Undergraduate Education* (New York: Henry Holt, 2000).

102. Ewing, op. cit.

103. Engh, op. cit., xi.

104. Ibid., 27–28.

105. Angela Lumpkin et al., op. cit., 65.

106. Troy Cross, "Assaults on Sports Officials," *Marquette Sports Law Journal* 8, no. 2 (Spring 1998): 4, article posted on the National Association of Sports Officials Web site, http://www.naso.org. See also Bob Still, *Special Report: The National Association of Sports Officials. Officials under Assault: Update 2002*, with Jim Arehart, ed. (Franksville, WI: The National Association of Sports Officials and Referee Enterprises, 2002).

107. Gano-Overway; op. cit.

108. Ibid.

109. Master Craig Peeples, "The Reason We Compete," flyer handed out to participants of the Georgia State Tae Kwon Do Championships in Kingsland, Georgia, May 1999.

110. Quote attributed to baseball's erstwhile "bad boy" Albert Belle, noted for his aggressive and combative demeanor both on and off the field. CNN-SI Television, December 2, 2001.

111. Quote attributed to Rick Reilly of *Sports Illustrated*, CNN-SI Television, interview, June 21, 2001. See also Matt Labash, "What's Wrong with Dodgeball? The New Phys Ed [*sic*] and the Wussification of America," *Weekly Standard* 6, no. 39 (June 25, 2001): 17–25.

112. Tutko and Bruns, op. cit., 7.

113. See, for example, Tamala M. Edwards, "Scourge of the Playground," with Anne Moffet, *Time* 157, no. 20 (May 21, 2001): 68, and Ellen R. Delisio, "New PE Trend Stresses Fitness and Fun," *Education World* On-Line, May 23, 2001, http://www.education-world.com.

114. Edwards, op. cit., 68.

115. See, for example, Teri Bostian, "Brutality in Our Schools: How Jock Culture Can Breed Violence," *SportsJones* On-Line, April 30, 1999, http://www.sportsjones.com. See also John Cloud, "The Legacy of Columbine," *Time* 157, no. 11 (March 19, 2001): 32–35, and Nadya Labi, "Let Bullies Beware," *Time* 157, no. 13 (April 2, 2001): 46–47. See also Brian Wilson, "The 'Anti-Jock' Movement: Reconsidering Youth Resistance, Masculinity, and Sport in the Age of the Internet," *Sociology of Sport Journal* 19, no. 2 (2002): 206–233.

116. In Edwards, op. cit., 68. Note: The reference to *Lord of the Flies* is particularly effective to Dr. Williams' argument. Beyond its being a recognizable reference to the Biblical Satan, it is a very popular teen novel that chronicles the behavior of marooned children left to govern themselves and their subsequent lapse into barbarism. See William Golding, *Lord of the Flies* (New York: Perigree Trade, 1959).

117. Delisio, op. cit.

118. Edwards, op. cit., 68.

119. See Labash, op. cit., 18, and Delisio, op. cit. See also Robert Rickover, "The New Physical Education," *Wellness Today On-Line* 4, no. 5 (March 2002), http://www.wellnesstoday.com.

120. This list may include jumping rope without the rope, cooperative musical hugs, and strike-outless baseball. See, for example, Terry Orlick, *The Cooperative Sports and Games Book: Challenge without Competition* (New York: Random House, 1978); Terry Orlick, *The Second Cooperative Sports & Games Book* (New York: Random House, 1982); and John Hichwa, *Right Fielders Are People Too: An Inclusive Approach to Teaching Middle School Physical Education* (Champaign, IL: Human Kinetics, 1998).

121. "Dodge This!" "Real Sports," HBO Sports, Bryant Gumbel, Host, Bernard Goldberg, Narr., Elizabeth Carp, Prod., February 28, 2002.

122. See Michael A. Messner and Donald F. Sabo, *Sex, Violence, and Power in Sports: Rethinking Masculinity* (Freedom, CA: Crossing Press, 1994).

123. Varda Burstyn, *The Rites of Men: Manhood, Politics, and the Culture of Sport* (Toronto: University of Toronto Press, 1999), 27.

124. Tara Kost Scanlon, "Social Evaluation and the Competition Process: A Developmental Perspective," in Smoll and Smith, op. cit., 306.

125. William Raspberry, "Accept Cheating in Sports and Society Suffers," *Savannah Morning News*, February 15, 2000.

126. ABC television commentator Diane Sawyer upon introducing a segment on adult misbehavior at youth sporting events. "Parental Violence, Losing It," "20/20," ABC Television, Tom Jarriel, Narrator, Nancy Kramer and James Altman, Producers, May 25, 1999.

127. Fred Engh speaking out on the issue of parental rage at youth sporting events. "Parental Guidance Is Suggested," op. cit.

128. Frankl, op. cit.

129. See, for example, Erica Thesing, "Sports Rage: The New Face of Violence," *New York Times*, July 10, 2000. See also Lumpkin, et al, op. cit., 65–70.

130. Cross, op. cit., 14.

131. See "Parental Guidance Is Suggested," op. cit.; "Goin' Deep," Fox Sports Network, Chris Myers, Host, Gary Foremen, Dir., October 11, 2000; "Parental Rage," "Real Sports," HBO Sports, Bryant Gumbel, Host, Bernard Goldberg, Narr., Alvin Patrick, Prod., October 12, 2000; and "Parental Violence, Losing It," "20/20," ABC Television, Tom Jarriel, Narr., Nancy Kramer and James Altman, Prods., May 25, 1999.

132. "Fan Violence Expert to Address Summit Attendees," NAYS Web site, June 5, 2001, http://www.nays.org. See also Wann, op. cit.

133. "Man Pleads Innocent to Manslaughter in Beating at Youth Hockey Match," *The Boston Globe* Online, July 10, 2000, http://www.boston.com. In what would became a highly publicized and contentious case, the accused, Thomas Junta, was subsequently found guilty of involuntary manslaughter and sentenced to six to ten years in a Massachusetts prison. See "'Hockey Dad' Gets 6 to 10 Years for Fatal Beating," CNN.com, January 25, 2002, http://www.cnn.com.

134. "Real Sports," op. cit. See also "Parental Guidance Is Suggested," op. cit. To note, the referee in question, Steve Feranocci, has become a regular commentator on the topic of adult violence at youth sporting events.

135. Donald F. Staffo, "Violence, Sportsmanship Still Problems in Youth Sports," *The Tuscaloosa News* Online, July 21, 2000, http://www.tuscaloosanews.com.

136. Dahlberg, op. cit.

137. Ibid.

138. Ibid.

139. See "This Week's Sign of the Apocalypse," *Sports Illustrated* 103, no. 3 (July 25, 2005): 26.

140. Dahlberg, op. cit.

141. Ibid.

142. Ibid.

143. Burnett quoted in Jon Sindell, "Lessons from Youth Hockey Mayhem," *My Prime Time* Web site, 2001, http://www.myprimetime.com. See also Darrell J. Burnett, "Teaching Youngsters How to Be Good Sports," Youth Sports Instruction Web site, February, 1998, http://youth-sports.com.

144. Smith, Shepherd, op. cit.

145. Ibid.

146. Gano-Overway, op. cit.

147. Mark Smith, "Youth Sports and Adult Violence," *The Caledonian Record* On-Line, January 8, 2001, http://www.caledonianrecord.com/.

148. See Bob Still, ed., "Assaults on Sports Officials: Based upon a Report Written by Troy Cross," National Association of Sports Officials Web site, http://www.naso.org. See also Troy Cross, "Assaults on Sports Officials," *Marquette Sports Law Journal* 8, no. 2 (Spring 1998). See also Still 2002, op. cit.

149. Op. cit., 65.

150. "JTAA Is the First Youth Sports Organization to Mandate Parent Training: An Interview with the JTAA President, Mr. Jeff Leslie," *National Association for Youth Sports* Web site, article posted on http://nays.org.

151. Ibid., 2. The NYSCA also advertises that it offers background checks at a reduced rate for members and league administrators that subscribe to the service. See insert. *Youth Sports Journal: A Publication of the National Alliance for Youth Sports* 3, Issue 3 (Fall 2001). This advertisement was also posted on the NAYS Web Site, http://www.nays.org.

152. Mike English, "JTAA Starts Sportsmanship Training," *The Jupiter Courier*, February 20, 2000.

153. Ibid.

154. "JTAA Is the First Youth Sports Organization to Mandate Parent Training: An Interview with the JTAA President, Mr. Jeff Leslie," op. cit.

155. Source: Bob Still, *Special Report: The National Association of Sports Officials. Officials under Assault: Update 2002*, with Jim Arehart, ed. (Franksville, WI: The National Association of Sports Officials and Referee Enterprises, 2002): 17.

156. Cited in Dahlbeg, op. cit.

157. Shepherd Smith, op. cit.

158. "Youth Sports Violence Is Spreading," MSNBC Web site, October 2001. Article posted on http://www.msnbc.com. See also Thesing, op. cit. and Cross, op. cit.

159. "Parental Guidance Is Suggested," op. cit.

160. Ibid.

161. Ibid. See also Overman, op. cit., 200.

162. Cited in "Outside the Lines," ESPN Television, Bob Ley, Host, July 23, 2001.

163. "Thin Ice," "Law & Order," Dick Wolfe, Exec. Prod., July 18, 2001. Note: This serial that prides itself on tackling matters "ripped from the headlines" and has branched out into no fewer than five separate franchises, is known for rushing into production with storylines that are as recent as possible. To further illustrate this, since the turn of the twenty-first century, the producers have aired programming related to the 9/11 attacks in 2001, the resignation of New Jersey's governor following his acknowledgement of a gay love affair in 2004, and a thinly veiled take on Michael Jackson's child sex abuse trial in 2005.

164. See "Real Sports," op. cit.

165. "Thin Ice," op. cit.

166. Ibid.

167. Burnett "Teaching Youngsters How to Be Good Sports," op. cit.

Chapter 6

1. Previous discussions of this nature can be found in Joel Nathan Rosen, "Self-Concept and the Discussion of Youth Sport—A Critique," *Journal of Mundane Behavior* 5, no. 1 (June 2004) and Joel Nathan Rosen, "The Contemporary Conundrum: Competition and the Therapeutic Undercurrent," paper presented at the American Sociological Association Conference, Chicago: Hilton Chicago, August 2002.

2. Matthew McKay and Patrick Fanning, *Self-Esteem*, 2nd ed. (New York: MJF Books, 1992): i-ii. Dr. McKay is the founding director of the Haight-Ashbury Psychological Services Organization in San Francisco, while Patrick Fan-

ning, who holds no advanced degree, has authored numerous books focusing specifically on men's mental health.

3. Wayne Smith, *Quest for High Self-Esteem* (Tustin, CA: Self-Esteem Publishing, 1995). Posted on the Self-Esteem Web page, http://www.self-esteem.com.

4. See, for example, Steven Ward, "Filling the World with Self-Esteem: A Social History of Truth-Making," *The Canadian Journal of Sociology Online* 21, no. 1 (Winter 1996): 5–8, http://www.ualberta.ca. Ward's analysis poses this shift in its varying contexts, looking at how Americans especially grew to become more aware of their individual identities primarily through the experience of being American.

5. Quote taken from *You Can Change Your Self-Esteem*, posted on the SOLO Lifestyles for Singles Web page, http://www.solosingles/esteem.htm.

6. Ward, op. cit., 9.

7. Quote taken from the Self-Esteem and Performance Web page, http://www.performance-unlimited.com.

8. Maureen Weiss, "Self-Esteem and Achievement in Children's Sport and Physical Activity," in Daniel Gould and Maureen R. Weiss, eds., *Advances in Pediatric Sport Sciences. Vol. 2: Behavioral Issues* (Champaign, IL: Human Kinetics Publishers Inc., 1987), 112.

9. See, for example, Frank Füredi, *Culture of Fear: Risk-Taking and the Morality of Low Expectations* (London: Cassell, 1997), 67–70. Füredi's discussion of self-esteem highlights the effect that the emphasis on its acquisition has on the more traditional achievement ethos, which he feels has degraded the efficacy of active human agency. See also James Heartfield, *The 'Death of the Subject' Explained* (Sheffield, UK: Sheffield Hallam University Press, 2002).

10. It must be noted that though he manifestly denied its existence, Hume, nonetheless, wrestled with the debates about the self, assuming what must have seemed then the alternate pose on the question. See David Hume, "The Doctrine of Substance," in E. Freeman, ed., *An Enquiry Concerning Human Understanding* (Chicago: Pacquin Printers, 1966), 256–257.

11. Ward, op. cit., 5–6. See also Stanley Coopersmith, *The Antecedents of Self-Esteem* (San Francisco: W.H. Freeman and Co., 1967); Daniel Gould and Maureen R. Weiss, eds., *Advances in Pediatric Sport Sciences. Vol. 2: Behavioral Issues* (Champaign, IL: Human Kinetics Publishers Inc., 1987); and James L. Nolan, Jr., *The Therapeutic State: Justifying Government at Century's End* (New York: New York University Press, 1998).

12. In Torsten Brian Neilands, *The Time Course of the Self-Concept Threat Reduction Process among Low and High Self-Esteem Individ-*

uals, Doctoral Dissertation (Austin, TX: The University of Texas at Austin, December 1993), 2. The formula Neilands works through is a common conception of James' basic theoretical understanding of self-esteem.

13. Gordon Allport, *Personality: A Psychological Interpretation* (New York: Henry Holt and Co., 1938), 172.

14. Neilands, op. cit., 9.

15. Morris Rosenberg, *Society and the Adolescent Self-Image* (Princeton, NJ: Princeton University Press, 1965). See also Ward, op. cit., 6.

16. Ward, op. cit., 6. See also George Sage, "Socialization of Coaches: Antecedents to Coaches' Beliefs and Behaviors," *Proceedings, The National College Physical Education Association for Men*, January 1975:124–32.

17. Coopersmith, op. cit., 5.

18. Ibid., 5.

19. Ibid., 88.

20. See Nolan, op. cit., 46–76. Nolan contends that the court system has undergone a recent transformation into the more acceptable world of the self and cites as evidence the trend among some judges to assume the guise of case workers rather than administers of justice who are prone to accept aspects of the self-esteem model and entertain once unthinkable claims that low self-esteem can be a mitigating factor in criminal behavior.

21. Guy W. Farmer, "We Need as Many 'Scholar Moms' as 'Soccer Moms,'" *Nevada Appeal*, October 31, 1999.

22. Weiss, op. cit., 92.

23. Vasconcellos cited in Ward, op. cit., 4. See also Andrew M. Mecca et al, eds., *The Social Importance of Self-Esteem* (Berkeley, CA: University of California Press, 1989).

24. Frank Füredi, "Why the 'Politics of Happiness' Makes Me Mad: If You're Unhappy with State-Sponsored Happiness Programmes, Clap Your Hands," *sp!ked online*, May 23, 2006, http://www.spiked-online.com.

25. Weiss, op. cit., 88.

26. Nolan, op. cit.

27. Ibid., 1–21.

28. See also Terry Eagleton, *The Illusions of Postmodernism* (Oxford, UK: Blackwell Publishers, 1996). Eagleton poses this issue of the human-centered liberation project in a much more historical context.

29. Nolan, op. cit., 152.

30. Ibid., 4.

31. Ibid., 178–179.

32. Janet Daley, "Progressive Ed's War on Boys," *City Journal* 9, no. 1 (Winter 1999): 32.

33. See John Fitzpatrick, "Spelling Fashism: Let's Stand up for Standard English," *Living Marxism*, 62 (December 1993): 28. Fitzpatrick, a law professor at the University of Kent at Canterbury, considers that this condition stems from not wanting the students to feel pressured by having to spell words correctly, which seems to offer solace by virtue of a nod toward their creative capacities. See also Onkar Ghate, "Say No to the 'Self-Esteem' Pushers: The Problem of Low Self-Esteem among Students Is Caused by the Very Approach Now Proposed as the Cure," Ayn Rand Institute Web site, Marina del Rey, CA, http://www.aynrand.org.

34. To note, American schools tend to place a cap on what age a repeater can stay at a given grade level. Therefore, some students are passed along to the next grade level because they have reached a certain age and not because they have demonstrated a mastery of the most basic elements that would qualify for actual promotion.

35. Rita Kramer, *Ed School Follies* (New York: Free Press, 1991): 209–210. This quote also appears in the Nolan text.

36. Martin V. Covington, "Self-Esteem and Failure in School: Analysis and Policy Implications," in Mecca et al., 1989, op. cit., 109.

37. Jackson State University physical education researcher Steven J. Overman reports that what David MacClelland once termed in his classic work "the achievement ethos" stemmed in part from eighteenth century Methodism and was later translated into the twentieth century through the Protestant ethic. This ethos in turn spilled over into adult life, creating a generational lineage fostering a high achievement orientation among both parents and their children. See Steven J. Overman, *The Influence of the Protestant Ethic on Sport and Recreation* (Brookfield, VT: Avebury, 1997), 245–246, and David C. MacClelland, *The Achieving Society* (New York: MacMillan Press, 1961).

38. The proliferation of self-help books, websites, and devotees share this particular view, that self-esteem supersedes success and achievement.

39. Christopher Lasch, "For Shame: Why Americans Should Be Wary of Self-Esteem," *The New Republic*, August 10, 1992, 34. Lasch had been an outspoken opponent of what he deemed countercultural objectives, finding many of them antithetical to human development and sophomoric in their most basic guise. See also Christopher Lasch, *The Culture of Narcissism: American Life in an Age of Diminishing Expectations* (New York: W.W. Norton & Co., Inc., 1978) and Melanie Phillips, *All Must Have Prizes* (London: Warner Books, 1997).

40. John K. Rosemond, "Raising Nonviolent Kids," illustrations by Reagan Dunnick, *Hemispheres: The Magazine of United Airlines*, August 2000, 126.

41. Nina H. Shokraii-Rees, "The Self-Esteem Fraud: Why Feel-Good Education Does Not Lead to Academic Success. An Executive Summary,"

Center for Equal Opportunity Web site, Washington DC, http://www.ceousa.org.

42. Ibid.

43. Ibid.

44. Herbert London, "Happiness in School Should Not Be Confused with Knowledge," *The Savannah Morning News*, January 10, 2000.

45. Farmer, op. cit.

46. Ghate, op. cit.

47. Ibid.

48. Ibid.

49. Nolan, op. cit., 305.

50. Covington, op. cit., 101.

51. Fred Engh, *Why Johnny Hates Sports: Why Organized Sports Are Failing Our Children and What We Can Do about It* (Garden City Park, NJ: Avery Publishing Group, 1999), xi.

52. Robin Williams as Professor John Keating in the film *Dead Poet's Societ*,. Peter Weir, Dir., 1989.

53. Quote attributed to a fifth grade student in Colorado and posted on the home page of Daniel Frankl, http://www.calstatelas.edu/faculty/dfrankl.

54. Taken from the "Children and Sports Fact Sheet" posted on a Web site that chronicles the so-called soccer mom phenomenon called iSoccer Mom, http://www.isoccermom.com.

55. Ibid.

56. Though commonly cited figures, these figures were presented in Engh, op. cit., 3.

57. The ubiquitousness of this quote renders it unable to be accurately assigned. Suffice it to say, however, that it is probably in the repertoire of nearly every coach with some ties to the more traditionally constructed sporting establishment.

58. See Overman, op. cit., 158–254. See also Daniel L. Wann, *Sport Psychology* (Upper Saddle, NJ: Prentice Hall, 1997), 1–16. Wann reports that while the first psychological studies of sport took place just prior to the turn of the twentieth century, sport psychology really begins to find its momentum during the 1960s, though much of their focus was on performance rather than the ramifications of sports participation, which has grown more popular as of late.

59. Brooks Clark, "I Stink: Handling the Pitfalls of Self-Esteem," article posted on *Sports Illustrated for Kids* Parents' Web, http://www.sportparents.com.

60. Marty Ewing. "Promoting Social and Moral Development through Sports," *Spotlight on Youth Sport* Online, Summer and Fall 1997, http://ed-web3.educ.msu.edu.

61. Ibid.

62. Source: Author's photograph. April 7, 2002.

63. Carolyn W. Sherif, "The Social Context of Competition," in *Social Problems in Athletics*, edited by Daniel M. Landers (Urbana: University of Illinois Press, 1976), 18–19.

64. Comedian Billy Crystal lampooning a twelve-year-old nominee by using the language of contemporary American youth sport. "2000 Academy Awards Show," Billy Crystal, Host, Richard D. and Lili Fini Zanuck, Prods., ABC Television, March 27, 2000.

65. Michael W. Passer, "At What Age Are Children Ready to Compete? Some Psychological Considerations," in Frank L. Smoll and Ronald E. Smith, eds., *Children and Youth in Sport: A Biopsychosocial Perspective* (Boston: WCB McGraw-Hill, 1996), 81.

66. Ibid., 81–83.

67. For more on this precautionary principle, see Christine Sismondo, "Why Cigs? Why Not Beef? The Vagaries of the Precautionary Principle," *The Toronto Star Online*, May 28, 2006, http://www.thestar.com, and Bill Durodié, "The Precautionary Principle Assumes That Prevention Is Better Than the Cure," *sp!ked online*, March 16, 2004, http://www.spiked-online.com. Sismondo sheepishly refers to the tendency to react fearfully to scientific advance as being a return to "our inner Puritan."

68. "Sports Lift Esteem in Young Athletes," The American Psychological Association Web site, Washington, D.C., 1996: 1, http://www.apa.org/.

69. Weiss, op. cit., 87.

70. "Sports Lift Esteem in Young Athletes," op. cit. See also Ronald Jeziorski, *The Importance of School Sports in American Education and Socialization* (Lanham, MD: University Press of America, 1994), 1–15.

71. Scanlon cited in "Sports Lift Esteem in Young Athletes," op. cit.

72. Weiss, op. cit., 103.

73. Ibid., 112–113.

74. Ewing, op. cit.

75. Ogilvie and Tutko, op. cit., 62.

76. Tara Kost Scanlon, "Social Evaluation and the Competitive Process," in Smoll and Smith, op. cit., 306.

77. See, for example, Mark Anshel, "Coping Styles among Adolescent Competitive Athletes," *The Journal of Social Psychology* 136, no. 3 (1996): 311–323.

78. Terry D. Orlick and Louise Zitzelberger, "Enhancing Children's Sport Experiences," in Smoll and Smith, op. cit., 330. To note, Zitzelberger was a graduate assistant of Dr. Orlick during the writing of this particular article.

79. James R. Whitehead and Charles B. Corbin, "Self-Esteem in Children and Youth: The Role of Sport and Physical Education," in Kenneth R. Fox, ed., *The Physical Self: From Motivation to Well-Being* (Champaign, IL: Human Kinetics Publishers, 1997), 199.

80. Ogilvie and Tutko, op. cit., 62.

81. Engh, op. cit., 120.

Chapter 7

1. James L. Nolan, Jr., *The Therapeutic State: Justifying Government at Century's End* (New York: New York University Press, 1998): 4.

2. Harry Edwards, *Sociology of Sport* (Homewood, IL: The Dorsey Press, 1973): 42.

3. Duleep Allarajah, "Who Wants a Footballer for a Role Model?" *sp!ked online*, December 28, 2001.

4. Andrew Calcutt, *Arrested Development: Pop Culture and the Erosion of Adulthood* (London: Cassell, 1998), 14. Calcutt maintains that with the election of President Clinton, former countercultural rebels would have finally realized what he deems the "old hippy fantasy," one that lacks the hallucinogenic component while offering a more muted yet certainly more refined depiction of the countercultural vision.

5. Hans Ulricht Gumbrecht, "Epiphany of Form: On the Beauty of Team Sports," *New Literary History* 30, no. 2 (1999): 352.

6. Todd Boyd, "Amerikkka's Most Hated," *SportsJones* On-Line, June 11, 1999.

7. See, for example, John C. Walter, "The Changing Status of the Black Athlete in the 20th Century United States," *American Studies Today Online*, 1996. Article posted on the John Carlos home page, http://www.johncarlos.com. See also Michael E. Lomax, "The African American Experience in Pro Football," *Journal of Social History* 33, no. 1 (1999): 163–178, and Harry Edwards, *Sociology of Sport* (Homewood, IL: The Dorsey Press, 1973).

8. Jon Entine, *Taboo: Why Black Athletes Dominate Sports and Why We're Afraid to Talk about It* (New York: Public Affairs, 2000), 19.

9. Source: Earl Smith, "The African American Student Athlete," in Charles K. Ross, ed., *Race and Sport: The Struggle for Equality on and off the Field* (Jackson: University of Mississippi Press, 2004), 137.

10. Source: "Highest-Paid Athletes," originally published in *Sports Illustrated*, posted on Steel Kaleidoscopes home page, July 5, 2005, http://steelkaleidoscopes.typepad.com/.

11. See, for example, Gary Ross Mormino, "The Playing Fields of St. Louis: Italian Immigrants and Sports, 1925–1941," in David K. Wiggins, ed., *Sport in America: From Wicked Amusement to National Obsession* (Champaign, IL: Human Kinetics, 1995), 225. Mormino's thesis revolves around the notion of the acculturation process of Italian American children through the embrace of the American competitive ethos and its effectiveness in terms of assimilating Italian immigrants into the mainstream. See also Peter Levine, "'Oy Such a Fighter!': Boxing and the Jewish-American Experience." In S.W. Pope, ed., *The New American Sport History: Recent Approaches and Perspectives* (Urbana: University of Illinois Press, 1997), 251–283 and chapter 2 of this work.

12. In Tutko and Bruns, op. cit., 129.

13. David Leonard, "The Decline of the Black Athlete: An Interview with Harry Edwards," *ColorLines* 3, no. 1 (Spring 2000): 21.

14. John Hoberman, *Darwin's Athletes: How Sport Has Damaged Black America and Preserved the Myth of Race* (Boston: Mariner/Houghton-Mifflin Company, 1997).

15. See, for example, Bonnie Berry and Earl Smith, "Race, Sport, and Crime: The Misrepresentation of African Americans in Team Sports and Crime," *Sociology of Sport Journal* 17, no. 2 (2000): 185–186.

16. To remind, Joe Louis would become the first African American athlete to enthrall the American public following his dramatic first-round knockout of German heavyweight champion Max Schmelling in their celebrated rematch in 1936.

17. Hoberman 1997, op. cit., 82.

18. Eric Michael Dyson, "Be Like Mike? Michael Jordan and the Pedagogy of Desire," in Robert G. Omeally, ed., *The Jazz Cadence of American Culture* (New York: Columbia University Press, 1998), 372–380. See also Michael Eric Dyson, *Reflecting Black: African-American Cultural Criticism* (Minneapolis: University of Minnesota Press, 1993) and the discussion of the remnants of minstrelsy in contemporary African American culture in W.T. Lhamon, Jr., *Raising Cain: Blackface Performance from Jim Crow to Hip Hop* (Cambridge, MA: Harvard University Press, 1998), 216–226.

19. Hoberman 1997, op. cit., 87.

20. In Dyson 1998, op. cit., 64.

21. Ibid., 74.

22. Ibid., 67.

23. Ibid., 67.

24. Hoberman 1997, op. cit., 87.

25. Cited in Harry Edwards, "The Black Athletes: 20th Century Gladiators for White America," *Psychology Today* 7 (November 1973): 45. This quote is also cited in the Hoberman 1997 text, op. cit., 76.

26. Hoberman 1997, op. cit., 83–84.

27. Berry and Smith, op. cit.

28. Ibid., 185

29. Ibid., 185.

30. Douglas Hartmann, "Rethinking the Relationships between Sport and Race in American Culture: Golden Ghettos and Contested Terrain," *Sociology of Sport Journal* 17, no. 3 (2000): 235.

31. Ibid., 235.

32. Ibid., 233.

33. Ibid., 240.

34. Ibid., 240.

35. Ibid., 240.

36. Edwards cited in Leonard, op. cit., 24.

37. Gerald Early, "Performance and Reality: Race, Sports and the Modern World," *The Nation* 267, no. 5 (August 10/17, 1998): 17.

38. Ibid., 19.

39. Michael Oriard, "A Review of Susan Faludi's *Stiffed: The Betrayal of the American Man*," *SportsJones* On-Line, December 1999.

40. Scoop Jackson, "White Man's Game," *SportsJones* On-Line, May 27, 2000.

41. Hoberman 1997, op. cit., 79.

42. Ibid., 79. This quote came from the essay "American Sexual Reference" in Amiri Baraka [Leroi Jones]. *Home: Social Essays* (New York: William Morrow, 1966), 216. See also Amiri Baraka [Leroi Jones]. *Blues People* (New York: William Morrow, 1963).

43. Hoberman 1997, op. cit., 155, 163, 235–236.

44. See, for example, Dave Zirin, "Sheryl Swoopes: Out of the Closet — and Ignored," *The Nation* Online, November 4, 2005.

45. Letter from 'Out' Editor, Special to ESPN.com: Page 2, article posted on ESPN.com, [Note: This letter was originally published in the May 2001 issue of *Out* magazine.] http://espn.go.com.

46. See "Speculation Renews Debate on Openly Gay Athletes," Gay & Lesbian Alliance against Defamation (glaad) On-Line, May 22, 2002. Article posted on http://www.glaad.org.

47. Cited in *Playing the Field: Sports and Sex in America*, Frank Deford, Writer, Rick Bernstein and Ross Greenberg, Exec. Prods., HBO Sports, 2000. To clarify, John Rocker, as notorious a figure there exists in modern sport, was suspended prior to the 2000 season for making insensitive remarks regarding minorities and homosexuals in New York City during an interview with a *Sports Illustrated* reporter. See Jeff Pearlman, "At Full Blast," *CNN-Sports Illustrated* On-Line, December 23, 1999. Article posted on http://sportsillustrated.cnn.com.

48. Berry and Smith, op. cit., 179.

49. See Eric Anderson, "The Mitigation of Homophobia in Sport," unpublished manuscript, 1998, 1–15. To note, Anderson's paper is an overview of what was to become a much broader assessment of sport and homosexuality entitled *Trailblazing: The True Story of America's First Openly Gay Track Coach* (Los Angeles: Alyson Books, 2000). See also "Review Symposium of Eric Anderson's *Trailblazing: The True Story of America's First Openly Gay Track Coach*," *Sociology of Sport Journal* 18, no. 4 (2000): 463–480.

50. See Clara B. Jones and Robert A. Dickerson, "Are Black Males Homophobic?—A Note," *African-American Male Research* On-Line 6, no. 1 (November/December 2001), http://www.pressroom.com/~afromale. The authors also note

Louis Farrakhan's 1995 "State of America" address when he equated homosexuality with prostitution and drug addiction.

51. Anderson, *Trailblazing: The True Story of America's First Openly Gay Track Coach.*

52. Eric Anderson, "Crunching Numbers," E-mail correspondence, June 7, 2002.

53. Brian Pronger, "Comments on Eric Anderson's *Trailblazing*," *Sociology of Sport Journal* 18, no. 4 (2000): 470.

54. Ibid., 470. To note, Dr. Pronger, often known for his polemical outbursts, once announced during a session on sport and homophobia at the twentieth annual conference of the North American Society for the Sociology of Sport in Cleveland, Ohio, in 1999 that he would like to "fuck sport right up the ass!"

55. Theresa Walton, "The Sprewell/Carlesimo Episode: Unacceptable Violence or Unacceptable Victim?" *Sociology of Sport Journal* 18, no. 3 (2001): 347–350.

56. Ibid., 346.

57. Emmanuel Oliver, "The Rape of Black America," *Living Marxism* 42 (April 1992). Posted on *LM* On-Line, http://www.informinc.co.uk.

58. Elizabeth Lasch-Quinn, *Race Experts: How Racial Etiquette, Sensitivity Training, and New Age Therapy HIJACKED the Civil Rights Revolution* (New York: W.W. Norton & Company, 2001), 56.

59. Andrew Sullivan, "Masculinities and Men's Magazines: Dumb and Dumber," *New Republic* On-Line, June 15, 2000, http://www.newrepublic.com.

60. Fred Engh, *Why Johnny Hates Sports: Why Organized Sports Are Failing Our Children and What We Can Do About It* (Garden City Park, NJ: Avery Publishing Group, 1999), 113.

61. Helen Longino, "The Ideology of Competition," in Valerie Miner and Helen E. Longino, eds., *Competition: A Feminist Taboo?* Foreword by Nell Irvin Painter (New York: The Feminist Press at the City University of New York, 1987), 254.

62. Ibid., 254.

63. Ibid., 254.

64. Teri Bostian, "A Review of Mariah Burton Nelson's *Embracing Victory: Life Lessons in Competition and Compassion*," *SportsJones* On-Line, August 24, 2001, http://www.sportsjones.com.

65. Mariah Burton Nelson in ibid.

66. Ruth Conniff, "The Joy of Women's Sports: A Whole Generation of Girls Know It's Not How a Body Looks, It's What It Can Do," *The Nation* 267, no. 5 (August 10/17, 1998): 26.

67. Cited in Akilah Monifa, "Niggas, Dykes, and Corporate Types: Some Notions on Racism and Homophobia in Sports," *ColorLines* On-Line 1, no. 2 (Fall 1998), http://www.arc.org/C_Lines/CLArchive.

68. Ibid.

69. The acronym stands for Strategic Press Information Network.

70. The NBA-sponsored professional women's basketball league.

71. Howard L. Nixon, II., "Gender, Sport, and Aggressive Behavior outside Sport," *Journal of Sport Social Issues* 21, no. 4 (November 1997): 381.

72. Jennifer Hargreaves, *Sporting Females: Critical Issues in the History and Sociology of Women's Sports* (London: Routledge, 1994), 242. See also M. Ann Hall, *Feminism and Sporting Bodies: Essays on Theory and Practice* (Champaign, IL: Human Kinetics, 1996), 89–107.

73. Nixon, op. cit., 381.

74. See, for example, Ray Ratto, "Sports Give Refuge to the 'Socially Touchy,'" special to ESPN.com, 1999, posted on ESPN.com, http://espn.go.com.

75. Frank Füredi, "In Praise of Masculine Men — and Women," *LM* 112 (July/August 1998): 13.

76. Mechelle Voepel, "Sales, Fans Wanted to Savor Final Games," ESPNET SportsZone, February 24, 1998, http://espn.go.com.

77. Eugen König, "Criticism of Doping: The Nihilistic Side of Technological Sport and the Antiquated View of Sport Ethics," *International Review for the Sociology of Sport* 30, no. 3+4 (1995): 249.

78. Füredi 1998, op. cit., 13.

79. Ibid., 13.

80. Ibid., 13. See also Gordon Graham, "Isn't This Where We Came In?" *LM* 123 (September 1999): 15. Dr. Graham, a professor at the University of Aberdeen, Scotland, discusses here the regressive ramifications of an attempt to "feminise [*sic*] knowledge."

81. Frank Deford, "Sweetness and Light," "Some Women Athletes Follow a Sordid Path," National Public Radio, May 24, 2006.

82. See, for example, Brian Pronger, "Homosexuality and Sport: Who's Winning?" In Jim McKay et al., *Masculinities, Gender Relations, and Sport* (Thousand Oaks, CA: Sage Publications, Inc., 2000), 222–244.

Conclusion

1. Bruce C. Ogilvie and Thomas A. Tutko, "Sport: If You Want to Build Character, Try Something Else," *Psychology Today*, October 1971: 61.

2. Quote attributed to veteran Major League Baseball player Sandy Alomar, Jr., in Sheldon Ocker, "Alomar's Advice: Let Kids Play," *Akron Beacon Journal*, March 14, 2000.

3. Clifford and Feezell have an excellent aside in regards to this point entitled "Human Excellence Is Worthy of Respect." See Craig Clifford

and Randolph M. Feezell, *Coaching for Character: Reclaiming the Principles of Sportsmanship* (Champaign, IL: Human Kinetics Publishers, Inc., 1997), 31. See also David Theo Goldberg, "Call and Response: Sports, Talk Radio, and the Death of Democracy," *Journal of Sport and Social Issues* 22, no. 2 (May 1998): 217. Additionally, many like to hearken back to Hemingway's remarkable narrative of a fisherman's appreciation for the athletic acumen of baseball great Joe DiMaggio. Ernest Hemingway, *The Old Man and the Sea* (New York: Charles Scribner, 1952), 22.

4. Frank Füredi, "Why the 'Politics of Happiness' Makes Me Mad: If You're Unhappy with State-Sponsored Happiness Programmes, Clap Your Hands," *sp!ked online*, May 23, 2006, http://www.spiked-online.com.

5. Fred Engh, *Why Johnny Hates Sports: Why Organized Sports Are Failing Our Children and What We Can Do About It* (Garden City Park, NJ: Avery Publishing Group, 1999), 128.

6. Ibid.

7. See, for example, Kenan Malik et al., *What Is It to Be Human? What Science Can and Cannot Tell Us. Conversations in Print* (London: Academy of Ideas Ltd., 2001).

8. Author Franklin Foer explaining why his parents, who themselves were products of a more baseball-friendly culture, ultimately made the choice to offer soccer as a way out for their troubled young son. In *How Soccer Explains the World: An Unlikely Theory of Globalization* (New York: HarperCollins, 2004), 236.

9. ESPN Radio's Colin Cowherd, host of "The Colin Cowherd Show," ESPN Radio, June 13, 2006.

10. I use exceptional here the way that Markovits and Hellerman would in terms of what separates America's sporting culture from other cultures. See Andrei S. Markovits and Steven L. Hellerman, *Offside: Soccer & American Exceptionalism* (Princeton, NJ: Princeton University Press, 2001).

11. John R. Kelly and Rodney B. Warnick, *Recreation Trends and Markets: The 21st Century* (Champaign, IL: Sagamore Publishing, 1999), 66.

12. Source: John R. Kelly and Rodney B. Warnick, *Recreation Trends and Markets: The 21st Century* (Champaign, IL: Sagamore Publishing, 1999), 66–68.

13. Sources: *Statistical Abstract of the United States: The National Data Book*, multiple editions (Washington, D.C.: U.S. Census Bureau, 1997–2006): 259; 259; 266; 270; 262; 762; 756; 778; 794; 796.

14. Eng, op. cit., 37. I should probably point out that the suburban embrace of soccer has a racial consideration that is often left unspoken but is certainly prevalent and deserving of challenge. See, for example, Carlton Brick, "Using

Our Religion. A Review of Gary Armstrong's and Richard Giulanotti's *Entering the Field: New Perspectives on World Football*," *LM* 104 (October 1997), 39.

15. Michael A. Clark, "Winning! How Important Is It in Youth Sports?" *Spotlight on Youth Sports* On-Line 17, no. 3 (June 16, 2000).

16. Numbers cited in Engh, op. cit., 3. See also Andrew Ferguson, "Sport: Inside the Crazy Culture of Kids' Sports," *Time* On-Line 154, no. 2 (July 12, 1999): 9.

17. Kenan Malik, "What Is It to Be Human?" Paper presented at The Institute of Idea's Conference "Science, Knowledge, and Humanity" (New York: The New School for Social Research) October 24, 2001. Article posted on http://www.kenanmalik.com.

18. *A Man for All Seasons*, with Robert Shaw and Paul Scofield, Fred Zinnemann, Prod. & Dir., Highland Films, 1966.

Appendix

1. Source: *Statistical Abstract of the United States: 2006. The National Data Book*, 125th ed. (Washington, D.C.: U.S. Census Bureau, 2006), 793–794.

Bibliography

Adelman, Melvin L. "The First Modern Sport in America: Harness Racing in New York City." In *Sport in America: From Wicked Amusement to National Obsession*, edited by David K. Wiggins, 3–12. Champaign, IL: Human Kinetics, 1995.

_____. *A Sporting Time: New York City and the Rise of Modern Athletics, 1820–1870*. Urbana: University of Illinois Press, 1986.

Allarajah, Duleep. "Football between God and Mammon: A Review of David Conn's *The Football Business*." *LM* 116 (December 1998/January 1999): 44.

_____. "Who Wants a Footballer for a Role Model?" *sp!ked*, December 28, 2001. http://www.spiked-online.com/.

Allen, Roger W., Sr. "Begin Now to Prepare Local School Children for Their Future." *Savannah Morning News*, June 11, 2001.

Allport, Gordon. *Personality: A Psychological Interpretation*. New York: Henry Holt and Co., 1938.

Altheide, David L. *Creating Fear: News and the Construction of Crisis*. Hawthorne, NY: Aldine de Gruyter, 2002.

Alzado, Lyle, and Shelley Smith. "I'm Sick and I'm Scared." *Sports Illustrated*, July 8, 1991, 21–27.

The American Academy of Child and Adolescent Psychiatry. "Children and Sports Fact Sheet No. 61." December 1997. http://www.aacap.org/page.ww?name=Children+And +Sports&section=Facts+for+Families.

American Academy of Pediatricians. "Steroids: Play Safe, Play Fair." http://www.aap. org/family/steroids.htm.

American College of Sports Medicine. "Steroids Threaten Health of Athletes and Integrity of Sport Performance: American College of Sports Medicine Calls for Increased Vigilance in Identifying Steroid Use." October 23, 2003. http://www.acsm.org/Content/ContentFolders/NewsReleases/2003/STEROIDS_THREATEN_HEALTH_OF_ATHLETES_ AND_INTEGRITY_OF_SPORTS_PERFORMANCE.htm.

American Psychological Association. "Sports Lift Esteem in Young Athletes." Washington, D.C. 1996. http://www.apahelpcenter.org/articles/article.php?id=18.

Anderson, Brian C., and Peter Reinharz. "Bring Back Sportsmanship." *City Journal* 10, no. 2 (Spring 2000): 44–51.

Anderson, David W. *More Than Merkle: A History of the Best and Most Exciting Baseball Season in Human History*. Lincoln: University of Nebraska Press, 2000.

Anderson, Eric. *Trailblazing: The True Story of America's First Openly Gay Track Coach*. Los Angeles: Alyson Books, 2000.

Andrews, John. "The World of Sport: Not Just a Game." *The Economist*, June 6, 1998, 5–23.

Anshel, Mark. "Coping Styles among Adolescent Competitive Athletes." *The Journal of Social Psychology* 136, no. 3 (1996): 311–23.

Aristides. "Trivial Pursuits." *American Scholar* 65, no. 4 (Autumn 1996): 487–94.

Armstrong, Gary, and Richard Giulianotti. *Entering the Field: New Perspectives on World Football*. Oxford: Berg Publishers, 1997.

Aronson, Elliot. "Look Beneath Surface of School Violence." *Savannah Morning News*, March 8, 2000.

Ashton, Alison. "Parents Need to Behave on the Playing Field." *Savannah Morning News*, May 13, 2001.

Atkinson, Michael. "Fifty Million Viewers Can't Be Wrong: Professional Wrestling, Sports-Entertainment, and Mimesis." *Sociology of Sport Journal* 1, no. 19 (2002): 47–66.

Axthelm, Pete. *The City Game: From the Garden to the Playground.* New York: Bantam Books, 1978.

Baker, Kevin. "NFL: National Felons League." *Wall Street Journal*. February 4, 2000.

Baker, William J. *Sports in the Western World.* Totowa, NJ: Rowan and Littlefield, 1982.

Baraka, Amiri [Leroi Jones]. *Blues People.* New York: William Morrow, 1963.

_____. *Home: Social Essays.* New York: William Morrow, 1966.

Bardwick, Judith. *Psychology of Women.* New York: Harper & Row, 1971.

Barzun, Jacques. *From Dawn to Decadence: 500 Years of Western Cultural Life. 1500 to the Present.* New York: Perennial, 2000.

Baseball Almanac. 2006. http://www.baseball-almanac.com.

Bekoff, Marc. "Social Play Behavior: Cooperation, Fairness, Trust, and the Evolution of Morality." *Journal of Consciousness Studies* 8 (2001): 80–91.

Benedict, Jeffrey R. *Athletes and Acquaintance Rape: Sage Series on Violence against Women.* Thousand Oaks, CA: Sage Publications, 1998.

Benedict, Jeffrey R., _____and Don Yaeger. *Pros and Cons: The Criminals Who Play in the NFL.* New York: Warner Books, 1998.

Berggren, Kris. "Lombardi and Little League Make a Poor Karmic Match." *National Catholic Reporter*, September 5, 1997, 15.

Berman, Morris. *The Twilight of American Culture.* New York: W.W. Norton and Co., 2000.

Berry, Bonnie, and Earl Smith. "Race, Sport, and Crime: The Misrepresentation of African Americans in Team Sports and Crime." *Sociology of Sport Journal* 17, no. 2 (2000): 171–97.

Berryman, Jack W. "The Rise of Boys' Sports in the United States, 1900 to 1970." In *Children and Youth in Sport: A Biopsychosocial Perspective*, edited by Frank L. Smoll and Ronald E. Smith, 4–14. Boston: WCB McGraw-Hill, 1996.

Best, Joel, ed. *How Claims Spread: Cross-National Diffusion of Social Problems.* Hawthorne, NY: Aldine de Gruyter, 2001.

Beutel, Ann, and Margaret Mooney Marini. "Gender and Values." *American Sociological Review* 60 (June 1995): 436–48.

Bloom, Allan. *The Closing of the American Mind.* New York: Touchstone Books, 1987.

Bly, Robert. *Iron John: A Book about Men.* New York: Vintage Books, 1992.

Bockrath, Franz, and Elk Franke. "Is There Any Value in Sports? About the Ethical Significance of Sport Activities." *The International Review for the Sociology of Sport* 3/4 (1995): 283–310.

Bostian, Teri. _____."Brutality in Our Schools: How Jock Culture Can Breed Violence." April 30, 1999. http://www.sportsjones.com/.

_____. "A Review of Mariah Burton Nelson's *Embracing Victory: Life Lessons in Competition and Compassion*." August 24, 2001. http://www.sportsjones.com/.

Boston Globe. "Man Pleads Innocent to Manslaughter in Beating at Youth Hockey Match." July 10, 2000. http://www.boston.com/.

Bouton, Jim. *Ball Four.* New York: Dell Publishing Co, Inc., 1970.

Bowie, Gary. "Winning Is Not Everything." http://calgaryschild.com/articles/winning.htm

Bowles, John. *The Imperial Achievement: The Rise and Transformation of the British Empire.* London: Secker and Warburg, 1974.

Boyd, Todd. "Amerikkka's Most Hated." June 11, 1999. http://www.sportsjones.com/.

Brady, Pat. "Blasphemy: Curt Flood's Suit against Baseball." December 1997. http//:xroads.virginia.edu.

Braunstein, Peter. "Forever Young: Insurgent Youth and the Sixties Culture of Rejuvenation." In *Imagine Nation: The American Counterculture of the 1960s and '70s*, edited by Peter Braunstein and Michael William Doyle, 243–73. New York: Routledge, 2002.

Braunstein, Peter, and Michael William Doyle. *Imagine Nation: The American Counterculture of the 1960s and '70s*. New York: Routledge, 2002.

Bredemeier, Brenda Light, and David Light Shields. "Moral Growth through Physical Activity: A Structural/Developmental Approach." In *Advances in Pediatric Sport Sciences. Vol. 2: Behavioral Issues*, edited by Daniel Gould and Maureen R. Weiss, 143–63. Champaign, IL: Human Kinetics Publishers Inc., 1987.

Breeding, John. *The Wildest Colts Make the Best Horses: The Truth about Ritalin, ADHD, and Other Disruptive Behavior Disorders*. nd2nd ed. Austin, TX: Bright Books, Inc, 1996.

Brick, Carlton. "Using Our Religion. A Review of Gary Armstrong's and Richard Giulanotti's *Entering the Field: New Perspectives on World Football*." *LM* 104 (October 1997): 38–39.

Bunyan, John. *The Pilgrim's Promise*. New York: Oxford University Press, 1998.

Burgess, Adam. *Divided Europe: The New Domination of the East*. London: Pluto Press, 1997.

Burnett, Darrell J. "Noticing Progress: The Key to Keeping Kids in Youth Sports." *Youth Sports Instruction*. February 1998. http://youth-sports.com.

_____. "Teaching Youngsters How to Be Good Sports." *Youth Sports Instruction*. February 1998. http://youth-sports.com.

Burstyn, Varda. *The Rites of Men: Manhood, Politics, and the Culture of Sport*. Toronto: University of Toronto Press, 1999.

Calcutt, Andrew. *Arrested Development: Pop Culture and the Erosion of Adulthood*. London: Cassell, 1998.

Califia, Pat. *Dick for a Day: What Would You Do If You Had One?* New York: Villard, 1997.

Canseco, José. *Juiced: Wild Times, Rampant 'Roids, Smash Hits, and How Baseball Got Big*. New York: Regan Books, 2005.

Carlson, M., A. Marcus-Newhall, and N. Miller. "The Effects of Situational Aggressive Cues: A Quantitative Review." *Journal of Personality and Social Psychology* 58 (1990): 622–33.

Center for the Study of Sport in Society. "Center for the Study of Sport in Society's 2001 Racial & Gender Report Card." Northeastern University, 2001. http://www.sportinsociety.org.

Chorbajian, Leon. "Toward a Marxist Sociology of Sport: An Assessment and a Preliminary Agenda." *Arena Review* 8 (1984): 55–69.

Citizenship through Sport Alliance. "Sports Culture in the New Millennium." Executive Summary for the Citizenship through Sport Alliance. Leawood, KS, June 27–29, 1999. http://www.sportsmanship.org/.

Clark, Brooks. "I Stink: Handling the Pitfalls of Self-Esteem." *Sports Illustrated for Kids*. http://www.sportparents.com.

Clark, Michael A. "Winning! How Important Is It in Youth Sports?" *Spotlight on Youth Sports* 17, no. 3 (June 16, 2000). http://ed-web3.educ.msu.edu/ysi/spotlight.

Clifford, Craig, and Randolph M. Feezell. *Coaching for Character: Reclaiming the Principles of Sportsmanship*. Champaign, IL: Human Kinetics Publishers Inc., 1997.

Cloud, John. "The Legacy of Columbine." *Time*, March 19, 2001, 32–35.

CNN. "Bucks' Robinson Faces Domestic Violence Charges." *CNN.com*, July 24, 2002. http://edition.cnn.com/2002/LAW/07/24/ctv.penalty.box/index.html.

CNN. "'Hockey Dad' Gets 6 to 10 Years for Fatal Beating." *CNN.com*, January 25, 2002. http://edition.cnn.com/2002/LAW/01/25/hockey.death.verdict/index.html.

CNN. "Orioles Pitcher Arrested on Assault Charges." *CNN.com*, July 24, 2002. http://www.cnn.com.

Coakley, Jay J. "Children and the Socialization Process." In *Advances in Pediatric Sport Sciences. Vol. 2: Behavioral Issues*, edited by Daniel Gould and Maureen R. Weiss, 43–60. Champaign, IL: Human Kinetics Publishers Inc., 1987.

_____. *Sport in Society: Issues & Controversies.* 6th ed. Boston: Irwin McGraw-Hill, 1998.

Coffey, Margaret A. "The Modern Sportswomen." In *Sport & Society: An Anthology,* edited by John T. Talamini and Charles H. Page, 277–301. Boston: Little, Brown and Company, 1973.

Cohen, Colleen Ballerino, Richard R. Wilk, and Beverly Stoeltje. *Beauty Queens on the Global Stage: Gender, Contests, and Power.* New York: Routledge, 1996.

Coleman, James S. *The Adolescent Society: The Social Life of the Teenager and Its Impact on Education.* New York: The Free Press of Glencoe, 1961.

Collins, Rick. "Teens and Testosterone." December 20, 2005. http://www.steroidlaw. com/?pageID=37.

Commission on the Reorganization of Secondary Education. *Cardinal Principles of Secondary Education.* Washington, D.C.: U.S. Bureau of Education Bulletin, 1918.

Conn, David. *The Football Business: Fair Game in the '90s?* London: Mainstream Publishing, 1998.

Conniff, Ruth. "The Joy of Women's Sports: A Whole Generation of Girls Know It's Not How a Body Looks, It's What It Can Do." *The Nation,* August 10/17, 1998, 26–31.

Coopersmith, Stanley. *The Antecedents of Self-Esteem.* San Francisco: W.H. Freeman and Co., 1967.

Cosell, Howard. *Cosell.* With Mickey Herskowitz. Chicago: Playboy Press, 1973.

Covington, Martin V. "Self-Esteem and Failure in School: Analysis and Policy Implications." In *The Social Importance of Self-Esteem,* edited by Andrew M. Mecca, Neil J. Smelser, and John Vasconcellos, 72–124. Berkeley, CA: University of California Press, 1989.

Cross, Troy. "Assaults on Sports Officials." *Marquette Sports Law Journal* 8, no. 2 (Spring 1998): 1–16. http://www.naso.org.

Crosset, Todd W., Jeffrey R. Benedict, and Mark A. McDonald. "Male Student-Athletes Reported for Sexual Assault: A Survey of Campus Police Departments and Judicial Affairs Offices." *Journal of Sport and Social Issues* 19, no. 2 (May 1995): 126–40.

Currie, Jeremy. "Violence in Sports." Malaspina University-College, Nanaimo, BC. 2000. http://www.mala.bc.ca.

Curry, Timothy Jon. "Booze and Bar Fights: A Journey to the Dark Side of College Athletics." In *Masculinities, Gender Relations, and Sport,* edited by Jim McKay, Michael A. Messner, and Donald F. Sabo, 162–75. Thousand Oaks, CA: Sage Publications, Inc., 2000.

Curtis, Mary C., and Christine H.B. Grant. "Overview of Title XI." University of Iowa Gender Equity in Sport Project. http://bailiwick.lib.uiowa.edu.

Dahlberg, Tim. "Youth Sport Violence Is Spreading." *ABC26,* June 2, 2001. http://www. sns.abc26.com.

Daley, Janet. "Progressive Ed's War on Boys." *City Journal* 9, no. 1 (Winter 1999): 26–32.

Delisio, Ellen R. "New PE Trend Stresses Fitness and Fun." *Education World,* May 23, 2001. http://www.education-world.com.

Dickey, Glenn. *The Jock Empire: Its Rise and Deserved Fall.* Radnor, PA: Chilton Book Co., 1974.

Dubois, Paul E. "Competition in Youth Sports: Process or Product?" *Physical Educator* 37 (1980): 151–54.

_____. "The Effect of Participation in Sport on the Value Orientation of Young Athletes." *Sociology of Sport Journal* 3 (1986): 29–42.

Dulles, Foster Rhea. *A History of Recreation: America Learns to Play.* nd2nd ed. New York: Appleton-Century-Crofts, 1965.

Durodié, Bill. "The Precautionary Principle Assumes That Prevention Is Better Than the Cure." *sp!ked,* March 16, 2004. http://www.spiked-online.com/.

Dworkin, Shari Lee, and Faye Linda Wachs. "The Morality/Manhood Paradox: Masculinity, Sport, and the Media." In *Masculinities, Gender Relations, and Sport,* edited by Jim McKay, Michael A. Messner, and Donald F. Sabo, 47–66. Thousand Oaks, CA: Sage Publications, Inc., 2000.

Dyreson, Mark. "The Emergence of Consumer Culture and the Transformation of

Physical Culture: American Sport in the 1920's." In *Sport in America: From Wicked Amusement to National Obsession*, edited by David K. Wiggins, 207–23. Champaign, IL: Human Kinetics, 1995.

_____. "Regulating the Body and the Body Politic: American Sport, Bourgeois Culture, and the Language of Progress, 1880–1920." In *The New American Sport History: Recent Approaches and Perspectives*, edited by S.W. Pope, 121–44. Urbana: University of Illinois Press, 1997.

Dyson, Michael Eric. "Be Like Mike? Michael Jordan and the Pedagogy of Desire." In *The Jazz Cadence of American Culture*, edited by Robert G. Omeally, 372–80. New York: Columbia University Press, 1998.

_____. *Reflecting Black: African-American Cultural Criticism*. Minneapolis: University of Minnesota Press, 1993.

Eagleton, Terry. *The Illusions of Postmodernism*. Oxford, UK: Blackwell Publishers, 1996.

Early, Gerald. "Performance and Reality: Race, Sports and the Modern World." *The Nation*, August 10/17, 1998, 11–20.

Eberstadt, Mary. "Home-Alone America." *Policy Review* 107 (June 2000). http://www.policyreview.org.

Edwards, Harry. "The Black Athletes: 20th Century Gladiators for White America." *Psychology Today* 7 (November 1973): 43–52.

_____. *Revolt of the Black Athlete*. New York: Free Press, 1970.

_____. *Sociology of Sport*. Homewood, IL: The Dorsey Press, 1973.

_____.Eitzen, D. Stanley, and George H. Sage. *Sociology of North American Sport*. 6th ed. Madison, WI: Brown & Benchmark, 1997.

Elleson, Vera J. "Competition: A Cultural Imperative?" *The Personnel and Guidance Journal* (December 1983): 195–98.

Elliott, James W. "Gentlemen or Gamesmen?" *The Middle Stump*. http://www.geocities.com/middlestump1/JWE3.html.

Engh, Fred. *Why Johnny Hates Sports: Why Organized Sports Are Failing Our Children and What We Can Do About It*. Garden City Park, NJ: Avery Publishing Group, 1999.

English, Mike. "JTAA Starts Sportsmanship Training." *The Jupiter Courier*, February 20, 2000.

Entine, Jon. "Breaking the Taboo: Why Black Athletes Dominate Sports and Why We're No Longer Afraid to Talk about It." *Skeptic* 8, no. 1 (2000): 29–35.

_____. *Taboo: Why Black Athletes Dominate Sports and Why We're Afraid to Talk about It*. New York: Public Affairs, 2000.

Ewing, Marty. "Promoting Social and Moral Development through Sports." *Youth Sport Institute*, Summer and Fall 1997. http://ed-web3.educ.msu.edu.

Fainaru-Wada, Mark, and Lance Williams. *Game of Shadows: Barry Bonds, BALCO, and the Steroids Scandal That Rocked Professional Sports*. New York: Gotham, 2006.

_____. "The Truth about Barry Bonds and Steroids." *Sports Illustrated*, March 13, 2006, 38–52.

Faludi, Susan. *Stiffed: The Betrayal of the American Man*. New York: Harperperennial Library, 2000.

"Fan Violence Expert to Address Summit Attendees." *NAYS*, June 5, 2001. http://www.nays.org.

Farmer, Guy. "We Need as Many 'Scholar Moms' as 'Soccer Moms.'" *Nevada Appeal*, October 31, 1999.

Feltz, Deborah, ed. *A Winning Philosophy of Youth Sports*. East Lansing, MI: Institute for the Study of Youth Sports, 1981.

Feminist Majority Foundation. "Empowering Women in Sports: A Publication of the Feminist Majority Foundation's Task Force on Women and Girls in Sports." Series No. 4, 1995. http://www.feminist.org.

Ferguson, Andrew. "Sport: Inside the Crazy Culture of Kids' Sports." *Time*, July 12, 1999, 1–11. http://www.time.com.

Fine, Gary Alan. "Sport as Play." *The World and I*, October 1988, 643–55.
Fitzpatrick, John. "Spelling Fashism: Let's Stand up for Standard English." *Living Marxism* 62 (December 1993): 28–29.
Fitzpatrick, Michael. "Tony Blair's Therapeutic State." *LM* 127 (February 2000): 8–9.
Flood, Curt. *The Way It Is*. With Richard Carter. New York: Trident Press, 1971.
Foer, Franklin. *How Soccer Explains the World: An Unlikely Theory of Globalization*. New York: HarperCollins, 2004.
Ford, Gerald. "In Defense of the Competitive Urge." In *Sport Inside Out: Readings in Literature and Philosophy*, edited by David L. Vanderwerken and Spencer K. Wertz, 246–56. Fort Worth, TX: Texas Christian University Press, 1985.
Ford, Gerald, and John Underwood. "In Defense of the Competitive Urge." *Sports Illustrated*, July 8, 1974, 16–23.
Fordyce, Tom. "America Wakes up to Doping Nightmare." *BBC Sport*, June 9, 2004. http://newsvote.bbc.co.uk/.
Fox, Kenneth R., ed. *The Physical Self: From Motivation to Well-Being*. Champaign, IL: Human Kinetics Publishers, 1997.
Freeman, E., ed. *An Enquiry Concerning Human Understanding*. Chicago: Paquin Printers, 1966.
Freeman, Scott. "John Rocker's Not Crazy: He's the Product of the Wrestlization of America." *Atlanta Magazine*, April 2000, 74–77, 150–53.
Friedan, Betty. *The Feminist Mystique*. Introduction by Anna Quindlen. New York: W.W. Norton & Co., 2001.
Fukuyama, Francis. *The End of History and the Last Man*. New York: Avon Books, 1993.
Füredi, Frank. *Culture of Fear: Risk-Taking and the Morality of Low Expectations*. London: Cassell, 1997.
_____. "Disciplining Parents." *sp!ked*, September 7, 2001. http://www.spiked-online.com/.
_____. "In Praise of Masculine Men — and Women." *LM* 112 (July/August 1998): 10–3.
_____. "Is It a Girl's World?" *Living Marxism* 79 (May 1995): 10.
_____. *Mythical Past, Elusive Future: History and Society in an Anxious Age*. London: Pluto Press, 1992.
_____. *Paranoid Parenting: Abandon Your Anxieties and Be a Good parent*. London: Allen Lane, 2001.
_____. "Robbing Kids of Their Childhood." *LM* 113 (September 1998): 24–26.
_____. "Towards a New Enlightenment." *Last Magazine*, Summer 2000, 36–38.
_____. "Why the 'Politics of Happiness' Makes Me Mad: If You're Unhappy with State-Sponsored Happiness Programmes, Clap Your Hands." *sp!ked*, May 23, 2006. http://www.spiked-online.com/.
Furlow, Bryant. "Play's the Thing: Kids Need the Playground Just as Much as the Classroom." *New Scientist*, June 9, 2001. http://www.newscientist.com/.
Galliher, John F., and Richard M. Hessler. "Sports Competition and International Competition." *Journal of Sport and Social Issues* 3, no. 1 (Spring/Summer 1978): 10–21.
Gano-Overway, Lori. "Emphasizing Sportsmanship in Youth Sports." *Education World*, May 3, 1999. http://www.education-world.com.
Garraty, John A. *A Short History of the American Nation*. th7th ed. New York: Longman, 1997.
Gary, Paul. "The Man Who Loved Children. Benjamin Spock: 1903–1998." *Time*, March 30, 1998. http://www.time.com.
Gaschnitz, K. Michael. *Professional Sports Statistics: A North American Team-by-Team, and Major Non-Team Events, Year-by-Year Reference, 1876–1996*. Jefferson, NC: McFarland & Company, Publishers, 1997.
Gaska, Carrie Loranger. "Parent Tech." *American Way*, June 15, 2001, 64–69.
Gay & Lesbian Alliance against Defamation. "Speculation Renews Debate on Openly Gay Athletes." May 22, 2002. http://www.glaad.org/media/np_archive_detail.php?id=343&PHPSESSID=.

Gems, Gerald R. "Selling Sport and Religion in American Society." In *The New American Sport History: Recent Approaches and Perspectives*, edited by S.W. Pope, 300–311. Urbana: University of Illinois Press, 1997.

Gent, Peter. *North Dallas Forty*. New York: Villard Books, 1989.

George Washington University. *Polling Report.com*. http:www.pollingreport.com/sport.htm.

Gerdy, John R. *Sports: The All-American Addiction*. Jackson: University of Mississippi Press, 2002.

Ghate, Onkar. "Say No to the 'Self-Esteem' Pushers: The Problem of Low Self-Esteem among Students Is Caused by the Very Approach Now Proposed as the Cure." *Ayn Rand Institute*. http://www.aynrand.org.

Gibbs, Nancy. "It's Only Me." *Time*, March 19, 2001, 22.

Giddens, Anthony. *Beyond Left and Right: The Future of Radical Politics*. Stanford, CA: Stanford University Press, 1994.

Gilbert, Bil. "Competition: Is It What Life's All About?" *Sports Illustrated*, May 16, 1988, 86–100.

Gitlin, Todd. *Media Unlimited: How the Torrent of Images and Sounds Overwhelms Our Lives*. New York: Metropolitan Books, 2001.

_____. *The Twilight of Common Dreams: Why America Is Wracked by Culture Wars*. New York: Owl Books, 1995.

Glassner, Barry. *The Culture of Fear. Why Americans Are Afraid of the Wrong Things: Crime, Drugs, Minorities, Teen Moms, Killer Kids, Mutant Microbes, Plane Crashes, Road Rage, & So Much More*. New York: Basic Books, 1999.

Goldberg, David Theo. "Call and Response: Sports, Talk Radio, and the Death of Democracy." *Journal of Sport and Social Issues* 22, no. 2 (May 1998): 212–23.

Golding, William. *Lord of the Flies*. New York: Perigree Trade, 1959.

Goldman, Robert. "We Make Weekends: Leisure and the Commodity Form." Posted on the Lewis and Clark College Web site. Originally published in *Social Text* 8 (Winter 1984). http://www.lclark.edu.

Goodman, Cary. *Choosing Sides*. New York: Schocken Books, 1979.

Gore, Tipper. "From the Visiting Experts: Be a Role Model." *National Parent and Teacher Association (PTA)*. http://www.pta.org.

Gorn, Elliott J., and Warren Goldstein. *A Brief History of American Sports*. New York: Hill and Wang, 1993.

Gould, Daniel. "Sportsmanship: Building 'Character' or 'Characters'?" In *A Winning Philosophy of Youth Sports*, edited by Deborah L. Feltz, 25–37. East Lansing, MI: Institute for the Study of Youth Sports, 1981.

Gould, Daniel, and Maureen R. Weiss, eds. *Advances in Pediatric Sport Sciences. Vol. 2: Behavioral Issues*. Champaign, IL: Human Kinetics Publishers Inc., 1987.

Graham, Gordon. "Isn't This Where We Came In?" *LM* 123 (September 1999): 15.

Guldberg, Helene. "Just Another Expert." *sp!ked*, May 23, 2001. http://www.spiked-online.com/.

Gumbrecht, Hans Ulricht. "Epiphany of Form: On the Beauty of Team Sports." *New Literary History* 30, no. 2 (1999): 351–72.

Gurian, Michael. *The Good Son: Shaping the Moral Development of Our Boys and Young Men*. New York: Jeremy P. Tarcher/Putnam, 1999.

Guttmann, Allen. *A Whole New Ballgame: An Interpretation of American Sports*. Chapel Hill: The University of North Carolina Press, 1988.

Halberstam, David. "Schaap Was a Pioneer ... and a Good Guy." ESPN.com: Page 2, December 24, 2001. http://espn.go.com/page2.

Hall, Alvin. *The Cooperstown Symposium on Baseball and American Culture, 1999*. Edited by Peter M. Ruskoff. Jefferson, NC: McFarland & Company, Inc., Publishers, 2000.

Hall, G. Stanley. *Adolescence*. Vol. I. New York: D. Appleton, 1905.

Hall, M. Ann. "Discourse of Gender and Sport: From Femininity to Feminism." *Sociology of Sport Journal* 5 (1988): 330–40.

_____. *Feminism and Sporting Bodies: Essays on Theory and Practice.* Champaign, IL: Human Kinetics, 1996.

Hanson, Sandra L., and Rebecca S. Kraus. "Women in Male Domains: Sport and Science." *Sociology of Sport Journal* 16, no. 2 (1999): 92–110.

Hargreaves, Jennifer. *Sporting Females: Critical Issues in the History and Sociology of Women's Sports.* London: Routledge, 1994.

Hartmann, Douglas. "Rethinking the Relationships between Sport and Race in American Culture: Golden Ghettos and Contested Terrain." *Sociology of Sport Journal* 17, no. 3 (2000): 229–53.

Heartfield, James. *The 'Death of the Subject' Explained.* Sheffield, UK: Sheffield Hallam University Press, 2002.

Heath, Stephen. "Male Feminism." In *Men in Feminism*, edited by Alice Jardine and Paul Smith, 1–32. New York and London: Methuen, 1987.

Heikkala, Juhu. "Modernity, Morality, and the Logic of Competing." *The International Review for the Sociology of Sport* 28, no. 4 (1993): 355–71.

Hemingway, Ernest. *The Old Man and the Sea.* New York: Charles Scribner, 1952.

Herbeck, Dale A. "Three Strikes and You're Out": The Role of Sports Metaphors in Political Discourse." In *The Cooperstown Symposium on Baseball and American Culture, 1999*, edited by Alvin Hall and Peter M. Ruskoff, 133–46. Jefferson, NC: McFarland & Company, Inc., Publishers, 2000.

Herman, Ken, and Jeffry Scott. "White House T-Ball? Bush Says He's Game." *Atlanta Journal Constitution*, March 31, 2001.

Herskowitz, Mickey, and Steve Perkins. *The Greatest Little Game.* New York: Sheed and Ward, 1974.

Hichwa, John. *Right Fielders Are People Too: An Inclusive Approach to Teaching Middle School Physical Education.* Champaign, IL: Human Kinetics, 1998.

Hitchens, Christopher. "The Obligatory Proto-Capitalist Worldview: Ayn Rand." *Business 2.0*, August 2001. http://www.business2.com.

Hoberman, John. *Darwin's Athletes: How Sport Has Damaged Black America and Preserved the Myth of Race.* Boston: Mariner/Houghton-Mifflin Company, 1997.

_____. "Totem and Taboo: The Myth of Race in Sports." *Skeptic* 8, no. 1 (2000): 35–38.

Hoch, Paul. *Rip Off the Big Game: The Exploitation of Sports by the Power Elite.* Introduction by Jack Scott. Garden City, NY: Anchor Books, 1972.

Holtzman, Jerome. *No Cheering in the Press Box.* Rev. ed. New York: Henry Holt and Company, 1995.

Horrocks, Roger. *Masculinity in Crisis.* London: MacMillan, 1996.

Hume, Mick. "Book Review: On the Moral High Ground." *New Statesmen*, July 9, 2001.

_____. "A Man's Game?" *LM* 11 (June 1998): 4–5.

_____._____. "Whatever Happened to the Heroes?" *Living Marxism* 94 (October 1996): 4–6.

Hunter, James Davison. *Culture Wars: The Struggle to Define America. Making Sense of the Battles over the Family, Art, Education, Law, and Politics.* New York: Basic Books, 1991.

Hymowitz, Kay S. "Parenting: The Lost Art." *American Educator*, Spring 2001: 4–9.

_____. "Raising Children for an Uncivil Society." *City Journal* 7, no. 3 (Summer 1997): 57–66.

_____. "Who Killed School Discipline?" *City Journal* 10, no. 2 (Spring 2000): 34–43.

Jackson, Scoop. "White Man's Game." *SportsJones*, May 27, 2000. http://www.sportsjones.com.

Jardine, Alice, and Paul Smith, eds. *Men in Feminism.* New York and London: Methuen, 1987.

Jeziorski, Ronald. *The Importance of School Sports in American Education and Socialization.* Lanham, MD: University Press of America, 1994.

Johnson, Jessica A. "Media Won't Give Bonds a Break." *The Columbus Dispatch*, December 17, 2004.

Johnson, William O., and Nancy P. Williamson. *"Whatta Gal": The Babe Didrikson Story.* Boston: Little, Brown & Co., 1977.

Jones, Clara B., and Robert A. Dickerson. "Are Black Males Homophobic?—A Note." *African-American Male Research* 6, no. 1 (November/December 2001). http://www.pressroom.com/~afromale.

Junker, Detlef. "The Americanization of the Holocaust." *Frankfurter Allgemeine Zeitung 2000,* October 20, 2000. http://www.faz.com.

Kashatus, William C. "Dick Allen, the Phillies, and Racism." In *Out of the Shadows: African American Baseball from the Cuban Giants to Jackie Robinson,* edited by Bill Kirwin, 147–193. Lincoln, NE: Bison Books, 2005.

Keil, Thomas. "Sport in Advanced Capitalism." *Arena Review* 8 (1984): 15–29.

Kelly, John R., and Rodney B. Warnick. *Recreation Trends and Markets: The 21st Century.* Champaign, IL: Sagamore Publishing, 1999.

Kent, Scott. "Some on Right Are Wrong about Knight." *Savannah Morning News,* September 14, 2000.

Kimball, Roger. "Francis Fukuyama and the End of History." *New Criterion* 10, no. 6 (February 1992). http://www.newcriterion.com/.

Kirwin, Bill, ed. *Out of the Shadows: African American Baseball from the Cuban Giants to Jackie Robinson.* Lincoln, NE: Bison Books, 2005.

Klatell, David A., and Norman Marcus. *Inside Big Time Sports: Television, Money & the Fans.* New York: MasterMedia Limited, 1996.

Klein, Alan. "Anti-Semitism and Anti-Somatism: Seeking the Elusive Sporting Jew." *Sociology of Sport Journal* 17, no. 3 (2000): 213–28.

Koch, Joanne Barbara, and Linda Nancy Freeman. *Good Parents for Hard Times: Raising Responsible Kids in the Age of Drug Use and Early Sexual Activity.* New York: Simon & Schuster, 1992.

Kohn, Alfie. *No Contest: The Case Against Competition. Why We Lose in Our Race to Win.* Rev ed. Boston: Houghton Mifflin Company, 1992.

_____. "Why Competition?" *The Humanist,* January/February 1980, 14–15, 49.

König, Eugen. "Criticism of Doping: The Nihilistic Side of Technological Sport and the Antiquated View of Sport Ethics." *International Review for the Sociology of Sport* 30, no. 3/4 (1995): 247–59.

Kornheiser, Tony. "What Is Fair for Carlesimo?" *Washington Post,* December 11, 1997.

Korr, Charles P. *The End of Baseball As We Knew It: The Players Union, 1960–81.* Urbana: University of Illinois Press, 2005.

Kramer, Rita. *Ed School Follies.* New York: Free Press, 1991.

Krauthammer, Charles. "If Enhancers Are OK for Others, Why Not for Bonds?" *The Morning Call,* June 5, 2006.

Kwon, Hye. "That Great All-American Pastime ... Gambling Fever." *The Daily Bruin,* October 31, 1996.

Labash, Matt. "What's Wrong with Dodgeball? The New Phys Ed and the Wussification of America." *Weekly Standard,* June 25, 2001, 17–25.

Laberge, Suzanne, and Mathieu Albert. "Conceptions of Masculinity and of Gender Transgressions in Sport among Adolescent Boys." *Men and Masculinities* 1, no. 3 (January 1999): 243–67.

_____. "Conceptions of Masculinity and Gender Transgressions in Sport among Adolescent Boys: Hegemony, Contestation, and the Social Class Dynamic." In *Masculinities, Gender Relations, and Sport,* edited by Jim McKay, Michael A. Messner, and Donald F. Sabo, 195–221. Thousand Oaks, CA: Sage Publications, Inc., 2000.

Labi, Nadya. "Let Bullies Beware." *Time,* April 2, 2001, 46–47.

Landers, Daniel M. *Social Problems in Athletics.* Urbana: University of Illinois Press, 1976.

Lapchick, Richard E. *Fractured Focus: Sport as a Reflection of Society.* Lexington, MA: Lexington Books, 1986.

Larson, Christina. "Reconstructing Rockwell: How an American Icon Became an Artist." *The Washington Monthly,* October 2001. www.washingtonmonthly.com/.

Lasch, Christopher. *The Culture of Narcissism: American Life in an Age of Diminishing Expectations.* New York: W.W. Norton & Co., Inc., 1978.

_____. "For Shame: Why Americans Should Be Wary of Self-Esteem." *The New Republic,* August 10, 1992, 29–34.

Lasch-Quinn, Elizabeth. *Race Experts: How Racial Etiquette, Sensitivity Training, and New Age Therapy HIJACKED the Civil Rights Revolution.* New York: W.W. Norton & Company, 2001.

Leonard, David. "The Decline of the Black Athlete: An Interview with Harry Edwards." *ColorLines* 3, no. 1 (Spring 2000): 20–24.

Levine, Peter. "'Oy Such a Fighter!' Boxing and the Jewish-American Experience." In *The New American Sport History: Recent Approaches and Perspectives,* edited by S.W. Pope, 251–83. Urbana: University of Illinois Press, 1997.

Levitt, Norman. "Adventures in the Thin Skin Trade." *Last Magazine,* Summer 2000, 46–47.

Lhamon, W.T., Jr. *Raising Cain: Blackface Performance from Jim Crow to Hip Hop.* Cambridge: Harvard University Press, 1998.

Library of Congress American Memory Project. Transcript of "Meet the Press" Television and Radio Broadcast. National Broadcasting Company, Sunday, April 14, 1957. Lawrence Spivak, Prod. Lawrence Spivak Papers, Library of Congress Manuscript Division. National Publishing Company, Washington, D.C., Vol. 1, No. 15. Article posted on *Baseball, the Color Line, and Jackie Robinson.* http://memory.loc.gov/ammem /collections/robinson/jrtimedivs.html.

Lipsyte, Robert. "The Emasculation of American Sports." *The New York Times Magazine,* April 2, 1995.

_____. *SportsWorld: An American Dreamland.* New York: Quadrangle, 1975.

_____. "SportsWorld Revisted." In *Fractured Focus: Sport as a Reflection of Society,* edited by Richard E. Lapchick, 313–17. Lexington, MA: Lexington Books, 1986.

_____._____. "The Varsity Syndrome: The Unkindest Cut." *The Annals of the American Academy* 445 (1979): 15–23.

Litsky, Frank. "Aggression Necessary, Hill Says." *New York Times,* January 22, 1987.

Livingston, Bill. "Let the Numbers Speak for Themselves." *The (Cleveland) Plain Dealer,* August 28, 2002.

Lomax, Michael E. "The African American Experience in Pro Football." *Journal of Social History* 33, no. 1 (1999): 163–78.

London, Herbert. "Happiness in School Should Not Be Confused with Knowledge." *Savannah Morning News,* January 10, 2000.

Longino, Helen. "The Ideology of Competition." In *Competition: A Feminist Taboo?* edited by Valerie Miner and Helen E. Longino, 248–60. Foreword by Nell Irvin Painter. New York: The Feminist Press at the City University of New York, 1987.

Lords, Erik. "Death Threat Spurs Critic of Bob Knight to Take Unpaid Leave from Indiana U." *The Chronicle of Higher Education,* June 15, 2000. http://chronicle.com.

Lovett, Karen. "Who Do You Consider a Role Model?" Extend Your Hand.com: The Web Seed Network. http://www.extendyourhand.com.

Lumpkin, Angela, Sharon Kay Stoll, Jennifer Marie Beller, and Jennifer Beller. *Sport Ethics: Applications for Fair Play.* nd2nd ed. Boston: WCB McGraw-Hill, 1999.

Lyness, D'Arcy. "The Story on Self-Esteem." *KidsHealth,* December 2002. http://kidshealth.org/.

MacClelland, David C. *The Achieving Society.* New York: MacMillan Press, 1961.

MacInnes, John. *The End of Masculinity: The Confusion of Sexual Genesis and Sexual Difference in Modern Society.* Milton Keynes, UK: Open University Press, 1998.

Macleod, David I. *Building Character in the American Boy: The Boy Scouts, YMCA, and Their Forerunners, 1870–1920.* Madison: The University of Wisconsin Press, 1983.

Mahoney, Ed. "Solving the Pete Rose Dilemma [*sic*]." *Elysian Fields Quarterly* 18, no. 1 (2001). http://www.efqreview.com.

Males, Mike. "The Culture War against Kids." *AlterNet*, June 1, 2001. http://alternet.org.
Malik, Kenan. *The Meaning of Race: Race, History and Culture in Western Society*. London: MacMillan, 1996.
_____. "Analysis: Tainted Gold: A Transcript of a Programme for a Radio 4 Analysis Strand." January 4, 2004. http://www.kenanmalik.com/tv/analysis_drugs.html.
_____. *What Is It to Be Human? What Science Can and Cannot Tell Us. Conversations in Print*. London: Academy of Ideas Ltd., 2001.
Malina, Robert M. "Sport, Violence, and Littleton: A Perspective." Youth Sport Institute, Spring 1999. http://ed-web3.educ.msu.edu.
Mangan, James A. *Athleticism in the Victorian and Edwardian Public School*. Cambridge: Cambridge University Press, 1981.
Mangan, James A., and Roberta J. Parks, eds. *From Fair Sex to Feminism: Sport and the Socialization of Women in the Industrial and Post-Industrial Eras*. London: Frank Cass, 1987.
Markovits, Andrei S., and Steven L. Hellerman. *Offside: Soccer & American Exceptionalism*. Princeton: Princeton University Press, 2001.
Marsh, Peter. "In Praise of Bad Habits." Social Issues Research Centre, November 17, 2001. http://www.sirc.org/index.html.
Martens, Rainer. "Competition: In Need of a Theory." In *Social Problems in Athletics*, edited by Daniel M. Landers, 9–17. Urbana: University of Illinois Press, 1976.
_____. "Competition: Misunderstood and Maligned." *Comparative Physical Education and Sport* 6 (1989): 29–51.
McCarthy, Terry. "Warning." *Time*, March 19, 2001, 24–28.
McChesney, Robert W. "Media Made Sport: A History of Sport Coverage in the United States." In *Media, Sports, & Society*, edited by Lawrence A. Wenner, 49–69. Newbury Park, CA: Sage Publications, 1989.
McIntire, Roger. *Raising Good Kids in Tough Times: Seven Crucial Habits for Parent Success*. Berkeley Spring, WV: Summit Crossroads Press, 1999.
McKay, Jim, Michael A. Messner, and Donald F. Sabo. *Masculinities, Gender Relations, and Sport*. Thousand Oaks, CA: Sage Publications, Inc., 2000.
McKay, Matthew, and Patrick Fanning. *Self-Esteem*. nd2nd ed. New York: MJF Books, 1992.
Mearsheimer, John J. "Why We Will Soon Miss the Cold War." *The Atlantic Monthly* 266, no. 2 (August 1990): 35–50.
Mecca, Andrew M., Neil J. Smelser, and John Vasconcellos, eds. *The Social Importance of Self-Esteem*. Berkeley: University of California Press, 1989.
Meggyesy, Dave. *Out of Their League*. New York: Ramparts Press, 1970.
Messner, Michael A. *Power at Play: Sports and the Problem of Masculinity*. Boston: Beacon Press, 1992.
_____. "Sports and Male Domination: The Female Athlete as Contested Ideological Terrain." *Sociology of Sport Journal* 5 (1988): 197–211.
Messner, Michael A., and Donald F. Sabo. *Sex, Violence, and Power in Sports: Rethinking Masculinity*. Freedom, CA: Crossing Press, 1994.
Michener, James A. *Sports in America*. Greenwich, CT: Fawcett Crest, 1976.
Miele, Frank. "An Introduction to [*sic*] Special Skeptic Symposium on Race & Sports." *Skeptic* 8, no. 1 (2000): 29.
Miller, Tim. "'Sportsex': Exploring the Sexuality of Sport. A Review of Toby Miller's *Sportsex*." *Outsports*, 2001. http://www.outsports.com.
Miller, Toby. *Sportsex*. Philadelphia: Temple University Press, 2001.
Miner, Valerie, and Helen E. Longino, eds. *Competition: A Feminist Taboo?* Foreword by Nell Irvin Painter. New York: The Feminist Press at the City University of New York, 1987.
Miracle, Andrew W., Jr., and C. Roger Rees. *Lessons of the Locker Room: The Myth of School Sport*. Amherst, NY: Prometheus Books, 1994.

Mitchell, Greg. "Putting the Play Back in Play Ball." Youth Leagues, April 12, 2000. http://www.youthleagues.com.

Mitsdarfer, Paul. "The Media's Portrayal of Athletes' Lives away from the Game." Bowling Green State University. http://www.bgsu.edu.

Monifa, Akilah. "Niggas, Dykes, and Corporate Types: Some Notions on Racism and Homophobia in Sports." ColorLines 1, no. 2 (Fall 1998). http://www.arc.org/C_Lines/CLArchive.

Moore, R.A. Sports and Mental Health. Springfield, IL: Charles C. Thomas Publishing, 1966.

Mormino, Gary Ross. "The Playing Fields of St. Louis: Italian Immigrants and Sports, 1925–1941. In Sport in America: From Wicked Amusement to National Obsession, edited by David K. Wiggins, 225–37. Champaign, IL: Human Kinetics, 1995.

Morse, Jodie. "Girlhoods Interrupted." Time, March 19, 2001, 28.

Mrozek, Donald J. _____."The Cult and Ritual of Toughness in Cold War America." In Sport in America: From Wicked Amusement to National Obsession, edited by David K. Wiggins, 257–68. Champaign, IL: Human Kinetics, 1995.

_____. Sport and American Mentality, 1880–1910. Knoxville: University of Tennessee Press, 1983.

MSNBC. "Youth Sports Violence Is Spreading." October 2001. www.msnbc.msn.com/.

Nack, William, and Lester Munson. "Sport's Dirty Secret." Sports Illustrated, July 31, 1995, 62–74.

National Association for Youth Sports, "JTAA Is the First Youth Sports Organization to Mandate Parent Training: An Interview with the JTAA President, Mr. Jeff Leslie." National Association for Youth Sports. http://www.nays.org.

National Collegiate Athletic Association. "National Collegiate Athletic Association (NCAA) Research Reports." 2002. http://www.ncaa.org.

National Review. "The Sporting Life." National Review, February 21, 1994, 20–21.

Nelson, Mariah Burton. Embracing Victory: Life Lessons in Competition and Compassion. New York: Avon Paperbacks, 1999.

_____. The Stronger Women Get, the More Men Love Football: Sexism and the American Culture of Sports. New York: Avon Books, 1994.

New York Times, "Flag Them for Illegal Use of the Hands," July 27, 2002. Article posted on The International Herald Tribune, http://www.iht.com.

Nietzsche, Friedrich Wilhelm. The Portable Nietzsche. Edited and Translated by Walter Kaufmann. New York: Penguin Books, 1982.

Nixon, Howard L., II. "Gender, Sport, and Aggressive Behavior outside Sport." Journal of Sport Social Issues 21, no. 4 (November 1997): 379–91.

Nolan, James L., Jr. The Therapeutic State: Justifying Government at Century's End. New York: New York University Press, 1998.

Nuechterlein, James. "The Weird World of Sports." First Things 84 (June/July 1998): 11–12.

Ocker, Sheldon. "Alomar's Advice: Let Kids Play." Akron Beacon Journal, March 14, 2000.

Ogilvie, Bruce C., and Thomas A. Tutko. "Sport: If You Want to Build Character, Try Something Else." Psychology Today, October 1971, 61–63.

O'Hanlon, Timothy P. "School Sports as Social Training: The Case of Athletics and the Crisis of World War I." In Sport in America: From Wicked Amusement to National Obsession, edited by David K. Wiggins, 189–206. Champaign, IL: Human Kinetics, 1995.

Oliver, Emmanuel. "The Rape of Black America." Living Marxism 42 (April 1992). http://www.informinc.co.uk.

Oliver, Paul. Screening the Blues: Aspects of the Blues Tradition. New York: Da Capo Press, 1968.

Omeally, Robert G., ed. The Jazz Cadence of American Culture. New York: Columbia University Press, 1998.

Oriard, Michael. "A Review of Susan Faludi's Stiffed: The Betrayal of the American Man." SportsJones, December 1999. http://www.sportsjones.com.

Orlick, Terry D. *The Cooperative Sports and Games Book: Challenge without Competition.* New York: Random House, 1978.

_____. *The Second Cooperative Sports & Games Book.* New York: Random House, 1982.

Orlick, Terry D., and Louise Zitzelberger. "Enhancing Children's Sport Experiences." In *Children and Youth in Sport: A Biopsychosocial Perspective,* edited by Frank L. Smoll and Ronald E. Smith, 330–337. Boston: WCB McGraw-Hill, 1996.

Overman, Steven J. *The Influence of the Protestant Ethic on Sport and Recreation.* Brookfield, VT: Avebury, 1997.

Paglia, Camille. "Feminists Must Begin to Fulfill Their Noble, Animating Ideal." *The Chronicle of Higher Education,* July 1997. Posted on the Bergen University Library On-Line. http://privat.ub.uib.no/bubsy/apollon.htm.

Park, Roberta J. "Sport, Gender, and Society in a Transatlantic Victorian Perspective." In *From Fair Sex to Feminism: Sport and the Socialization of Women in the Industrial and Post-Industrial Eras,* edited by James A. Mangan and Roberta J. Parks, 58–93. London: Frank Cass, 1987.

Passer, Michael W. "At What Age Are Children Ready to Compete? Some Psychological Considerations." In *Children and Youth in Sport: A Biopsychosocial Perspective,* edited by Frank L. Smoll and Ronald E. Smith, 73–86. Boston: WCB McGraw-Hill, 1996.

Pearlman, Jeff. "At Full Blast." *Sports Illustrated,* December 23, 1999. http://sportsillustrated.cnn.com/.

Peeples, Master Craig. "The Reason We Compete." Flyer Distributed to participants of the Georgia State Tae Kwon Do Championships in Kingsland, Georgia. May 1999.

Perry, Dayn. "Are Steroids Ruining Sports, and Should Cheating Athletes Be Held Accountable?" Hi International, 2006. http://hiinternational.com/.

Peters, Ruth. *Are Your Kids Driving You Nuts? Don't Be Afraid of Discipline: The Commonsense Program for Low-Stress Parenting That Improves Kids' Behavior in a Matter of Days, Stops Nagging and Hassling, Restores the Parent-Child Relationship, Creates Lasting Results.* New York: Golden Books, 1997.

Peterson, Robert. *Only the Ball Was White: A History of Legendary Black Players and All-Black Professional Teams.* New York: Oxford University Press, 1970.

Peterson, Robert W. *Cages to Jump Shots: Pro Basketball's Early Years.* New York: Oxford University Press, 1990.

_____. "Helping Children Learn Positive Values." *Scouting Magazine,* January-February 2001. http://www.bsa.scouting.org/mags.

Pfeil, Fred. *White Guys: Studies in Postmodern Domination and Difference.* London: Verso, 1996.

Phillips, Melanie. *All Must Have Prizes.* London: Warner Books, 1997.

Pope, S.W. "American Sport History — Toward a New Paradigm." In *The New American Sport History: Recent Approaches and Perspectives,* edited by S.W. Pope, 1–32. Urbana: University of Illinois Press, 1997.

—, ed. *The New American Sport History: Recent Approaches and Perspectives.* Urbana: University of Illinois Press, 1997.

Pronger, Brian. "Comments on Eric Anderson's *Trailblazing.*" *Sociology of Sport Journal* 18, no. 4 (2000): 467–71.

_____. "Homosexuality and Sport: Who's Winning?" In *Masculinities, Gender Relations, and Sport,* edited by Jim McKay, Michael A. Messner, and Donald F. Sabo, 222–44. Thousand Oaks, CA: Sage Publications, Inc., 2000.

Puma, Mike. "Not the Size of the Dog in the Fight." A SportsCentury Biography. *ESPN.com.* http://espn.go.com.

Pyke, Karen D. "Class-Based Masculinities: The Interdependence of Gender, Class, and Interpersonal Power. *Gender & Society* 10, no. 5 (October 1996): 527–49.

Rader, Benjamin. *American Sports: From the Age of Folk Games to the Age of Televised Sports.* th4th ed. Upper Saddle, NJ: Prentice Hall, 1999.

Rail, Geneviève, ed. *Sport and Postmodern Times.* Albany: State University of New York Press, 1998.

Ratto, Ray. "Sports Give Refuge to the 'Socially Touchy.'" Special to ESPN.com, 1999. http://espn.go.com.

Reilly, Rick. "Get the Message?" *CNN-Sports Illustrated*, August 9, 1999. http://sportsillustrated.cnn.com/inside_game/magazine/life_of_reilly/news/1999/06/15/reilly.

Remnick, David. "How Muhammad Ali Changed the Press." *SportsJones*, October 29, 1999. http://www.sportsjones.com.

Reston, James, Jr. *Collision at Home Plate: The Lives of Pete Rose and Bart Giamatti.* Lincoln: University of Nebraska Press, 1997.

"Review Symposium of Eric Anderson's *Trailblazing: The True Story of America's First Openly Gay Track Coach.*" *Sociology of Sport Journal* 18, no. 4 (2000): 463–80.

Rickover, Robert. "The New Physical Education." *Wellness Today* 4, no. 5 (March 2002). http://www.wellnesstoday.com.

Rieff, Philip. *The Triumph of the Therapeutic.* Chicago: University of Chicago Press, 1966.

Riess, Steven A. "Sport and the Redefinition of Middle-Class Masculinity in Victorian America." In *The New American Sport History: Recent Approaches and Perspectives*, edited by S.W. Pope, 173–97. Urbana: University of Illinois Press, 1997.

Roiphe, Katie. *The Morning After: Sex, Fear, and Feminism.* Boston: Little, Brown and Company, 1994.

Rosemond, John K. *John Rosemond's Six Point Plan for Raising Happy, Healthy Children.* Kansas City, MO: Andrews and McMeel, 1989.

_____. *Parent Power! A Common Sense Approach to Parenting in the '90's and Beyond.* Kansas City, MO: Andrews and McMeel, 1990.

_____. "Raising Nonviolent Kids." Illustrations by Reagan Dunnick. *Hemispheres: The Magazine of United Airlines*, August 2000, 122–28.

Rosen, Joel Nathan. "All-Sports Radio: The Development of an Industry Niche." *Media History Monographs* 5, no. 1 (2001–2002). http://www.elon.edu/dcopeland/mhm/mhm.htm.

_____. "Review of *Athletes and Acquaintance Rape.*" *Reviewing Sociology* 11, no. 2 (1999). http://www.reading.ac.uk/RevSoc/volumeII/RSII2.web.htm#Athletes%20Acquaintance%20Rape.

_____. "Self-Concept and the Discussion of Youth Sport — A Critique." *Journal of Mundane Behavior* 5, no. 1 (June 2004). http://mundanebehavior.org/index2.htm.

Rosenberg, Morris. *Society and the Adolescent Self-Image.* Princeton: Princeton University Press, 1965.

Rosentraub, Mark S. *Major League Losers: The Real Cost of Sports and Who's Paying for It. What Governments and Taxpayers Need to Know.* Rev ed. New York: Basic Books, 1999.

Ross, Charles K., ed. *Race and Sport: The Struggle for Equality on and off the Field.* Jackson: University of Mississippi Press, 2004.

Rossinow, Doug. "The Revolution Is about Our Lives." In *Imagine Nation: The American Counterculture of the 1960s and '70s*, edited by Peter Braunstein and Michael William Doyle, 99–124. New York: Routledge, 2002.

Roszak, Theodore. *The Making of a Counter Culture: Reflections on the Technocratic Society and Its Youthful Opposition.* Garden City, NY: Anchor Books, 1969.

Rothman, Howard. *All That Once Was Good: Inside America's National Pastime.* Denver: Pendleton Clay Publications, 1995.

Russell, Bill, and Taylor Branch. *Second Wind: The Memoirs of an Opinionated Man.* New York: Random House, 1979.

Sabo, Don, et al. "Domestic Violence and Televised Athletic Events." In *Masculinities, Gender Relations, and Sport*, edited by Jim McKay, Michael A. Messner, and Donald F. Sabo, 127–46. Thousand Oaks, CA: Sage Publications, Inc., 2000.

Sage, George. "Socialization of Coaches: Antecedents to Coaches' Beliefs and Behaviors." In *Proceedings, The National College Physical Education Association for Men.* Meeting held January 9–12, 1975, in Phoenix, Arizona.

Sarup, Madan. *An Introductory Guide to Post-Structuralism and Postmodernism.* 2nd ed. Athens: The University of Georgia Press, 1993.

Scanlon, Tara Kost. "Social Evaluation and the Competition Process: A Developmental Perspective." In *Children and Youth in Sport: A Biopsychosocial Perspective*, edited by Frank L Smoll and Ronald E. Smith, 298–308. Boston: WCB McGraw-Hill, 1996.

Schmaltz, Jim. "Panic Room: The Baseball-Steroid Issue Reaches the Senate, and Legal Supplements Get Smeared in the Process." *LookSmart* Online. http://www.findarticles.com/.

Schwalbe, Michael L. "A Humanist Conception of Competition in Sport." *Humanity & Society* 13, no. 1 (1989): 43–60.

Scott, Jack. *The Athletic Revolution*. New York: The Free Press, 1971.

Searls, Helen. "An English Woman in Washington." *sp!ked*, March 8, 2001. http://www.spiked-online.com/.

Seefeldt, Vern. "The Future of Youth Sports in America" In *Children and Youth in Sport: A Biopsychosocial Perspective*, edited by Frank L. Smoll and Ronald E. Smith, 423–35. Boston: WCB McGraw-Hill, 1996.

Sennett, Richard. *The Corrosion of Character: The Personal Consequences of a Work in the New Capitalism*. New York: W.W. Norton & Company, 1998.

Sewart, John J. "The Rationalization of Modern Sport: The Case of Professional Football." *Arena Review* 5 (1981): 45–51.

Shaw, Gary. *Meat on the Hoof: The Hidden World of Texas Football*. New York: St. Martin's Press, 1972.

Sheaffer, Robert. "Feminism, the Noble Lie." *Free Inquiry*, Spring 1995. Article posted on http://www.debunker.com.

Sherif, Carolyn W. "The Social Context of Competition." In *Social Problems in Athletics*, edited by Daniel M. Landers, 18–36. Urbana: University of Illinois Press, 1976.

Shields, David. "Taboo Topics, True Subjects." *Austin Chronicle*, November 19, 1999.

Shields, David, and Brenda Light Bredemeier. "Moral Reasoning in the Context of Sport." Studies in Moral Development and Education Web page. Chicago: University of Illinois at Chicago. October 1999. http://tigger.uic.edu/~lnucci/MoralEd/index.htm. [Note: This paper was originally delivered at the annual meeting of The Association for Moral Education in Minneapolis, MN.]

Shields, David Lyle Light, B.J.L Bredemeier, D.E. Gardner, and A. Bostrom. "Leadership, Cohesion, and Team Norms Regarding Cheating and Aggression." *Sociology of Sport Journal* 12 (1995): 324–36.

Shokraii-Rees, Nina H. "The Self-Esteem Fraud: Why Feel Good Education Does Not Lead to Academic Success." The Center for Equal Opportunity. http://www.ceousa.org.

Simmons, Mark. "Pro Sports Salaries." 1999. http://www.askmen.com.

Sindell, Jon. "Lessons from Youth Hockey Mayhem. *My Prime Time*, 2001. http://www.myprimetime.com.

Sismondo, Christine. "Why Cigs? Why Not Beef? The Vagaries of the Precautionary Principle." *The Toronto Star*, May 28, 2006. http://www.thestar.com.

Smith, Earl. "The African American Student Athlete." In *Race and Sport: The Struggle for Equality on and off the Field*, edited by Charles K. Ross, 121–45. Jackson: University Press of Mississippi, 2004.

Smith, Lynn. "Putting a Spin on the Truth with Statistics and Studies." *LA Times*, June 6, 2001. http://www.latimes.com.

Smith, Mark. "Youth Sports and Adult Violence." *The Caledonian Record*, January 8, 2001. http://www.caledonianrecord.com/.

Smith, Shepherd. "Is the Choice Sportsmanship or Death?" *Savannah Morning News*, August 1, 2000.

Smith, Wayne. *Quest for High Self-Esteem*. Tustin, CA: Self-Esteem Publishing, 1995. http://www.self-esteem.com.

Smoll, Frank L., and Ronald E. Smith, eds. *Children and Youth in Sport: A Biopsychosocial Perspective*. Boston: WCB McGraw-Hill, 1996.

_____. "The Coach as a Focus of Research and Intervention." In *Children and Youth in*

Sport: A Biopsychosocial Perspective, edited by Frank L. Smoll and Ronald E. Smith, 125–41. Boston: WCB McGraw-Hill, 1996.

Sommers, Christina Hoff. "The New Mythology." *National Review*, June 27, 1994. http://www.nationalreview.com.

Sowell, Mike. *One Pitch Away: The Players' Stories of the 1986 League Championships and World Series*. New York: MacMillan Books, 1995.

Sperber, Murray. *Beer and Circus: How Big Time College Sports Is Crippling Undergraduate Education*. New York: Henry Holt, 2000.

Spock, Benjamin, and Steven Parker. *Dr. Spock's Baby and Childcare: A Handbook for Parents of the Developing Child from Birth through Adolescence*. th7th ed. New York: Dutton, 1998.

Sports Illustrated. "This Week's Sign of the Apocalypse." July 25, 2005, 26.

Spring, Joel H. *Images of American Life: A History of Ideological Management in School, Movies, Radio, and Television*. Albany: State University of New York Press, 1992.

_____. "Mass Culture and School Sports." *History of Education Quarterly* 14 (Winter 1974): 483–98.

Springhall, John. *Youth, Popular Culture and Moral Panics: Penny Gaffs to Gangsta Rap, 1830–1996*. New York: St. Martin's Press, 1998.

Staffo, Donald F. "Violence, Sportsmanship Still Problems in Youth Sports." *The Tuscaloosa News*, July 21, 2000. http://www.tuscaloosanews.com.

Stange, Mary Zeiss. "Point of View: The Political Intolerance of Academic Feminism." *The Chronicle of Higher Education*, June 21, 2002. http://chronicle.com.

Statistical Abstract of the United States: The National Data Book. Multiple editions. Washington, D.C.: U.S. Census Bureau, 1997–2006.

Steel Kaleidoscopes Web site. "Highest-Paid Athletes." (Originally published in *Sports Illustrated*.) http://steelkaleidoscopes.typepad.com/steel_kaleidoscopes/2005/07/highest_paid_at.html, July 5, 2005.

Still, Bob, ed. "Assaults on Sports Officials: Based upon a Report Written by Troy Cross." National Association of Sports Officials. http://www.naso.org.

_____. *Special Report: The National Association of Sports Officials. Officials under Assault: Update 2002*. With Jim Arehart, ed. Franksville, WI: The National Association of Sports Officials and Referee Enterprises, 2002.

Stoelje, Beverly. "The Snake Charmer." In *Beauty Queens on the Global Stage: Gender, Contests, and Power*, edited by Cohen, Colleen Ballerino, Richard R. Wilk, and Beverly Stoeltje, 13–30. New York: Routledge, 1996.

Story, Ronald. "The Country of the Young: The Meaning of Baseball in Early American Culture." In *Sport in America: From Wicked Amusement to National Obsession*, edited by David K. Wiggins, 121–32. Champaign, IL: Human Kinetics, 1995.

Strong, Jerald M. "A Dysfunctional and Yet Winning Youth Football Team." *Journal of Sport Behavior* 15, no. 4 (December 1992): 319–26.

Stuber, Robert, and Jeff Bradley. *Smart Parents, Safe Kids: Everything You Need to Protect Your Family in the Modern World*. Kansas City, MO: Andrews and McNeel, 1997.

Sullivan, Andrew. "Masculinities and Men's Magazines: Dumb and Dumber." *New Republic*, June 15, 2000. http://www.newrepublic.com.

Sullivan, Tim. "Running the Option: College Sports Don't Need Las Vegas.' *The Hoya*, September 15, 2000.

Taffel, Ron. "Teaching Kids Respect." *Parents*, June 1999, 1–6. http://www.parentsmagazine.com.

Talamini, John T., and Charles H. Page. *Sport & Society: An Anthology*. Boston: Little, Brown and Company, 1973.

Tatum, Jack, and Bill Kushner. *They Call Me Assassin*. New York: Morrow/Avon Reading, 1980.

Taylor, Tracy, and Kristine Toohey. "Sport, Gender, and Cultural Diversity: Exploring the Nexus." *Journal of Sport Management* 13 (1999): 1–13.

Telender, Rick. *The Hundred Yard Lie: The Corruption of College Football and What We Can Do to Stop It.* Urbana: University of Illinois Press, 1996.

Thesing, Erica. "Sports Rage: The New Face of Violence." *New York Times,* July 10, 2000.

Tiger, Lionel. "Constituency Esthetics." *New York Press* 13, no. 1010 (March 2000). http://www.nypress.com.

Tocqueville, Alexis de. *Democracy in America.* Vol. I. http://www.tocqueville.org.

Tucker, Lori W., and Janet B. Parks. "Effects of Gender and Sport Type on Intercollegiate Athlete's Perceptions of the Legitimacy of Aggressive Behaviors in Sport." *Sociology of Sport Journal* 18, no. 4 (2001): 403–413.

Tutko, Thomas, and William Bruns. *Winning Is Everything and Other American Myths.* New York: MacMillan Publishing Co., 1976.

Turner, Frederick Jackson. *The Frontier in American History.* New York: Henry Holt, 1935.

"Two Important Resolutions." *The Journal of Health and Physical Education* 9 (1938): 488–89.

Tygiel, Jules. *Baseball's Great Experiment.* New York: Oxford University Press, 1983.

USA Today baseball Web site. 2006. http://www.usatoday.com/sports/baseball/front.htm.

Vail, Kathleen. "It's How You Play the Game." *The American School Board Journal* 184, no. 8 (August 1997): 16–18.

Vanderwerken, David L., and Spencer K. Wertz, eds. *Sport Inside Out: Readings in Literature and Philosophy.* Fort Worth: Texas Christian University Press, 1985.

Vincent, Ted. *Mudville's Revenge: The Rise & Fall of American Sport.* Lincoln: University of Nebraska Press, 1981.

Voepel, Mechelle. "Sales, Fans Wanted to Savor Final Games." *ESPNET SportsZone,* February 26, 1998. http://espn.go.com.

Volkwein, Karin A.E. "Ethics and Top-Level Sport — A Paradox?" *The International Review for the Sociology of Sport* 3/4 (1995): 311–19.

"Volunteer Checks Necessary." *Sporting Kid: The Parents Guide to Youth Sports & Fitness,* November/December 2001, 31–32.

Walker, Don. "Selig Says Steroids Plague Sport: Female Journalists Hear His Message." *Milwaukee Journal-Sentinel,* June 5, 2004. http://www.jsonline.com.

Walker, Martin. *The Cold War: A History.* New York: Henry Holt and Company, Inc., 1993.

Walker, Stuart H. *Winning: The Psychology of Competition.* New York: W.W. Norton, 1980.

Walter, John C. "The Changing Status of the Black Athlete in the 20th Century United States." *American Studies Today* On-Line. 1996. Article posted at http://www.johncarlos.com.

Walton, Theresa. "The Sprewell/Carlesimo Episode: Unacceptable Violence or Unacceptable Victim?" *Sociology of Sport Journal* 18, no. 3 (2001): 345–357.

Wann, Daniel L. *Sport Psychology.* Upper Saddle, NJ: Prentice Hall, 1997.

Wann, Daniel L., Merrill J. Melnick, Gordon W. Russell, and Dale G. Pease. *Sport Fans: The Psychology and Social Impact of Spectators.* New York: Routledge, 2001.

Ward, Steven. "Filling the World with Self-Esteem: A Social History of Truth-Making." *The Canadian Journal of Sociology* 21, no. 1 (Winter 1996). http://www.ualberta.ca.

Weber, Max, and Talcott Parsons. *The Protestant Ethic and the Spirit of Capitalism.* nd2nd ed. Translated by Anthony Giddens. London: Routledge, 2001.

Weiss, Maureen. "Self-Esteem and Achievement in Children's Sport and Physical Activity." In *Advances in Pediatric Sport Sciences. Vol. 2: Behavioral Issues,* edited by Daniel Gould and Maureen R. Weiss, 87–119. Champaign, IL: Human Kinetics Publishers Inc., 1987.

Weiss, Philip. "Is Sprewell Still a Black Menace?" *Jewish World Review,* June 18, 1999. http://www.jewishworldreview.com.

Wenner, Lawrence A., ed. *Media, Sports, & Society.* Newbury Park, CA: Sage Publications, 1989.

Wenzel, Lisa R. "Position Paper: Athletes and Domestic Violence." The Program for Public Policy in Sports, University of North Carolina at Chapel Hill, May 1998. http://www.unc.edu/depts/ppps/.

Wickham, DeWayne. "Treat Criminal Jocks Like Anyone Else." *USA Today*, March 14, 2000.

Wiggins, David K. "A History of Organized Play and Highly Competitive Sport for American Children." In *Advances in Pediatric Sport Sciences. Vol. 2: Behavioral Issues*, edited by Daniel Gould and Maureen R. Weiss, 1–24. Champaign, IL: Human Kinetics Publishers, Inc., 1987.

_____, ed. *Sport in America: From Wicked Amusement to National Obsession*. Champaign, IL: Human Kinetics, 1995.

Will, George. *Bunts: Curt Flood, Camden Yards, Pete Rose, and Other Reflections on Baseball*. New York: Scribner, 1998.

_____. "... Liberals Left out in the Cold." *Washington Post*, December 13, 2001. www.washingtonpost.com/.

_____. "Steroids Ruin Sport with Chemistry and Bad Character." *The Morning Call*, December 8, 2004.

Williamson, Peter. *Good Kids, Bad Behavior: Helping Children Learn Self-Discipline*. New York: Simon and Schuster, 1990.

Willis, George. "2 Raised Fists Still Breaking Down Barriers." *New York Post*, August 22, 1999. http://promotions.nypost.com.

Wilson, Brian. "The 'Anti-Jock' Movement: Reconsidering Youth Resistance, Masculinity, and Sport in the Age of the Internet." *Sociology of Sport Journal* 19, no. 2 (2002): 206–233.

Wilson, Woodrow. *The New Freedom: A Call for the Emancipation of the Generous Energies of a People*. Compiled by Bayard Hale. New York: Doubleday & Page, 1914.

Wojnarowski, Adrian. "Boorish Behavior Knows Few Bounds." *ESPN.com*, October 19, 1999. http://espn.go.com.

Wolton, Suke, ed. *Marxism, Mysticism and Modern Theory*. London: Palgrave Macmillan, 1996.

Wooden, John. "Developing a Coaching Philosophy." March 28, 2000. *http://www.calstatela.edu/faculty/dfrankl/dfrankl.htm*

Wright, Michael P. "A Critical Look at Rape Awareness Week at the University of Oklahoma: How Accountable Is the Women's Studies Program?" *Clarion* 4, no. 4. (March/April 2000). http://www.popecenter.org.

Youth Sports Journal: A Publication of the National Alliance for Youth Sports. Initial Issue. n.d.

Youth Sports Journal: A Publication of the National Alliance for Youth Sports 3, no. 3 (Fall 2001).

Zion, Sidney. ""What about the Fans? Fuhgeddaboutit [*sic*]." *The Nation*, August 10/17, 1998, 31–35.

Zirin, Dave. "Sheryl Swoopes: Out of the Closet — and Ignored." *The Nation*, November 4, 2005. http://www.thenation.com/doc/20051121/sheryl_swoopes_out_of_the_closet.

Theses, Conference Papers, and Other Unpublished Works

Anderson, Eric. "The Mitigation of Homophobia in Sport." Unpublished manuscript. 1998:1–15.

Cantrell, Tamia H. "Media, Women and Sport: A Cultural Theory Approach to Explaining Women's Fight against Hegemony." Paper presented at the Refereed Roundtable Category Marriage, Family, Work, Gender, and Feminism Session of The American Sociological Association 2000 Annual Meeting. Washington, D.C.: The Washington Hilton, August 2000:1–17.

Grant, Christine and H.B. Grant. "A Basic Title IX Presentation." Paper presented in Cedar Rapids, IA, September 25, 1995. Posted on the University of Iowa Gender Equity in Sport Project Web Site. http://bailiwick.lib.uiowa.edu.

Lee, Ellie. "Marxism and Feminist Theory." In *Marxism, Mysticism and Modern Theory*, edited by Suke Wolton, 48–60. London: Palgrave Macmillan, 1996.

Malik, Kenan. "What Is It to Be Human?" Paper presented at The Institute of Idea's Conference "Science, Knowledge, and Humanity." New York: The New School for Social Research, October 24, 2001.

Malszecki, Greg. "The Virile Paradigm: The Political Linguistics of Sport." Paper presented at The North American Society for the Sociology of Sport 20th Annual Conference. Cleveland, OH: Marriott Key Center, November 1999.

Neilands, Torsten Brian. *The Time Course of the Self-Concept Threat Reduction Process among Low and High Self-Esteem Individuals*. PhD diss., The University of Texas at Austin, December 1993.

Riess, Steven A. "Sports Inner Dynamic." E-mail correspondence, October 30, 2000.

Rosen, Joel Nathan. "Separating Wheat from Chaff: Looking for Jackie Robinson in an Uncritical Age." Paper presented at the conference From Jack Johnson to Marian Jones: Gains Made-Struggles Remain for African Americans in Sport. Ithaca, NY: Ithaca College, January 2005.

_____. *A Clashing of Cultural Imperatives: Contemporary American Sport and the Recoil from the Traditional Competitive Ethos*. PhD diss., University of Kent, December 2002.

_____. "Competition in the New Millennium: Have We Lost Our Nerve?" Paper presented at The North American Society for the Sociology of Sport 20th Annual Conference. Cleveland, OH: Marriott Key Center, November 1999.

_____. "The Contemporary Conundrum: Competition and the Therapeutic Undercurrent." Paper presented at the American Sociological Association Conference. Chicago: Hilton Chicago, August 2002.

_____. *"Your Question or Comment Please": A Sociological Study of All-Sports Radio*. Master's thesis, University of Mississippi, August 1995.

Schafer, Walter E. "Sport and Youth Counterculture: Contrasting Socialization Themes." Paper presented at The Conference on Sport and Social Deviancy. Brockport, NY: SUNY-Brockport. December 10, 1971:1–21.

Special Olympics "The Special Olympics Oath." Bundled Mail. November 10, 2005.

Miscellaneous Electronic Media Sources

"2000 Academy Awards Show." Billy Crystal, host. Richard D. and Lili Fini Zanuck, prods. ABC Television. March 27, 2000.

A Man for All Seasons. With Robert Shaw and Paul Scofield. Fred Zinnemann, prod. & dir. Highland Film,. 1966.

"All Things Considered." National Public Radio, November 4, 2000.

"Arli$$." "Episode 75: Moments to Remember." With Robert Wuhl. HBO Television, July 28, 2002.

Back to School. With Rodney Dangerfield. Alan Metter, dir. Orion, 1986.

Baseball. Nineteen Parts. John Chancellor, narr. Ken Burns, exec. prod, 1994.

"Black Athletes— Fact or Fiction." Tom Brokaw, narr. Tom Brokaw and Jon Entine, coprods. NBC Television, April 1989.

CNN-SI Television. Daily Programming. Air Dates December 2, 2001, and June 21, 2001.

"Citizenship through Sports." The Citizenship through Sports Alliance and the National Federation of State High Schools. Todd Erlich, prod., 2000.

"Colin Cowherd Show, The." ESPN Radio, June 13, 2006.

"Contrarian View, The." "Real Sports." Bryant Gumbel, host. HBO Sports. Armen Keteyian, narr. Tim Walker, prod., January 25, 2006.

Courtney, Alan and Homer, Benjamin. "Joltin' Joe DiMaggio." *Baseball: A Film by Ken Burns. Original soundtrack recording*. New York: Elektra Entertainment, 1994.

"Curt Flood." *ESPN's Sport Century*. Chris Fowler, narr. ESPN2, February 27, 2001.

Dare to Compete: The Struggle of Women in Sports. Mary Carillo and Frank Deford, writers. Ross Greenberg, exec. prod. HBO Sports, 1999.
David Halberstam's The Fifties. Edward Herrmann, narr. Nancy Button, prod., 1997.
Deford, Frank. "Gene Therapy and the Future of Competition." National Public Radio, November 17, 2004.
_____. "Sweetness and Light." "Some Women Athletes Follow a Sordid Path." National Public Radio, May 24, 2006.
"Dodge This!" "Real Sports." HBO Sports. Bryant Gumbel, host. Bernard Goldberg, narr. Elizabeth Carp, prod., February 28, 2002.
Dylan, Bob. "Love Minus Zero/No Limit." *Bringing It Back Home.* New York: Columbia Records, 1965.
Fists of Freedom: The Story of the '68 Summer Games. Ross Greenberg, exec. prod. HBO Sports, 1999.
"Goin' Deep." "Sport and Civility" Fox Sports Network. Chris Myers, host. Gary Foremen, dir., October 11, 2000.
Graduate, The. With Anne Bancroft and Dustin Hoffman. Mike Nichols, dir. MGM, 1967.
Hendrix, Jimi. "The Star Spangled Banner." *Jimi Hendrix: Woodstock.* Universal City, CA: MCA Records, 1994.
Hoop Dreams. With William Gates and Arthur Agee. Steve James, dir. Fine Line Features, 1994.
"Jim Rome's Jungle." Premiere Radio Network, March 1, 2000.
Kicking & Screaming. With Will Ferrell and Robert Duvall. Jesse Dylan, dir. MCA Home Vide,. 2005.
Legally Blond. With Reese Witherspoon. Robert Luketic, dir. MGM, 2001.
"Letter from 'Out' Editor." Special to ESPN.com: Page 2. [Note: This letter was originally published in the May 2001 issue of *Out* magazine.] http://espn.go.com/page2.
"Letters." "M*A*S*H." Charles S. Durbin, dir. FX Network. March 21, 2001. This episode originally aired November 24, 1980.
Making Sense of the Sixties. Kirk Wolfinger, prod. Carol Rissman, narr., 1991.
McDaniel, Elias. "I'm a Man." Chicago: Chess Records, 1955.
"Meet the Press" Television and Radio Broadcast. National Broadcasting Company, Sunday, April 14, 1957. Lawrence Spivak, prod. Lawrence Spivak Papers, Library of Congress Manuscript Division. National Publishing Company, Washington, D.C., Vol. 1, No. 15.
"Morning Edition." National Public Radio, June 12, 2002.
North Dallas Forty. With Nick Nolte and Charles Durning. Ted Kotcheff, dir. Paramount, 1979.
"Outside the Lines." ESPN Television. Bob Ley, narr., July 23, 2001.
"Parent-Proof Baseball Field." "All Things Considered." National Public Radio. Robert Siegel, narr., July 9, 2002.
"Parental Guidance Is Suggested." "Outside the Lines." ESPN Television. Bob Ley, narr., July 5, 2001.
"Parental Rage." "Real Sports." HBO Sports. Bryant Gumbel, host. Bernard Goldberg, narr. Alvin Patrick, prod., October 12, 2000.
"Parental Violence, Losing It." "20/20." ABC Television. Tom Jarriel, narr., Nancy Kramer and James Altman, prods., May 25, 1999.
Playing the Field: Sports and Sex in America. Frank Deford, writer. Rick Bernstein and Ross Greenberg, exec. prods. HBO Sports, 2000.
"Real Sports." Bryant Gumbel, host. HBO Sports, March 20, 2000.
Simon, Paul and Art, Garfunkel. "Mrs. Robinson." *Bookends.* New York: Columbia Records, 1968.
"Sports Center." ESPN Television. Daily Sport News Program. Air date February 27, 2006.
"Sports Reporters, The." ESPN Television. Weekly Series. Air dates 2 May 1999, 5 March 2000, 5 March 2006, 30 April 2006, and 18 June 2006.
"Thin Ice." "Law & Order." NBC Television. Dick Wolfe, exec. prod., July 18, 2001.

Travis, Merle. "Sixteen Tons." New York: Capitol Records, 1946.
Trouble along the Way. With John Wayne. Michael Curtiz and John Wayne, dirs. Warner Bros., 1953.
When It Was a Game. Parts I-III. HBO Sports. Ross Greenberg, exec. prod., 2000.

Internet Sites

ABC26. http://www.sns.abc26.com Accessed July 21, 2001.
African-American Male Research On-Line. http://www.pressroom.com/~afromale Accessed December 30, 2001.
AlterNet On-Line. http://alternet.org Accessed June 1, 2001.
Amazon.com. http://www.amazon.com Accessed October 13, 1997.
American Academy of Child and Adolescent Psychiatry. *http://www.aacap.org/* Accessed November 10, 2001.
American Academy of Pediatricians home page. http://www.aap.or/family/steroids/htm Accessed February 6, 2006.
American College of Sports Medicine home page. http://www.acsm.org Accessed February 6, 2006.
American Psychological Association. http://www.apa.org/ Accessed November 2, 1999.
Arthur Agee Role Model Foundation Web Site. http://www.edgesportsintl.com/Arthur.htm Accessed November 25, 2001.
askmen.com http://www.askmen.com Accessed June 2, 2002.
Ayn Rand Institute. http://www.aynrand.org Accessed January 7, 2000.
"Baseball Labor History: An Old Fashioned Game with Old Fashioned Traditions." Authored by Pat Brady. http://xroads.Virginia.edu Accessed June 2, 1998.
Baseball Almanac Online. http://www.baseball-almanac.com Accessed June 3, 2006.
BBC Sport On-line. http://newsvote.bbc.co.uk/ Accessed June 17, 2005.
Bergen University Library. http://privat.ub.uib.no/bubsy/apollon.htm Accessed December 19, 2001.
Boston Globe On-Line. http://www.boston.com Accessed August 1, 2000.
Bowling Green State University. http://www.bgsu.edu Accessed September 4, 2001.
Business 2.0. http://www.business2.com Accessed September 17, 2001.
Caledonian Recor On-Line. http://www.caledonianrecord.com/ Accessed July 26, 2001.
Calgary's Child. http://calgaryschild.com Accessed July 21, 2001.
Canadian Journal of Sociology On-Line. http://www.ualberta.ca Accessed January 7, 2000.
Center for Equal Opportunity. http://www.ceousa.org Accessed January 5, 2000.
Children Today, Inc. http://www.childrentoday.org Accessed June 14, 2001.
Chronicle of Higher Education On-Line. http://chronicle.com Accessed June 30, 2000, and June 21, 2002.
Citizenship through Sports Alliance. http://www.sportsmanship.org/main.html Accessed August 12, 2000.
Clarion On-Line. Published by the Pope Center for Higher Education Policy. http://www.popecenter.org. Accessed December 17, 2001, and December 19, 2001.
ColorLines On-Line. http://www.arc.org/C_Lines/CLArchive Accessed December 30, 2001.
CNN.com. http://www.cnn.com Accessed January 26, 2002.
CNN-Sports Illustrated Online. http://sportsillustrated.cnn.com Accessed January 8, 2000, and November 27, 2001.
Crossroads On-Line. http//: xroads.virginia.edu Accessed June 2, 1998, and May 17, 2000.
Daniel Frankl. http://www.calstatela.edu/faculty/dfrankl/dfrankl.htm Accessed 2 April 1999, 25 March 2000, and 6 July 2000.
Democracy in America On-Line. http://www.tocqueville.org Accessed March 9, 2001.
Education World On-Line. *http://www.education-world.com* Accessed August 12, 2000, and March 2, 2002.

Elysian Fields Quarterly On-Line. http://www.efqreview.com Accessed December 25, 2001.
ESPN.com http://espn.go.com Accessed December 1, 1999, and July 17, 2006.
ESPN.com: Page 2. http://espn.go.com/page2 Accessed December 21, 2001, and December 25, 2001.
ESPNet SportsZone. http://espn.go.com Accessed April 4, 1999.
Extend Your Hand.com: The Web Seed Network. http://www.extendyourhand.com Accessed November 15, 2001.
Feminist Majority Foundation. http://www.feminist.org Accessed December 19, 2001.
Frankfurter Allgemeine Zeitung 2000 On-Line. http://www.faz.com Accessed October 21, 2000.
Gay & Lesbian Alliance against Defamation (glaad) On-Line. http://www.glaad.org Accessed June 13, 2002.
George Washington University's Polling Report.com. http:www.pollingreport.com/ sport.*htm* Accessed June 8, 2002.
Hi International home page. 2006. http://hiinternational.com/ Accessed February 6, 2006.
International Herald Tribune Online. http://www.iht.com Accessed July 29, 2002.
Jewish World Review On-Line. http://www.jewishworldreview.com Accessed December 26, 2001.
John Carlos home page. http://www.johncarlos.com Accessed December 30, 2001.
Kenan Malik home page. http://www.kenanmalik.com Accessed November 24, 2001, and June 23, 2006.
KidsHealth Online. http://kidshealth.org/ Accessed August 25, 2003.
Lewis and Clark College. http://www.lclark.edu Accessed February 4, 2001.
Library of Congress' American Memory Project Webpage. http://memory.loc.gov/ammem/ collections/robinson/meetpres.html Accessed December 30, 2004.
LM On-Line. http://www.informinc.co.uk Accessed June 19, 1997.
Los Angeles Times On-Line. http://www.latimes.com Accessed July 16, 2001.
LookSmart Online. http://www.findarticles.com/ Accessed February 6, 2006.
Malaspina University-College. http://www.mala.bc.ca Accessed December 21, 2001.
Media History Monographs. http://www.elon.edu/dcopeland/mhm/mhm.htm Accessed February 27, 2002.
Middle Stump, The On-Line. http://www.geocities.com/middlestump1/JWE3.html Accessed June 8, 2002.
Milwaukee Journal-Sentinel Online. http://www.jsonline.com Accessed February 6, 2006.
MSNBC On-Line. http://www.msnbc.com Accessed October 23, 2001.
My Prime Time. http://www.myprimetime.com Accessed June 2, 2001.
The Nation Online. http://www.thenation.com Accessed May 29, 2006.
National Alliance for Youth Sports. http://www.nays.org Accessed 2 March 2000, 1 July 2001, and 19 December 2001.
National Association of Sports Officials. http://www.naso.org Accessed July 26, 2001.
National Collegiate Athletic Association (NCAA) On-Line. http://www.ncaa.org/library/ research.html Accessed June 8, 2002.
National Parent and Teacher Association (PTA). http://www.pta.org Accessed November 27, 2001.
National Review On-Line. http://www.nationalreview.com November 24, 2001.
New Criterion On-Line. http://www.newcriterion.com/ Accessed. July 1, 2001.
New Republic, The On-Line. http://www.newrepublic.com Accessed July 11, 2000.
New Scientist On-Line. http://www.newscientist.com/ Accessed July 1, 2001.
New York Post On-Line. http://promotions.nypost.com Accessed August 22, 2001.
New York Press On-Line. http://www.nypress.com Accessed July 1, 2000.
Northeastern University's Center for the Study of Sport in Society Web Site. http://www.sportinsociety.org Accessed February 27, 2000, and June 2, 2002.
OutSports On-Line. http://www.outsports.com Accessed December 30, 2001.
Parents On-Line. http://www.parentsmagazine.com Accessed April 11, 2001.

Policy Review On-Line. http://www.policyreview.org Accessed May 24, 2001.
Pope Center for Higher Education Policy, The. http://www.popecenter.org Accessed December 19, 2001.
Program for Public Policy in Sports On-Line. http://www.unc.edu/depts/ppps/ Accessed July 29, 2002.
"Prosperity and Thrift: The Coolidge Era and the Consumer Economy, 1921–1929." Designed by the American Library of Congress. http://lcweb2.l0c.gov/ammem/cool-html/coolhome.html Accessed June 22, 2000.
Reviewing Sociology. http://www.rdg.ac.uk/RevSoc/ Accessed May 21, 2006.
Robert Sheaffer's The Debunker's Domain. http://www.debunker.com Accessed December 18, 2001.
Scouting Magazine On-Line. http://www.bsa.scouting.org/mags Accessed November 28, 2001.
Self-Esteem and Performance. http://www.performance-unlimited.com Accessed January 5, 2000.
Self-Esteem. http://www.self-esteem.com Accessed January 5, 2000.
1Soccer Mom! http://www.isoccermom.com Accessed January 11, 2000.
Social Issues Research Centre. http://www.sirc.org/index.html Accessed November 27, 2001.
SOLO Lifestyles for Singles. http://www.solosingles/esteem.htm Accessed January 7, 2000.
sp!ked. http://www.spiked-online.*com* Accessed 8 March 2001, 23 May 2001, 8 September 2001, 28 December 2001, and 23 May 2006.
SportsJones On-Line. http://www.sportsjones.com Accessed 1 July 2000, 17 September 2001, and 17 December 2001.
Sports Illustrated for Kids Parents' Web. http://www.sportparents.com Accessed January 8, 2000.
Spotlight on Youth Sports On-Line. Michigan State University's Youth Sport Institute. http://ed-web3.educ.msu.edu/ysi/spotlight Accessed 2 June 2000, 15 December 2000, 2 February 2001, and 12 May 2001.
Steel Kaleidoscopes Web page. http://steelkaleidoscopes.typepad.com/ Accessed June 1, 2006.
SteroidLaw.com http://www.steroidlaw.com Accessed June 23, 2006.
Studies in Moral Development and Education. University of Illinois at Chicago. http://tiger.uic.edu/~lnucci/MoralEd/index.htm Accessed November 7, 2001.
Time On-Line. http://www.time.com Accessed April 7, 2001, and May 24, 2001.
Toronto Star Online. http://www.thestar.com Accessed May 29, 2006.
Tuscaloosa News On-Line. http://www.tuscaloosanews.com Accessed August 10, 2001.
University of Iowa Gender Equity in Sport Project. http://bailiwick.lib.uiowa.edu Accessed December 17, 2001, and June 11, 2002.
USA Today Online. Baseball Page. http://asp.usatoday.com/sports/baseball/salaries/default.aspx Accessed June 3, 2006.
US Census Bureau home page. http://www.census.gov/ Accessed June 2, 2006, and June 3, 2006.
Wellness Today On-Line. http://www.wellnesstoday.com Accessed March 2, 2002.
Youth Leagues. http://www.youthleagues.com Accessed June 2, 2000.
Youth Sport Institute. http://ed-web3.educ.msu.edu Accessed June 2, 2000, and December 15, 2000.
Youth Sports Instruction. http://youth-sports.com Accessed January 5, 2001.

Index